The Palestine Question

HENRY CATTAN

Licencié en Droit [Paris];
LL.M. [London], of the Middle Temple;
Barrister-at-Law;
Formerly Member of the Palestine Bar and
   Tutor at the Jerusalem Law School;
Member of the Bars of Syria, Jordan and Lebanon

CROOM HELM
London ● New York ● Sydney

© 1988 Henry Cattan
Croom Helm Ltd, Provident House, Burrell Row,
Beckenham, Kent BR3 1AT

Croom Helm Australia, 44–50 Waterloo Road,
North Ryde, 2113, New South Wales

British Library Cataloguing in Publication Data

Cattan, Henry
    The Palestine question.
    1. Palestine — Politics and government
    I. Title
    956.94′04   DS126
    ISBN 0–7099–4860–3
    ISBN 0–7099–4878–6 (Pbk)

Published in the USA by
Croom Helm
in association with Methuen, Inc.
29 West 35th Street
New York, NY 10001

Library of Congress Cataloging-in-Publication Data

Cattan, Henry.
    The Palestine question.

    Includes index.
    1. Israel-Arab conflicts. I. Title.
DS119.7.C377 1987   956′.04   87-17114
ISBN 0-7099-4860-3
ISBN 0-7099-4878-6 (pbk.)

Photoset by Mayhew Typesetting, Bristol, England
Printed and bound in Great Britain by Mackays of Chatham Ltd. Kent

Contents

Preface

The history of Palestine has been marked by many dramatic events that have left a lasting impact not only on the region, but also on the world at large. Closely linked with history, with three world religions, with Palestine and Zionist Jewish nationalism, as well as with the strategic interests of the two superpowers, the Palestine Question has been the cause of several wars in the Middle East. It constitutes one of the most explosive, intractable and unresolved issues of modern times that threatens not only the stability of the region, but also the peace of the world.

Yet, despite its crucial importance, and the mass of literature written about the subject, ignorance about the Palestine Question is fairly widespread. What are its basic issues? Which of its protagonists is right or wrong? Who are the aggressors and who are the victims? Very few are in a position to give the correct answers. Much confusion exists with regard to these questions. The average person has a vague idea that the Palestine Question concerns an area located somewhere in the Middle East over which Jews and Arabs have been quarrelling and going to war for years. Others who are influenced by Zionist and Israeli propaganda claim that the Palestine Question concerns the heroic struggle of the Jews to defend 'their' country against Palestinian 'terrorists' who want to wrest it from them. The same ignorance explains the failure, sometimes the inanity, of the so-called solutions that have been proposed for the settlement of the Palestine Question.

There exist two main reasons for ignorance about the true nature and dimensions of the Palestine Question. The first is the systematic, well-planned and expertly organized misinformation and distortion which are spread in the Western media by Zionist and Israeli propaganda concerning the question generally. This process of misinformation and distortion is coupled with a deliberate concealment of the history of Palestine which for 1800 years, and until recent times, was an exclusively Arab country. The Israelis are anxious to bury that part of the past during which the Jews did not live or exist in Palestine. For this reason the history of Palestine for that period is ignored, distorted or is not even taught in Israeli schools. The purpose of Israel's suppression of the historical Arab character of Palestine is to give the false impression of continuity of Jewish presence in the country and hence of a non-existent historical connection between the two Jewish monarchies of biblical times and the State of Israel that was established 25 centuries later.

The second reason is that each new wrong committed against the Palestine people blots out the preceding one. Bertrand Russell observed that for over 20 years Israel had expanded by force of arms and, after every stage in this expansion, it had appealed to 'reason' and suggested 'negotiations'. 'Every new conquest', he said, 'became the new basis of the proposed negotiation from strength, which ignores the injustice of the previous aggression.'[1]

The ignorance that exists with regard to the Arab-Israeli conflict surprised General Odd Bull, Chief of Staff of the UN Truce Supervision Organization from 1963 to 1970. Although he spoke about Norway, his comment is valid for Europe and America. General Odd Bull wrote with reference to the Arab-Israeli conflict:

Few people in the outside world appreciated the true situation. When I went to Norway for Christmas, six months after the war, not one in a hundred of those I talked to had any understanding of the facts. An uncritical acceptance of the Israeli point of view in all its aspects was the rule . . .

Gradually, it is true, the Norwegian press shed some of its bias, but for a variety of reasons public opinion in Norway has remained consistently favourable to Israel and unfavourable to the Arabs. In the first place most Norwegians are profoundly ignorant about the politics and problems of the Middle East. Then the Bible naturally disposes them to favour God's chosen people, and their sympathies were profoundly stirred by the appalling fate that befell the Jews in Europe at the hands of the Nazis. Norwegians, like most other Europeans and almost all Americans, found it in no way inappropriate that the Arabs should pay for crimes committed by Hitler.[2]

A proper understanding of the Palestine Question is not simply a matter of curiosity or of historical interest. Just as a disease cannot be treated without knowledge of its cause, so also the Palestine Question cannot be resolved unless there exists a full and proper knowledge of its dimensions.

The solution of the Palestine Question is a necessity as well as an international obligation. Every citizen of the world has an interest in world peace and security. Arab-Israeli wars have threatened world peace on more than one occasion, whether in 1948, 1956, 1967, 1973 or 1982. Former US President Richard Nixon who had declared 'a nuclear alert' during the Arab-Israeli War of 1973 recently disclosed that he took such action because the two super-powers came close to a nuclear confrontation on account of the Arab-Israeli conflict.[3]

Lastly, the Palestine Question should weigh heavily on the con-science of the many nations who bear the responsibility for having created the unjust situation that exists today in Palestine. The failure to appreciate the real facts and responsibilities that underlie the Palestine Question has prevented its equitable solution. It is, therefore, necessary to set forth the essentials of the Palestine Question concisely and objectively in broad outline, without bias, partiality or partisanship, its evolution from the concept of a Jewish national home to a Jewish state expanding territorially by war decade after decade. This would present a clear picture of the Palestine drama which has been obscured by deceptive propaganda and mis-information. This, in essence, is the basic objective of this book.

Part I of this book gives the background to the Palestine Question and includes a discussion of the Balfour Declaration, the British mandate over Palestine and the UN resolution for the partition of the country into Arab and Jewish States. Part II is devoted to a review of the main events which have taken place in Palestine since 1948. The emergence that year of the State of Israel in the historic land of Palestine caused a tremendous political upheaval, ignited the war of 1948 and led to the expulsion or exodus of most of the Palestinians from their homeland. It also led to the usurpation by the new state of most of the territory of Palestine and the confiscation of Arab land and started a chain of wrongs, injustices and wars, which have convulsed and still convulse the Middle East to the present day. Part III deals with the all-important problem of Jerusalem which lies at the heart of the Palestine Question. Finally, Part IV examines past initiatives for securing a settlement and discusses the principles for achieving a fair and equitable solution of the Palestine Question. These principles deviate from current so-called peace initiatives and suggest a peaceful and political solution which is squarely based on right and justice.

Henry Cattan

NOTES

1. *Middle East International*, 21 January 1983, p. 19.
2. General Odd Bull, *War and Peace in the Middle East*, (Leo Cooper, London, 1973), pp. 126–7.
3. *Time*, 21 July 1985.

Part I

Background to the Palestine Question

1

Palestine until 1917

The Palestine Question cannot be fully understood without knowledge of the early history of Palestine. The claims of the parties to the conflict, Jews and Palestinians, are rooted deep in early history and it is incumbent, therefore, to examine their respective association with Palestine as well as the events that went into the making of the Palestine problem before it exploded in 1948. It goes without saying that a cursory historical survey only can be attempted in this book.

Although history, and particularly the Bible, mention the existence at one time or another of several peoples in ancient Palestine, only three peoples played a leading role in that country and left a lasting impact on it. These peoples are the Canaanites, the Philistines and the Israelites. The Palestinians are the descendants of the Canaanites and the Philistines.

The Canaanites are the earliest known inhabitants of Palestine and are thought to have settled there after 3000 BC. They lived in cities and possessed an economy based upon agriculture and commerce. Each city was ruled by a priest-king. The Canaanites gave to the country its early biblical name of 'the land of Canaan' (Numbers, 34:2; 35:10) and 'the country of the Canaanites' (Exodus, 3:17). Among their cities was Jerusalem which may have come into existence some 18 centuries BC.

The Philistines and the Israelites came to the land of Canaan almost contemporaneously with each other in the latter part of the second millennium BC. The Philistines came to the land of Canaan about 1175 BC, probably from Illyria. (It should here be remembered that this date, like other dates of biblical events, are approximate.) They occupied its southern part and eastern coast and remained for several centuries in control of the territory which became known as Philistia. It was the Philistines who gave to Palestine its modern name. According to the biblical account, the Israelites wandered in the desert after their exodus from Egypt, reaching the eastern part of the land of Canaan about 1200 BC. During the following two centuries they slowly infiltrated into the country and settled in it as the twelve tribes of Israel. They were ruled by the Patriarchs.

Modern historians discount the biblical account of Joshua's violent capture of Jericho because according to archaeologist Miss K.M. Kenyon, Jericho had already been destroyed several centuries before.[1] Similarly, historians reject some biblical accounts of the massacre of the Canaanites by the newcomers and assert that the Israelites and the Canaanites cohabited and even merged together. Professor Noth observes that the Israelites did not conquer or destroy Canaanite cities, but in general settled in unoccupied regions without displacing the original inhabitants.[2] Professor Adolphe Lods stated:

> The people of Israel at the royal period were a mixture of Hebrews and Canaanites . . . In this amalgamation, the Canaanite element was by far the most numerous . . . Being more civilized, the Canaanites naturally compelled the newcomers to adopt their culture, and in this sense one can say that the Canaanites conquered their victors. But, on the other hand, the Hebrews possessed and preserved the consciousness of conquerors; they succeeded in imposing their social framework, their name, their God, on the entire population of Palestine.[3]

Unlike the situation that prevailed between the Canaanites and the Israelites, there was never peaceful coexistence between the Philistines and the Israelites. They were constantly at war with each other. As a result of their constant wars with the Philistines, the twelve Israelite tribes united under Saul who became their first king about 1030 BC. Saul was slain by the Philistines at Gilboa. After his death, his son-in-law David, who had been in the service of a Philistine prince, reunited the Israelite tribes, assumed their leadership and became their king. In or about the year 1000 BC, David captured Jerusalem from the Jebusites, a Canaanite subgroup, and made the city the capital of his kingdom. By his conquests David expanded the territory of his kingdom. But even at the height of his power, he was unable to dominate or subdue the Philistines who remained in control of the maritime plain to a point south of Acco

(Acre) and to a point north of Japho (Jaffa). David ruled his kingdom for a period of 33 years (1006 to 972 BC) and his son Solomon ruled it for 40 years (972 to 932 BC). Solomon built a temple at Jerusalem which was given his name. After his death, the Israelite tribes revolted and, as a result, the unified kingdom established by David was split into the kingdom of Israel in the north and the kingdom of Judah in the south. The unified kingdom had lasted 73 years.

The two new kingdoms collapsed, one after the other. The kingdom of Israel was destroyed by the Assyrians in 721 BC and thereafter became extinct. The other kingdom, described by archaeologist K.M. Kenyon as the 'pseudo-autonomous' kingdom of Judah, survived precariously for a while. Its capital, Jerusalem, was periodically besieged, taken and sacked by the Assyrians, the Philistines, the Arabs, the Syrians, the Babylonians and the Egyptians.[4] It became a vassal state and paid tribute to Assyria, Egypt and Babylon in turn. When in 705 BC Judah failed to pay the tribute, the Assyrian King Sennacherib occupied it and gave its territory to the Philistines, leaving to the king of Judah the city of Jerusalem. Then in 587 BC, the kingdom of Judah was destroyed by the Babylonians who burned Solomon's Temple and carried the Jews into captivity to Babylon. With the exile of the Jews, the Hebrew language disappeared from Palestine and was replaced by Aramaic which was used alongside the Arabic language for several centuries. Aramaic was the language of Jesus Christ.

After the destruction of Judah, a succession of peoples ruled over Palestine. The Babylonians ruled the country from 587 to 538 BC when it was captured by the Persians who remained in occupation for two centuries. It was during this period that Cyrus, King of Persia, issued an edict allowing the Jews who had been deported to Babylon to return to Palestine. Few, however, did return as a great number had settled in Babylon or had emigrated to other lands.[5] Those who returned built a second but more modest temple in Jerusalem.

In 332 BC, Alexander the Great captured Palestine. In 166 BC, the Jews revolted against their Greek rulers and established the Maccabean kingdom. But Maccabean independence did not last long because in 134 BC Antiochus Sidetes, King of Syria, besieged Jerusalem and levied a tribute upon the Jews. Then in 63 BC Pompey captured Palestine for the Romans and put an end to Maccabean rule. Palestine became the Roman province of Judea and Herod, an Idumean, was placed at its head as a vassal king. During the Roman era one of the great events in the history of mankind occurred in Palestine: this was the birth of Christ at Bethlehem. From that time, Bethlehem, where Christ was born, Nazareth and Galilee, where he lived, and Jerusalem, where he was crucified and buried, became Christianity's holiest places, and Palestine itself became the Holy Land of Christendom.

The Jews revolted twice against the Romans, first in AD 66 to 70 and again in AD 132 to 135. During the first revolt Titus destroyed Jerusalem and the second Temple. After the second revolt the Jews were either killed or dispersed to the four corners of the Roman Empire. From that time until the middle of the nineteenth century there were practically no Jews in Jerusalem, and only a small number lived in Palestine, mainly at Tiberias and Safad.

Roman Emperor Constantine, who was converted to Christianity, ordered in AD 323 the adoption of Christianity as the religion of the Roman Empire. Except for an invasion of the country by the Persians between 614 and 628, Palestine remained under Christian rule for over three centuries. In 638 the Moslem Arabs burst out from the Arabian peninsula and occupied the country. Palestine remained under Moslem Arab rule until 1099 when the Crusaders conquered Palestine and established the Latin Kingdom of Jerusalem. This kingdom extended from Aqaba to Beirut, and from the Mediterranean to the Jordan River. In 1187, however, Palestine was reconquered by Saladin (Salah-ud-Din Ayoubi) who restored Moslem Arab rule. The Latin Kingdom of Jerusalem lasted 88 years in Palestine, though longer in other areas. Apart from a period of ten years between 1229 and 1239, when Jerusalem was temporarily ceded by its Moslem ruler to the German Emperor Frederick II, who had undertaken a crusade for the liberation of the city, Palestine was ruled by the Arab Caliphs — Omayyads, Abbassids and Fatimids — until the Turkish conquest in 1517.

The Moslem Arab conquest of Palestine did not involve any alteration in the country's demographic structure, but only a change of rule and, to a large extent, a change of religion. It is essential to observe that the Moslem Arabs did not colonize Palestine. They brought to the country no immigrants, but only their religion and culture. A number of the original Christian inhabitants were converted to Islam, largely in order to escape the tribute (*Jizia*) imposed on non-Moslems, and, as a result, 'the predominantly Christian population became predominantly Muslim'.[6] A Christian minority, however, remained after the conquest until the present day. This Christian minority constitutes the earliest Christian community in the world.

The absence of any colonization of Palestine by the Moslem Arabs after their conquest exposes the fallacy of imagining that the Arabs first came to Palestine in the seventh century at the time of the Moslem Arab occupation.

The Palestine Arabs have, in fact, been indigenous to Palestine since the dawn of history. The Arabs are a pre-Islamic people who lived in Palestine and in various other parts of the Middle East before the advent of Islam. The term 'Arab' is a generic description of all peoples that live in the Middle East whose mother tongue is Arabic, regardless of their race, creed or religion. Accordingly, there are Moslem Arabs, Christian Arabs and Jewish Arabs.

In 1517 the Ottoman Turks conquered Palestine and occupied it until 1917. Like the Moslem Arab conquest in the seventh century, the Turkish occupation of Palestine involved no colonization or immigration. The administration of the country remained in Arab hands, except for certain key posts which were held by the Turks.

In the summer of 1917 British forces in Egypt launched a campaign against the Turks for the seizure of Palestine, Lebanon and Syria. Jerusalem surrendered on 9 December 1917 and Turkish rule came to an end in Palestine shortly after.

The year 1917 marks a turning point in the history of Palestine not only because of the end of Turkish rule, but also because of the issuance in November of that year by Britain of the Balfour Declaration which constitutes the root cause of the Palestine Question. But before discussing the Balfour Declaration and the events that followed it, it is necessary to pause and to examine the demographic structure in the country at that time as well as the political rights which the Palestinians enjoyed in Turkish times because subsequent events have blurred these basic facts.

The Palestinians of today are the descendants of the Canaanites, the Philistines, and the other early tribes which inhabited the country.[7] Professor Maxime Rodinson points out that the Arab population of Palestine was native in all senses of that word.[8] There were infusions of other racial elements into the Palestinian stock, mainly from the Greeks, the Romans, the Moslem Arabs and the Crusaders. But this Palestinian stock, which comprises both Moslems and Christians, continued to constitute the main element of the population despite the large number of invasions and conquests until the majority of the original inhabitants of Palestine were displaced by the Israelis in 1948.

Although for four centuries Palestine was then an integral part of Turkey, or the Ottoman Empire as it was then called, its inhabitants

7

were not a subject people, but were citizens of a sovereign and independent country. The Palestinians enjoyed full civil and political rights equally with Ottoman citizens. The principle of equality of rights, regardless of race, creed or religion, which had existed in fact in the Ottoman Empire was reaffirmed by the Ottoman Constitution of 23 December 1876. Article 48 of the Constitution recognized the right of every Ottoman citizen to elect and to be elected for national representation. The same rights for all citizens were again reaffirmed in the Ottoman Constitution of 1908. In the parliamentary elections of 1908 the deputies elected to the Ottoman parliament comprised, *inter alia*, 142 Turks, 60 Arabs and 5 Jews.[9] Several Arab deputies represented Palestine,[10] Syria, Lebanon and Iraq.

Such was the political and constitutional position of the Palestinians at the end of Turkish rule in Palestine. Yet, although the Palestinians enjoyed full and equal civil and political rights with the Turks during the Ottoman regime, they, like other Arab citizens in the Ottoman Empire, had been for years attempting to secede and to establish a separate Arab state. Accordingly, when the First World War broke out and Turkey joined Germany's side in the war, the British government and its allies encouraged the Arabs to revolt against the Turks. To this end, they gave them several pledges to recognise their independence from Turkey at the end of the war. These pledges included a pledge for the independence of Palestine. The first of those pledges was given in 1915–16 by the British government in the correspondence exchanged between the Sharif of Mecca and Sir Henry McMahon, British High Commissioner in Egypt. Other pledges by the Allied Powers followed.[11] Although the Arabs revolted against the Turks, all the pledges given to them in regard to Palestine were not honoured as we shall see in the next chapter.

NOTES

1. K.M. Kenyon, *Digging up Jericho* (London, 1957), pp. 256–265; R. de Vaux, *Histoire Ancienne d'Israël* (Gabalda, Paris, 1971), p. 562; Martin Noth, *Histoire d'Israël*, (Payot, Paris, 1970), p. 159.

2. Martin Noth, *Histoire d'Israël* (Payot, Paris, 1970), p. 93.

3. Adolphe Lods, *Israël, Des Origines au Milieu du VIIe Siècle* (Albin Michel, Paris, 1949), p. 386.

4. Albert M. Hyamson, *Palestine Old and New* (Methuen, London, 1928), p. 76.

5. A.S. Rappoport, *Histoire de la Palestine* (Payot, Paris, 1932), p. 121.

6. *Encyclopedia Britannica* (1966), vol. 17, p. 166.

7. 'The Palestinian Arab of today, then, is a descendant of the Philistines, the Canaanites and other early tribes, and of the Greeks, Romans, Arabs, Crusaders, Mongols and Turks'. Moshe Menuhin, *The Decadence of Judaism in our Times* (Exposition Press, New York, 1965), p. 18.

8. Maxime Rodinson, *Israel and the Arabs* (Penguin, London, 1968).

9. S.N. Fisher, *The Middle East* (Routledge and Kegan Paul, London, 1960), p. 322.

10. The Palestinian deputies elected in 1913 for the Jerusalem district, for example, were Faidi Alami, Said Husseini and Ragheb Nashashibi, all from Jerusalem.

11. For the text of these pledges, see George Antonius, *The Arab Awakening* (Hamish Hamilton, London, 1938) and British Government's Report, *Cmd.* 5974, 16 March 1939.

2

The Balfour Declaration

The withdrawal of the Turks from Palestine during the First World War did not lead to Palestinian independence, as in the case of other peoples who were liberated from Turkish domination, on the basis of the pledges given to the Arabs by Great Britain and its allies. This was because of a contradictory pledge given to Zionist Jews by Great Britain on 2 November 1917 in a letter addressed by Arthur James Balfour, British Foreign Secretary, to Lord Rothschild. This letter, which became known as the Balfour Declaration, changed the course of history in Palestine and the rest of the Middle East. In his letter, Balfour stated:

> I have much pleasure in conveying to you, on behalf of His Majesty's Government, the following declaration of sympathy with Jewish Zionist aspirations which has been submitted to and approved by the Cabinet.
>
> His Majesty's Government view with favour the establishment in Palestine of a national home for the Jewish people, and will use their best endeavours to facilitate the achievement of this object, it being clearly understood that nothing shall be done which may prejudice the civil and religious rights of existing non-Jewish communities in Palestine, or the rights and political status enjoyed by Jews in any other country. I should be grateful if you would bring this declaration to the knowledge of the Zionist Federation.

The Balfour Declaration was issued by the British government with the object of winning the support of Zionist Jews during the war as it had previously done by giving several pledges to the Arabs to gain them on its side. But who were the Zionist Jews and what were their aspirations with respect to Palestine?

10

SPIRITUAL AND POLITICAL ZIONISM

In discussing Zionist aspirations it is necessary to distinguish between spiritual Zionism which has always existed and reflected the religious and mystical attachment of the Jews to Jerusalem, particularly after their deportation by the Romans, on the one hand, and political Zionism which developed at the end of the nineteenth century in consequence of the persecution of Jews in Eastern Europe, on the other hand. Spiritual Zionism did not involve any political, territorial or nationalist aims and caused no concern to the Arabs or to the Palestinians in whose midst the Jews lived and even sought refuge after their expulsion from Spain in 1492. As Rabbi Elmer Berger observed, spiritual Zionism threatens no one's political rights, does not use bombs, and drives no one from their homes.

Political Zionism, on the contrary, implies nationalist and territorial ambitions. The founder of political Zionism is Theodor Herzl, an Austrian journalist, who, influenced by the persecution of Jews in Europe, advocated the idea of the creation of a Jewish state either in Palestine or in Argentina in a pamphlet named *Der Judenstaat* (*The Jewish State*) which he published in 1896. Herzl approached Turkey with a request for the colonization of Palestine, but was turned down. He then approached the British government and obtained its approval for the Jewish colonization of what is now known as Uganda in East Africa. Herzl convened a Zionist Congress at Basle in the following year, but the idea of the creation of a Jewish state was not accepted by the Congress, which recommended instead the creation in Palestine of a 'home' for the Jewish people which would be secured by public law. The Zionist plan, which was endorsed by a small number of Jews, lay dormant until the First World War when Zionist activists under the leadership of Chaim Weizmann, a Russian Jew, saw the opportunity of winning the support of the British government to the Zionist cause. The Balfour Declaration represented the successful culmination of their efforts.

MEANING OF 'NATIONAL HOME'

The meaning of 'a national home for the Jewish people' in the Balfour Declaration was vague, presumably so as a matter of deliberation. Zionist Jews spoke in different tones about the concept, some claiming that the national home would eventually involve the

11

creation of a Jewish state while others denied that such was its intention or meaning. Among the latter category, mention may be made of a leading Zionist historian, Nahum Sokolov, who participated in the drafting of the Balfour Declaration. Writing in 1919, he said:

> It has been said, and is still being obstinately repeated by anti-Zionists again and again, that Zionism aims at the creation of an independent 'Jewish state'. But this is wholly fallacious. The 'Jewish state' was never a part of the Zionist programme.[1]

Likewise, Norman Bentwich, a Zionist Jew and at one time Attorney-General of Palestine, wrote:

> State sovereignty is not essential to the Jewish national idea. Freedom for the Jew to develop according to his own tradition, in his own environment, is the main, if not the whole demand.[2]

An authoritative interpretation of the Balfour Declaration was that given by Sir Herbert Samuel, himself a leading British Jew who had participated in the negotiation of the Declaration with the British government and was appointed the first High Commissioner in Palestine, a post which he held for a period of five years. Sir Herbert Samuel stated in the House of Lords in 1947:

> The Jewish state has been the aspiration of the Jewish people for centuries. It is an aspiration which at the present day cannot be realized. It is not contained in the Balfour Declaration. If the Balfour Declaration had intended that a Palestine state should be set up, it would have said so . . . There was no promise of a Jewish state. What was promised was that the British Government would favour the creation of a Jewish National Home — the term was carefully chosen — in Palestine. The Declaration did not say that Palestine should be the Jewish National Home, but that it favoured a Jewish National Home in Palestine, without prejudice to the civil and religious rights of the Arab population.[3]

Describing the situation in Palestine on his assumption of his post as High Commissioner, Sir Herbert Samuel said:

From the outset it was obvious to the Government at home and to the administration in Palestine, that the Arab question was the predominant issue. There were over 600,000 Arabs in the country. Rooted there for a thousand years, regarding themselves as trustees of Moslem interests and Moslem Holy Places, on behalf of the Mohammedan world, they were apprehensive as to the ownership of their lands, and anxious as to the possibility of being supplanted by the incursion into Palestine of millions of Jews, drawn from the reservoirs of Jewish population and backed by the resources of Jewish wealth all over the world. It was necessary to show that those anxieties were unjustified and to allay those fears. It was plain that the establishment of the Jewish National Home must be conditioned not only by safeguards for the existing rights of the Arab population, but also by a constant and active care, on the part of the mandatory power, for their economic and cultural progress.[4]

In several statements of policy the British government declared that the Balfour Declaration 'need not cause alarm to the Arab population of Palestine' for it did not involve the creation of a Jewish state or the subordination of the Palestinian Arabs to the Jewish immigrants.[5]

A VOID, MORALLY WICKED AND MISCHIEVOUS DECLARATION

But whatever may have been the intended meaning of the Jewish 'national home', the Balfour Declaration was legally void, morally wicked and politically mischievous. Firstly it was legally void, because the consent of the people of Palestine, who were the indigenous and sovereign inhabitants of the country (sovereign in the full sense of the term after their detachment from Turkey), was never asked or obtained. The Balfour Declaration was also void because Turkey, as the legal sovereign over Palestine at the time of the issue of the Balfour Declaration, did not consent to it. This basic flaw did not escape the attention of Chaim Weizmann, the principal Zionist negotiator of the Balfour Declaration, because he stressed to the British government 'the importance of the Balfour Declaration being included in the Treaty of Peace with Turkey'.[6] The British government dutifully complied with his request and insisted upon the inclusion of a reference to the Balfour Declaration in the peace

13

treaty concluded with Turkey known as the Treaty of Sèvres of 10 August 1920. This Treaty provided in Article 95 that the parties agreed to entrust, by application of Article 22 of the Covenant of the League of Nations, the administration of Palestine to a Mandatory who would be responsible for putting into effect the Declaration made on 2 November 1917 by the British government, in favour of the establishment in Palestine of a national home for the Jewish people.[7] Turkey, however, refused to subscribe to this provision and to ratify the treaty. As a result, the provision about the Balfour Declaration was dropped from the Treaty of Lausanne of 24 July 1923 which replaced the Treaty of Sèvres. In addition, the Balfour Declaration was also void because the British government, a foreign power in regard to Palestine, did not possess, nor had it ever possessed, any sovereignty, right of disposition, or jurisdiction over Palestine, that enabled it to grant any rights, be they political or territorial, to an alien people over the territory of Palestine. A donor cannot give away what he does not own. It is noteworthy that on the date that the British government issued the Balfour Declaration, not only did it possess no sovereignty over Palestine, but it was not even in occupation of the country. The Balfour Declaration was tantamount to the issue of a false promissory note.

The Balfour Declaration was morally wicked because it amounted to 'one nation solemnly promising to a second nation the country of a third'.[8] In effect, by its promise of a national home for the Jews in Palestine, Britain denied to the people of Palestine the attainment of their independence in exercise of their right of self-determination. The intention to deny to the Palestinians their natural right of self-determination in their own homeland was admitted by the author of the Declaration. In a letter to the Prime Minister dated 19 February 1919 Balfour declared:

> The weak point of our position is that in the case of Palestine we deliberately and rightly decline to accept the principle of self-determination. If the present inhabitants were consulted they would unquestionably give an anti-Jewish verdict. Our justification for our policy is that we regard Palestine as being absolutely exceptional; that we consider the question of the Jews outside Palestine as one of world importance and that we conceive the Jews to have an historic claim to a home in their ancient land; provided that home can be given them without either dispossessing or oppressing the present inhabitants.[9]

The Balfour Declaration, which was aptly described by John

Reddaway, Director of the Council for Arab-British Understanding, as 'the folly of Balfour', was politically mischievous because it has sown the seeds of a bloody conflict between Arabs and Jews who had previously co-existed in peace and harmony for centuries in Palestine and in other Arab countries. Moreover, it brought the most disastrous consequences to the people of Palestine. These consequences were prophetically foreseen when the English House of Lords debated the Palestine mandate in 1922. The Lords opposed the inclusion of the Balfour Declaration in the British mandate over Palestine. Lord Islington said that the proposed mandate violated the pledges made by His Majesty's government to the people of Palestine. Moreover, its provisions concerning the establishment of a Jewish national home were inconsistent with Article 22 of the Covenant of the League of Nations, which had laid the foundations of the mandatory system. Lord Islington continued:

The mandate imposes on Great Britain the responsibility of trusteeship for a Zionist political predominance where 90 per cent of the population are non-Zionist and non-Jewish . . . In fact, very many orthodox Jews, not only in Palestine but all over the world, view with the deepest misapprehension, not to say dislike, this principle of a Zionist Home in Palestine . . . The scheme of a Zionist Home sought to make Zionist political predominance effective in Palestine by importing into the country extraneous and alien Jews from other parts of the world . . . This scheme of importing an alien race into the midst of a native local race is flying in the very face of the whole of the tendencies of the age. It is an unnatural experiment . . . It is literally inviting subsequent catastrophe . . .[10]

Answering this criticism, the author of the Declaration, Lord Balfour, said:

Zionism may fail . . . this is an adventure . . . Are we never to have adventures? Are we never to try new experiments? . . . I do not think I need dwell upon this imaginary wrong which the Jewish Home is going to inflict upon the local Arabs.[11]

Lord Sydenham replied that the Zionist experiment would fail,

but the harm done by dumping down an alien population upon an Arab country — Arab all round in the hinterland — may never

15

be remedied . . . What we have done is, by concessions, not to the Jewish people but to a Zionist extreme section, to start a running sore in the East, and no one can tell how far that sore will extend.[12]

These prophetic words still ring true today and the sore has become an appalling tragedy for the original inhabitants of Palestine.

Although the House of Lords then rejected the British mandate by 60 votes to 29 because of its inclusion of the Balfour Declaration, the British government managed to ignore such rejection and to secure the approval of the Council of the League of Nations to the mandate and to its inclusion in the Declaration. It is noteworthy that not only was the Balfour Declaration rejected by the House of Lords, but it was never approved by the British Parliament. In fact, an examination of the records of the House of Commons for the period 1917–23 that was carried out at the request of the author, shows that the governments of the time made strenuous efforts to prevent any debate in Parliament on the Balfour Declaration.

NOTES

1. Nahum Sokolow, *History of Zionism* (Ktav, New York, 1919), p. xxiv.
2. Norman Bentwich, *Palestine of the Jews* (London, 1919), p. 195.
3. From Viscount Samuel's speech in the Palestine debate in the House of Lords, 23 April 1947.
4. From a lecture delivered by Sir Herbert Samuel on 25 November 1935 at University College, London, *The Jewish Historical Society of England*, pp. 19–20.
5. *Cmd.* 1700, June 1922; *Cmd.* 3692, October 1930 and *Cmd.* 6019, May 1939.
6. Doreen Ingrams, *Palestine Papers 1917–1922, Seeds of Conflict* (John Murray, London, 1972), p. 89.
7. For the Treaty of Sèvres, see J.G. Hurewitz, *Diplomacy in the Near and Middle East* (Van Nostrand, New York, 1956), vol. II, p. 84.
8. Arthur Koestler, *Promise and Fulfilment* (Macmillan, New York, 1949), p. 4.
9. Doreen Ingrams, *Palestine Papers*, p. 61.
10. *Hansard's Reports*, House of Lords, 21 June 1922, p. 997.
11. *Ibid.*, p. 1015.
12. *Ibid.*, p. 1025.

3

Zionist Claim to Palestine

Armed with the Balfour Declaration, the World Zionist Organization (which, despite its high-sounding name, represented only a
small number of Zionist Jews) submitted in 1919 to the Paris Peace
Conference at Versailles a claim 'to recognize the historic title of the
Jewish people to Palestine and the right of the Jews to reconstitute
in Palestine their national home'.[1] In its memorandum dated 3
February 1919 the World Zionist Organization referred to the
endorsement of the Balfour Declaration by the Principal Allied
Powers in the First World War and requested that Palestine be
placed by the League of Nations under a mandate to be entrusted to
Great Britain. The Zionist case was heard on 27 February 1919.

The Paris Peace Conference did not accept the Zionist case or
admit the Zionist claim for recognition of an historic title to
Palestine for the Jews. The Peace Conference decided in Article 22
of the Covenant of the League of Nations (which it adopted in April
1919 and incorporated in the Treaty of Versailles) that the Arab
territories detached from Turkey would be administered by a
mandatory on behalf of the League (see Chapter 4). It was agreed
between the Principal Allied Powers that Britain would have the
Palestine mandate while France would have the mandate over Syria
and Lebanon. It was not until 25 April 1920 that the Supreme
Council of the Principal and Allied Powers formally agreed to
entrust to Britain the mandate over Palestine. Its terms, however,
were not then defined, but were formulated in consultation between
the British government and the Zionists. It is noteworthy that in
discussing the terms of the mandate with the British government
Chaim Weizmann sought to insert therein what was denied to the

Zionists by the Peace Conference, namely, a recognition by the Principal Allied Powers 'of the historic rights of the Jews to Palestine'. This, however, was rejected by the British government, as we shall see in Chapter 5.

DOES THE ZIONIST CLAIM OF A HISTORIC RIGHT HAVE ANY LEGAL OR FACTUAL BASIS?

Zionist Jews claim a historic title of the Jewish people to Palestine. But unlike the Palestinians, who are the descendants of the original inhabitants of the country, the Jews are not descendants of the original inhabitants. Historically, the Jews were emigrants from Pharaonic Egypt. Although they lived together with the Canaanites and even ruled the country for a while, as we have seen in the first chapter, they disappeared from Palestine following the destruction of the kingdoms of Israel and Judah. Commenting upon the destruction of the last of those two kingdoms by the Babylonians in 587 BC, Georges Friedman, a Jewish commentator, observed:

> The twelve tribes were deported to the Caucasus, Armenia and in particular Babylonia, and disappeared; and with them the Jewish people in the plenitude of their existence as a simultaneous ethnic, national and religious community also disappeared for ever.[2]

Furthermore, Jewish rule in Palestine was not longer than, or even as long as, the rule of other peoples. The longest rule was that of the pagans: Canaanites, Babylonians, Persians, Greeks and Romans. Jewish rule, in varying degrees of independence, did not exceed four centuries. As Professor Noth observes, the Israeli monarchy lasted two and a half centuries as an independent institution in the two states of Israel and Judah, and one century and a half in the vassal monarchy of Judah.[3] Christian rule, Byzantine and Crusader, lasted four centuries while Moslem rule, Arab and Turkish, continued for twelve centuries.

The Jewish population was deported from Palestine by the Babylonians and the Romans (Chapter 1). Jews virtually disappeared from Palestine after their deportation by the Romans following their second revolt in AD 132–5. Benjamin of Tudela, a Jewish pilgrim who visited the Holy Land about AD 1170–1, found only 1,440 Jews in all Palestine.[4] Until the nineteenth century only a small number of

Jews were found in religious centres in Jerusalem, Safaed and Tiberias. In 1837, Jews in Palestine numbered 8,000 out of a total population of 350,000;[5] in 1845 they were 11,000; in 1880 they numbered 20,000 out of a total population of 500,000[6] and in 1918 they were 56,000 or 8 per cent of a total population of 700,000.[7] It may be remarked that while the Jewish presence in Palestine was of short duration and for many centuries actually ceased, in contrast, the presence of the Palestinians as the indigenous descendants of the original inhabitants was continuous until the twentieth century. The Zionist claim of title to Palestine also has no basis in fact. The Jews who migrated to Palestine in the twentieth century and established the state of Israel are mostly descendants of converts to Judaism and possess no racial links with the Israelites or Hebrews who lived in Palestine in biblical times and had disappeared from the country some eighteen centuries previously. According to Joseph Reinach, a French writer of Jewish origin:

> The Jews of Palestinian origin constitute an insignificant minority. Like Christians and Moslems, the Jews have engaged with great zeal in the conversion of people to their faith. Before the Christian era, the Jews had converted to the monotheistic religion of Moses other Semites (or Arabs), Greeks, Egyptians and Romans, in large numbers. Later, Jewish proselytism was not less active in Asia, in the whole of North Africa, in Italy, in Spain and in Gaul . . . There were many converted Iberians among the Jews who were expelled from Spain by Ferdinand the Catholic and who spread to Italy, France, the East and Smyrna. The great majority of Russian, Polish and Galician Jews descend from the Khazars, a Tartar people of southern Russia who were converted in a body to Judaism at the time of Charlemagne. To speak of a Jewish race, one must be either ignorant or of bad faith. There was a semitic or Arab race; but there never was a Jewish race.[8]

Likewise, Arthur Koestler traces the origin of the Jews of Eastern Europe called *Ashkenazis* to the Khazars who, as mentioned by Joseph Reinach, were converted to Judaism.[9] The small number of Jews who lived in Palestine in Turkish times were mostly descendants of the *Sephardic* Jews who were expelled from Spain in 1492, some of whom sought refuge in Palestine. Most of the other Jews who lived in Arab countries were either Arabs or Berbers of North Africa who were converted to Judaism. In neither case can their origins be traced to the biblical Israelites.

19

ZIONIST EXPLOITATION OF THE BIBLE

In order to give support to their spurious claim of title to Palestine and to gain the sympathy of Western statesmen to the concept of a Jewish state, the Zionists have exploited and continue to exploit the Bible and the religious association of the Jews with Palestine. Zionists have often quoted God's promise to Abraham: 'To your descendants I will give this land' the land of Canaan (Genesis 12:7). However, this rests upon a distortion of the Bible. The term 'descendants' is not restricted to the Jews for it includes the Arabs, both Moslems and Christians, who claim descent from Abraham's son Ishmael and all are children of Abraham.

In addition, biblical texts have been misinterpreted in order to justify the creation of the State of Israel. Some evangelical fundamentalist Christians believe, or are made to believe, that the restoration of the Jewish people to the Holy Land augurs the imminent end of the world and the arrival of the kingdom of God. But the biblical texts that are invoked in this regard refer to a spiritual kingdom and not to a secular state of Israel which was established by Russian, Romanian and Polish immigrants with a heterogeneity of other Jews many of whom do not even believe in the Bible. Unlike the evangelicals, the position of the mainstream Protestant churches and the Roman Catholic Church on the Israeli-Palestinian issue is based on considerations of justice and human rights, rather than on biblical prophecy.[10]

Commenting upon the misuse of biblical texts, the Rev. Tony Crowe observed:

> The Bible is a dangerous book, and a happy hunting ground for cranks, who can prove anything by quoting texts out of context, and applying them to contemporary events. Manipulation of texts was ruthlessly employed by Weizmann, the man behind the Balfour Declaration. His biblical language moved British and American politicians to further the Zionist cause.[11]

The Zionist exploitation of the Bible has generated support not only for the Balfour Declaration, but also for the UN partition resolution and the creation of a Jewish state. Nowadays the Bible is also relied upon for the annexation of the West Bank and Gaza which the Israeli authorities like to describe by their biblical names of Judea and Samaria.

The Hebrew or Israelite occupation of Palestine was a biblical episode which came to an end centuries ago, as did other invasions. It is evident that the Zionist claim to a 'historic right' to Palestine is based on false historical premises and lacks any juridical basis. The addition of religious considerations derived from the Bible does not improve its quality. The claim was designed to justify the Zionist plan to usurp the land of Palestine from its original inhabitants. J.P. Alem, the French commentator on Middle Eastern affairs, has observed: 'The concept of historical rights claimed by the Zionists has served the purpose for which it was conceived and is nowadays quite worn out'.[12]

NOTES

1. For the text of the Zionist memorandum to the Paris Peace Conference, see J.C. Hurewitz, *Diplomacy in the Near and Middle East* (Van Nostrand, New York, 1956), vol. II, p. 45.

2. Georges Friedmann, *The End of the Jewish People?* (Doubleday Anchor Books, New York, 1968), p. 266.

3. Martin Noth, *Histoire d'Israël* (Payot, Paris, 1970), p. 299.

4. Rev. Charles T. Bridgeman's letter to the President of the Trusteeship Council, 13 January 1950, UN Doc. A/1286, p. 13.

5. Nevill Barbour, *Nisi Dominus* (Institute of Palestine Studies, Beirut, 1969), p. 32.

6. *Dictionnaire Diplomatique*, Paris, p. 294.

7. Government of Palestine, *Survey of Palestine* (Palestine Govt Printing Press), vol. 1, p. 144.

8. Translation from *Journal des Débats*, 30 March 1919, Paris.

9. Arthur Koestler, *The 13th Tribe, the Khazar Empire and its Heritage* (Hutchinson, 1976), London.

10. On evangelical beliefs and influence on the Palestine Question in US policy, see Ruth W. Mouly, *The Evangelical Dimension* (National Council on US-Arab Relations, New York, 1985) and Grace Halsell, *Prophecy and Politics*, Lawrence Hill, Westport, Conn., 1986.

11. *Middle East International*, August 1971.

12. Translation from J.P. Alem, *Juifs et Arabes* (Grasset, Paris, 1968), p. 35.

4

Article 22 of the
Covenant of the League of Nations

The ideas which President Wilson propounded towards the end of the First World War — namely, the rejection of any territorial acquisition by conquest and the recognition of the right of self-determination of peoples — came to be generally accepted and were incorporated in 1919 in Article 22 of the Covenant of the League of Nations. The Covenant laid down that, to the peoples inhabiting territories which have ceased to be under the sovereignty of the state which formerly governed them, there should be applied 'the principle that their well-being and development form a sacred trust of civilisation'. Moreover, and specifically with regard to the communities detached from the Ottoman Empire, namely, the peoples of Palestine, Syria, Lebanon and Iraq, Article 22 laid down that 'their existence as independent nations can be provisionally recognized subject to the rendering of administrative advice and assistance by a mandatory until such time as they were able to stand alone'. The Covenant of the League of Nations was approved by the Paris Peace Conference on 28 April 1919 and was incorporated in the Treaty of Versailles which was signed two months later.

ARTICLE 22 APPLIED TO ARAB TERRITORIES DETACHED FROM TURKEY

Article 22 of the Covenant was applied in the Arab territories detached from Turkey at the end of the First World War. Four new states then came into existence: Iraq, Lebanon, Syria and Palestine. In accordance with Article 22 these four states were subjected to temporary mandates designed to assist them and to lead them to complete independence. It might be observed that the mandate over

Iraq did not come into operation by reason of strong opposition on the part of its inhabitants and, as a result, the mandate was replaced by a treaty relationship between Great Britain and Iraq, which became a fully independent state. Referring to the new Arab states that were then placed under mandates, H. Duncan Hall observed:

> These were cradles of western civilisation and of great religions of Europe and Asia; and their peoples were capable of becoming independent states within a short period of time if they could in fact devise constitutions based on the consent of the main elements of the population.[1]

Emirate of Transjordan

A fifth territory located in the area lying east of the Jordan River was entrusted to Britain and attached to the Palestine mandate. This territory, which was called Transjordan, had not formed part of historical Palestine. In Ottoman times, it had been administratively part of the province of Syria and was called the district of Al Balqa'. When the question of delimiting the British and French mandates arose, Britain insisted on the inclusion of the district of Al Balqa' in its mandate over Palestine because it wished to entrust its administration to Emir Abdullah, son of King Hussein Ben Ali, the Sharif of Mecca, to reward him for his help during the war against the Turks. The new territory assumed the name of Transjordan and was set up as an Emirate. The Emirate of Transjordan remained under a protective treaty relationship with Britain until 25 May 1946 when it was formally detached from the Palestine mandate and Emir Abdullah was recognized as King of Transjordan. In 1949 the new kingdom assumed the name of the Hashemite Kingdom of Jordan.

Palestine after the First World War

Palestine became a state after its detachment from the Ottoman Empire. It is necessary to emphasize that the various Arab countries, including Palestine, which were subjected to mandates under Article 22 of the Covenant became states under international law, even though their powers of self-government were restricted and were exercised by a Mandatory. Their international status was akin to protected states. Discussing the international status of Palestine and

23

Syria, the Earl of Birkenhead said:

> The position of Palestine and Syria is that they were integral portions of the Turkish Empire (which has renounced all right or title to them: Article 16 of the Treaty of Lausanne, 1923), they have become administratively, partially dependent now upon an appointed mandatory state, but they are acknowledged — in the terms of Article 22 of the Covenant — to be entitled to provisional recognition of independence . . . The status of Palestine and Syria resembles very closely that of states under suzerainty.[2]

Palestine possessed, therefore, its own statehood, its own international personality and its own government which were distinct from those of the Mandatory. Although under the control of Britain, the government of Palestine concluded agreements with the Mandatory and became party, through the instrumentality of the Mandatory, to a number of international treaties and conventions.[3] Although Palestine then became a state and its people were 'provisionally recognized as an independent nation', it was in fact deprived of the powers of legislation and administration which were vested in the Mandatory. This was done in order to enable the Mandatory to facilitate Jewish immigration into Palestine and otherwise implement the Balfour Declaration against the will and the wishes of the original inhabitants.

NOTES

1. H. Duncan Hall, *Mandates, Dependencies and Trusteeships* (Carnegie Endowment for International Peace, New York, 1948), pp. 33–4.
2. Earl of Birkenhead, *International Law*, 6th edn. (J.M. Dent, London), p. 40.
3. For a discussion of the status and sovereignty of states under mandate, see Henry Cattan, *Palestine and International Law*, 2nd edn. (Longman, London, 1976), pp. 116–21.

5

The British Mandate 1922–1948

TERMS OF THE MANDATE

The Palestine mandate was approved by the Council of the League of Nations on 24 July 1922. It recited in its first preamble that the Principal Allied Powers had agreed, 'for the purpose of giving effect to the provisions of Article 22 of the Covenant of the League of Nations', to entrust to a Mandatory the administration of the territory of Palestine. In its second recital, the mandate stated that the Principal Allied Powers had also agreed that the Mandatory should be responsible for putting into effect the declaration originally made by the government of His Britannic Majesty in favour of the establishment in Palestine of a national home for the Jewish people, 'it being clearly understood that nothing should be done which might prejudice the civil and religious rights of existing non-Jewish communities in Palestine', or the rights and political status enjoyed by Jews in any other country. In its third recital, the mandate declared that recognition was thereby given to the 'historical connection' of the Jewish people with Palestine and to the grounds for reconstituting their national home in that country.

In his autobiography, Chaim Weizmann, the author and principal Zionist negotiator of the Balfour Declaration, states that instead of the phrase in the preamble which refers to 'the historical connection' of the Jewish people with Palestine, the Zionists wanted to have: 'Recognizing the historic rights of the Jews in Palestine'.[1] But the British government rejected this wording and Balfour suggested 'historical connection' as a compromise.

It is remarkable that although the mandate speaks of 'Jews', 'the Jewish people' and 'the Jewish population of Palestine', it does not once mention the Palestinians or the Palestinian Arabs who are the original inhabitants and then constituted 92 per cent of the population. It merely refers to them as 'non-Jewish communities' in Palestine. Was such language used to create the implication that the Palestinians were of little significance or consisted of an insignificant number?

The principal provisions of the mandate are contained in Articles 1, 2 and 6. Article 1 gave the Mandatory full powers of legislation and administration. Article 2 imposed upon the Mandatory three contradictory obligations, namely,

(a) to place the country under such political, administrative and economic conditions as would secure the establishment of the Jewish national home;
(b) to develop self-governing institutions and
(c) to safeguard the civil and religious rights of all the inhabitants.

Article 6 provided that, 'while ensuring that the rights and position of other sections of the population are not prejudiced', the Administration of Palestine should facilitate Jewish immigration.

The terms of the mandate were formulated by the World Zionist Organization and were settled by the British government 'in consultation with Zionist representatives'.[2] The people of Palestine who were the party most affected were neither consulted about the mandate, nor their consent obtained to its terms. The Palestinians never accepted the mandate as it violated their national rights and their opposition to it was expressed by several congresses, and riots and disturbances.

Incompatibility with Article 22 of the Covenant

The Palestine mandate was clearly incompatible with Article 22 of the Covenant under whose authority it purported to have been formulated. The statement in its preamble that its purpose was to give effect 'to the provisions of Article 22 of the Covenant of the League of Nations' was contradicted by its very terms. This incompatibility was shamelessly admitted by the author of the Balfour Declaration. In a memorandum to the British government dated 11 August 1919, Balfour wrote to Curzon:

the contradiction between the letters of the Covenant and the policy of the Allies is even more flagrant in the case of the 'independent nation' of Palestine than in that of the 'independent nation' of Syria. For in Palestine we do not propose even to go through the form of consulting the wishes of the present inhabitants of the country, though the American Commission has been going through the form of asking what they are.

The Four Great Powers are committed to Zionism. And Zionism, be it right or wrong, good or bad, is rooted in age-long traditions, in present needs, in future hopes, of far profounder import than the desires and prejudices of the 700,000 Arabs who now inhabit that ancient land . . .

Whatever deference should be paid to the views of those living there, the Powers in their selection of a mandatory do not propose, as I understand the matter, to consult them. In short, so far as Palestine is concerned, the Powers have made no statement of fact which is not admittedly wrong, and no declaration of Policy which, at least in the letter, they have not always intended to violate.[3]

One really wonders whether this is callous frankness or frank callousness.

The injustice of the mandate

The injustice done to the Palestinians by the Balfour Declaration and the mandate was described by Professor John Garstang in the following terms:

For more than a thousand years, almost as long as English folks have inhabited this country, an Arab people has dwelt in undisputed possession of the soil of Palestine. Gentle by nature, hospitable and courteous in bearing, they form an ordered society, with their own doctors, lawyers, judges, government officials, landed gentry, small owners, agriculturists and peasants . . . The Arabs gave a cordial welcome to Lord Allenby's Proclamation of November 1918, with its definite promise to the peoples of Syria and Palestine of 'National Governments and Administrations deriving their authority from the initiative and free choice of the indigenous populations'. . . . What has clouded the horizon for Palestine — and for Palestine alone of all the mandated territories — has been the imposition . . . of a difficult and hazardous experiment. 'The Jewish National Home', as a Jewish writer

27

recognises, 'is quite novel and finds no counterpart in international law . . . It is being created in a territory largely occupied by another race' . . . It is on record that in 1921 Mr Winston Churchill affirmed to a deputation at Jerusalem: 'We cannot tolerate the expropriation of one set of people by another, or the violent trampling down of one set of national ideals for the sake of erecting another.'

The Arabs found that, though constituting more than 90 per cent of the population, their status was not recognised in the mandate, which omits all mention of their name. They found that their request in 1922 for the creation of a national independent Government was dismissed as incompatible with the pledges made to the Jews . . . This meant in so many words that the pledge given in 1918 to the 'indigenous populations' must be broken. This was the first blow to British good faith, whereon the Arabs had relied.[4]

Jewish immigration during the mandate

The British mandate in Palestine did not achieve the basic purpose of Article 22 of the Covenant of the League of Nations to lead the people to full independence, nor, as we have seen, was it intended to do that. After almost three decades of the mandate there was no sign of self-governing institutions. All that the mandate achieved in a quarter of a century was to permit a massive Jewish immigration into Palestine which resulted in the modification of the demographic structure in the country from a largely Palestinian Arab population to a mixed Arab-Jewish population. During the mandate, the Jewish population increased more than tenfold: from 56,000 in 1918[5] the number of Jews in Palestine increased to 83,794 according to the census of 1922, to 174,610 according to the census of 1931, and to 608,230 in 1946 out of a total population of 1,972,560.[6] According to the statistics of the government of Palestine, the provenance of most of the Jewish immigrants was Eastern Europe. This immigration and demographic change in the structure of the population were achieved against the will of the original inhabitants and despite their opposition which was demonstrated in riots and a civil war that lasted from 1936 to 1939.

Riots and commissions of inquiry

After each serious disturbance the British government appointed a commission of inquiry to determine its causes. Commissions of inquiry were appointed in 1920, 1921, 1929 and 1936.[7] In all cases the causes for the disturbances were found to be the same: Palestinian opposition to Jewish immigration, their fear of the establishment of a Jewish national home and their desire for national independence. Nevertheless, the findings of these commissions failed to arrest the flow of Jewish immigration. The last commission, known as the Peel Commission, which investigated the unrest in 1936, recommended the termination of the mandate and partition of the country between Arabs and Jews, save for enclaves covering Jerusalem, Bethlehem and Nazareth, which would remain under a British mandate.[8] On further investigation of the form and practicabilities of partition by another commission called the Woodhead Commission, the British government came to the conclusion that the difficulties involved in the proposal to create Arab and Jewish states within Palestine were so great as to make partition impracticable.[9]

Jewish opposition to self-government in Palestine

The Jewish immigrants showed no disposition to a normal co-existence with the Palestinians. Spurred on by Zionist political ambitions, they were determined to establish, not a national home in Palestine, but to create a Jewish state. For this reason, they opposed the attempt made by the Mandatory in 1923 to set up a Legislative Council comprising Moslems, Christians and Jews. They were also hostile to the creation of any form of self-government as long as they were a minority.

British White Paper of 1939 on proposed termination of the mandate

In 1939 the British government remembered its obligation to safeguard the rights of the original inhabitants and also the fact that its tutelage was not intended to be permanent but should lead to the independence of Palestine. It, therefore, announced in a white paper[10] its intention to limit Jewish immigration into Palestine to

75,000 during the following five years and to grant Palestine its independence within ten years.

This decision of the British government was somewhat belated because the rights, position and future of the Palestinians had already been considerably prejudiced. By increasing through immigration the number of the Jews in Palestine from one-twelfth to one-third of the population, the British government had substantially and dangerously altered the demographic structure in the country and thus laid the foundations for a separatist movement by the Zionist Jews and the establishment of a Jewish state.

Violent Jewish opposition

The Zionist Jews fought the attempt by the British government to limit Jewish immigration and to grant to Palestine its independence by a campaign of violence and terror directed at the British and Palestinians alike. Jewish terrorists blew up the King David Hotel at Jerusalem which was the seat of the government, killing 91 of its senior officials; captured and hanged British officers; raided military stores; dynamited homes over the heads of their occupants in Arab residential quarters and bombed Arab market places.[11]

On the political level, the Jews pressed for the partition of Palestine into Jewish and Arab states. They rejected the idea of a binational state which was suggested by one of their leading intellectuals, Judah Magnes, president of the Hebrew University of Jerusalem. Judah Magnes opposed the partition of Palestine because he believed that it would lead to war between Arabs and Jews. What he did not foresee was that partition would lead to several wars and perhaps, as things stand at present, to perpetual war.

British government refers the question of Palestine to the UN

Harassed by the Jewish campaign of violence and terror, unable to permit any further Jewish immigration against the wishes of the original inhabitants, and subjected to pressure by American President Harry Truman to open the gates of Palestine to Jewish immigrants while the US government closed to them its own doors, the British government decided in April 1947 to refer the question of the future government of Palestine to the UN.

NOTES

1. Chaim Weizmann, *Trial and Error* (Hamish Hamilton, London, 1949), p. 348.

2. H.W.V. Temperley, *History of the Peace Conference of Paris* (Hodder and Stoughton, London, 1924), vol. VI, p. 174. See also John Marlowe, *The Seat of Pilate* (Cresset Press, London, 1959), pp. 60–2.

3. Doreen Ingrams, *Palestine Papers 1917–1922, Seeds of Conflict* (John Murray, London, 1972), p. 73.

4. Professor John Garstang, *The Observer*, 20 September 1936.

5. Government of Palestine, *Survey of Palestine* (Palestine Govt Printing Press), vol. I, p. 144.

6. Appendix I to Report of Sub-Committee I, Official Records of the 2nd Session of the General Assembly, Ad Hoc Committee on the Palestine Question, p. 270.

7. For the reports of these Commissions, see Government of Palestine, *A Survey of Palestine* (Palestine Govt Printing Press, 1946), vol. I, pp. 18–25.

8. *Cmd.* 5479, July 1937.

9. *Cmd.* 5854, November 1938.

10. *Cmd.* 6018, May 1939.

11. For details about this campaign of violence, see *A Survey of Palestine*, vol. I, pp. 56–7; *The British Statement on Acts of Violence, Cmd.* 6873, July 1946; S.N. Fisher, *The Middle East* (Routledge and Kegan Paul, London, 1960), p. 579; G. Kirk, *The Middle East, 1945–1950* (Oxford University Press, London, 1954), pp. 209–13 and 218–23.

6

UN Resolution
for the Partition of Palestine

PALESTINE AND THE UN

In its letter to the Secretary-General of the UN dated 2 April 1947 the British Government requested that the Question of Palestine be placed on the agenda of the General Assembly at its next session at which it would ask the Assembly to make recommendations, under Article 10 of the Charter, concerning the future government of Palestine. A special session of the General Assembly was convened on 28 April 1947 to consider the matter.

Five Arab States, Egypt, Iraq, Syria, Lebanon and Saudi Arabia requested the Secretary-General to include as an additional item in the agenda of the special session the question of the termination of the mandate over Palestine and the declaration of its independence.

MANDATE ENDED WITH THE DISSOLUTION OF THE LEAGUE OF NATIONS

It should be observed that the Palestine mandate had already come to an end legally as a result of the dissolution of the League of Nations in April 1946. Since the mandate was exercised as a tutelage on behalf of the League, it is obvious that it came to an end with the termination of the League's existence. In a resolution adopted at its last meeting on 18 April 1946 the League of Nations recalled that Article 22 of the Covenant applied to certain territories placed under mandate the principle that the well-being and development of their inhabitants form a sacred trust of civilization and also recognized that, on the termination of the League's existence, its functions with respect to the mandated territories would come to an end. The League took note of the intentions of the members of the League then administering mandated territories to continue to administer them for the well-being and development of the peoples concerned until arrangements were made between the UN and the Mandatory Powers under the UN Charter. Certain of the Mandatories had declared their intention to conclude trusteeship agreements under the Charter, but the Egyptian delegate pointed out that the mandates had terminated with the dissolution of the League and that, therefore, Palestine could not be placed under trusteeship.[1]

PROCEEDINGS AT THE UN IN 1947: PLAN TO PARTITION PALESTINE

When the Question of Palestine came up for discussion at the UN in 1947, the Jews and the Palestinians were invited to submit their views. The former, represented by Rabbi Hillel Silver, asked for the reconstitution of the Jewish national home in Palestine in accordance with the Balfour Declaration, referred to the plight of the Jews during the Second World War and appealed for the establishment of a Jewish State in Palestine.[2] The author of this book presented the Palestinian viewpoint as spokesman of the Arab Higher Committee which represented the people of Palestine.[3] He opposed the plan to partition Palestine and emphasized that the Palestine Arabs were entitled to their independence on the basis of the Charter and their natural and inalienable rights.[4]

The Arab States argued that the only course open to the UN was to recognize the termination of the mandate and the independence of Palestine. However, by reason of political manoeuvring by the Zionists and their supporters, the Arab proposal failed to obtain the required majority. Instead, the General Assembly established on 15 May 1947 a Special Committee on Palestine (UNSCOP) to prepare a report on the Question of Palestine to be submitted to its next regular session. The Palestinians, however, boycotted UNSCOP and did not participate in its investigations. UNSCOP submitted two plans, a majority and a minority plan. The majority plan proposed the termination of the mandate and the partition of Palestine, the creation of an Arab State and a Jewish State with economic union between them, and a *corpus separatum* for the City of Jerusalem which would be subjected to a special international régime to be administered by the UN. The minority plan also envisaged the termination of the mandate, but proposed the establishment of a

33

federal state which would comprise an Arab and a Jewish State with Jerusalem as the capital of the federation.

In the debate that followed, the Arabs rejected the partition proposal and questioned the competence or power of the UN to recommend the partition of their homeland into two States and thus to destroy its territorial integrity. They also raised the issues of the invalidity of the Balfour Declaration and of the mandate. Sub-Committee 2 to the Ad Hoc Committee on the Palestine Question recommended that these issues be referred to the International Court of Justice for an advisory opinion.[5] However, the recommendation of Sub-Committee 2 as well as several Arab requests to refer these issues to the International Court of Justice were defeated in the General Assembly.[6]

Jewish opposition to partition

The partition of Palestine was opposed not only by the Palestinian Arabs and by the Arab States, but also by the indigenous Orthodox Jews of Palestine who lived on good terms with their Arab neighbours. In fact, the concept of a Jewish national home was foreign to the indigenous religious Jews in Palestine. Ronald Storrs, the first British Governor of Jerusalem, wrote: 'The religious Jews of Jerusalem and Hebron and the *Sephardim* were strongly opposed to political Zionism'.[7]

Opposition also came from leading Jewish statesmen. Notable among the opponents of partition were Sir Herbert Samuel, the first British High Commissioner in Palestine and J.L. Magnes, President of the Hebrew University of Jerusalem. Both men, as we have seen in discussing the Balfour Declaration, had proclaimed their opposition to its leading to a Jewish State. In a speech at the House of Lords on 23 April 1947, Sir Herbert Samuel, then Viscount Samuel, said: 'I do not support partition, because knowing the country as I do, it seems to be geographically impossible. It would create as many problems as it would solve.'[8] In his testimony before the Anglo-American Committee of Inquiry on Palestine, J.L. Magnes declared:

> The Arabs have great natural rights in Palestine. They have been here for centuries. The graves of their fathers are here. There are remains of Arab culture at every turn. The Mosque of Aksa is the third Holy Mosque in Islam . . .[9]

34

In a memorandum to UNSCOP dated 23 July 1947, J.L. Magnes formulated the case against partition in the following terms:

> We have been asked for a statement as to why we are against the partition of Palestine . . . We believe genuine segregation to be impossible. No matter where you draw the boundaries of the Jewish state, there will always be a very large Arab minority . . . It is impossible to draw satisfactory economic boundaries . . . The larger the Jewish state, the more impossible becomes the economic existence of the Arab state . . .
>
> Satisfactory 'national boundaries', if the object is to promote peace, cannot be drawn. Whenever you draw these boundaries, you create irredentas on either side of the border. Irredentas almost invariably lead to war . . . There are those who say that we should accept partition now, because 'borders are not eternal' . . . In other words, the partitioned Jewish Palestine would be a bridge-head for the further conquest of the whole of the country.
>
> Many Jews are in favour of partition . . . But there are many Jews, moderates and extremists, religious and not religious, who are opposed to partition. Almost all the Arabs are opposed to partition . . . Imposing partition would therefore be a hazardous undertaking.
>
> Under all these circumstances, we find it strange that anyone should claim for partition that it, at least, gives finality. To us it seems to be but the beginning of real warfare . . . perhaps between Jew and Jew, and warfare between Jew and Arab.[10]

US and Soviet Union support partition

Although the Zionist ambition of creating a Jewish State was not shared by all Jews, the Zionists mobilized all their forces to secure a vote by the UN in favour of partition. They succeeded in enlisting the aid of Harry Truman, President of the USA, who for electoral reasons connected with the Jewish vote used his immense influence to persuade several members of the UN to vote in favour of partition.[11] The Soviet Union also favoured partition mainly for two reasons: first, in order to eliminate the British Administration from Palestine and second, it hoped that since the great majority of the Jewish immigrants to Palestine came from the Soviet Union, Poland and Central Europe, a Jewish State would become its ally in the Middle East.[12]

Under the combined influence of the US and the Soviet Union and their satellites, the General Assembly adopted on 29 November 1947, Resolution 181(II) for the partition of Palestine into Arab and Jewish States by a vote of thirty-three to thirteen with ten abstentions. The UK abstained. The negative votes comprised those of six Arab States: Egypt, Iraq, Lebanon, Saudi Arabia, Syria and Yemen; four Moslem countries: Afghanistan, Iran, Pakistan, Turkey; and Cuba, Greece and India.

The boundaries of the two states were delimited in the resolution. According to the boundaries defined in the resolution, the Arab State would have an area of 11,800 square kilometres representing 43 per cent of the territory of Palestine while the Jewish State would have an area of 14,500 square kilometres representing 57 per cent of the area of Palestine. The resolution further provided for the establishment of a *corpus separatum* for the City of Jerusalem which would be subject to a special international régime to be administered by the UN. The resolution also provided that the independent Arab and Jewish States would have an economic union since a partition of Palestine without economic union would leave the Arab State economically non-viable.

It was envisaged that the new States and the special régime for the City of Jerusalem would come into existence two months after the evacuation of the armed forces of the Mandatory had been completed. In December 1947, the British Government informed the UN that it would terminate the mandate and withdraw its forces on 15 May 1948.

The role played by the US and the Soviet Union in influencing the UN to vote in favour of partition is recognized by the State Department in a *Report of the Policy Planning Staff* on the position of the US with respect to Palestine, dated 19 January 1948. The Report stated:

The US and USSR played leading roles in bringing about a vote favourable to partition. Without US leadership and the pressures which developed during UN consideration of the question, the necessary two-thirds majority in the General Assembly could not have been obtained . . . It has been shown that various unauthorized US nationals and organizations, including members of Congress, notably in the closing days of the Assembly, brought pressure to bear on various foreign delegates and their home governments to induce them to support the US attitude on the Palestine Question. Evidence to this effect is attached under Tab A.[13]

Although the US backed the partition of Palestine and the creation of a Jewish State, it is necessary for the record to mention the dissenting voices of at least three leading members of the US administration. James Forrestal, Secretary of Defence, condemned the manoeuvres used in order to secure a favourable vote on partition in his *Diaries*. Forrestal said that 'our Palestine policy had been made for "squalid political purposes" . . . '[14] Warren Austin, US representative at the UN, opposed partition in discussions with his delegation and was reported to have said:

In line with the US stated principle of backing the UN by defending political independence and integrity, Ambassador Austin did not see how it was possible to carve out of an area already too small for a state a still smaller state. He thought it was certain that such a state would have to defend itself with bayonets for ever, until extinguished in blood. The Arabs, he said, would never be willing to have such a small state in their heart.[15]

The strongest indictment of the partition of Palestine was voiced by Loy Henderson, Director of the Office of Near Eastern and African Affairs at the Department of State. In a report to the Secretary of State dated 22 September 1947 he criticized UNSCOP's majority report recommending partition and declared that it was not in the interests of the US to support the partition plan or the setting up of a Jewish State. He also referred to the finding of the Anglo-American Committee of Inquiry which did not recommend partition. Loy Henderson continued:

We are under no obligation to the Jews to set up a Jewish State. The Balfour Declaration and the mandate provided not for a Jewish State, but for a Jewish national home.

He also emphasized that partition would be:

in definite contravention to various principles laid down in the Charter as well as to principles on which American concepts of government are based.[16]

Invalidity of the partition resolution

The partition resolution is vitiated by several gross irregularities which are summarized below.

(1) Incompetence of the General Assembly of the UN to partition Palestine. The UN possessed no sovereignty over Palestine, nor the power to deprive the people of Palestine of their right of independence in the whole of their homeland or to impair their national rights. Hence, the UN resolution for the partition of Palestine possesses no value, in law or in fact, as acknowledged by a number of leading jurists. P.B. Potter has observed that:

> The United Nations has no right to dictate a solution in Palestine unless a basis for such authority can be worked out such as has not been done this far.
>
> Such a basis might be found by holding that sovereignty over Palestine, relinquished by Turkey in the Treaty of Lausanne, passed to the League of Nations, and has been inherited by the United Nations, a proposition which involves two hazardous steps. Or it might be held that the Mandate is still in force and that supervision thereof has passed to the United Nations, which is much more realistic but still somewhat hazardous juridically. The Arabs deny the binding force of the Mandate, now or ever, as they deny the validity of the Balfour Declaration on which it was based, and again they are probably quite correct juridically.[17]

Professor Quincy Wright recently expressed the view that 'The legality of the General Assembly's recommendation for partition of Palestine was doubtful'.[18]

The same view was expressed by Professor I. Brownlie:

> It is doubtful if the United Nations 'has a capacity to convey title', *inter alia* because the Organization cannot assume the rôle of territorial sovereign . . . Thus the resolution of 1947 containing a Partition plan for Palestine was probably *ultra vires* [outside the competence of the United Nations], and, if it was not, was not binding on member states in any case.[19]

It follows, therefore, that the partition resolution was not legally effective or binding on the Palestinian people.

(2) Denial of justice in the rejection by the General Assembly of several requests to refer the questions of the incompetence of the General Assembly and of the illegality of the Balfour Declaration and of the mandate for an advisory opinion of the International Court of Justice. P.B. Potter has observed that the rejection of the Arab

requests to refer the question of UN jurisdiction over the Palestine situation to the International Court of Justice 'tends to confirm the avoidance of international law' in this regard.[20] Such avoidance of international law constituted a denial of justice which deprived the partition resolution of any juridical value.

(3) Violation of Article 22 of the Covenant of the League of Nations which provisionally recognized the independence of the people of Palestine and envisaged a temporary mandate over Palestine with a view to leading its inhabitants to full independence.

(4) Violation of the Charter of the UN and the principle of self-determination of the people of Palestine.

(5) Violation of the most elementary democratic principles by the flagrant disregard of the will of the majority of the original inhabitants who opposed partition of their homeland.

(6) Undue influence exercised by the American administration, and personally by the President of the USA, to secure a General Assembly vote in favour of partition.

(7) Iniquity of the plan of partition. The iniquity of the plan of partition adopted by the General Assembly is glaring.

On the one hand, more than half a million Palestinians would be subjected to Jewish rule in the Jewish State by immigrants brought into the country against the will of its original inhabitants. As delineated by the plan of partition, the population of the proposed Jewish State would consist of 509,780 Moslems and Christians and 499,020 Jews.[21] On the other hand, in accordance with the Palestine Government's *Village Statistics* the Jews owned at the end of the mandate 1,491,699 *dunoms* of land (the *dunom* being equal to one thousand square metres) out of a total of 26,323,023 *dunoms* representing the area of Palestine. Thus, Jewish land ownership amounted to 5.66 per cent of the total area of Palestine. This was acknowledged by David Ben Gurion, then Chairman of the Jewish Agency, and later the first Prime Minister of Israel, in his testimony before UNSCOP in 1947. He then said: 'The Arabs own 94 per cent of the land, the Jews only 6%'.[22]

And yet, despite the insignificant area owned by the Jews in Palestine in 1947, the partition plan attributed to the Jews — who constituted less than one-third of the population, who were largely foreigners and who owned less than 6 per cent of the land — an area almost ten times greater than what they owned, i.e., 57 per cent of Palestine while it left 43 per cent of their homeland to the Palestinians. This was not a partition, but a spoliation.

The Arab States proclaimed their opposition to the partition resolution which they considered to be a violation of the Charter and totally lacking in legal validity.[23] The Palestinians also rejected the partition of their homeland, but the Jews accepted it 'with reluctance'. The Palestinians and the Arabs generally have been criticized for their rejection of partition as being intransigent, uncompromising and mistaken in their attitude, while the Jews were praised for their conciliatory attitude, in their acceptance, albeit 'reluctant', of partition. This criticism has been convincingly answered by a neutral observer, J. Bowyer Bell, in these terms:

> In retrospect it is all too easy to point out the Arab blunders, their missed opportunities, their intransigence. It is only just, however, to note that it is easy to urge compromise of another's principle, to urge someone else to give up half a loaf of his own bread. Surely, the Arab argument had much justice . . . Whittled down to basics, the Zionist position was that, given the Palestine dilemma, they would settle for half whereas the Arabs unfairly continued to demand all. It was ingenious, it was evil, and it threw the entire Arab argument into the wrong frame of reference. More devastating still, it proved effective.[24]

SOLOMON'S JUDGEMENT?

The UN resolution for the partition of Palestine may appear to some to have been a kind of Solomon's judgement. Yet when King Solomon had to give judgement in the dispute between the two women who claimed the same child and he ordered that it be cut in two so as to 'give half to the one, and half to the other', (1 Kings 3:25), he only intended to find out the truth as to who of the two was the real mother. And when he did, he ordered that the child be not slain, but that it be given to its mother. But in the case of Palestine, King Solomon's wisdom was not followed and Palestine was effectively cut in two and, as a result, it has been bleeding ever since.

NOTES

1. Regarding the effect of the dissolution of the League of Nations on mandates, see H. Duncan Hall, *Mandates, Dependencies and Trusteeships*, (Carnegie Endowment for International Peace, 1948), pp. 272–4.
2. *UN Official Records of the first special session*, 1947, vol. III, pp. 108 *et seq.*

3. The Arab Higher Committee was formed in 1936 by the six Arab political parties which then existed in Palestine. It was recognized by the mandatory Government and subsequently by the UN as the representative of the Palestinian people.

4. *UN Official Records of the first special session*, 1947, vol. III, pp. 189 *et seq.*

5. *UN Official Records of the second session of the General Assembly*, Ad Hoc Committee on the Palestine Question, p. 300.

6. *Ibid.*, p. 203. For the several denials in 1947 by the General Assembly of requests for an advisory opinion on the Palestine Question, see UN Documents A/AC/14/21, 14 October 1947; A/AC 14/24, 16 October 1947; A/AC 14/25, 16 October 1947; A/AC 14/32, 11 November 1947.

7. Ronald Storrs, *Orientations* (Nicholson and Watson, London, 1945), p. 340.

8. From Viscount Samuel's speech at the House of Lords, 23 April 1947.

9. J.L. Magnes, *Palestine — Divided or United* (Jerusalem, 1947), p. 32.

10. J.L. Magnes, 'The Case against Partition', a memorandum presented to UNSCOP, 23 July 1947.

11. Regarding the rôle played by President Harry Truman to secure the acceptance of partition by the UN, see Henry Cattan, *Palestine and International Law*, 2nd edn. (Longman, London 1976), pp. 82–7.

12. Government of Palestine, *Statistical Abstract 1944–1945* (Palestine Govt Printing Press), p. 42.

13. *Foreign Relations of the United States* (Department of State, Washington, 1948), vol. V, p. 548.

14. *The Forrestal Diaries* (Viking Press, New York, 1951), pp. 345, 347, 357–8, 363 and 508.

15. *Foreign Relations of the United States* (Department of State, 1947), vol. V, p. 1150.

16. *Ibid.*, pp. 1153–8.

17. Pitman B. Potter, 'The Palestine Problem Before the United Nations', *American Journal of International Law*, vol. 42, 1948, p. 860.

18. Quincy Wright, *The Middle Eastern Crisis*, address to the Association of the Bar of the City of New York, November 1968.

19. I. Brownlie, *Principles of International Law* (Clarendon Press, Oxford, 1966), pp. 161–2.

20. Pitman B. Potter, *The Palestine Problem*, op cit., p. 860.

21. Appendix I to Report of Sub-Committee 2 to the Ad Hoc Commission on the Palestine Question, Official Records of the 2nd session of the General Assembly, Doc. A/AC 14/32, p. 304.

22. Jorge Garcia Granados, *The Birth of Israel* (Knopf, New York, 1949), p. 130.

23. UN Doc. A/PV 128, 29 November 1947, pp. 91–101.

24. J. Bowyer Bell, *The Long War: Israel and the Arabs since 1946* (Prentice-Hall, Englewood Cliffs, N.J., 1969), p. 67.

7

Termination of the Mandate in Chaos and Turmoil

THE TURMOIL FOLLOWING THE PARTITION RESOLUTION

The partition resolution precipitated the country into anarchy and chaos. The chronology of events, murders, arson, bombings and massacres during the remaining period of the mandate reads like a sequence of horrors. The Mandatory was unwilling to commit its forces to establish law and order. Insecurity reigned all over the country. The Palestinians sought to prevent the partition of their ancestral homeland. The Zionist Jews sought to establish a Jewish State, not on the lines recommended by the UN General Assembly, but a Jewish State that would be free of Arabs.

The Security Council could not bring the situation under control. The Palestinian Commission which was set up under the partition resolution to progressively take over from the Mandatory the administration of Palestine, to establish Provisional Councils of Government in the Arab and Jewish States and generally to implement the resolution, was unable to assume or exercise its functions in Palestine. The Security Council considered the situation in February and March 1948 without any concrete results.

US MOVES TO SUSPEND PARTITION AND IMPOSE TRUSTEESHIP

In view of the turmoil and the impossibility of implementing partition by peaceful means, the US Government asked the Security Council on 19 March 1948 to suspend action on the partition plan and to call a special session of the General Assembly at once to work out a new solution. Warren R. Austin, the US representative at the

UN, advocated a temporary trusteeship for Palestine under the UN Trusteeship Council until the establishment of a government approved by Arabs and Jews. On 30 March, he presented to the Security Council a resolution asking that the General Assembly be convened 'to consider further the question of the future government of Palestine'. On 16 April 1948 a second special session of the General Assembly was convened for this purpose. Discussions both at the Security Council and at the General Assembly revealed that some governments questioned the wisdom of the partition plan. The UK, as the retiring Mandatory Power, declared that it was not prepared to participate in the enforcement of a settlement which was not acceptable to both Arabs and Jews, and further asserted that lack of co-operation on its part sprang from the fact that the partition had not been impartially conceived. The Jews opposed any reversal of attitude concerning partition. The suggestion made by the US Government for the establishment of a temporary UN trusteeship over Palestine was attacked by the Jews as 'a shocking reversal of the United States position'.

THE JEWS PUT INTO EFFECT THEIR PLAN TO SEIZE PALESTINE

While the UN was immersed in debate about the future government of Palestine, the Zionist Jews put into effect their own plan to seize Palestine and to establish a Jewish State. It has now been disclosed that this plan had been hatched for years, in fact several years before the adoption by the UN of the partition resolution. Uri Millstein reported in *Hadashot* newspaper of 11 January 1985 a conversation which he had had with Yigael Yadin, Acting Chief of Staff in the War of 1948 hours before the latter's death. Yigael Yadin said that he distributed on 10 March 1948 the 'D-Plan' to the General Staff and battalion commanders. The D-Plan was based on previous plans drawn up by the Haganah, a Jewish paramilitary organization in Palestine, in 1945, 1946, 1947 and 1948. The purpose of the plan was to 'seize control of the area of the Jewish State and to defend its borders and also to defend Jewish settlements and populations outside the borders . . .'. In addition, the following specific points were laid down in the D-Plan: 'the destruction of Arab villages' near Jewish settlements or main arteries of transportation and 'the evacuation of their inhabitants, the siege of Arab cities that were not located inside the Jewish State according to the UN resolution and

43

direct actions against Arab targets in Western Palestine, outside the borders of the Jewish State.'

It is clear that the D-Plan had two objectives: the first was to establish a Jewish State, not within the boundaries defined by the UN, but in all such territory as Jewish forces could seize even outside such borders; the second was to establish such a state free from Arabs by requiring 'the evacuation' — meaning the deportation — of the villagers.

The implementation of the D-Plan before the termination of the mandate possessed the advantage of enabling the Jews to act immediately through their paramilitary organizations — the Haganah, the Irgun, and the Stern Gang — without opposition or interference either from the Mandatory which was not prepared to risk its forces to prevent the realization of the plan, or from the Arab States which could not intervene while the mandate was still in force and the British Government maintained its troops in the country. Not much organized opposition could be expected from the Palestinians who possessed no military training and no arms since they had been systematically disarmed by the Mandatory during the mandate because of their opposition to the Balfour Declaration and to Jewish immigration.

The D-Plan was put into force at the beginning of April 1948. In execution of its first objective, the Jewish paramilitary organizations seized several hundred villages and most of the Arab cities in Palestine before the termination of the mandate on 15 May 1948, even though most of them were located outside the area of the Jewish state as defined by the UN. Tiberias was occupied on 19 April 1948, Haifa on 22 April, Jaffa on 28 April, the Arab quarters in the New City of Jerusalem on 30 April, Beisan on 8 May, Safad on 10 May and Acre on 14 May 1948.[1] The second objective, namely 'the evacuation' of the Arab inhabitants, was successfully achieved principally by means of a notoriously heinous outrage: the massacre of Deir Yassin, a peaceful and undefended village lying west of Jerusalem. The purpose of the massacre was to create terror and to force the Arabs to flee.

Deir Yassin massacre

On 9 April 1948, the Irgun massacred 300 men, women and children 'without any military reason or provocation of any kind' as reported by Jacques de Reynier, the Chief Delegate of the International Red

Cross.[2] The Irgun was a terrorist organization which was led by Menachem Begin. This did not prevent him from subsequently becoming Israel's Prime Minister or from being awarded a Nobel Peace Prize.

The Deir Yassin massacre achieved its purpose of terrorizing the Palestinians and they began an exodus which assumed catastrophic dimensions. The effect of the Deir Yassin massacre upon the Palestinians is described by Menachem Begin who speaks of the panic which overwhelmed the Palestinians:

> The Arabs began to flee in terror . . . of the about 800,000 Arabs who lived in the present territory of the state of Israel, only some 165,000 are still there.[3]

Dr Stephen Penrose, then President of the American University of Beirut, explained the connection between the Deir Yassin massacre and the exodus of the Palestinian Arabs in 1948:

> On both sides dreadful deeds were committed but, in the main, the Zionists made better use of terrorist tactics which they learned only too well at the hands of Nazi taskmasters. There is no question but that frightful massacres such as that which took place at Deir Yassin in April 1948 were perpetrated for the major purpose of frightening the Arab population and causing them to take flight. The Zionist radio repeated incessantly for the benefit of Arab listeners 'Remember Deir Yassin'. It is small wonder that many Arab families began a hasty exodus from the battle area and from sectors which might soon become battlegrounds. Terror is contagious, and it built up the tremendous migration which has led to the results which may be witnessed in the refugee camps.[4]

Where the Deir Yassin massacre did not achieve its objective in removing the Palestinians from territory which the Jews had seized, they did not hesitate to expel them physically, as happened at the time of the occupation of Tiberias on 19 April, Haifa on 22 April, Jaffa on 28 April and Safad on 10 May 1948. Expulsions of Arabs and destruction of Arab villages in accordance with the D-Plan continued after the emergence of the State of Israel as will be seen in Part II of this book.

MANDATE ENDS IN CHAOS AND TURMOIL

When the UN General Assembly realized that while it had been debating the question of the future government of Palestine the Jews had practically occupied not only the area of the proposed Jewish State, but also a substantial part of the area destined by the partition resolution for the Arab State, it decided on 14 May 1948 to put the Question of Palestine in the hands of a mediator and charged him with the unenviable task of promoting 'a peaceful adjustment of the future situation of Palestine'. The idea of trusteeship was implicitly abandoned. As for the British Government, it terminated the mandate on the following day and hastened to withdraw its last forces from Palestine, leaving the country in a state of complete chaos and confusion.

Thus came to an inglorious end the Palestine mandate which had originally been devised by the League of Nations to lead the country to full independence in discharge of 'a sacred trust' for the welfare of its inhabitants. Instead of realizing such a praiseworthy ideal, the mandate's purpose was perverted and, in fact, it was used to prevent the Palestinians from exercising their national rights and to bring into the country an alien people determined to seize power and to usurp the land of Palestine from its owners. This misuse and deviation of the mandate from its original purpose sowed the seeds of what was to become a long and bloody conflict in the Holy Land and created one of the most iniquitous, dangerous and still unresolved problems of the twentieth century.

NOTES

1. See Henry Cattan, *Palestine, The Arabs and Israel* (Longman, London, 1969), pp. 21–32; *Middle East Journal*, 1948, vol. 2, pp. 329–32, Washington, DC; G. Kirk, *The Middle East, 1945–1950* (Oxford University Press, London, 1954), pp. 262–6.

2. See the account of this massacre by the Chief Delegate of the International Red Cross, Jacques de Reynier, *A Jérusalem un drapeau flottait sur la ligne de feu* (Editions de la Baconnière, Neuchâtel, Switzerland, 1950).

3. Menachem Begin, *The Revolt* (Henry Schuman, New York, 1951), pp. 164–5.

4. Stephen B.L. Penrose, *The Palestine Problem: Retrospect and Prospect* (American Friends of the Middle East, New York), p. 12.

Part II

The 1948 Upheaval and its Sequels

8

The Emergence of Israel

PROCLAMATION OF THE STATE OF ISRAEL

The State of Israel was proclaimed by the Jews on 14 May 1948 on the eve of the termination of the British mandate over Palestine. The declaration was made by the 'members of the people's council, representative of the Jewish community of Eretz-Israel and of the Zionist movement' who by virtue of their 'natural and historic right and on the strength of the resolution of the United Nations General Assembly, hereby declare the establishment of a Jewish State in Eretz-Israel, to be known as the State of Israel'.

The declaration of the establishment of the State of Israel calls for the following comments.

Incompetence of the parties issuing the proclamation

First, the parties which issued the declaration, whether they were the Jews of Palestine — who in their majority were alien immigrants and were neither indigenous nor citizens of the country[1] or whether they were the representatives of the World Zionist Movement — a foreign political organization — possessed no competence or capacity to proclaim a Jewish State in Palestine.[2]

Grounds invoked for the proclamation

The declaration invoked two grounds for the proclamation of the State of Israel: a so-called 'historic right' and the UN partition resolution.

The Jewish 'historic right' to Palestine, as we have seen in Chapter 3, was not accepted by the Paris Peace Conference and was rejected by the British Government when it formulated with the Zionists the terms of the Palestine mandate (Chapter 5). Hence, one of the grounds for the declaration of Israel's independence was without foundation.

As to the other ground, apart from its doubtful validity and legality, as pointed out in Chapter 6, it was not, in fact, respected because the state which emerged did not conform to the UN partition resolution on which it purported to be based, either demographically or territorially. Demographically, in advance of the proclamation the Jews had evicted several hundred thousand Palestinian Arabs who lived in the territory of the Jewish State as defined by the UN. Territorially, the newly proclaimed state ignored the boundaries fixed for it by the UN. In this regard, one may observe that the proclamation omitted any reference to the boundaries of the Jewish state. Such omission was in no way an oversight. Any doubt that may exist regarding the significance of the omission to mention Israel's boundaries is removed by the publication in 1978 of Israel's national archives for the year 1948. These reveal that the question of boundaries was discussed at the time but that Ben Gurion opposed their delimitation in the proclamation claiming that 'the war will determine the dimensions of the Jewish State'. It is clear then that the proclamation of the State of Israel relied more on war than on a UN resolution.

US POSITION ON ISRAEL'S BOUNDARIES

Although the Jews carefully avoided any reference to boundaries in proclaiming the State of Israel, they were unable to avoid the issue when it came to securing recognition from the US government. President Truman was pressed by some of his advisers to promise recognition to Israel and by others to wait. According to Under-Secretary of State Lovett 'the President had decided to do something about recognizing the new state if it was set up but that he would agree to wait until the request had been made and until there was some definition of boundaries.'[3] Hence, assurances on those two points were furnished by the new state in the letter addressed on 14 May 1948 by Eliahu Epstein, Agent of the Provisional Government of Israel to President Truman requesting recognition of Israel. The letter notified the President that:

The State of Israel has been proclaimed as an independent republic *within frontiers approved by the General Assembly of the United Nations in its resolution of November 29, 1947,* and that a provisional government has been charged to assume the rights and duties of government for preserving law and order within the boundaries of Israel . . .[4] (emphasis added).

No sooner did President Truman receive the letter than he recognized Israel within minutes, even though the Question of Palestine was still being considered by the General Assembly. Such recognition which was made in 'indecent haste' almost precipitated the US delegation at the UN to resign *'en masse'.*[5]

Israel is bound by partition resolution

Despite the omission to fix boundaries, Israel's reliance in the proclamation of independence on the UN partition resolution obligates it to observe the provisions of the resolution in all respects, including boundaries. Moreover, the proclamation stated that 'the State of Israel is prepared to cooperate with the agencies and representatives of the United Nations in implementing the resolution of the General Assembly of the 29th November 1947'. However, Israel did not co-operate in any way to implement the resolution, but, on the contrary, occupied and usurped most of the territory of the Arab State which was to emerge side by side with it, as well as modern Jerusalem, thus belying its commitment in its proclamation of independence to implement the partition resolution. Legally, however, Israel's inobservance of the boundaries of the UN partition resolution does not discharge it from its obligation to respect and to implement the resolution and to withdraw, as will be pointed out in Chapter 34, from all territories it seized in excess of its provisions.

RELATIONSHIP BETWEEN THE STATE OF ISRAEL AND JUDAISM

The state of Israel does not possess a genuine relationship with Judaism. As we have seen in Chapter 3, the Zionist Jews who founded Israel possessed no racial links with the biblical Jews. The concept of a Jewish State which was preached by Herzl had no direct link with Judaism and was planned for nationalistic reasons by

European Jews in order to escape discrimination or persecution in Eastern Europe. They exploited the Bible and Judaism to secure support for their ambition to form a Jewish State and they succeeded in deceiving the world.

This explains why we find today that the majority (54 per cent) of the Israelis are secular Jews. Moreover, the National Religious Party, Aguda, Morasha, Shas and the racist Kach Party, form a small minority in the Knesset. The two main dominant parties which control the administration, i.e. Labour and Likud, are secular but because neither can form a government alone, they need the support of one or more of the religious parties.

Condemnation of the state of Israel by Orthodox Jews

In addition to the secular and national religious Jews in Israel there exist a number of Orthodox Jews who are opposed on religious grounds to political Zionism and to the State of Israel. An important group of non-Zionist Jews are members of *Naturei Karta*. This group which comprises a number of learned rabbis is active in Jerusalem and in New York. In a statement published in the *New York Times* (21 April 1980) the American *Naturei Karta* declared

> The establishment of a 'Jewish' pre-messianic State is a most serious aberration and a blasphemous act that has been condemned by the leading *Talmidei Chachomin* (Torah sages) of the past generations and of our own time.

The same group stated in the *New York Times* (26 April 1985):

> Zionism in its nature is the very enemy of the Jews and Judaism . . . According to Jewish law the Jews are forbidden to have their own state before the coming of the Messiah . . . It is not the ambition of the Jewish people to have a strong navy or air force and in our opinion the defense of the State of Israel is neither practicable nor desirable. For the name of Israel was usurped by the Zionists to mislead the Jews and the nations of the world . . .

NOTES

1. Out of the roughly half a million Jews who came to Palestine as

immigrants during the mandate, less than one-third, *viz.* 132,616 had acquired Palestinian citizenship: see *Statistical Abstract*, Government of Palestine, 1944–1945, pp. 36 and 46, Palestine Govt Printing Press.

2. For a discussion of the absence of a legal basis for the proclamation of the Jewish state see Henry Cattan, *Palestine and International Law*, 2nd edn. (Longman, London, 1976), p. 95.

3. *Foreign Relations of the United States* (Department of State, Washington, D.C., 1948), vol. V, p. 1005.

4. *Ibid.*, p. 989.

5. *Ibid.*, pp. 993 and 1006.

9

The War of 1948

INTERVENTION OF ARAB STATES

On 15 May 1948, that is on the day following the proclamation of the Jewish State and the withdrawal of British forces from Palestine, the Arab States intervened in the hostilities which Jewish forces had opened against the Palestinians in the month of April as we have noted in Chapter 7. Contrary to what was misrepresented by Israeli propaganda, the War of 1948 between Israel and the neighbouring Arab States did not involve an all-out offensive by the Arabs against the Jews, nor did it aim at wiping them out of Palestine. The Arab States intervened essentially to protect the Palestinians from massacre such as that at Deir Yassin and hopefully to prevent the partition of the country. The purpose of the Arab States' intervention was explained by Azzam Pasha, the Secretary-General of the League of Arab States in a cablegram to the UN dated 15 May 1948 (UN Doc. S/745) as being to restore law and order, to prevent disturbances from spreading into their territories and to check further bloodshed. The cablegram stated that, in consequence of Jewish aggression, over a quarter of a million Arabs had been compelled to leave their homes. It was necessary, therefore, for the Arab Governments to intervene in order to fill the vacuum resulting from the termination of the mandate and the failure to replace it by any legally constituted authority.

The absence of a resolve on the part of the Arab States to launch a war against the Jews of Palestine is confirmed by John Bagot Glubb, British Commander of the Arab Legion of Transjordan. He declared that on the very day before the fighting began in Palestine, the Secretary-General of the League of Arab States, Azzam Pasha, admitted to him that they had never believed that the issue would come to fighting. 'We believed that the solution would be political,' he said.[1] Strictly speaking, therefore, the Arab States did not launch a war against Israel, but undertook an armed intervention which was both lawful and justified.

But, as mentioned in Chapter 7, Jewish forces had already commenced military operations in Palestine before the end of the mandate. Hence, by the time that the Arab States could and did intervene, that is after the departure of the British troops from Palestine on 15 May 1948, the Jews had occupied not only most of the area allotted to the Jewish State by the UN partition resolution, but also most of the area allotted to the Arab State as well, including several Arab towns. This was the basic reason why the Arab intervention failed. But there were also other reasons for the failure of the intervention: the inequality in numbers, in resolve and in preparedness.

Inequality in numbers, resolve and preparedness

The number of men which the Arab States engaged in the conflict disproves any suggestion that they launched an all-out offensive against the Jews in 1948. The Arab armies which then moved into Palestine represented token forces from Egypt, Syria, Transjordan, Lebanon, Iraq and Saudi Arabia which totalled 20,000 men[2] while the Jews put into the field 60,000 to 80,000 fully trained men of the Haganah, and 5,000 to 10,000 of the Irgun and Stern Gang. As to the Palestinians, they possessed no military training or organization and their military potential was limited to small groups of volunteers with little or no military experience. The largest group of volunteers was the Arab Liberation Army with an estimated strength of 6,000 to 7,500 men. Another factor of weakness for the Palestinians was their having been systematically disarmed by the British Government, as previously noted, because of their opposition to its policy in Palestine. Between 1937 and 1947, over 7,600 rifles had been confiscated by the Palestinian Government from the Arabs, while only 135 rifles were confiscated from the Jews.[3]

In the War of 1948, not only were the parties unequal in numbers, but they were unequal in resolve and organization, whether military or political. The Arab States put into the field 'four armies with no central command, no concerted aim, and no serious and sustained will to win', to face the Israelis, who had proceeded with a total mobilization of their manpower on modern lines.[4]

As to preparedness, this was completely absent on the Arab side. In contrast with the Jews who had been preparing the occupation of Palestine and drawing military plans to this end since 1945, as noted in Chapter 7, neither the Arab States, nor their military staffs, made any preparation of any kind despite their threats of military intervention if the partition of Palestine were carried out.

END OF WAR BUT NOT OF ISRAEL'S EXPANSION

The War of 1948 was short in duration, but its catastrophic consequences still endure. The war commenced on 15 May 1948 and was interrupted on 11 June by a four-weeks' truce ordered by the Security Council and arranged by the UN Mediator, Count Folke Bernadotte. On the expiry of the truce, hostilities resumed. This time the fighting lasted only ten days, for a second truce was ordered by the Security Council and came into force on 18 July 1948.

The Israelis, however, violated this last truce on several occasions to make other territorial gains. On 15 October 1948 the Israelis, in breach of the truce, launched a general offensive against the Egyptians on the southern front. The Israelis, now enjoying for the first time a superiority in the air, made substantial gains of territory, capturing Beersheba on the 21st, Bait Hanun (only five miles north-east of Gaza) on the 22nd, and Bait Jibrin (in the direction of Hebron) soon afterwards. The parties accepted a cease-fire with effect from 22 October 1948 but on 31 October the Israelis defied a warning by the UN Chief of Staff and launched an attack on the Lebanese front and occupied fifteen villages situated within Lebanese territory. Also, in November, they moved forward in the Negeb in the direction of the Gulf of Aqaba. On 22 December 1948 the Israelis launched another offensive in the south, occupied the area of Auja and made substantial penetration into the Sinai. This was not their last violation of the truce. On 10 March 1949, in breach of their Armistice Agreement with Egypt, the Israelis again moved further south until they reached the Gulf of Aqaba and occupied the Palestine Police post of Umm Rashrash, which they afterwards named Eilat.

The Palestine war was theoretically concluded by four Armistice Agreements signed by Israel with Egypt on 24 February 1949, with Lebanon on 23 March 1949, with Jordan on 3 April 1949 and with Syria on 20 July 1949. The Armistice Agreements did not lay down political boundaries, but only armistice lines. In fact, they specifically provided that the armistice lines were delineated 'without prejudice to the ultimate settlement of the Palestine Question'. It is necessary to emphasize this fact because it is erroneously assumed today in many quarters that Israel has possessed political boundaries since 1949 and that its withdrawal from the West Bank and Gaza to the 1949 armistice lines would settle the problem.

In addition to seizing Arab territories in breach of the Armistice Agreements, Israel gradually seized the demilitarized zones that were set up by those Agreements between it and Egypt and Syria.[5] Such seizures were carried out by Israel after the dates of the Armistice Agreements, despite the fact that the territorial situation was frozen by the Tripartite Declaration issued by the UK, France and the US on 25 May 1950 which proclaimed that they would oppose any violations of frontiers or armistice lines between Israel and the Arab States. But the situation was not frozen for long because Israel committed several new aggressions, the principal ones being in 1956, 1967 and 1982. The areas seized by Israel in excess of the UN Partition Plan are indicated in Appendix V.

Commenting on the War of 1948, Commander Hutchison of the UN armistice staff, observed:

It was a short war marked by outside intervention, Arab disunity and unlimited aid to Israel from the West, in addition to timely and substantial shipments of arms from behind the Iron curtain, primarily from Czechoslovakia. This aid, sent in against the orders of the United Nations, was sufficient to turn the tide and to grant Israel considerable land gains.[6]

Czechoslovakia, however, was only the conduit pipe, because the real supplier of arms to Israel in 1948 was the Soviet Union. This fact, which was kept secret for a long time, was however, disclosed by Ben Gurion, Israel's Prime Minister. He stated in May 1973 in an interview with the *Jerusalem Post* that the Soviet Union was a major factor in the Arabs' defeat by Israel in 1948, because it supplied Israel with vital arms through Czechoslovakia. Conversely, the Arab States received no military assistance from anyone.

FACT AND FICTION: ZIONIST PROPAGANDA

The Zionist Jews showed their ability at the time of the War of 1948 to completely mislead world public opinion. In those days, war accounts and news reporting were rudimentary or non-existent in the Middle East, unlike the present day when radio, TV and the press report world events on the same day. These facts, allied to Zionist influence on the media, enabled Israel to make the world believe in 1948:

(1) That Jewish little David was the subject of a savage onslaught by several Arab Goliaths when, in fact, the Arab forces that were used were symbolic and inconsequential.

(2) That the war had started on 15 May 1948 when, in fact, during the two preceding months Jewish forces had seized several Arab towns and hundreds of Arab villages.

(3) That the Jews were fighting heroically in order not to be thrown into the sea when, in fact, they themselves expelled most of the Palestinian inhabitants out of their country, creating one of the worst refugee and politically explosive problems in this century.

(4) That for the Jews the war was a defensive war and a war of independence when, in reality, the war was nothing but an aggression by Jewish forces against undefended Arab towns and villages and unarmed civilians.

RESULT OF THE WAR

The result of the Palestine conflict of 1948 was summed up by the American Chairman of the Israeli-Jordan Armistice Commission in the following terms:

> The brief official Palestine war of 1948–1949 is now part of history — it settled none of the basic issues of the Arab-Israeli contention. The major powers of the West and the East, losing sight of the true value of a friendly Arab World in the swirling clouds of Zionist propaganda, overran the rights of the indigenous population of Palestine — the Arabs. Every step in the establishment of a Zionist state had been a challenge to justice.[7]

Not only did the War of 1948 settle none of the basic issues of the Palestine Question, it created new and very grave ones. Its catastrophic consequences will be examined in the following chapters.

NOTES

1. John Bagot Glubb, *Britain and the Arabs* (Hodder and Stoughton, London, 1959), p. 284.

2. For an account of military operations during the Palestine War of 1948 and the respective military strength of Arabs and Jews, see Edgar O'Balance, *The Arab-Israeli War, 1948* (Faber, London, 1956).

3. Government of Palestine, *A Survey of Palestine*, vol. II, pp. 594–5 (Palestine Govt Printing Press, 1946).

4. Albert Hourani, 'Arab Refugees and the Future of Israel', *The Listener*, 28 July 1949; S.G. Thicknesse, *Arab Refugees*, p. 2 (Royal Institute of International Affairs, London, 1949), p. 2.

5. See a reference to those seizures in Henry Cattan, *Palestine and International Law*, 2nd edn. (Longman, London, 1976), pp. 154–5.

6. E.H. Hutchison, *Violent Truce* (Devin-Adair, New York, 1956), p. 95.

7. *Ibid.*

10

Exodus of the Palestine Refugees

CAUSES OF THE EXODUS

Rarely in history — at least in modern history — has a majority of
the population of a country been forcibly displaced and uprooted by
a militant minority of foreign origin. Yet this happened in Palestine
in 1948 when nearly a million Palestinians were expelled or otherwise forced to leave their homes, towns and villages; were robbed
of their lands, properties and possessions and became refugees
without homes and without any means of livelihood. The bulk of
them went to Jordan and the Gaza Strip, the remainder to Syria and
Lebanon. Why were so many displaced? The exodus of the Palestine
refugees in 1948 was due to three causes: Jewish terrorism, expulsion, and the breakdown of security and government machinery for
the preservation of law and order during the last few months of the
mandate. In his Progress Report the late Count Bernadotte, United
Nations Mediator for Palestine, summarized these causes as follows:

> The exodus of Palestinian Arabs resulted from panic created by
> fighting in their communities, by rumours concerning real or
> alleged acts of terrorism, or expulsion.[1]

Jewish terrorism

It can safely be said that the Deir Yassin terrorist massacre (see
Chapter 7) was the principal cause of the Palestinian exodus in 1948.
Although some Palestinians took refuge in neighbouring countries as
a result of murders and bombings, the exodus began to assume
catastrophic proportions only after the outrage of Deir Yassin.

60

The resort to terror by the Jews to force the exodus of the Palestinians that began during the mandate continued after the emergence of the State of Israel and was carried out by the organized troops of the new state. Having occupied most of the Arab towns in Palestine, with the exception of the Old City of Jerusalem, Nablus and Hebron, Jewish terrorist action was concentrated on Arab villages in areas which the Jews wanted to occupy and annex. Notwithstanding the Mediator's protests (UN Doc. A/648, 16 September 1948), the destruction of Arab villages by Israel proceeded on a large scale. The intention was to prevent their inhabitants who had fled or had been forced to evacuate their homes from returning. Many villages were even destroyed after the UN resolution of 11 December 1948 calling upon Israel to permit the return of the refugees to their homes. By November 1953 one hundred and sixty-one Arab villages had been razed to the ground after occupation by Israeli forces.[2] But the total of Arab villages destroyed exceeded that number. Israel Shahak, President of the Israeli League for Human Rights, listed in 1975 the names and number of Arab villages destroyed by Israel since 1948 and their total reached the figure of 385.[3]

Jewish terrorism was condemned all round, by Jews and non-Jews. Viscount Samuel, who was himself a Zionist Jew and the first High Commissioner of Palestine, said:

> The Jewish people have always taken pride in the good deeds performed and the distinctions won by their members; in the number of scientists, writers, musicians, philosophers and statesmen, who have come from the Jewish ranks . . . Today these same people have given birth to a set of assassins, who, disguised in false uniforms, waylay soldiers and policemen, hurl bombs promiscuously, blow up trains . . . I feel bound to say . . . that the Jewish population of Palestine and the Jewish Agency are blameworthy for not having . . . extirpated this curse which has brought shame upon all members of the Jewish community.[4]

Expulsion

Where terrorism failed to force the departure of the Palestinians, Jewish forces resorted to expulsion. The expulsion of the Palestinians was carried out in Haifa, Lydda and Ramleh,[5] Tiberias, Safad,

Beersheba and several other towns and villages. On various occasions Israeli forces used loudspeakers to threaten the civilian population and to order it to leave. Describing the occupation of Haifa, George Kirk wrote:

> The Jewish combatants there and elsewhere made skilful use of psychological warfare to break their opponents' morale, and the effect upon the civilians was only what was to be expected. At a later stage, the Israeli armed forces did not confine their pressure on the Arab civilian population to playing upon their fears. They forcibly expelled them: for example the population of 'Akka (including refugees from Haifa) in May; the population of Lydda and Ramleh (including refugees from Jaffa) in July; and the population of Beersheba and Western Galilee in October.[6]

The creation of a Jewish state in Palestine has been described as a 'process which either by accident or intent rid Israel of the majority of its large Arab population'.[7] In fact, there was little accident in the process. I.F. Stone observed:

> Jewish terrorism, not only by the Irgun, in such savage massacres as Deir Yassin, but in milder form by the Haganah itself, 'encouraged' Arabs to leave the areas the Jews wished to take over for strategic or demographic reasons. They tried to make as much of Israel as free of Arabs as possible.[8]

Lieutenant-General E.L.M. Burns, Chief of Staff of the UN Truce Supervision Organization in Palestine, declared that 'Israelis had a record of getting rid of Arabs whose lands they desired'.[9] John H. Davis, Commissioner-General of the UN Relief and Works Agency for Palestine Refugees in the Near East for five years, has remarked that 'the extent to which the refugees were savagely driven out by the Israelis as part of a deliberate master-plan has been insufficiently recognized'. Dr Davis went on to explain how the Zionist concept of a Jewish state called for the ousting of the indigenous Arab population from its homeland, and emphasized that this objective was achieved by means ranging from 'expert psychological warfare to ruthless expulsion by force'.[10]

For a long time the Israeli authorities succeeded in preventing any official acknowledgement of the expulsions of the Palestinians in 1948 despite the facts having been established beyond doubt. The blackout on official admission of the expulsions continues to the present day. According to the *New York Times* of 23 October 1979, Y. Rabin who commanded the Jewish brigade which occupied Ramleh and Lydda, and subsequently held several ministerial posts, stated in his *Memoirs* that the inhabitants of those two towns were expelled in 1948. But a censorship committee composed of five Israeli cabinet ministers forbade such disclosure and the passage relating to expulsions was expunged from the book when published. But the Israeli press is free from censorship. *Al Hamishmar* of 17 March 1985, quoted an Israel soldier:

> In the Independence War we expelled whole villages of Palestinians. We took trucks and transferred them, quickly, to the other side of Jordan. It is a fact that today is not denied any more.

Israel, however, cannot permanently conceal the inhuman and shameless expulsion of the Palestinians from their homeland. The truth is emerging slowly. Recent revelations in the Israeli press and disclosures from Israeli sources have shattered the myth spread by Israeli propaganda that the Palestinian exodus of 1948 was voluntary or was ordered by the Arab states. On the contrary, such revelations and disclosures essentially support the view that the expulsion of the Palestinians was a deliberate act, intended to rid the new state of Israel of those who were not wanted as citizens and to enable Jewish colonists to settle on Arab lands. David Gilmour summarized the evidence on this matter in the *Middle East International* magazine No. 286 of 24 October 1986 and No. 288 of 21 November 1986.

Breakdown of security and government before the end of the mandate

The last of the causes that contributed to the exodus of the Palestine Arabs in 1948 was the breakdown of security and government machinery during the last six months of the mandate. After the outbreak of violence and terrorism following the partition vote by the UN, the British government was neither able to maintain law and order in Palestine nor willing to commit its forces for that purpose. The mandate was coming to an end on 15 May 1948 and the British government concerned itself mainly with the evacuation of its personnel and equipment.

In December 1947 the British government withdrew its forces from Jaffa and Tel Aviv and notified the UN that during their gradual withdrawal British troops would maintain order in the area which they still occupied, but would not be available to maintain order on behalf of the Palestine Commission which was charged with the implementation of partition. On 20 January 1948 the British government stated that 'the policy of allowing both the Jewish and Arab communities to make arrangements for their own security, in areas where either community was in the great majority, had been carried further, so that the British police could be concentrated in Jerusalem and other mixed localities'. At the beginning of February 1948, British personnel in the principal cities were concentrated in enclosed and guarded zones. What happened outside the guarded zones ceased to be of concern to the Mandatory government. In so far as law, order and security were concerned, the people were left to fend for themselves. During March 1948 the evacuation of British personnel began. Notwithstanding that hundreds were being killed or wounded, not a single prosecution or police inquiry was even attempted. An indication of the complete absence of any government machinery at the time is afforded by the fact that when the massacre of Deir Yassin occurred on 9 April 1948 no government authority lifted a finger either to prevent the massacre or to assist and save the wounded or even bury the dead.

ISRAEL REJECTS REPATRIATION OF THE PALESTINE REFUGEES

In resolution 194 of 11 December 1948 the General Assembly called for the repatriation of the Palestine refugees and the restitution of their property. It declared:

> that the refugees wishing to return to their homes and live at peace with their neighbours should be permitted to do so at the earliest practicable date, and that compensation should be paid for the property of those choosing not to return and for loss of or damage to property which, under principles of international law or in equity, should be made good by the Governments or authorities responsible.

But Israel was adamant. It refused and still refuses to implement the resolution. In its Third Progress Report the UN Conciliation Commission declared that it had not succeeded in securing from Israel the acceptance of the principle of the repatriation of Palestine refugees.

On only one occasion, as a result of pressure from the US government, did Israel make an offer to take back a limited number of refugees. In May 1949, the US government addressed a note to Israel in which it insisted that Israel should make tangible concessions on the question of refugees, boundaries and the internationalization of Jerusalem, failing which the US government would reconsider its attitude towards it. The US note 'interpreted Israel's attitude as dangerous to peace and as indicating disregard of the UN General Assembly resolutions of 29 November 1947 and 11 December 1948'.[11] This produced an Israeli offer to the Conciliation Commission to permit the return of 100,000 refugees, subject to conditions, one of which was that Israel 'reserved the right to resettle the repatriated refugees in specific locations, in order to ensure that their re-installation would fit into the general plan of Israel's economic development'. Obviously, a proposal to permit the return of some 10 per cent of the refugees and to resettle them in specific locations away from their homes did not constitute a compliance with the UN repatriation resolution. The Conciliation Commission's comment was that it considered the Israeli proposal unsatisfactory.[12]

Resolution 194 has been reaffirmed each year by the General Assembly to no avail. Israel's opposition to the repatriation of the Palestine refugees has not changed or diminished.

In the face of Israel's refusal to comply with its resolution for the repatriation of the refugees and the restitution of their property, the General Assembly gave a directive to the Conciliation Commission on 14 December 1950 in resolution 394 to ensure the protection of the rights, property and interests of the refugees. However, the efforts of the UN to protect Arab refugee property and to save it from confiscation were defeated by Israel's intransigence. The Conciliation Commission for Palestine mentioned in its Third Progress Report that it had presented to the Israeli Government a list of preliminary measures which it considered fair and just for the protection of Arab refugee property. Israel ignored the request. Another request made by the Conciliation Commission for the appointment of a mixed committee to deal with the question of the preservation of Arab orange groves was rejected. The Conciliation Commission also asked Israel to abrogate the Absentee Property Law and to suspend all measures of requisition and occupation of Arab houses and lands. Again, this effort bore no fruit. The Conciliation Commission reported that 'the Israeli delegation informed the Commission that its Government was unable to abrogate the Absentee Act or to suspend measures of requisition of Arab immovable property'.[13]

OUSTER OF PALESTINIANS REMAINS AN ISRAELI OBJECTIVE

Although Israel's objective to oust the Palestinians from their homeland was largely achieved in 1948, and was also continued in 1967, as we shall see in Chapter 17, it still remains in some quarters a means to settle the Palestine Question. In an article published by *Davar* on 29 September 1978 under the title 'A Solution for the Refugee Problem' which quotes Joseph Weitz, former Deputy-Chairman of the Jewish National Fund, it was stated:

> Among ourselves, it must be clear that there is no place in the country for both peoples together . . . With the Arabs we shall not achieve our aim of being an independent people in this country. The only solution is Eretz-Israel, at least the west part of Eretz-Israel, without Arabs . . . And there is no other way but to transfer the Arabs from here to the neighbouring countries. Transfer all of them, not one village or tribe should remain . . .

Rabbi Meir Kahane, who leads a campaign for the expulsion of all Palestinians from Israel and the West Bank, and was elected to the Knesset on such a platform, is today saying the same thing.[14]

The forced exodus of the Palestinians is a necessary consequence of the implementation of the Zionist aim which Chaim Weizmann stated to be to 'take over the country'.[15]

The number of refugees

In consequence of Jewish terror and expulsions the majority of the Palestinians were transformed in 1948 almost overnight into refugees, deprived of food, shelter and homeland. In June 1949 the Secretary-General of the UN reported to the General Assembly that the number of Palestinian refugees was 960,000[16] out of a total Arab population in 1947 of 1,348,840.[17] The estimate of the number of Palestinian refugees in 1948 was given by the Delegate of Red Cross Societies to the Middle East as being close to one million.[18] These official figures are mentioned because it is the policy of Israel and its apologists to reduce substantially the number of the refugees.

With natural increase and the additional number of refugees of the War of 1967, the total number of Palestinian refugees has considerably increased. The number of refugees registered with UNRWA (United Nations Relief and Works Agency for Palestinian Refugees) on 30 June 1986, was 2,145,794. This figure, however, does not represent the total number of refugees because it is limited to those who are 'registered' with the organization for rations or services, a large number of refugees not being registered. In his Annual Report dated 27 August 1962 the Commissioner-General of UNRWA estimated the number of unregistered refugees at 20 per cent of the total. If one takes into account unregistered refugees, the total number of Palestinian refugees may be estimated at over 2,500,000. They are scattered in various countries, but are principally found in Jordan, the West Bank and Gaza, Lebanon, Syria, the Arabian Gulf and the Americas.

Assistance to refugees

UNRWA was established on 1 May 1950 by a decision of the General Assembly to furnish assistance to the Palestinian refugees. It alleviated the conditions of deprivation and starvation of a large number of the refugees by providing them with food, shelter and medical care. Not all refugees receive assistance. For a number of years attention has been given to vocational training.

UNRWA's annual expenditure, which is derived from contributions by governments, in particular, the US, has risen from $26 million in 1950 to $191 million in 1984. The budget estimate for 1985 is $231 million. Until 1966 the average per capita assistance amounted to less than $30 a year for each refugee (UN Doc. A/5214, p. 1) but the present average reaches about $100 per year. These amounts stand in striking contrast with the annual aid paid by the US Government to Israel which is roughly equal to $1,500 for every Israeli man, woman and child.[19]

NOTES

1. UN Doc. A/648, p. 14.
2. A list giving the names of these villages was published with a letter

of protest to the Israeli Government in *Al Rabitah*, No. 12, November 1953, a church magazine of the Greek Catholic Episcopate in Israel.

3. Israel Shahak, *Le Racisme de l'Etat d'Israël* (Guy Authier, Paris, 1975), p. 156.

4. From Viscount Samuel's speech in the Palestine Debate in the House of Lords, 23 April 1947.

5. In Lydda and Ramleh 60,000 persons, many of whom were refugees from other places, were expelled by the Israelis: G. Kirk, *The Middle East 1945–50* (Oxford University Press, Oxford, 1954), p. 281.

6. G. Kirk, *The Middle East*, p. 264.

7. *Middle East Journal*, 1948, p. 447.

8. I.F. Stone in *New York Review of Books*, 3 August 1967.

9. E.L.M. Burns, *Between Arab and Israeli* (Harrap, London, 1962, and Institute for Palestine Studies, Beirut, 1969), p. 191.

10. John H. Davis, *The Evasive Peace* (John Murray, London, 1968), pp. 57–60.

11. Don Peretz, *Israel and the Palestine Arabs* (Middle East Institute, Washington, D.C., 1958), pp. 41–2; James G. McDonald, *My Mission in Israel* (Simon and Schuster, New York, 1951), pp. 181–2.

12. UN Doc. A/1367, p. 14.

13. Fourth Progress Report of the Conciliation Commission, Doc. A/992, 22 September 1949.

14. See Chapter 26.

15. Chaim Weizmann, *Trial and Error* (Hamish Hamilton, London, 1949), p. 224.

16. Annual Report of the Secretary-General on the work of the UN, 1 July 1948–30 June 1949, p. 102.

17. Appendix 1 to Report of Sub-Committee 1, Official Records of the 2nd Session of the General Assembly, Ad Hoc Committee on the Palestinian Question, 1947, p. 270.

18. *Middle East Journal*, 1949, p. 251.

19. George W. Ball, *Error and Betrayal in Lebanon* (Foundation for Middle East, Washington, D.C., 1984), p. 118.

11

Territorial Consequences of the War of 1948

We have seen that before and during the War of 1948 Israel seized not only the areas designated for the Jewish State by the partition resolution, but also more than half the territory reserved for the Arab State by the same resolution. The areas which Israel seized before and after 15 May 1948, in excess of the territorial limits of the Jewish State as fixed by the partition resolution, include Western Galilee, the City of Jerusalem, the area west of Jerusalem to the Mediterranean, the Arab cities of Jaffa, Acre, Lydda, Ramleh, and several hundred Arab villages. The total areas which the Israelis seized in 1948 and 1949 amounted to 20,850 square kilometres[1] out of 26,323 square kilometres representing the total area of Palestine. This meant that Israel increased the territory of the Jewish State as proposed by the UN from 14,500 square kilometres to 20,850 square kilometres, that is, to almost 80 per cent of the territory of Palestine, in striking contrast to the 6 per cent Jewish land owner- ship in the whole of the country.

The Arabs, on their part, were thus left with one-fifth of the original territory of their country. And what remained to them was the bone, mainly infertile land and mountainous desert. In contrast, the Palestine Arabs did not seize any of the territories reserved for the Jewish State under the partition resolution. Even when the Arab states did intervene militarily on 15 May 1948, an express restriction was imposed on one of their armies (the Arab Legion of Trans- jordan) not to move into territory earmarked for the Jews by the partition plan.[2] Sir John Glubb, the Commander of the Arab Legion, stated that the Jordanians did not enter territory allotted to Israel, but defended the area allotted to the Arabs.[3] However, in the latter objective, the Arabs failed hopelessly.

The Israelis have pretended that they did not respect the territorial limits set by the resolution of 29 November 1947 because the Arabs refused to accept partition. In actual fact, they themselves defeated the partition resolution by occupying by force, and even before the end of the mandate, the major part of the territories allocated to the Palestine Arabs by the resolution.

NOTES

1. Israeli Government, *Government Yearbook*, English edition, 5712 (1951/1952), p. 315.
2. S.N. Fisher, *The Middle East* (Routledge & Kegan Paul, London, 1960), p. 585.
3. Sir John Glubb, *The Middle East Crisis* (Hodder and Stoughton, London, 1967), p. 39.

12

Plunder and Confiscation
of Arab Property

As regards Israel's plunder of Arab property a distinction should be made between Palestinian refugees and Palestinian Arabs who remained under occupation.

PALESTINIAN REFUGEES

All the property, movable and immovable, of a million Palestinian refugees was plundered by Israel in 1948. This plunder is one of the greatest mass robberies in the history of Palestine, about which little has been said, and much less done.

In the case of movables, there was an orgy of looting which is reminiscent of days before the advent of civilization. The testimony about this large-scale looting is unanimous. In his Progress Report, Count Bernadotte observed that most of the refugees left practically all their possessions behind.[1] He then added:

> Moreover, while those who had fled in the early days of the conflict had been able to take with them some personal effects and assets, many of the latecomers were deprived of everything except the clothes in which they stood, and apart from their homes (many of which were destroyed) lost all furniture and assets, and even their tools of trade.[2]

Writing later, Ralph Bunche, the Acting Mediator on Palestine, stated in his Progress Report that 'the bulk of the refugees left their homes on foot at short notice taking little or nothing with them'.[3] Similarly, the Director of Field Operations for the UN's Disaster Relief Project observed: 'While a few were able to carry personal effects and some money, flight was generally disorderly and with almost no possessions.'[4] Referring to the exodus of the Palestine refugees, Edwin Samuel stated: 'The next stage in this tragedy was widespread Jewish looting of Arab property.'[5] George Kirk wrote:

> It was apparently at Jaffa that Jewish troops first succumbed to the temptation to indulge in wholesale looting . . . and within a few days Jewish troops were looting the newly captured Arab suburbs of Jerusalem (see Kimche, *Seven Fallen Pillars*, p. 224; Levin, *Jerusalem Embattled*, pp. 116, 135–6, 226). Ben Gurion himself afterwards admitted that the extent to which respectable Jews of all classes became involved was a shameful and distressful spectacle (*Israel, Government Handbook*, 5712, London, Seymour Press, 1951/52).[6]

Don Peretz has cited the Israeli Custodian of Absentee Property as follows:

> In a statement describing the early period, the Custodian of Absentee Property reported to the Knesset's Finance Committee early in 1949 that, during the violent transition from mandatory to Israeli control, before a firm authority was established, the Arabs abandoned great quantities of property in hundreds of thousands of dwellings, shops, storehouses and workshops. They also left produce in fields and fruit in orchards, groves and vineyards, placing 'the fighting and victorious community before serious material temptation'. (Extract from Custodian's report to the Knesset Finance Committee given on 18 April 1949.)[7]

In the case of immovables, the spoliation comprised the bulk of the land of Palestine and a number of cities and towns, namely, the wholly Arab cities and towns of Jaffa, Acre, Nazareth, Lydda, Ramleh, Beersheba, Beisan, Majdal, Isdud, Beit Jibrin and Shafa Amr, the Arab quarters of the New City of Jerusalem, Haifa, Tiberias, Safad and over eight hundred villages.[8] As their Arab inhabitants were terrorized or expelled, or fled in conditions of chaos and confusion, all these cities, towns and villages were taken over, in almost all cases, complete with their contents which were confiscated.

The confiscation of immovable property was carried out in two phases. In the first phase, Arab refugee property which was described as 'absentee property' was seized under the Absentee

Property Regulations (1948) and vested in the Custodian of Absentee Property who was given the power to administer the property, but not to sell it, nor to lease it for a period exceeding five years. Then in 1950 Israel took the next step, namely, the confiscation of refugee property. This was achieved by the Absentee Property Law (1950) which again vested 'absentee property' in the Custodian and authorized him to sell it at its 'offical value' to a Development Authority established by the Knesset (Article 19). Such 'official value' would be determined by the Custodian on the basis of tax records. This was, in fact, a formula for the confiscation of Arab refugee property at a symbolic consideration.

The extent of Arab refugee property which the Israeli government euphemistically described as 'absentee' property and admitted was 'acquired' by the Custodian of Absentee Property was stated to be the following:

'Village property', belonging to all Arab absentees, whether they are outside the country or living in Israel, 'acquired' by the Custodian of Absentee Property, includes some 300 abandoned or semi-abandoned villages with a total area of 3½ million dunums. The agricultural property includes 80 thousand dunums of orange groves and more than 200 thousand dunums of orchards . . . Property in the towns includes 25,416 buildings, consisting of 57,497 residential apartments, and 10,729 shops and light industry workshops . . .[9]

Without going into the correctness or otherwise of the extent of Arab refugee property confiscated by Israel since 1948, it is pertinent to cite Don Peretz in this regard:

The CCP (United Nations Conciliation Commission of Palestine) Refugee Office estimated that although only a little more than a quarter was considered cultivable, more than 80 per cent of Israel's total area of 20,850 square kilometres represented land abandoned by the Arab refugees . . . Abandoned property was one of the greatest contributions towards making Israel a viable state. The extent of its area and the fact that most of the regions along the border consisted of absentee property made it strategically significant. Of the 370 Jewish settlements established between 1948 and the beginning of 1953, 350 were on absentee property. In 1954, more than one-third of Israel's Jewish population lived on absentee property and nearly a third

73

of the new immigrants (250,000 people) settled in urban areas abandoned by Arabs.[10] They left whole cities like Jaffa, Acre, Lydda, Ramleh, Baysan, Majdal; 338 towns and villages and large parts of 94 other cities and towns, containing nearly a quarter of all the buildings in Israel. Ten thousand shops, businesses and stores were left in Jewish hands. At the end of the mandate, citrus holdings in the area of Israel totalled about 240,000 dunums of which half were Arab owned. Most of the Arab groves were taken over by the Israel Custodian of Absentee Property.[10]

Palestinians who remained under occupation

As to the Palestinians who remained in territory under Israeli control, i.e. in Israel and whose number in 1948 was originally estimated at 300,000 (at the time of writing over 700,000), they did not fare much better because most of their lands were also confiscated by Israel. Different means and methods — some military and others legislative, but all invariably unlawful under international law — were used to confiscate the land of Palestinian Arab residents in Israel. A series of measures taken by the authorities empowered the military to declare vast areas as 'closed areas' which the public and the owners of the land were forbidden to enter. Other areas were seized, their inhabitants expelled, and then were given for Jewish settlement on the grounds of 'security and development'.

Among the confiscatory measures disguised in the form of legislation, mention may be made of the extension of the Absentee Property Law to Arab residents who had changed their place of residence before 1 August 1948; the Regulations of 1949 enabling the Minister of Defence to declare certain areas 'security zones' and evict all their Arab inhabitants; the Law Concerning Uncultivated Lands, 1949; the Expropriation Law, 1950; the Land Acquisition Law, 1953, and the Law of Limitation, 1958. The effect of some of these laws is briefly mentioned hereafter. By the Absentee Property Law of 1950 the term 'absentee' was extended to include Arabs who, though they remained in Israeli-occupied territory in 1948, had the misfortune of leaving temporarily their ordinary place of residence. The effect of this law was that if an Arab left his village in 1948 and sought refuge in a city or a neighbouring village so as to avoid a possible fate such as that of the villagers of Deir Yassin, he was classified as an 'absentee' and his property was seized and given away to the Development Authority. By this means nearly half the Arab lands belonging to owners who had remained in Israeli-controlled territory was taken and confiscated. The Land Acquisition Law (1953) validated the seizure of land belonging to resident Arabs made prior to 1953 which had allegedly been taken for 'security reasons or development purposes' and vested title to such land in the Development Authority. The owners were offered in exchange either some land which was to be allotted by the authorities or some nominal compensation in cash which they never received. Another means which was adopted by Israel to dispossess the Arab minority of its lands was the Law of Limitation (1958). This law required the claimant of unregistered land to prove continuous undisputed possession for a period of 15 years. Failing such proof, the land would be forfeited to the Israeli government. Since most of the land of Palestine was unregistered and claims thereto rested upon a possessory title, and since the required proof was in many cases almost impossible to adduce by reason of the prevailing circumstances, the Law of Limitation meant, in effect, the confiscation of all unregistered Arab-owned land.

It is clear from this review of Israel's confiscatory land legislation that its policy not only was to create an exclusively Jewish state by displacing the non-Jewish inhabitants, but also aimed at the dispossession of the Arabs, both refugees and residents, of all their lands, houses and buildings. This was the position until 1967 in the territories which Israel seized in 1948 and 1949 and considered as part of the Israeli state. Israel's occupation of the West Bank and Gaza in 1967 led to further massive seizures and confiscations amounting to 52 per cent of Arab land in the occupied territories for the creation of Jewish settlements, as will be explained in Chapter 25.

In conclusion, it may be observed that, as a result of confiscations and other unlawful measures which have been described as constituting institutional robbery, Israel has increased its land holding in Palestine from less than 6 per cent in 1948 to at least 85 per cent in 1983 as we shall see in Chapter 31. The process of dispossessing Arab owners is still continuing.

NOTES

1. UN Doc. A/648, p. 14.
2. *Ibid.*, p. 47.
3. UN Doc. A/689, p. 1.

4. W. de St. Aubin, 'Peace and Refugees in the Middle East', *Middle East Journal*, 1949, p. 252.

5. *Middle East Journal*, 1949, p. 14.

6. George Kirk, *The Middle East 1945–1950* (Oxford University Press, London, 1954).

7. Don Peretz, *Israel and the Palestine Arabs* (The Middle East Institute, Washington, D.C., 1958), p. 148.

8. The number of Arab villages which existed in 1945 in the territories occupied by Israel was 863: A. Granott, *Agrarian Reform and the Record of Israel* (Eyre and Spottiswode, London, 1956), p. 89.

9. *Israel Government Yearbook*, 1959, pp. 74–5. A dunum equals 1,000 square metres.

10. Don Peretz, *Israel and the Palestine Arabs* (Middle East Institute, Washington, D.C., 1958), p. 143.

13

Palestine Independence Thwarted

POLITICAL AND TERRITORIAL BREAKING UP OF PALESTINE

In 1948, the independence of Palestine was thwarted and its territory was split into three areas which were occupied by Israel, Jordan and Egypt. As already noted, Israel seized and annexed 80 per cent of the territory of Palestine, Jordan occupied the West Bank and Egypt, the Gaza Strip. However, the West Bank and Gaza were not annexed by Jordan and Egypt because the avowed purpose of the Arab States' intervention was to protect the people of Palestine and to prevent the partition of their country. The League of Arab States specifically decided that the territories of Palestine occupied by Arab forces would be held 'in trust' for the people of Palestine until settlement of the Palestine Question.

The fiduciary character of the occupation of Palestinian territory which was decided by the League of Arab States was not much to the liking of King Abdullah of Jordan who harboured the design to incorporate into his kingdom the Palestinian territories that his army had occupied. When at the end of September 1948 Palestinian leaders proclaimed at Gaza the 'Government for All Palestine', King Abdullah did not relish the idea of a separate Palestinian entity and he countered the move by convening at Jericho on 1 September 1948 a congress of a few hundred Palestinians. This congress recommended the union of Palestine with Jordan. This recommendation was 'accepted' by the King who in April 1950 organized elections in Transjordan and in the occupied territories of Palestine, and on the 24th of the same month a national assembly convened at Amman and adopted a resolution which proclaimed the unification of Transjordan and Palestine. The resolution laid down three conditions for the union:

That all Arab rights in Palestine shall be safeguarded, that those rights shall be defended by all legal means, and that the union shall not prejudice the final settlement of the Palestine Question.

These reservations clearly meant that Palestinian rights and sovereignty over Palestine were preserved despite the unification of Palestine and Jordan.

Egypt, for its part, duly respected its position as trustee in regard to the Gaza Strip and at no time manifested any annexationist intention regarding such territory.

In consequence of the occupation of the territory of Palestine by the three powers and the dispersal of the majority of the Palestinian population in different countries as refugees, the statehood of Palestine was shattered, the Palestinians were prevented from attaining their independence and Palestine ceased to exist as an independent and separate political entity.

RESPONSIBILITIES

Many parties share the responsibility for the situation which came into existence upon termination of the mandate and prevented the concretization of the independence of Palestine. Britain was to blame for its failure to discharge its obligation under the mandate to develop self-government and for leaving the country in a state of utter chaos, confusion and turmoil without handing over the administration to an organized authority. The UN was largely responsible because of its adoption of the partition resolution which gave the Zionist Jewish immigrants a pretext to establish a state in Palestine in violation of the rights of the original inhabitants. Finally, the Palestinian leadership and the Arab States showed a lack of foresight in not taking proper and reasonable steps to prevent the deterioration of the situation.

The Palestinian leadership and the Arab States had laboured under the mistaken belief that the British were not planning to withdraw from Palestine at the end of the mandate. The author was told by a responsible Palestinian leader: 'If the British were to leave by the door, they would come back by the window.' Accordingly, the Palestinian leaders did not prepare to take over the country in the due exercise of Palestinian sovereignty. Unlike the Jews who had prepared their planning years and months ahead and who, on the eve of the termination of the mandate, proclaimed the State of Israel and established a provisional government with all that it required as administrative organs and personnel, the Arab Higher Committee, as representative of the Palestinians, was not structured or equipped to administer the country on the Mandatory's withdrawal. In a memorandum which he presented to them in January 1948, the author drew the attention of the Arab Higher Committee and the League of Arab States to the legal, political and practical reasons which made it imperative to establish a government contemporaneously with the termination of the mandate in order to fill the vacuum that would occur upon withdrawal of the Mandatory and to ensure the maintenance of public services, supplies and security whose disruption was to be expected and was already becoming apparent.

Having rejected the partition resolution, boycotted the UN Palestine Commission which was charged with its implementation, and being opposed to the establishment of a provisional government in accordance with the partition resolution, the only logical and consistent step for the Arab Higher Committee to take was to form a Palestinian government. With the termination of the mandate, the establishment of a Palestinian government by the majority of the people would have constituted a democratic measure as well as a proper and legal exercise of Palestinian sovereignty.

Regrettably, this was not done. When the Palestinian leadership established on 26 September 1948 in Gaza 'the Government For All Palestine', it was too late. Four-fifths of the territory of Palestine had already been seized by Jewish forces and the majority of the Palestinians had been evicted from their homes. Moreover, although the Government For All Palestine was recognized by the League of Arab States, it was not recognized by Jordan which, as previously mentioned, entertained its own plans regarding the future of the territories that had been occupied by its forces. As a result, the people of Palestine remained without any effective political representation until the creation of the Palestine Liberation Organization (PLO) in 1964.

14

UN Measures for Redress

In 1948 and subsequent years the UN took measures for redress of
the situation. These measures related to hostilities (truces and truce
supervision) and armistice agreements, to humanitarian assistance to
the refugees (UNRWA) and to settlement of the conflict. Measures
intended to settle the conflict aimed at mediation, conciliation,
repatriation of the refugees, the internationalization of Jerusalem,
Israeli withdrawal from territories occupied in 1967 and creation of
settlements. In this chapter, we shall review UN efforts at mediation, conciliation and implementation of the international régime of
Jerusalem; other measures are discussed in chapters 10, 18 and 25.

MEDIATION

On 14 May 1948 the General Assembly adopted resolution 186
which empowered a UN Mediator, chosen by the five permanent
members of the Security Council, to exercise certain functions, the
principal one being 'to promote a peaceful adjustment of the future
situation in Palestine'. Count Folke Bernadotte, a Swedish
Ambassador, was nominated as the UN Mediator on Palestine. The
account of the Mediator's activities is given in his Progress Reports,
in particular, in his last report to the General Assembly dated 16
September 1948 (UN Doc. A/648) and in his diary published
posthumously in 1951 by Hodder and Stoughton, London, under the
title *To Jerusalem*.[1]

Count Bernadotte did not embark on his mission with any sense
of unqualified acceptance of the partition resolution or of the situation created on the ground by force of arms. Without questioning
the provision for the creation of a Jewish State, he made suggestions

for a peaceful solution which were not in conformity with the partition plan or with the boundaries prescribed therein. To the objection made by the Provisional Government of Israel that his suggestions constituted 'deviations from the General Assembly resolution of 29 November 1947', he replied on 6 July 1948 as follows:

> In paragraph 1 of your letter it is stated that my suggestions 'appear to ignore the resolution of the General Assembly of 29 November 1947 . . .' I cannot accept this statement. As United Nations Mediator, it is true that I have not considered myself bound by the provisions of the 29 November resolution, since, had I done so, there would have been no meaning to my mediation. The failure to implement the resolution of 29 November 1947, and the open hostilities to which the Arab opposition to it led, resulted in the convoking of the second special session of the General Assembly 'to consider further the future Government of Palestine'. This special Assembly, taking into account the new situation, adopted on 14 May 1948 the resolution providing for a Mediator.[2]

His main conclusions in his report dated 16 September 1948 were as follows:

As regards the territorial question, Count Bernadotte stated that the boundaries of the Jewish State must finally be fixed either by formal agreement between the parties concerned or failing that, by the UN. He suggested certain revisions to be made in the boundaries defined in the partition resolution with regard to the Negeb and Galilee. He suggested that the disposition of the territory of Palestine not included within the boundaries of the Jewish State should be left to the governments of the Arab states in full consultation with the Arab inhabitants of Palestine, with the recommendation that in view of the historical connection and common interests of Transjordan and Palestine, there would be compelling reasons for merging the Arab territory of Palestine with the territory of Transjordan.

As to the refugees, he recommended that 'the right of the Arab refugees to return to their homes in Jewish-controlled territory at the earliest possible date should be affirmed by the United Nations, and their repatriation, resettlement and economic and social rehabilitation, and payment of adequate compensation for the property of those choosing not to return, should be supervised and assisted by the United Nations conciliation commission . . .'

On the question of Jerusalem, he stated that the city of Jerusalem should be placed under effective UN control with maximum feasible local autonomy for its Arab and Jewish communities and full safeguards for the protection of the Holy Places and religious freedom.

Count Bernadotte put on record Israel's unco-operative attitude in regard to his mediation. In his diary, he condemned the inhuman attitude adopted by Israel towards the refugees and mentioned Israel's 'arrogance',[3] its 'blatant unwillingness for co-operation',[4] 'the uncompromising and stiff-necked behaviour of the Jewish Government'[5] and how the latter 'had shown nothing but hardness and obduracy towards these refugees'.[6]

Count Bernadotte was assassinated with UN observer Colonel André Sérot at Jerusalem on 17 September 1948 by Jewish terrorists. With the death of Count Bernadotte, UN mediation effectively came to an end. After the elimination of Count Bernadotte, Dr Ralph Bunche was appointed as Acting Mediator until the establishment of the Conciliation Commission for Palestine.

Conciliation

The Conciliation Commission for Palestine was established by the General Assembly in its resolution 194 dated 11 December 1948 and was constituted of representatives of France, Turkey and the US, all nominated by the permanent members of the Security Council. Its mission was to assume the functions entrusted to the Mediator on Palestine and to carry out the specific directives given to it by the General Assembly or by the Security Council. The Conciliation Commission held discussions with Israel and the Arab States concerned, but no discussions were held with the Palestinians, the principal parties affected by the conflict.

The principal achievement of the Conciliation Commission was to secure the agreement of the four neighbouring Arab states (Egypt, Jordan, Syria and Lebanon) on the one hand, and Israel, on the other hand, to the Lausanne Protocol which was signed on 12 May 1949. The Protocol stated that the parties accepted the proposal made by the Conciliation Commission that the working document attached thereto (map of the partition resolution of 29 November 1947) would be taken as a basis for discussion with the Commission. In fact, however, and despite its signature of the Lausanne Protocol, Israel refused in its discussions with the Conciliation Commission to take the UN partition resolution as a basis for discussion. The Third Progress Report of the Commission (UN Doc. A/927 dated 21 June 1949) sets out the position taken by Israel in this regard.

On the territorial issue, the Commission found that Israel's attitude was in no way conducive to a settlement. Rejecting the partition resolution as a basis for discussion, Israel insisted on taking instead the armistice lines as a basis, even demanding more Arab territories, namely Western Galilee and the Gaza Strip. The Third Progress Report of the Conciliation Commission mentioned that on the territorial question Israel proposed that its frontiers with Egypt and Lebanon should be the frontiers of Palestine that existed under the British mandate. This proposal, if accepted, would have meant Israel's annexation of Western Galilee and the Gaza Strip, both of which were wholly Arab areas that had been reserved for the Palestine Arabs under General Assembly resolution 181 of 29 November 1947. As regards its frontier with Jordan, Israel proposed a boundary corresponding to the armistice lines. The proposal again implied the annexation by Israel of several Arab territories which it had seized in 1948 and 1949 but which were reserved for the Palestine Arabs under the General Assembly resolution. In effect, Israel's territorial proposals at the Lausanne discussions in 1949 meant that the Palestine Arabs would be left with about 20 per cent of the area of their own country.

In adopting this attitude, Israel was asserting as a source of title to territory a right of conquest rather than the UN partition resolution. James G. McDonald, the first American Ambassador to Israel, reports Israel's Prime Minister Ben Gurion saying to him: 'What Israel has won on the battlefield, it is determined not to yield at the council table.'[7] Israel's insistence on retaining the territorial gains it realized outside the boundaries of the Jewish State as defined by the partition resolution wrecked any possibility of achieving any settlement by mediation or conciliation. Likewise, its attitude on the questions of the repatriation of the refugees and of Jerusalem was totally inflexible and in disaccord with the General Assembly's resolutions.

Jerusalem

Notwithstanding the occupation of Modern Jerusalem (New City) by Israel and of the Old City by Jordan, the General Assembly instructed the Conciliation Commission to place the City of Jerusalem under an international régime as envisaged by its 1947 resolution. It issued its directives in this respect in its resolutions 194 of 11 December 1948 and 303 of 9 December 1949. The Concilia-tion Commission held discussions on the matter with the Arab States and Israel. While the Arab representatives showed themselves, in general, prepared to accept the principle of an international régime for Jerusalem, Israel declared itself unable to accept such a régime; it did, however, accept an international régime of the Holy Places in the Old City[8] which were then under Jordan's control.

Ineffectiveness of the Conciliation Commission

Although the Conciliation Commission has been in existence since 1948, one cannot credit it with any substantial achievement. One must concede that its mission was severely hampered by Israel's obduracy and its refusal to comply with UN resolutions. Furthermore, unlike Count Bernadotte, it made no proposals that were constructive. When it did eventually make certain proposals to the parties in September 1951, they were closer to the *fait accompli* than to equity and justice. Thus the Commission's proposals on territory amounted, in effect, to the conversion of the armistice lines into frontiers. Regarding the refugee problem, the Commission proposed that 'Israel should agree to the repatriation of a certain number in categories which can be integrated into the economy of Israel'. As to compensation for refugee property, the commission suggested a global sum which it evaluated at the ridiculously low figure of £120 million sterling. Both Arabs and Jews rejected the Commission's proposals.

Having failed in its principal mission, the Conciliation Commis-sion confined its efforts to secondary matters, such as the identifica-tion of Arab refugee property and the release of Arab bank accounts blocked in Israel. Since then the Conciliation Commission has continued to report annually to the General Assembly on its inability to achieve a settlement for which it is regularly and courteously thanked by the General Assembly.

Failure of UN measures of redress

The only UN measure of redress that has been successful has been the assistance and relief of the refugees by UNRWA. All other measures for redress were wrecked by Israel: mediation was thwarted, conciliation was defeated, repatriation of refugees was denied, the international régime of Jerusalem was rejected, refugee property was pillaged and the Armistice Agreements were violated by Israel's aggressions, principally in 1956, 1967 and 1982.

84

NOTES

1. See also on Count Bernadotte's mission, Sune O. Persson, *Mediation and Assassination* (Ithaca, London, 1979).

2. Progress Report of the UN Mediator for Palestine, 16 September 1948, UN Doc. A/648, p. 9.

3. F. Bernadotte, *To Jerusalem* (Hodder and Stoughton, London, 1951), p. 118.

4. *Ibid.*, p. 210.

5. *Ibid.*, p. 222.

6. *Ibid.*, p. 209.

7. James G. McDonald, *My Mission in Israel, 1948–1951* (Simon and Schuster, New York, 1957), p. 86.

8. See the Report of the Conciliation Commission for Palestine dated 2 September 1950, UN Doc. A/1367/Rev. I, pp. 10–11.

15

Admission of Israel to the UN

INVESTIGATION BEFORE ADMISSION

Israel's admission to the UN differed from the admission of other states to UN membership in two important respects. First, it was preceded by a long and searching examination by the General Assembly of Israel's future policy and intentions concerning frontiers, the internationalization of Jerusalem, and the Palestine refugees.[1] Second, admission was granted after Israel had given formal assurances concerning the implementation of General Assembly resolutions.

The reason for such a procedure was that Israel's original application for admission, which had been made on 29 November 1948, was rejected by the Security Council because several governments opposed Israel's admission on the ground that the questions of boundaries, refugees and the status of Jerusalem had not been settled. When Israel renewed its application for admission on 24 February 1949, the General Assembly invited it to clarify its attitude concerning the execution of the resolutions of the General Assembly on the internationalization of Jerusalem and on the problem of refugees. Several meetings of the Ad Hoc Political Committee of the General Assembly were held during which Israel's representative, Aubrey Eban, was questioned in detail and at length about Israel's intentions regarding the execution of General Assembly resolution 181 (II), the repatriation of the Palestine refugees, and the international status of Jerusalem. Among the questions which were directed to Israel's representative was a specific inquiry as to whether Israel had made the required Declaration to the UN for the guarantee of Holy Places, human rights, fundamental freedoms and minority rights as required by the resolution of 29 November 1947.

Israel's representative replied that 'only the State of Israel gave the requested formal undertaking to accept its provisions' and he referred to Security Council document S/747 which embodied the cablegram containing such undertaking, addressed by Israel's Foreign Minister to the Secretary-General of the UN on 15 May 1948.

During the meetings Israel made formal declarations and gave explanations with regard to the basic issues involved. It proclaimed its readiness to implement General Assembly resolutions and not to invoke Article 2, paragraph 7 of the Charter, which relates to domestic jurisdiction. In particular, it gave assurances regarding the implementation of General Assembly resolution 181 of 29 November 1947 (concerning the territory of the Arab and Jewish States, the City of Jerusalem, the Holy Places and minority rights) and General Assembly resolution 194 of 11 December 1948 (concerning repatriation of refugees and Jerusalem). It assured the General Assembly that it would co-operate with it in seeking a solution to all problems that had arisen. It saw no difficulty with regard to Jerusalem 'since the legal status of Jerusalem is different from that of the territory in which Israel is sovereign . . .'[2]

Conditions of Israel's admission

Israel was admitted to UN membership on 11 May 1949 subject to the 'declarations and explanations' which it had made to the General Assembly before its admission. These declarations and explanations were referred to in the General Assembly's resolution which admitted Israel to membership. The preamble of the resolution stated:

> *Noting* furthermore the declaration by the State of Israel that it 'unreservedly accepts the obligations of the United Nations Charter and undertakes to honour them from the day when it becomes a Member of the United Nations',
> *Recalling* its resolutions of 29 November 1947 and 11 December 1948 and taking note of the declarations and explanations made by the representative of the Government of Israel before the *Ad Hoc* Committee in respect of the implementation of the said resolutions.

It is evident that Israel's admission to UN membership was not unqualified or unconditional but was made subject to its compliance with its declarations and explanations relative to the implementation of General Assembly resolutions.

Israel's violation of its commitments

Israel's actions after its admission to UN membership have been at variance with the declarations and explanations it gave to the UN as a condition of its admission. The position it took before the Conciliation Commission in considering the armistice lines as its boundaries conflicted with its undertaking to respect General Assembly resolutions, and in particular, resolution 181. Its refusal to repatriate the Palestine refugees violated resolution 194. Its annexation of Jerusalem violated General Assembly resolutions 181, 194 and 303 as well as specific assurances before admission. In opposing the establishment of a Palestinian State, it violated resolution 181 and also repudiated its own birth certificate. Lastly, in launching general wars of aggression in 1956, 1967 and 1982 it flouted the principles of the UN Charter and international law.

Legal effect of Israel's admission to UN membership

Israel's admission to UN membership did not imply a recognition of its territorial integrity or of its title or sovereignty over the territories which it seized in excess of the borders of the Jewish State as defined in 1947. This is quite obvious from the fact that Israel's admission was conditional upon its commitment to implement resolution 181 which excluded from the area of the Jewish State the territories reserved for the Arab State and for the city of Jerusalem.

Moreover, admission to the UN did not involve recognition of Israel's legitimacy or a legitimation of its creation. Admission to membership of the UN, like recognition by other states, did not affect the status of Israel or cure its illegitimacy: admission to the UN is not a kind of religious sacrament which, like baptism in accordance with Christian belief, washes away human sin. The violations of UN resolutions as well as of the UN Charter involving the seizure and annexation of territory reserved for the Arab State, the uprooting and expulsion of the Palestinians, the denial of their repatriation, the plunder of their property and the annexation of the city of Jerusalem are not condoned by Israel's admission to UN membership. On the contrary, such admission obligates Israel all the more to respect and honour scrupulously the principles of the Charter, to observe and implement UN resolutions and to redress the wrongs it has committed.

NOTES

1. See the report of these meetings in Official Records of the General Assembly, Part II *Ad Hoc* Political Committee, 1949, pp. 179–360.

2. Official Records of the 3rd Session of the General Assembly, Part II, *Ad Hoc* Political Committee, 1949, pp. 286–7.

16

The Suez War

ITS UNDERLYING OBJECTIVES

On 26 July 1956 President Nasser nationalized the Suez Canal. The decree of nationalization provided that shareholders would be compensated at the closing prices of the shares on that day on the Paris Bourse. Although the nationalization was legal in accordance with international law, Britain and France invoked it as a pretext to launch an invasion of Egypt ostensibly for the protection of the Canal. In fact, however, a secret agreement had been made with Israel to join in the operation and even to initiate the hostilities.[1]

Although the nationalization of the Suez Canal was ostensibly invoked as the reason for the invasion of Egypt, the motivations for the Suez War existed in the minds and in the plans of the three invaders long before there was any thought of nationalization of the Canal. In launching the Suez War, France and Britain planned the elimination of Nasser for political reasons while Israel aimed at the realization of territorial gains.

France wanted to eliminate Nasser because of his political support and material aid to the Algerian rebellion against French rule. Britain wanted to eliminate Nasser, amongst other reasons, because of his opposition to its political plans in the Middle East, and, in particular, to the Baghdad Pact which it was sponsoring in the area. British hostility to Nasser reached its peak in March 1956 as a result of Jordan's ouster of General Glubb, British Commander of the Jordanian army, an act which the British attributed to Nasser's growing influence in the Middle East. Anthony Eden, the British Prime Minister, then vowed 'to destroy' Nasser.[2] This was several months before the nationalization of the Canal provided a pretext for the war.[3]

Unlike France and Britain, the plans of Israel's Prime Minister, David Ben Gurion, were concerned more with territorial gains than with the overthrow of Nasser. Ben Gurion did not consider that Israel's Armistice Agreement with Egypt, and for that matter, its Armistice Agreements with other Arab states had put an end to its territorial ambitions. There was here in his mind a piece of unfinished business to be attended to. Allen Dulles is reported to have said: 'Ben Gurion never intended peace.'[4] Israel's encroachments on the demilitarized zones set up by its Armistice Agreement with Egypt were preparations for a resumption of the war. Israel's pre-Suez occupation of El Auja indicated its aggressive intentions against Egypt. El Auja, a strategic area in Sinai and a gateway to an invader, was, for that reason, set up as a demilitarized zone by the Egyptian-Israeli Armistice Agreement. Its inhabitants, some 3,500 Bedouins, were expelled by the Israelis in 1950, and a number of them killed in 1953. Military bases disguised as agricultural settlements were established by Israel in the zone in violation of the Armistice Agreement.[5] Israel thus became the unchallenged master of the El Auja zone which it transformed into a stronghold and an invasion base from which it mounted its invasion in 1956.[6] In 1955 definite war preparations were made by Israel's purchase of Mystère jets from France. In November 1955 Ben Gurion uttered war threats against Egypt at the Knesset for its blockade of the Gulf of Aqaba and the closure of the Suez Canal to Israeli navigation. These two measures, however, were not in any way new developments: these had been in force for years, that is from the very day on which Israel came into existence.

COLLUSION

Thus, despite differences in motivations, there was a convergence between Britain, France and Israel on their war aims against Egypt. Secret discussions took place among them and a plan was evolved whereby Israel would be the first to attack Egypt and would move towards the Suez Canal so as to furnish a pretext for an Anglo-French armed 'intervention' which would be described to the world as 'a police action' intended to separate the combatants and to protect the waterway. As a further dressing up the plan envisaged that after commencement of hostilities an ultimatum would be addressed by Britain and France to Egypt and to Israel asking them to withdraw from the Canal area to permit an Anglo-French

91

occupation of the waterway. Upon refusal of the ultimatum by one or both, Anglo-French forces would then land in Egypt supposedly 'to separate the combatants'.

The plan was reviewed during a meeting held at Sèvres, a suburb of Paris, among the three parties on 22 to 24 October 1956. The meeting was called on the initiative of Ben Gurion who wished to obtain Britain's written acceptance of the plan, and also a commitment from the allies to destroy the Egyptian air force on the ground simultaneously with the launching of Israel's attack so as to forestall Egyptian bombing of Israeli cities. The meeting was attended by Selwyn Lloyd, the British Foreign Secretary, Guy Mollet, the French Premier, Pineau, the French Foreign Minister, Bourges-Maunoury, the French Defence Minister, Ben Gurion and Moshe Dayan, Israel's Prime Minister and Defence Minister, respectively. Ben Gurion obtained satisfaction on all points and a precise timetable for the scenario was laid down. The war plan was approved by Anthony Eden, the British Prime Minister and the British Cabinet on 25 October. For Israel the Suez War was a golden opportunity: it enabled it with the support of two major powers to invade the Sinai and the Gaza Strip, seize Sharm El Sheikh which controlled the Gulf of Aqaba and destroy the Egyptian army, the largest and strongest of all Arab armies. As an additional bonus, the Egyptian air force would be smashed up by the allies on the ground.

EXECUTION OF THE SCENARIO

The war began as planned by Israel's invasion of the Sinai Peninsula and the Gaza Strip on 29 October 1956. Egypt responded by sending troops eastward across the Canal to Sinai to halt the invasion. On 30 October, as agreed at Sèvres, the Anglo-French ultimatum was issued to Egypt to withdraw all forces to a distance of ten miles from the Canal and to accept the temporary occupation of Anglo-French forces of Port Said, Ismailia and Suez. As was foreseen and intended, the ultimatum was not accepted and on 31 October British aircraft bombed all Egyptian airfields and destroyed the Egyptian air force. Thereupon, as soon as Nasser realized that an Anglo-French invasion of Egypt was imminent, he recalled the troops he had despatched to Sinai, in order to meet the Anglo-French invasion. With the Egyptian air force destroyed and Egyptian forces withdrawn from Sinai, Israel had no difficulty in seizing the whole Sinai Peninsula, including the Gaza Strip. Two resolutions presented by the US and the Soviet Union to the Security Council that called for Israel's withdrawal were vetoed by Britain and France.

The seizure of the Sinai Peninsula and the Gaza Strip was completed on 5 November thus ending Israel's war operations. This was an advance by Israel ahead of its schedule, but this fact did not prevent Anglo-French forces from landing at Port Said ostensibly 'to separate combatants' who were not combating each other any longer. The Anglo-French forces captured Port Said and made a 23-mile advance down the Suez Canal.

SUCCESS FRUSTRATED

The Suez adventure caused a worldwide uproar and failed by reason of political and economic pressures that were exercised against Britain, France and Israel.

At the UN, although the Security Council was paralysed by the British and French vetoes, an emergency special session of the General Assembly was convened in accordance with the Assembly's resolution 377 A(V) of 3 November 1950 in order to deal with the situation. That resolution, called 'The Uniting for Peace' resolution, was adopted at the time of the Korean crisis of 1950. It declared that if the Security Council, because of lack of unanimity of the permanent members, should fail to exercise its primary responsibility for the maintenance of international peace and security, the General Assembly would make appropriate recommendations to members for collective measures, including the use of armed force. On the strength of such a resolution, the General Assembly called for an immediate cease-fire and a prompt withdrawal by the invaders. At the same time the Soviet Union addressed to the UN and to the US a proposal to use, jointly with other UN members, naval and air forces to smash the aggressors and to end the war. The Soviet Union's proposal was not accepted, but on 5 November 1956 Soviet Premier Bulganin addressed warnings to Eden, Mollet and Ben Gurion. To Eden and Mollet, he mentioned the possibility of the use of rockets against their countries. As to Ben Gurion, he warned him that by its action Israel was putting in jeopardy its very existence as a state.

In addition to the condemnation of the Suez invasion by world opinion, there was an uproar in the House of Commons against the British Government. From the start, in the words of Anthony Nutting, British Labour opposition 'smelt a rat' and accused Eden's government of collusion with the French and the Israelis. This accusation was vigorously denied in the House of Commons by Selwyn Lloyd who said 'There was no prior agreement' with the Israelis and by Anthony Eden who declared that 'There was not foreknowledge that Israel would attack Egypt'.[7] These denials, however, did not silence the Labour opposition which continued to press for withdrawal from Egypt.

Economic factors and in particular, the use of the oil weapon, were no less effective in bringing the war to an end. Following the blocking up of the Suez Canal by Egypt sinking in it several ships and the blowing up by Syria of the British-owned Iraq Petroleum Oil Company's pumping stations the movement of oil from the Middle East to Western Europe was almost completely stopped. Only a small American pipeline which passed through Syria and Lebanon continued to function. In a gesture of Arab solidarity against aggression, Saudi Arabia placed an embargo on oil shipments to France and Britain. In addition, the UK faced a serious financial crisis caused by a run on the pound. The fall of dollar reserves and the shortage of oil supplies threatened to paralyse British industry. The US Government further increased the pressure upon Britain and France in order to obtain their withdrawal from Egypt by withholding from them oil deliveries and dollar credits.[8]

On 5 November 1956 the General Assembly established a UN Emergency Force (UNEF) to supervise the cessation of hostilities. Egypt accepted the stationing of the international force on its territory along the armistice lines, but Israel refused its presence on its side of the armistice lines. On the following day, Britain and France agreed to a cease-fire and ten days later announced that their forces would be withdrawn from Egypt. On 22 December their withdrawal was completed.

ISRAEL RESISTED WITHDRAWAL

In the case of Israel, however, its withdrawal proved to be more difficult. Israel resisted withdrawal for two reasons. Unlike the British and French whose purposes were political, not territorial, Israel invaded the Sinai Peninsula and the Gaza Strip with the aim of keeping these territories. Having seized them, it was reluctant to abandon its spoils. Moreover, it possessed what it thought would be powerful weapons in manipulating US policy in its favour: the Jewish vote, the Zionist lobby and influential friends in Congress.

In contrast with Britain and France who withdrew unconditionally,

Israel demurred to the resolutions of the General Assembly of 2, 4, 7, 24 November 1956, 19 January 1957 and 2 February 1957 which called on it to withdraw its forces behind armistice lines. Israel observed the cease-fire requested by the UN because it had achieved its territorial objectives but to get it to withdraw was another matter.

The battle became one of political pressures behind the scenes between Israel and President Eisenhower. In fact, Israel had initiated its political pressures on the US President as part of its war plan prior to the date of the invasion. It sought to intimidate President Eisenhower by influencing the Jewish vote in the American presidential election due to take place in the first week of November 1956. Alfred Lilienthal mentioned one form of Zionist Jewish pressure on the White House: the distribution of hundreds of thousands of pamphlets in New York and other large urban areas saying: 'A vote for Ike is a vote for Nasser . . .'.[9] Twice during the month of October, Eisenhower warned Ben Gurion that he should not act in Israel's warlike plans against Egypt on the assumption that he, Eisenhower, would be influenced by considerations of the Jewish vote in the forthcoming election. In fact, he is reported to have declared in response to the threat of an adverse Jewish vote that 'he didn't give a damn whether he was re-elected'.[10] Israel's pressures, however, had not the slightest effect upon Eisenhower's success in the election which he won by a landslide on 6 November 1956 obtaining the biggest popular vote in American history.

Yet Eisenhower's warnings did not deter Israel from invading Sinai, nor Ben Gurion from resisting withdrawal. On the day the war ended, Ben Gurion proclaimed before the Knesset his intention to keep the occupied territories claiming that Israel possessed a 'historical title' to Sinai and Gaza and that Egypt possessed no sovereignty over those areas. On 7 November, Eisenhower wrote to Ben Gurion expressing deep concern over Israel's decision not to withdraw to the armistice lines and urged him to comply with UN resolutions. Concurrently with this letter it appears from Ben Gurion's biography by Michel Bar-Zohar that 'a simultaneous message from Hoover to Golda Meir raised the prospect of economic sanctions against Israel and of a broad-based movement in the UN to expel Israel'.[11] This had the desired effect because Ben Gurion replied on the following day to Eisenhower that Israel 'has never planned to annex Sinai' and that on arrival of the UN Emergency Force which it had been decided to despatch to Egypt, 'we will willingly withdraw our forces'.[12]

But despite the despatch of the UN Emergency Force to Egypt,

Israel's stated willingness to withdraw did not materialize. It pulled back from most of Sinai, but clung to the Aqaba Straits and to the Gaza Strip. It formalized its attitude by the adoption of a resolution by the Knesset which vowed to hold the Aqaba Straits until free navigation was assured 'by real guarantees' and to keep the Gaza Strip, but without the 210,000 Palestinian refugees who in 1948 had lost their homes and sought refuge in the area.

It should be observed that the Israeli demand for guarantees to assure free navigation through the Aqaba Straits represented the assertion of a claim which was unacceptable to Egypt. Since 1948, in exercise of its sovereignty, and because of the existence of a state of war with Israel, Egypt had prevented the passage of Israeli shipping through the waterway which lay entirely within its territorial waters. As to Israel's demand to keep the Gaza Strip, this was subsequently abandoned in favour of an equally unacceptable condition, namely, to retain the civil administration and policing over the area.

Having laid its conditions for withdrawal from Egyptian and Palestinian territories, Israel then proceeded through the Jewish lobby to develop public pressure on the White House to make it abandon the idea of forcing it to withdraw under the threat of sanctions. In justification of its stand, Israel invoked the two stock arguments which it has since used in subsequent expansionist adventures, namely, its 'historical connection' with those areas and its need for 'security'.

The US resisted Israel's pressure since to give in would have meant in the words of Dulles that 'Israel could control United States policy'.[13] Furthermore, in a statement made on 17 February, Eisenhower rejected Israel's contentions and conditions concerning the Gulf of Aqaba and the Gaza Strip and declared that members of the UN were bound by their undertakings under the Charter which 'preclude using the forcible seizure and occupation of other lands as bargaining power in the settlement of international disputes'.[14]

EISENHOWER THREATENS ISRAEL WITH SANCTIONS

From the outset Eisenhower saw in recourse to sanctions the most effective weapon to secure Israel's withdrawal. However in his resolve to apply sanctions, he faced not only Israeli pressures but also the opposition of influential Congress leaders, such as Lyndon Johnson who led the pro-Israel group of Democratic senators, and William F. Knowland, the Senate Republican leader, both of whom argued against the application of sanctions to Israel. In a meeting at the White House, Eisenhower reminded them that the US had previously applied sanctions against Britain and France by withholding from them oil shipments and dollar credits in order to force them to withdraw.[15]

On 20 February 1957 Eisenhower warned Ben Gurion in a cable that the US might vote for sanctions in the UN and prohibit private assistance from Americans to Israel. That same evening he delivered a televised address in which he publicly rejected Israel's conditions for withdrawal and warned it about the use of 'pressure' by the UN implying its recourse to sanctions. After describing the unsuccessful efforts which he made to secure the Israeli withdrawal, President Eisenhower declared:

Should a nation which attacks and occupies foreign territory in the face of United Nations disapproval be allowed to impose conditions on its own withdrawal?

If we agree that armed attack can properly achieve the purposes of the assailant, then I fear we will have turned back the clock of international order. We will, in effect, have countenanced the use of force as a means of settling international differences and through this gaining national advantages.

I do not, myself, see how this could be reconciled with the Charter of the United Nations. The basic pledge of all the members of the United Nations is that they will settle their international disputes by peaceful means and will not use force against the territorial integrity of another state.

If the United Nations once admits that international disputes can be settled by using force, then we will have destroyed the very foundation of the organization and our best hope of establishing a world order. That would be a disaster for us all.

I would, I feel, be untrue to the standards of the high office to which you have chosen me if I were to lend the influence of the United States to the proposition that a nation which invades another should be permitted to exact conditions for withdrawal.[16]

On the following day Ben Gurion defiantly rejected any change in his position before the Knesset. But the threat of sanctions became more imminent with the submission of a resolution to the General Assembly requiring the termination of all aid to Israel by all members of the UN if it failed to withdraw in accordance with UN resolutions.

SANCTIONS DID IT

With the certainty that such a resolution would receive an over-whelming vote from the General Assembly as well as the full support of the US and would result in cutting off from Israel both government and private aid, Israel yielded and announced on 1 March 1957 at the General Assembly of the UN its intention to carry out 'a full and prompt withdrawal' from the Sharm El Sheikh area and the Gaza Strip. The withdrawal to the armistice lines was completed a few days later.

The story of Suez is not of historical interest only: it is of actuality because history sometimes repeats itself as exemplified by Israel's repetition in 1967 of the Suez aggression. In 1967, as we shall see in the following Chapter, it seized again the Sinai Peninsula and the Gaza Strip and, in addition, the West Bank and the Syrian Golan. As in 1956, it refused and still refuses to withdraw from the territories which it occupied — other than the Sinai Peninsula from which it withdrew under the Egyptian-Israeli Peace Treaty of 1979 — invoking the same arguments of 'security'[17] and 'historical association' which it put forward at the time of Suez. As in 1956, it used the Jewish vote and the Zionist lobby to influence US policy and has succeeded in persuading successive American administrations to bar any recourse to sanctions the threat of which proved so effective in securing its withdrawal after the Suez aggression. But unlike 1956, Eisenhower's successors have failed to restrain Israeli excesses for fear of incurring the displeasure of the Zionist Jewish electorate. This continues to be the situation at the present time.

NOTES

1. On the Suez War, see Kennett Love, *Suez* (McGraw-Hill, New York, 1969); Anthony Nutting, *The Story of Suez* (Constable, London, 1967) and Moshe Dayan, *Story of My Life* (Weidenfeld and Nicolson, London, 1976).

2. Anthony Nutting, *The Story of Suez*, p. 34.

3. Kennett Love, *Suez*, p. 215.

4. Kennett Love, *Suez*, p. 53.

5. E.L.M. Burns, *Between Arab and Israeli* (Harrap, London, 1962), pp. 92-3.

6. Kennett Love, *Suez*, p. 110.

7. The whole story is given by Anthony Nutting, *The Story of Suez*. Anthony Nutting, who was at the time Minister of State for Foreign Affairs, resigned from office in October 1956 in protest against the landings at Suez.

8. Regarding the withholding by the US of oil and dollar credits from Britain and France during the Suez crisis, see Anthony Nutting, *The Story of Suez*, pp. 146 and 156.

9. Alfred Lilienthal, *The Zionist Connection* (Dodd, Mead and Co, New York, 1978), p. 338.

10. See Kennett Love, *Suez*, p. 454 and Anthony Nutting, *The Story of Suez*, p. 114.

11. Bar-Zohar, *The Armed Prophet*, p. 251 cited by Kennett Love, *Suez*, p. 639. This biography was published in French by Fayard, Paris, in 1966 and its English translation by Prentice-Hall in 1967.

12. See Eisenhower's correspondence with Ben Gurion in J.W. Moore (ed.), *The Arab-Israeli Conflict* (Princeton University Press, New Jersey, 1974), vol. III, p. 635.

13. Sherman Adams, *First Hand Report, The Inside Story of the Eisenhower Administration* (Greenwood Press, Westport, Conn., 1961), p. 283.

14. J.W. Moore (ed.), *The Arab-Israeli Conflict*, vol. III, p. 641.

15. Sherman Adams, *First Hand Report*, p. 281.

16. J.W. Moore (ed.) *The Arab-Israeli Conflict*, pp. 647–8.

17. The argument of 'security' was again invoked by Israel to justify its retention of a 'security zone' in south Lebanon following its war against the PLO in 1982.

17

The War of 1967

REAL CAUSE OF THE WAR

Notwithstanding the immensely deceptive propaganda which at the time succeeded in concealing the real cause of the War of 1967 and made it appear to be a defensive response by Israel to an Egyptian attack, there can be no doubt that it was a war of aggression waged by Israel in order to seize the rest of the territory of Palestine, namely, the West Bank and the Gaza Strip.

In this connection, it must be borne in mind that although the Jews had accepted the UN partition resolution in 1947 with a feigned reluctance, the purpose of their acceptance was merely to enable them to implant a Jewish State in Palestine, and then to expand its area to the whole of the country in furtherance of the Zionist programme, which was outlined to the Paris Peace Conference by the World Zionist Organization at the end of the First World War. This explains why in 1948 Israel did not respect the boundaries of the Jewish State as defined by the UN but seized in addition most of the territory of the Arab State, including Modern Jerusalem. This also explains why Israel did not observe the Armistice Agreements, but seized additional territories, including the demilitarized zones that were set up by such Agreements. This explains also Israel's seizure in the Suez War of the Gaza Strip and the Sinai Peninsula which, as we have seen in the previous chapter, it was forced to disgorge. The same Zionist objective also explains the War of 1967.

However, in order to launch a war in 1967 and to seize more territory after the Suez fiasco, Israel needed a pretext so that world opinion would not condemn its action as it had done in 1956. The pretext was fairly easy to create. A careful examination of the chain of events that preceded the War of 1967 reveals who struck the first blow and why. Two months before the outbreak of the war, that is on 7 April 1967, Israel launched a massive attack against Syria which has been described as 'the curtain-raiser to the six-day war'.[1] This incident arose from the provocative cultivation by an Israeli armoured tractor, backed by regular armed forces, of two Arab-owned parcels of land in the Syrian-Israeli demilitarized zone. Their cultivation had been approved by the Israeli Cabinet on 3 April 1967 and advertised in advance in the press (see the Syrian complaint to the Security Council, S/7845, 9 April 1967). This action was part of the Israeli programme for dispossession of Arab farmers and for seizure of the demilitarized zone, contrary to the Syrian-Israeli Armistice Agreement. The Israeli armoured tractor was met by Syrian small-arms fire. This was answered by a massive Israeli military action which included the use of artillery, tanks and aircraft. Several Syrian villages were bombarded and Israeli jet fighters reached the Damascus area. Six Syrian aircraft were shot down. In reporting this incident to the Security Council, Syria stated:

Several times during the past two weeks the Israelis continued to cultivate the disputed areas in the Demilitarized Zone for the sole purpose of instigating hostilities. This they did by armoured tractors protected by tanks and every armament, illegally placed in the Demilitarized Zone, in violation of the General Armistice Agreement. This demonstrates beyond any doubt a clear criminal intent to provoke a large-scale war with Syria [UN Doc. S/7845 9 April 1967, p. 5].

Israel followed the incident of 7 April by overt and public threats of military action against Syria. On 10 May 1967, General Rabin, the Israeli Chief of Staff, said that Israeli forces might 'attack Damascus and change its Government'. On 11 May, Israel's Prime Minister Eshkol declared in a public speech that in view of past incidents, 'we may have to adopt measures no less drastic than those of 7 April'. On 13 May, in a radio interview, Israel's Prime Minister spoke of drastic measures to be taken against Syria 'at the place, the time, and in the manner we choose', including the seizure of Damascus and the overthrow of the Syrian Government. It is significant that these threats were also whispered by the Israelis in the ears of 'journalists and foreign diplomats including the Soviets'.[2] On 15 May 1967 Syria drew the attention of the Security Council to the threatening statements made by Israeli leaders which evidenced an intent to launch military action against it.

What could have been the purpose behind Israel's threats against Syria and behind its troop concentrations, real or simulated? One can only presume that Israel's aim was to exert such pressure on Syria as to bring Egypt into the fray. The invasion of Syria would not realize Israel's basic objectives, both military and territorial. Israel was more interested in engaging Egypt, which possessed the only Arab army that stood in the way of its territorial and expansionist ambitions into the rest of Palestine. If, as is likely, this was Israel's plan, it succeeded perfectly.

Faced with Israel's threats of military action, Syria sought Egypt's assistance under the Mutual Defence Pact concluded between them in November 1966. Egypt responded by moving troops to Alexandria and Ismailia. At the same time, Egypt requested on 16 May the withdrawal of UNEF (United Nations Emergency Force) from Egyptian territory and, after the withdrawal, ordered on 22 May the closure of the Strait of Tiran in the Gulf of Aqaba to Israeli shipping and strategic war material destined for Israel.

Although the purpose of the measures taken by Egypt immediately preceding the war was misunderstood and even deliberately misconstrued, reliable evidence shows that they were essentially defensive in character and were meant to deter Israel from attacking Syria. In several public declarations President Nasser declared that Egypt would not unleash war, though it would resist Israeli aggression against any Arab country. His purpose was clearly 'to deter Israel rather than provoke it to a fight'.[3]

The defensive objective behind Egyptian troop movements prior to the outbreak of war is now becoming obvious to world opinion:

By May of 1967 limited mobilizations had occurred on both sides of the armistice lines, and the United Arab Republic, believing with considerable justification that Israel was about to make a major military move against Syria, began a substantial build-up of forces in the Sinai Peninsula.[4]

The same defensive consideration explains Egypt's request for the withdrawal of UNEF from the Egyptian side of the armistice lines. This move has been tendentiously presented as an indication of Egypt's aggressive intentions against Israel. Yet such action was both legal and necessary. That it was legal was recognized by the Secretary-General of the UN in his report dated 19 May 1967. The Secretary-General declared that Egypt had 'a perfect right to move

its troops up to its frontier' and that 'the United Nations Emergency
Force (UNEF) had no right to remain against the will of the govern-
ing authority'.[5] It was also necessary to meet the situation that
would arise if Israel carried out its threat to invade Syria, and Egypt
was compelled to extend effective assistance to the victim of aggression. It is significant that prior to ordering the withdrawal of UNEF
at Egypt's request, the Secretary-General of the UN suggested to
Israel that the force be stationed on the Israeli side of the armistice
lines. But Israel's representative quickly turned down the suggestion
as being 'entirely unacceptable to his government'.[6] It is clear that
the retention of the UN Emergency Force along the armistice lines
with Egypt did not suit Israel's plans. In any event, 'if Israel merely
wanted to defend itself, it should have allowed the United Nations
Force to come to its side of the boundary, as suggested by U Thant.
There is a great deal of evidence that Israel desired more
territory'.[7]

The evidence shows that it was not Egypt, but Israel, which had
a firm intention to attack the other. In his memoirs, President Lyndon
Johnson mentions the findings of Secretary of Defence Robert
McNamara concerning the situation: 'Three separate intelligence
groups had looked carefully into the matter, McNamara said, and it
was our best judgment that a UAR attack was not imminent.'[8] As
to the Israelis, the situation was different: 'The Israeli service chiefs,
for their part, became increasingly insistent on attack, and accused
the pacifists of treason for their shilly-shallying.'[9]

ISRAEL FABRICATES A FALSE CHARGE OF EGYPTIAN
AGGRESSION

The war started by a false charge which Israel fabricated against
Egypt. At 03.10 New York time on the morning of 5 June 1967,
Israel's Permanent Representative at the UN awoke the President of
the Security Council (Hans R. Tabor of Denmark) from his sleep to
inform him that he had just received reports 'that Egyptian land and
air forces have moved against Israel and Israeli forces are now
engaged in repelling the Egyptian forces' [UN Doc. S/PV 1347, 5
June 1967, p. 1]. The Israeli Representative asked that the Security
Council be convened to hear an urgent communication which he
wished to make to the body.

Twenty minutes later, the President of the Security Council was
informed by the Egyptian Permanent Representative to the UN that

'Israel has committed a treacherous premeditated aggression against the United Arab Republic this morning. The Israelis launched attacks against the Gaza Strip, Sinai, airports in Cairo, in the area of the Suez Canal and at several other airports within the United Arab Republic.'

The Security Council convened on the morning of 5 June. The Israeli representative again repeated the false charge that Israeli defence forces 'are now repelling the Egyptian Army and Air Force'. And in order to appear convincing he furnished to the Council the following false details:

> In the early hours of this morning Egyptian armoured columns moved in an offensive thrust against Israel's borders. At the same time Egyptian planes took off from airfields in Sinai and struck out towards Israel. Egyptian artillery in the Gaza Strip shelled the Israel villages of Kissufim, Nahal-Oz and Ein Hashelosha. Netania and Kefar Javetz have also been bombed. Israeli forces engaged the Egyptians in the air and on land and fighting is still going on . . .
>
> In accordance with Article 51 of the Charter, I bring this development to the immediate attention of the Security Council' [UN Doc. S/PV 1347, 5 June 1967, p. 4].

Most radio stations and newspapers spread the fabricated story of an Egyptian aggression against Israel and the whole world sympathized with the supposed victim. On the following day, Abba Eban, Israel's Foreign Minister, did not hesitate to repeat this fabricated story to the Security Council. Addressing the Council on 6 June, the Israeli Minister declared:

> *When the approaching Egyptian aircraft appeared on our radar screens*, soon to be followed by artillery attacks on our villages near the Gaza Strip, I instructed Ambassador Rafael to inform the Security Council, in accordance with Article 51 of the Charter. I know that that involved arousing you, Mr President, at a most uncongenial hour of the night, but we felt that the Security Council should be most urgently seized [UN Doc. S/PV 1348, 6 June 1967].

The great deception practised by Israel on the UN and the whole world could not last very long. The story that it was Egypt that commenced the war by an attack against Israel is now completely discredited. Even the Israelis themselves have abandoned the pretence. (The pretence was officially abandoned for the first time by Israel on 4 June 1972 when it published the Israeli Government's decision adopted on 4 June 1967 to attack Egypt, Syria and Jordan. The further pretence that Israel was threatened with extermination in June 1967 was shown to be false by three Israeli generals and was described as an exaggeration designed to justify the further annexation of Arab territory: see *Le Monde*, 3 June 1972.)

AGGRESSION AGAINST EGYPT, SYRIA AND JORDAN

The true facts were that on the morning of 5 June 1967, at 07.45 Egyptian time, that is shortly before Israel's Permanent Representative at the UN awoke the President of the Security Council to inform him of the alleged Egyptian aggression, wave after wave of Israeli bombers began to attack Egyptian airfields at ten minute intervals, destroying aircraft on the ground and putting runways out of action. In less than three hours, over 300 out of 340 Egyptian aircraft — representing almost the totality of the Egyptian air force — were destroyed, mostly on the ground. Nineteen Egyptian airfields were hit and rendered unserviceable on the first day of the attack. Then, within half an hour of the beginning of the Israeli airstrikes, Israeli ground forces launched an offensive against Egyptian positions in the Gaza Strip and the Sinai Peninsula and within days reached the eastern bank of the Suez Canal.

The Israeli air-strike on 5 June 1967 was not confined to Egypt. After destroying the Egyptian air force in a matter of hours, the Israelis attacked Syrian and Jordanian airfields before noon on the same day and destroyed a number of aircraft on the ground.[10] At the same time as its invasion of Sinai, Israeli ground forces pressed their attacks on Syria and Jordan. Within six days, Israel had occupied the whole of the Sinai Peninsula, the Old City of Jerusalem, the West Bank, the Gaza Strip and the Syrian Golan. The Security Council issued four cease-fire orders which Israel ignored until it had achieved its territorial objectives.

American secret participation in the war

One of the well-kept secrets of the war was a covert participation in the war by the US Government. This was disclosed recently by

Stephen Green in his book *Taking Sides: America's Secret Relations with a Militant Israel*.[11] This participation took the form of providing tactical support by US reconnaissance aircraft brought on 3 June 1967 from US bases in Germany and the UK to a NATO base in Spain. The date is of significance since it shows that the US was privy in advance to Israel's plans. The American pilots were instructed on arrival at the Spanish base to proceed to the Negeb desert and to provide tactical support for the IDF (Israel Defence Forces) by filming certain objectives in a war which Israel planned to launch on 5 June against the Arabs. Disguised as civilian employees of Israel and their planes painted with Israeli markings and the Star of David, the American pilots filmed the movements of Arab armies at night. The films were then passed on to the IDF which made devastating use of the information. The American 'ultrasecret' collaboration lasted until the very last day of the war. Once their work was completed, the Americans returned to their bases after being 'told that they were never, under any circumstances, to reveal what they had been doing the previous week'.

ISRAEL'S ATTEMPTED JUSTIFICATION OF THE WAR

After the discovery of the true facts about Israel's aggression, Israel invoked two arguments to justify its launching the war. Its first argument was that it acted by way of a preventive strike which, in its view, is equivalent to self-defence under Article 51 of the UN Charter. Such argument has no basis in fact or in law. In fact, Israel, as we have seen, created the crisis and attacked its neighbours. In law, the Charter recognizes the right of self-defence against an armed attack, but not of a pre-emptive strike in advance of any attack. None of the Arab States had attacked or threatened to attack Israel and as D.P. O'Connell observes, the invasion of a neighbouring country's territory is not an exercise of the right of self-defence.[12]

Israel's second argument was that Egypt's closure of the Strait of Tiran constituted a *casus belli*. Such an argument is unacceptable. The closure of the Strait of Tiran to Israeli shipping and to strategic war material designed for Israel was part of Egypt's response to the threats made by Israel against Syria. This action was defensive in its object and in its nature. Such closure was in conformity with international law. The Strait of Tiran lies within Egypt's territorial waters and its navigable channel is situated less than a mile from the Egyptian coast. In these circumstances, the action was a legal exercise by Egypt of its right of sovereignty over its territorial sea and an assertion of a right of belligerence recognized by international law.

Yet, despite the clear fabrication of the cause of the war and the deceit practised on the UN and on world opinion, Israeli and Zionist propaganda still continues to refer to the War of 1967 as one of 'the four defensive wars' which Israel had to wage for its existence.

SEQUELS OF THE WAR

The sequels of the War of 1967 were almost as catastrophic as those of the War of 1948 and may be summed up as follows:

(1) Territorial occupation

The war involved Israel's occupation of the West Bank, including the Old City of Jerusalem, the Gaza Strip, the Sinai Peninsula and the Syrian Golan. Except for the Sinai Peninsula (which Israel returned to Egypt under their Peace Treaty of 1979) the other territories still remain under Israeli occupation. The continued occupation of those territories has no justification whatsoever, particularly since the two false pretexts which Israel invoked for their seizure, i.e., the threat of an Egyptian attack and the closure of the Strait of Tiran, were settled by the peace concluded between Egypt and Israel. But Israel has shown its true face as well as the real motivation for its waging the War of 1967: it has annexed the Old City of Jerusalem and the Syrian Golan and, by means of a feverish colonization, it is proceeding with a rampant annexation of the West Bank and the Gaza Strip.

(2) Creation of another refugee tragedy

In accordance with an estimate made by the Government of Jordan, 410,248 Palestinians, comprising 145,000 refugees of the 1948 conflict, were displaced in 1967 and crossed into Jordan. Some left in consequence of the hostilities, others were expelled by force or threats. Under the pressure of world opinion and UN resolutions, Israel announced in July 1967 that it would allow the return of the refugees of the last conflict. However, it hemmed in its offer of repatriation by such conditions and time limits that only 14,000 of the 410,248 refugees were permitted to return while at the same time Israel expelled some 17,000 Palestinians out of the country.[13]

(3) Annexation of the Old City of Jerusalem

On the first day of the war, Levi Eshkol, Israel's Prime Minister, and Moshe Dayan, its Defence Minister, declared that Israel had no aim of territorial conquest. But no sooner did the war come to an end with the defeat of the Arabs than the tone changed and Levi Eshkol denounced the 1949 Armistice Agreements and proclaimed before the Knesset on 12 June that there would be no return to the armistice lines fixed by these Agreements. 'Today', said Levi Eshkol, 'the world realizes that no force can uproot us from this land'.

Accordingly, the Old City of Jerusalem was annexed without delay. On 28 June the Israeli Government issued an order which declared that the Old City of Jerusalem 'shall be subject to the law, jurisdiction and administration of Israel'. Although this clearly amounted to annexation of the Old City, Israel attempted to deceive world opinion and to explain it away as an innocent action which possessed no political significance.[14] However, no such diffidence was shown thirteen years later when in July 1980 Israel adopted a law which proclaimed Jerusalem its 'eternal capital'.

(4) Subjection of Arab inhabitants of occupied territories to domination and repression

Some 1,400,000 Palestinians in the West Bank and Gaza are subjected to Israeli domination. The treatment to which the inhabitants of the occupied territories, including the inhabitants of Jerusalem, have been subjected, the repression of any resistance and the violations of their human rights will be discussed in Chapter 26.

(5) Colonization of the occupied territories

Immediately after its occupation of Arab territories in 1967, Israel commenced its colonization with the creation of Jewish settlements. More than one hundred settlements were established in the occupied territories in violation of international law, the Fourth Geneva Convention of 1949 and UN resolutions. The colonization of the West Bank and Gaza will be discussed in Chapter 25.

(6) The blotting out of the Palestine Question

The most devastating consequence of the War of 1967, however, was psychological: the enormity of the damage caused and its sequels have overshadowed the Palestine Question itself, including the wrongs that went into its making: the Balfour Declaration, the partition resolution, the upheaval of 1948, the massive refugee problem and the usurpation of 80 per cent of Palestine. These wrongs have been blurred by the War of 1967 and the main concern since then has been how and at what price to secure Israel's withdrawal from the territories it occupied in that year. This has become the dominant consideration which since then has inspired current plans for peace in the Middle East.

NOTES

1. Charles W. Yost, 'The Arab-Israeli War: How It Began', *Foreign Affairs*, vol. 46, no. 2 (January, 1968), p. 310.
2. Charles W. Yost, *op. cit.*, p. 310.
3. *The Observer*, 4 June 1967.
4. 'The Arab-Israeli Conflict and International Law', *Harvard International Law Journal*, vol. 9 (1968), p. 242.
5. UN Doc. S/7896 (1967).
6. Charles W. Yost, 'The Arab-Israeli War', p. 313. As to the circumstances of UNEF's withdrawal and Israel's rejection of the Secretary-General's offer to move the UN Force to the Israeli side of the armistice line, see U Thant's address in UN publication OPI/429–01419, January, 1971.
7. Quincy Wright, *AJIL*, vol. 64, no. 4 (1970), p. 80.
8. Lyndon Johnson, *The Vantage Point* (Holt, Rinehart and Winston, New York, 1971), p. 293.
9. Maxime Rodinson, *Israel and the Arabs* (Penguin Books, Harmondsworth, 1968), p. 199.
10. For an account of military operations during the Israeli-Arab War of 5 June 1967, see Randolph and Winston Churchill, *The Six-Day War* (Heinemann, London, 1967); Yves Cuau, *Israël Attaque* (Laffont, Paris, 1968); E. Rouleau, J.F. Held, J. and S. Lacouture, *Israël et les Arabes* (Seuil, Paris, 1967).
11. Stephen Green, *Taking Sides: America's Secret Relations with a Militant Israel* (William Morrow, New York, 1984), pp. 204–11.

12. D.P. O'Connell, *International Law*, vol. I (Stevens and Sons, London, 1965), p. 342.

13. See details in Henry Cattan, *Palestine, The Arabs and Israel* (Longman, London, 1969), pp. 108 *et seq.*

14. See the declaration of Abba Eban, Israel's Foreign Minister, at the 1,541st meeting of the General Assembly, 29 June 1967.

18

Security Council Resolution 242

ORIGIN OF RESOLUTION 242

In the summer of 1967 the General Assembly and the Security Council attempted without success to secure Israel's withdrawal from the territories it had occupied in June of that year. The attempt failed by reason of disagreement between the two superpowers on the manner of resolving the issue. Unlike the unanimous reprobation which the two superpowers showed towards Israel's military adventure in 1956, they were divided this time in their attitude towards its new aggression. On the one hand, the Soviet Union requested the condemnation of Israel as aggressor and demanded its immediate withdrawal. On the other hand, the US Government showed no disposition to condemn Israel. It sought to enlarge the issues and to secure a political settlement between the Arab States and Israel. In consequence, neither the Security Council nor the General Assembly, could agree on a resolution to resolve the crisis and liquidate its territorial consequences.

Nothing concrete happened until November 1967 when the Security Council convened at Egypt's request in order to examine the situation again. Two draft resolutions were discussed. The first was submitted by the US on 7 November and the second was submitted by Britain on 16 November. The only difference between the two drafts was the emphasis of the latter on 'the inadmissibility of the acquisition of territory by war'. The British draft was adopted on 22 November 1967 and became known as resolution 242.

ITS MAIN PROVISIONS

Resolution 242 purported to lay down a formula for 'a just and lasting peace in the Middle East'. It emphasized the inadmissibility of the acquisition of territory by war and affirmed that the fulfilment of the principles of the Charter required the establishment of a just and lasting peace in the Middle East which should include the application of both the following principles:

(i) Withdrawal of Israeli armed forces from territories occupied in the recent conflict.

(ii) Termination of all claims or states of belligerency and respect for and acknowledgement of the sovereignty, territorial integrity and political independence of every state in the area and their right to live in peace within secure and recognized boundaries free from threats or acts of force.

The resolution further affirmed the necessity:

(i) For guaranteeing freedom of navigation through international waterways in the area;

(ii) For achieving a just settlement of the refugee problem;

(iii) For guaranteeing the territorial inviolability and political independence of every state in the area, through measures including the establishment of demilitarized zones.

Finally, the resolution requested the Secretary-General to designate a Special Representative to proceed to the Middle East to establish and maintain contact with the states concerned, in order to promote agreement and assist efforts to achieve a peaceful settlement in accordance with the principles of the resolution.

FAILURE OF ATTEMPT TO IMPLEMENT RESOLUTION 242

Dr Gunnar Jarring, the Swedish Ambassador to Moscow, was appointed by the Secretary-General of the UN as his Special Representative to implement Security Council resolution 242. However, his efforts bore no fruit, on account of Israel's refusal to withdraw, or to give an undertaking to withdraw, from the territories it had occupied. The failure of Ambassador Jarring's mission led to a resumption of hostilities in 1969 between Egypt and Israel in a positional war which Egypt intended to be 'a war of attrition'. Egypt's aim was to force Israel's withdrawal, because it considered that the cease-fire which it had observed since June 1967 was not intended to perpetuate Israel's occupation of its territory. This incidental war was suspended as a result of a proposal made to the parties by William P. Rogers, US Secretary of State, who suggested a temporary cease-fire and the reactivation of the Jarring mission. A cease-fire was arranged and came into force on 7 August 1970. The initiative taken by William P. Rogers was restricted to a cease-fire and reactivation of the Jarring mission with the aim of implementing resolution 242.

Ambassador Jarring resumed his discussions with Israel and the neighbouring Arab States. Under the pressure of military occupation of their territories, Egypt and Jordan agreed to implement resolution 242. Syria rejected it. Despite the fact that the resolution was basically in its favour, Israel refused to implement its provision concerning withdrawal of its armed forces from the occupied territories because it wanted to retain some of them, in particular Jerusalem, Sharm El Sheikh in the Gulf of Aqaba, parts of the West Bank and the Golan Heights of Syria. Although its attitude on this matter had been apparent since July 1967, Israel's refusal to withdraw from the occupied territories was formally notified to Ambassador Jarring several years later in a communication dated 26 February 1971 which stated: 'Israel would not withdraw to the pre-5 June 1967 lines' (UN Doc. A/8541, 30 November 1971). Israel claimed that it would withdraw only to 'safe and secure boundaries' to be determined by negotiations between the parties. This meant, in effect, that under the pretext of obtaining 'safe and secure boundaries' Israel planned to retain and annex some of the territories it had occupied in a war of aggression which it had itself initiated.

Thus Ambassador Jarring's mission foundered upon Israel's refusal to withdraw. He made some further efforts to persuade Israel to change its mind but he failed, and in March 1972 he abandoned his fruitless mediation.[1]

It should be remarked that Israel's attitude about resolution 242 has been ambivalent. Politically, Israel accepted the resolution because it was premised on the recognition of Israel by the Arab States and implied ratification of its conquests in 1948 and 1949. But territorially, Israel rejected the resolution, as explained above, because it wished to retain some, if not all, of the territories it had seized in 1967.

It should be noted that Ambassador Jarring did not conduct any negotiations with the Palestine Liberation Organization (PLO). Presumably, this was because resolution 242 ignored the existence of the Palestinians, except as refugees. But the PLO made its position known and proclaimed its rejection of resolution 242 on the ground that it overlooked the Palestine Question which it treated simply as 'a refugee problem'.

Whether resolution 242 provides a fair and equitable plan for the settlement of the Palestine Question will be examined in Chaper 32.

NOTE

1. The efforts made by Ambassador Jarring during his mission are described in the Secretary-General's reports S/10070, 4 January 1971 and S/10929, 18 May 1973.

19

The Palestine Liberation Organization

PALESTINIAN NATIONALISM

During Ottoman times, Palestinian nationalism was merged in the general Arab nationalist movement which had developed in the middle of the nineteenth century and sought secession of the Arab territories from the Ottoman Empire.[1] In the First World War Palestinian nationalists joined the Arab war effort against Turkey and allied themselves to its leader King Hussein of the Hedjaz. The Allied Powers encouraged the Arabs to rebel and secede from Turkey. To this end, they gave them pledges for their independence as mentioned in Chapter 1. But these pledges were not honoured with respect to Palestine.

In the crisis that developed in Palestine over the Balfour Declaration, Jewish immigration and partition, the Arab States assumed the role of guardians of the Palestinian cause. As a result, the Palestinians relied mainly on the Arab States to safeguard their rights. However, the poor showing which the Arab States made in defending Palestine in 1948 and the failure of the UN to redress the wrongs done to them convinced the Palestinians that they should take matters into their own hands. Israel's aggression in 1967 and its seizure of the rest of Palestine reinforced the Palestinians' determination to liberate their country, which had already taken shape in the creation of a national movement.

THE PLO: STRUCTURE AND OBJECTIVES

On 28 May 1964 a Palestinian National Congress convened at Jerusalem and proclaimed the establishment of the Palestine Liberation Organization (PLO). The Congress also adopted a national

115

Charter which set out the Palestinian national programme. The PLO comprises three main organs:

(1) The Palestine National Council which is composed of representatives of the main guerrilla organizations (*Fatah*, the principal organization which was founded by Yasser Arafat in 1959 and whose name is an acronym in reverse order of the first letters of 'Movement for the Liberation of Palestine' in Arabic; the Popular Front for the Liberation of Palestine founded by George Habash; the Democratic Front for the Liberation of Palestine; the Front for the Liberation of Palestine and the Saiqa), of the Army for the Liberation of Palestine, of trade unions and the Palestinian communities in the diaspora, refugees and independent individuals. The Council holds annual meetings and comprises 430 members who represent the constituent elements of the Council in the following proportions: 19.3 per cent from the guerrilla organizations, 10.2 per cent from the Army for the Liberation of Palestine, 26 per cent from trade unions and popular associations and 44.1 per cent from Palestinian communities, refugees and independent individuals from the diaspora.

(2) The Central Council was created in 1973 by the National Council to implement its resolutions and to act as an advisory body. It consists of 60 members elected by the National Council.

(3) The Executive Committee which was established in 1964 and consists of 15 members elected by the Council and functions as the executive branch of the organization.

Since its establishment and during the last two decades, the PLO developed, in addition to its military and political organs, an infrastructure which includes a national fund, a Red Crescent, and a number of cultural, social and educational institutions. In effect, the PLO has become a quasi-government. Since its withdrawal from Beirut in 1982 its headquarters have been located in Tunis.

The political programme of the PLO was set out in the Palestine National Charter of 1964 and was amended in 1968.[2] It originally aimed at the restoration of the national rights of the Palestinians in their own country. Accordingly, its objective is not restricted to securing Israel's withdrawal from the territories which it seized in excess of the partition plan, but extends to the liberation of all the land of Palestine, the repatriation of its people, and the establishment of a lay, unitary and democratic state in which Moslems, Christians and Jews will live together enjoying equal rights and subject to the same duties.

116

The Charter also proclaimed the illegality of the Balfour Declaration, the British mandate, the partition resolution and the establishment of Israel. Although no formal amendment of the Charter has been made, an evolution in the PLO's political programme has taken place in recent times. The PLO is now prepared to accept a political solution based on UN resolutions, as will be discussed in Chapter 32.

INTERNATIONAL RECOGNITION OF THE PLO

Official recognition as a full member was accorded to the PLO by the League of Arab States in June 1964. In addition, the PLO is recognised by the Arab States as the sole legitimate representative of the Palestinian people.

On the international level, the PLO was recognized by the General Assembly of the UN as the representative of the Palestinian people in its resolution 3210 of 14 October 1974. It invited it to participate in its deliberations on the Question of Palestine. Moreover, in its resolution 3236 of 22 November 1974, the General Assembly requested the Secretary-General to establish contacts with the PLO on all matters concerning the Question of Palestine and in its resolution 3237 of the same date it invited the PLO to participate in the capacity of observer in the sessions and the work of the General Assembly and all international conferences convened under the auspices of the General Assembly or other organs of the UN.

The PLO is recognized not only by all Arab states but also by most states in Asia, Africa and Latin America, in all 130 states, 61 of them according to it full diplomatic status. The states that accord to the PLO diplomatic status include India, Pakistan, China, the Soviet Union, Austria, Greece and Spain. In the case of other states that recognize it, the PLO maintains an information office. It may be remarked in this connection that a greater number of countries recognize the PLO than recognize Israel.

GUERRILLA ACTIONS

Before there was any thought of a political solution to the Palestine Question, the PLO's basic aim was the liberation of Palestine. The only means available to it was guerrilla action. Hence the question which must be posed is whether guerrilla action is justifiable.

Rationally, the answer can only be in the affirmative. When a people have been uprooted from their ancestral homeland, dispossessed of homes, lands and all other possessions, denied the human right to return to their country and deprived of all civil and political rights, is it surprising that they should fight to recover their homes and the land of their forefathers? When the Arab-Israeli War of 1973 broke out, French Foreign Minister Michel Jobert was questioned on 8 October 1973 by newsmen as to whether the Arabs could really be blamed for trying to regain their lost territories. His answer was: 'Do you think that trying to get back into your own home really constitutes an unforeseen act of aggression?'

International law and the conscience of mankind recognize the right of the Palestinians to struggle for the recovery of their homeland. In its resolution 2787 of 6 December 1971 and in subsequent resolutions, the UN General Assembly confirmed:

The legitimacy of the struggle of the Palestinians (amongst other peoples), for self-determination and liberation from colonial and foreign domination and alien subjugation by all available means consistent with the UN Charter.

The truth about guerrilla actions

It is not the intention here to give an account of Palestinian guerrilla actions against Israel as this would fill volumes. Nor is it the intention to justify all Palestinian guerrilla action. There exist, however, two important considerations that should be borne in mind.

First, the guerrilla organizations possess, in fact, a politico-military character and do not share identical views about the manner of conducting the struggle against the Israeli state. Hence, they differ in methods and ideology. Thus, they have differed among themselves over policy following their withdrawal from Beirut, over the need to adopt a political solution and finally over the Jordan–PLO agreement of 11 February 1985 (Chapter 32) which broke down in 1986. Such differences have resulted in the formation of a dissident group of guerrilla organizations which came to be described as 'the rejection front'. However, although they differ in methods, they are in perfect harmony in their opposition to Israel.

Second, it is essential to realize that not *all* aggressions that are committed against the Israelis are the work of the Palestinians or of the PLO. Many acts are committed either by splinter or independent

118

groups over whom the PLO has no control or by *agents pro-vocateurs*. There are persons and organizations not belonging to the PLO whose objective is to discredit and destabilize the PLO because of its policy to seek a political solution to the Palestine Question. They resort to terrorism both against PLO represent-atives, many of whom have been assassinated (including PLO representatives in Paris, London, Brussels and Rome), and also against Jewish institutions or synagogues in Europe. In both cases, the perpetrators remain anonymous, in order that public opinion, influenced by Zionist propaganda, will impute the terrorist acts to the PLO.

But Israel's propaganda automatically and without any evidence, or even contrary to the facts, invariably attributes responsibility for guerrilla actions to the PLO. A fairly recent example of such false accusations is to be found in the attempted assassination of the Israeli Ambassador in London on 3 June 1982 which served as one of the pretexts for the War of 1982. This aggression was falsely and maliciously imputed to the PLO by Israel despite the fact that the investigation carried out by the British authorities established that the PLO had no connection whatsoever with it and further showed that the next victim on the assassins' list was the PLO representative in London.

In many cases Israel has deliberately falsified and distorted details of guerrilla actions in order to attract sympathy for the Israeli cause. Examples are the hijacking of aeroplanes and the seizure of hostages, events which attracted worldwide attention and concern. These examples have been chosen for discussion here because Israel's propaganda still invokes them as illustrations of Palestinian terrorism.

Hijacking of aeroplanes

Before discussing the hijacking of aeroplanes by Palestinians, it may be necessary to remind the reader that Israel carried out the first (but not the last) hijacking in the Middle East. On 14 December 1954 Israeli fighters intercepted a Syrian civilian airliner after take-off from Damascus and forced it to land at Lydda in Israel, its passengers held hostage for 48 hours. The US Government described the action as 'without precedent in international practice'. Israeli Prime Minister Moshe Sharett, who had not been consulted about the hijacking, arranged the release of the aircraft and the hostages and condemned the act as behaviour 'according to the laws of the jungle'.[3]

Turning to Palestinian hijackings, the most spectacular were carried out in 1970. On 6 September three airliners were hijacked by the Popular Front for the Liberation of Palestine, one of the Palestinian guerrilla organizations, and were forced to land at Zerka, in Jordan. A fourth airliner was also hijacked three days later. The hijacking of a fifth Israeli airliner failed and one of the hijackers was killed. In all, 450 passengers were kept as hostages during six days. They were given an explanation of the Palestine Question and the injustices suffered by the Palestinians. The hostages were then released unharmed. But the hijacked airliners — two American and one British — were blown up as an expression of disapproval of Anglo-American policy in regard to the Palestine Question.

These hijackings were carried out primarily to focus world attention on the Palestine injustice which had almost come to be forgotten. This objective fully succeeded because for the first time many people began to ask: 'Who are the Palestinians?', 'What is the Palestine problem?', 'What do the Palestinians want?'. A subsidiary aim of the hijackings was to secure the liberation of seven Palestinian commandos who were detained in Switzerland, West Germany and the UK. These were released following the liberation of all the hijacked passengers.

The hijackings were generally condemned or deplored, but their underlying political objective was recognized. UN Secretary-General U Thant condemned the hijackings despite the fact that, as he observed, 'some of the grievances of the perpetrators are understandable, and even justifiable'. After the spectacular hijackings of September 1970 which achieved their purpose in focusing world attention on the Palestine Question, this method of publicity has been abandoned by Palestinian resistance although Israeli propaganda always seeks to link any hijacking with the PLO.

The hijacking of the *Achille Lauro*

A recent example of the exploitation of a hijacking to discredit the PLO when it was completely innocent is the hijacking of the Italian cruise liner, the *Achille Lauro*, in October 1985. The hijacking was carried out by three Palestinians, belonging to a small guerrilla group, without the knowledge or approval of the PLO. The original objective of the guerrillas was to travel as tourists on the cruise ship and to disembark at Ashdod in Israel to carry out a raid on a military objective. However, when a member of the crew discovered that the Palestinian 'tourists' possessed arms, the guerrillas hijacked the ship and a Jewish American passenger was killed and his body was thrown into the sea.

The guerrillas subsequently surrendered to the Egyptian authorities and were to be sent to Tunis where the PLO planned to put them on trial. US forces intercepted the Egyptian aeroplane however, and forced it to land at a NATO base in Sicily. Until today responsibility and blame for the incident are ascribed without reason or justification to the PLO in order to smear its reputation when, in fact, it had no responsibility whatsoever for it.

Seizure of hostages

Another form of Palestinian guerrilla action which has received considerable publicity and has been and is still exploited by Israeli propaganda against the Palestinians is the seizure of Israeli hostages with the aim of securing the release of Palestinians unlawfully detained or imprisoned in Israel. There are several thousand Palestinians detained in Israeli prisons at any given time. They are detained without trial, under the so-called 'Emergency Defence Regulations' which Israel inherited from the British Mandatory Power. Such Emergency legislation was first enacted by the British in 1936 in order to detain without trial Palestinian Arabs for their opposition to the Balfour Declaration and to Jewish immigration. The Israeli authorities have preserved this exceptional legislation and have made and still make liberal use of its provisions against political opponents, journalists and students.

One of the much publicized and tragic cases of such an action occurred on 5 September 1972 at the Olympic Games at Munich. On that day members of 'Black September'[4] seized eleven Israeli participants at the Games as hostages and offered to exchange them for 200 Palestinians detained in Israel under the Emergency Defence Regulations. In negotiations with the German authorities, the captors offered to carry out the exchange in Cairo to which city the hostages and their captors would be flown in a Lufthansa aeroplane. The German authorities feigned acceptance of this plan and persuaded the Palestinian commandos to proceed with their hostages in two helicopters to the military airfield of Furstenfeld where a Lufthansa aeroplane would be waiting to take them to Cairo. An ambush was prepared at the airfield for no sooner had one of the Palestinians disembarked from the first helicopter and moved towards the waiting Lufthansa plane than the German sharpshooters began firing at the Palestinians and their hostages. The result was a tragic ending for captors and hostages alike.

It is regrettable that no official inquiry took place to clarify the facts and circumstances of the Munich affair and, in particular, who was responsible for the killings and the ambush which occasioned them. Several high German officials were involved in the negotiations, including the federal Minister of the Interior (D. Genscher) and the Bavarian Minister of the Interior (B. Merk) as well as Abba Eban, Israel's Foreign Minister, who stated that Israel had requested that the German authorities use force in order to rescue the hostages. No attempt was made to establish who killed who. But regardless of the facts, Israel's propaganda has since then laid the blame squarely on what it describes as Palestinian terrorists and constantly refers to 'Munich' as the outstanding example of Palestinian terrorism.

To avenge 'Munich' Israel launched several massive air raids on 8 September 1972 hitting ten Palestinian refugee camps in Lebanon and Syria which caused some 200 casualities — mostly civilian refugees. These two states requested the Security Council to condemn Israel for its violation of their territories and the bombing of innocent civilians. However, a US veto on 10 September 1972 defeated the adoption of any resolution by the Security Council. The official explanation of the veto by the US representative was his government's insistence upon mentioning in the resolution the 'cause' of Israeli retaliation. But the very cause of the Munich tragedy would be ignored. As Rabbi Elmer Berger pointed out, the US government could reach back into memory no farther than Munich and did not recall Deir Yassin, Qibya, Es-Samu', or Israel's continuing defiance of UN resolutions.[5] Rabbi Berger, founder of an American organization advocating alternatives to Zionism, quotes a pathetic will left by one of the Munich Palestinian 'terrorists' which was published by *The Times* on 8 September and which stated:

We are neither killers nor bandits. We are persecuted people who have no land and no homeland.

Rabbi Berger claimed that the veto amounted to a 'blank check' for the Israelis to pursue with impunity their war against the Palestinians. In fact, Israel lost no time in using this 'blank check' for on 16 and 17 September 1972 Israeli forces, killed and injured some 200 persons and destroyed a large number of houses in air and land attacks on south Lebanon, in retaliation for the shooting of two Israeli soldiers. The 'blank check' has been in use ever since.

Another instance of hostage taking — Maalot — will be discussed here because, like Munich, the facts have been distorted by Israeli propaganda which exploits it as a horrible case of Palestinian 'terrorism'. The discussion is not intended to justify or excuse the guerrilla action but to illustrate the distortion of facts which is made by Israeli propaganda in this and other similar cases in order to lay the blame on the Palestinians.

The facts of the Maalot incident were as follows:

In the early morning of 15 May 1974 three Palestinian guerrillas seized a school at Maalot in northern Galilee in which there were 90 children. The guerrillas sent two children out with a list of 26 Palestinian prisoners held in Israeli jails whose release they demanded before 6.00 p.m. in exchange for freeing the hostages. As a result of negotiations between the guerrillas and the Israeli authorities it was agreed that the prisoners (23 Palestinians, 2 Israelis and 1 Japanese) would be flown to Damascus. In a radio and TV broadcast, Prime Minister Golda Meir claimed her government had accepted the guerrillas' terms although it had no intention of doing so. She said: 'Since we do not wage war on the backs of our children, we decided that we must accept the terrorists' demands and free the prisoners.' She added that General Dayan, Defence Minister, and General Gur, Chief of Staff, had conveyed this decision to the guerrillas. The Dayan-Gur statement to the Palestinian guerrillas (that they accepted their terms) was nothing but a tactical and delaying action while preparations were being made for the army to storm the school. This took place half an hour before the expiration of the ultimatum. According to eyewitnesses, Israeli forces blazed away with bazookas as they attacked the school: 16 school children and the 3 guerrillas were killed as a result. There is little doubt but that the school children were shot by the Israeli army. Irene Benson, the *Guardian* correspondent made the following comment:

> The sequence of events of that tragic day does not support the
> Israeli contention that the aim of the three guerrillas was to
> murder innocent victims and spread terror . . . The aims of the
> Palestinians in operations like the one at Maalot are to continue
> the protest begun with the Balfour Declaration of November 2,

123

1917 — which promised, without consulting the Palestinian people, to hand over their country to foreign immigrants; to reaffirm that places like Tarshiha (Maalot) are occupied territory recognized as such by the international organization; and finally to seek the release of some of the thousands of Palestinians held in Israeli jails.

By her statement that Tarshiha (Maalot) was 'occupied territory recognized as such by the international organization' Irene Benson meant that this village was located in Western Galilee which formed part of the Arab State as defined by the UN partition resolution of 1947.

As in the case of Munich, Israel wreaked vengeance on the innocent Palestinian refugees in their camps. From 16 to 21 May 1974, Israeli Phantoms bombed Palestinian refugee camps in various parts of Lebanon killing 48 people and wounding 208.

There is little doubt but that the seizure of hostages is an unlawful deed, but it should not be overlooked that in many cases its root cause is the unlawful detention by Israel of innocent civilians, which is equivalent to taking them as political hostages for an indefinite duration without trial or justification.

ISRAEL'S WAR ON PALESTINIAN NATIONALISM

While the Palestinians conduct a guerrilla campaign against Israel with limited means, Israel responds with a fully fledged war conducted with the state's resources. The reason is not difficult to perceive. Despite its tactical acceptance of the resolution for the partition of Palestine into Arab and Jewish States, and despite the Armistice Agreements, Israel wanted and wants the whole territory of Palestine. Palestinian nationalism, and in particular the existence of the PLO, stands in the way of the success of this plan. Hence, the Wars of 1956, 1967 and 1982.

In its war against Palestinian nationalism Israel has pursued three objectives:

(i) To seize and annex the territory of the whole of Palestine so as to deprive the Palestinians of any territorial base for the establishment of a state.

(ii) To stamp out guerrilla action and to annihilate the PLO which, since its creation, has become the embodiment of Palestinian nationalism.

124

(iii) To crush political opposition and to terrorize the Palestinians who are under its domination in order to force them into submission or cause their exodus from their homeland.

Israel's weapons

In execution of its objectives, Israel has recourse to the following weapons: war and massive bombings of Palestinian villages and refugee camps, massacres of civilians, political assassinations, oppression and repression in territories under its control and a smear campaign against the PLO. These actions will be briefly discussed hereinafter.

War and bombings of Palestinian villages and refugee camps

The Wars of 1948, 1956, 1967 and 1982 were carried out in execution of the Israeli objectives noted above. In addition to these wars, mention must be made of Israel's invasion of south Lebanon in March 1978 in retaliation for a Palestinian raid on the Haifa-Tel Aviv road which caused 35 deaths. Israel withdrew its forces three months later after the establishment by the Security Council of the UN Interim Force in Lebanon (UNIFIL).

In implementation of its objective to stamp out guerrilla action, Israel has launched hundreds of attacks on Arab villages and refugee camps. For some of them, such as Qibya (1953), Nahalin (1954), Samou' (1966) and Karameh (1968), Israel was condemned by the Security Council for its flagrant violations of the cease-fire and the UN Charter. In all cases, the Security Council rejected Israel's excuse that it acted in retaliation for guerrilla actions. The Council denied the existence of any right of reprisal or retaliation.[6]

After the PLO had been forced to move to Lebanon in 1970 following a conflict with Jordan (see Chapter 20), Israel conducted hundreds of air raids between 1970 and 1987 against Palestinian refugee camps in Lebanon during which it killed tens of thousands of refugees. Israel was condemned by the Security Council for several of these attacks, but was not deterred. In fact, the bombings of refugee camps, particularly in Lebanon, became a current and almost a daily operation. Mention will be made of only one of these murderous bombing raids because it represented a turning point in the US attitude regarding the condemnation of Israeli bombings of Palestinian refugee camps. On 2 December 1975 Palestinian refugee camps near Tripoli and Nabatieh in Lebanon were attacked by 30

125

Israeli jets. More than 100 men, women and children were killed and 140 wounded. Although the Israelis pleaded in justification their false excuse that the raids were directed against 'terrorist' bases, the Security Council adopted on 8 December 1975 a resolution that condemned this savage attack on innocent people. The US Government was alone to vote against the resolution; this veto together with that which defeated the condemnation of Israel for the attacks made on refugee camps after Munich, as mentioned above, discouraged the Lebanese Government from submitting complaints to the Security Council in respect of subsequent attacks. The bombing of refugee camps in Lebanon continued and continues to the present day. Its intensity may be judged by the fact that one of those camps, the Rashidieh refugee camp near Tyre, was shelled or bombed 500 times between 1977 and 1982. Finally, it was razed to the ground in 1982 during the Israeli invasion.

Massacres

In addition to the massive bombings of refugee camps, Israel's objective of terrorizing the Palestinians has been carried out by means of several massacres. Apart from the massacre of Deir Yassin (already discussed in Chapter 7), the most notorious of these massacres were perpetrated at Qibya (1953), Qufr Qassem (1956), Nahalin (1954), Samou' (1966), Salt (1968) and Karameh (1968). For these massacres, except that of Qufr Qassem which was concealed for several weeks, Israel was condemned by the Security Council. Two of those massacres, namely, those of Qibya and Qufr Qassem may be mentioned briefly here.

According to Major-General Vagn Bennike, Chief of the UN Truce Supervision Organization (UNTSO) the Qibya massacre was perpetrated on 14 October 1953 by 250 to 300 Israeli soldiers. Fifty-three Arab villagers, regardless of age and sex were killed and their homes destroyed. It was an indiscriminate killing of innocent civilians with the obvious purpose of spreading terror among the Palestinians. The Security Council condemned the attack on 24 November 1953.

The massacre of Qufr Qassem was committed on 29 October 1956. The victims were 47 civilians: men, women and children. Here is the account of what happened as given by Kennett Love:

At 4.30 p.m. the Israeli Border Police told the village *mukhtar* (headman) that a curfew had been imposed from 5 p.m. until 6 a.m. and that anyone found out of doors after five would be shot.

The *mukhtar* protested that it would be impossible to warn villagers in the fields or working in nearby towns. After a brief argument the police set up a roadblock on the only road to the village.

For an hour, between 5 and 6 o'clock, the police stopped men, women and children returning home, . . . and machine-gunned them in batches . . . By 6 o'clock, sixty bodies lay in the road, thirteen of whom survived by feigning death as the police moved about finishing off those who stirred . . . News of the massacre was suppressed by the Israeli censors for six weeks.[7]

General Burns, Chief of Staff of the UN Truce Supervision Organization, said the case was 'a very sad proof of the fact that the spirit that inspired the notorious Deir Yassin massacre in 1948 is not dead among some of the Israeli armed forces'.[8]

Israel's responsibility for the massacre of Sabra and Chatila in 1982 will be discussed in Chapter 24.

Political assassinations of Palestinian leaders

This new tactic began on 8 July 1972 with the assassination in Beirut of Ghassan Kanafani, spokesman of the Popular Front for the Liberation of Palestine, one of the Palestinian commando organizations, who was killed by a bomb which exploded as he switched on the ignition of his car. Then followed the assassination of representatives of the PLO in Paris, Rome, Nicosia and Sweden by Israeli murder squads. A murder squad 'belonging to the state of Israel' was found by an Italian court to have been responsible for the assassination of the PLO representative in Rome in 1972 (*Wall Street Journal*, 15 April 1982). Likewise, the existence of a Scandinavian murder squad at the service of Israel was also confirmed by a Swedish court. The Israelis were to crown their crimes in this field by the assassination of three Palestinian resistance leaders in the heart of Beirut on the night of 10 April 1973. Israeli commandos had entered Lebanon with forged passports as European 'tourists' a few days before, and assisted by others who came by sea and landed surreptitiously on the coast, they smashed their way in the middle of the night into the homes of three Palestinian leaders whom they coolly murdered under the eyes of their families. Unlike the assassination of representatives of the PLO by Israeli agents in Rome, Paris and Nicosia, this criminal deed was openly admitted by the Israeli Government and was even the subject of boasting by the Israeli leaders. At the Security Council, to which Lebanon submitted

127

a complaint, the condemnation of Israel's action as a violation of the sovereignty of Lebanon and an act of state gangsterism was almost unanimous.

In addition to the assassination of targeted individuals, Israel has undertaken mass bombings. On 17 July 1981 Israel undertook a massive operation to destroy by bombing the PLO's offices in Beirut; 300 persons were killed, 800 wounded, mostly civilians. On 1 October 1985 Israel carried out a bombing raid on the PLO headquarters at Tunis which killed over 70 persons. This bombing raid, which was purportedly undertaken by Israel in retaliation for the murder of three Israelis at Larnaca a week before (allegedly Mossad observers of Palestinian movements in Cyprus) was, in fact, an attempt to assassinate Yasser Arafat and the PLO personnel at its headquarters. The intention to kill the PLO leaders was not even denied. Israel's Defence Minister, Yitzhak Rabin, then stated: 'The time has arrived to hit those who make the decisions, who guide the PLO terror acts against us' (*International Herald Tribune*, 7 October 1985). And this massacre was perpetrated despite the fact that the PLO had denied any connection with or responsibility for the Larnaca murders.

Oppression and repression in territories under Israeli control

The repressive measures taken in territories under Israeli occupation which aim at crushing political opposition by the Palestinians will be discussed in Chapter 26.

Israel's smear campaign against the PLO

In addition to military action, bombings, repression, massacres and assassinations, Israel resorts to a formidable psychological weapon in its war upon Palestinian nationalism: the smear campaign. Essentially, this smear campaign aims at representing Palestinian nationalism as a form of international terrorism.

Infuriated by the awakening of Palestinian nationalism and by guerrilla action, in particular after the War of 1967 when it thought it had settled the Palestine Question by the conquest of the whole territory of Palestine, Israel has sought to vilify Palestinian nationalism by labelling it as 'terrorism' and the PLO as a 'band of assassins'. Possessing a great expertise in deception, distortion and propaganda as well as an immense influence on the media, Israel distorts the facts and imputes to the PLO acts, deeds and outrages which it did not commit. By the label of Palestinian terrorism, the Israelis hope to make the world forget their own terrorist outrages which have caused a much larger number of victims among the Palestinians as compared with Israeli victims of Palestinian guerrilla action.

A recent example of Israel attributing to the PLO automatically, without justification or a shred of evidence, any terrorist act is found in the attacks on 27 December 1985 on the check-in counters of El Al, the Israeli airline, at the Rome and Vienna airports, as a result of which 19 people were killed and over 100 injured. On the same day and the following days Israel's leaders held the PLO responsible and threatened reprisals. The press reported that: 'Although the PLO issued a denial that it was responsible for the attacks, Israeli leaders laid the blame squarely on the PLO and hinted broadly that armed retribution would soon follow.' It took several days before Israel had to abandon its false accusation against the PLO, but the smear remained.

However, despite Israel's influence over the media and its systematic brainwashing, it is remarkable to find an American newspaper, such as the *Washington Post* piercing the veil of Israel's deceptive misinformation and pointing out that:

The Israelis wish to label all elements and activities of the PLO as 'terrorist' not simply for the necessary purpose of combating terrorism but for the purpose of suppressing Palestinian national-ism . . . (cited by the *International Herald Tribune* of 3 January 1984).

A scathing criticism of Israel's expertise at distortion of facts was made by Swedish General Carl von Horn, Chief of Staff of the UN Truce Supervision Organization in Palestine. Referring to an incident in which a UN observer and some Israelis were killed, he states:

Feelings in Israel ran high. There was great bitterness about their dead and, as we might have anticipated, it was now the United Nations who were painted in the blackest colours . . . We were amazed at the ingenuity of the falsehoods which distorted the true picture. The highly skilled Israeli Information Office and the entire press combined to manufacture a warped, distorted version which was disseminated with professional expertise through every available channel to their own people and their sympathizers and supporters in America and the rest of the world. Never in all my life had I believed the truth could be so cynically, expertly bent.[9]

Objectives of the smear campaign

The primary purpose of the vilification of the PLO is obvious: it is to disguise the usurpation of Palestine and to give Israel the appearance of a lawfully established authority against which some disorderly elements, described as terrorists, are rebelling. Many people now understand the real nature and objectives of the Palestinian national movement which in no way differ from similar movements resisting foreign military occupation at other times and places. Unfortunately, however, the Israeli smear campaign has yielded political results: it has influenced US policy. Since the 1970s, it has become a principle of US policy to reject any contact with the PLO because, in its view, the latter is a terrorist organization. To a lesser degree, British Prime Minister Mrs. Thatcher also subscribed to the fabricated charge against the PLO for she was reported to have said that Britain did not have ministerial meetings with the PLO 'because of their association with terrorism' (*Middle East International*, 2 October 1981). Apart from its being unfounded, such aspersion is inadmissible coming from the Prime Minister of a state which issued the Balfour Declaration and thereby became largely responsible for the tragedy of Palestine.

It is necessary to emphasize that the objectives of the Israeli smear campaign against the Palestinians go much further than the intent to misrepresent or weaken Palestinian nationalism. One of the objectives that has not escaped the attention of political observers is the dehumanization of the Palestinians with a view to creating psychological conditions conducive to their destruction. Commenting upon the responsibility of certain Israeli leaders for the massacre of Palestinians in 1982 in the Sabra and Chatila refugee camps, Anthony Lewis wrote in the *New York Times*

> Mr Begin and Mr Sharon always spoke of Palestinians in Lebanon as 'terrorists'. It was a dehumanizing device, a deliberate one: as if there were no Palestinians except bomb-throwers. Of all human beings on earth, Mr Begin should have known that calling people brutal names makes it easier to hate and kill them. The women and children massacred in the refugee camps are one more testament in man's history to the dehumanizing power of hatred.

The same conclusion was reached by the International Commission which inquired into the massacre of Sabra and Chatila.[10]

NOTES

1. For a history of the Arab nationalist movement from the middle of the nineteenth century to the 1930s see George Antonius, *The Arab Awakening: The Story of the Arab National Movement* (Hamish Hamilton, London and Khayat's, Beirut, 1938).

2. The text of the Palestine National Charter is set forth in J.W. Moore (ed.), *The Arab-Israeli Conflict* (Princeton University Press, Princeton, 1974), vol. III, pp. 699–711.

3. *Middle East International*, p. 12, No. 253, 28 June 1985.

4. 'Black September' is a secret Palestinian organization which is not affiliated with the PLO. It had its origin in, and derived its name from, the events which took place in Amman in September 1970 when, as a result of a difference between the Palestinian resistance and the Jordanian Government, a bloody conflict broke out which caused thousands of casualties among the Palestinians (see Chapter 20).

5. Elmer Berger, *American Jewish Alternatives to Zionism Inc.*, Report 16, September 1972.

6. For those condemnations and denial by the Security Council of Israel's claim of a right of reprisal, see Henry Cattan, *Palestine and International Law*, 2nd edn. (Longman, London, 1976), p. 156.

7. Kennett Love, *Suez* (McGraw-Hill, New York, 1969), p. 47.

8. E.L.M. Burns, *Between Arab and Israeli* (Institute for Palestine Studies, Beirut, 1969), p. 306.

9. Carl von Horn, *Soldiering for Peace* (Cassell, London, 1966), p. 85.

10. *Israel in Lebanon, The Report of the International Commission* (Ithaca Press, London, 1983), p. 181.

20

Jordan and the Palestinians

We have seen in Chapter 4 how the state of Jordan came into existence after the end of the First World War, first as an Emirate under Emir Abdullah, son of the Sheriff of Mecca, and then in 1946 as the Hashemite Kingdom of Jordan. There followed in April 1950 the union between Jordan and Palestine by a vote of the National Assembly under the condition, amongst others, that such union should not prejudice the final settlement of the Palestine Question (Chapter 13). After the union, King Abdullah considered himself the representative and spokesman of the Palestinians, and he did not allow or encourage the manifestation of any Palestinian personality or identity.

King Hussein, who succeeded his grandfather King Abdullah, did not share his grandfather's aversion to a Palestinian entity and he did not, therefore, frown upon the Palestinian guerrilla movement. He was even present and delivered an encouraging address at the opening of the Palestinian National Congress which convened at Jerusalem on 28 May 1964 and proclaimed the formation of the Palestine Liberation Organization.

CONFLICT BETWEEN PLO AND JORDAN

The Bedouin elements in Transjordan, despite the union with the Palestinians, still controlled the army and the administration, and did not look favourably on the presence of the Palestinian guerrillas in the country. The tension developing between the army and the guerrillas increased when King Hussein showed readiness in 1970 to accept an American peace initiative which was incompatible with Palestinian national objectives and with the conditions of the union laid down in 1950. This peace initiative, which was taken by William P. Rogers, US Secretary of State, aimed at the implementation of Security Council resolution 242, which the Palestinians opposed because it treated the Palestinian Question as involving merely a refugee problem (Chapter 18).

The first few months of 1970 were fertile in incidents of violence between the Jordanian army and the Palestinian guerrillas. Then, on 17 September the army attacked and bombarded the Palestine refugee camps around Amman in which over 100,000 lived in tents, huts and shacks. Thousands of them were killed or injured. The fighting spread to other towns. Arab public opinion was alarmed at what was rumoured to be the existence of a plan to liquidate the Palestinian resistance. The Arab heads of state met at Cairo and called for a cease-fire in this fratricidal fighting. King Hussein then went to Cairo and an agreement was reached on 27 September which provided for an immediate cease-fire and for the appointment of an Arab ministerial commission to supervise it and to work out an arrangement that would guarantee the continuance of guerrilla action and at the same time ensure respect for Jordanian sovereignty.

This agreement, and others that followed it, did not, however, succeed in clearing the atmosphere. The Government of Jordan was apparently bent on putting an end to the presence of the Palestinian guerrillas in Jordan. On 13 July 1971 and during the following days the Jordanian army attacked Palestinian guerrilla bases in the north of the country, near Ajlun and Jarash, killing several hundred Palestinian fighters and taking two thousand prisoners. This represented the liquidation of Palestinian resistance in Jordan, a fact which caused great satisfaction in Israel.

THE PLO MOVES TO LEBANON

In consequence of the bloody conflict between the Palestinian guerrillas and Jordan in 1970–71, the PLO moved to Lebanon where it established its headquarters and infrastructure. The withdrawal of the PLO to Lebanon did not terminate or diminish King Hussein's interest in the Palestine Question since the majority of the inhabitants of Jordan are Palestinian refugees. Nor did such withdrawal sever the relationship between Jordan and the PLO. Two issues, however, arose between them. These were the question of the representation of the Palestinians and the future relationship between Jordan and the Palestinians.

133

ISSUES BETWEEN JORDAN AND THE PLO

The question of who was qualified to represent and speak on behalf of the Palestinians arose in connection with the Geneva Peace Conference which first convened in December 1973 in execution of Security Council resolutions 242 and 338. This question divided King Hussein of Jordan and the PLO. The latter took the position that it alone was competent to represent the Palestinians. King Hussein, on the other hand, claimed that his Government was the representative of the Palestinians since they formed two-thirds of the population of his kingdom, but conceded that the PLO could represent the Palestinian refugees who lived outside Jordan. Later, he qualified his position and declared that after the liberation of the territories occupied by Israel in 1967, a plebiscite would be held to decide whether the Palestinians wished to remain united with Jordan, or whether they preferred a federation or independence.

The difference between Jordan and the PLO was settled by the UN and by an Arab Summit Conference. On 14 October 1974 the General Assembly of the UN adopted a resolution which invited the PLO as *the* representative of the Palestinian people to take part in its debate on the Palestine Question. On the other hand, the Conference of Arab Heads of States which met at Rabat on 28 October 1974 recognized the PLO as 'the sole legitimate representative of the Palestinian people'. King Hussein bowed to this unanimous decision of the Arab states and declared that he would respect it.

The second question as to the future relationship between Jordan and the Palestinians has been the subject of discussions between King Hussein and the PLO since 1972. The King's proposals in this regard evolved from a unified Kingdom between Jordan and the West Bank to a federation and finally to a confederation. Since these proposals form part of the 'Jordanian option', one of the peace initiatives for the settlement of the Palestinian Question, they will be discussed in Chapter 32 in Part IV.

21

The War of 1973

CAUSE OF THE WAR

The War of 1973 stands apart from the other wars fought in the Middle East. In the War of 1948 Jewish forces had commenced hostilities in Palestine, seized several towns including Modern Jerusalem, before the end of the mandate and before the Arab States intervened. In 1956, 1967 and 1982 Israel was plainly an aggressor. But the War of 1973 was commenced by Egypt and Syria for a legitimate reason, namely, the recovery of their territories (the Sinai Peninsula and the Golan) which Israel had seized in 1967.

We have seen in Chapter 18 that, despite Egypt's acceptance of Security Council resolution 242, Ambassador Jarring's mission foundered over Israel's refusal to withdraw to the pre-5 June 1967 lines and that in consequence he abandoned his mediation. The resulting immobility of the situation which came to be described as being one of 'no war, no peace' suited Israel perfectly, both politically and economically. Israel's creeping annexation of the occupied territories was proceeding quietly with the creation of new facts and new settlements. The occupation was even financially profitable to Israel, which, as a result, was provided with cheap Arab labour, a profitable trade with Jordan, and with substantial quantities of crude oil from the Egyptian oil-fields of Abu Rodeis in Sinai, which covered 55 per cent of its consumption needs.

Such a situation could not continue indefinitely. Accordingly, in the summer of 1973, Egypt made another effort to secure Israel's withdrawal by pacific means. To this end, it requested a meeting of the Security Council to consider the situation. During the debate eight members of the Council submitted a draft resolution which reaffirmed resolution 242, endorsed Ambassador Jarring's proposal for an Israeli withdrawal linked to an Egyptian peace pledge, and stressed respect for the rights of the Palestinians. This draft resolution was opposed by Israel, which insisted that it would not withdraw until new boundaries were fixed by negotiations between the parties. Israel further opposed any reference in the draft resolution to 'the rights and legitimate aspirations of the Palestinians'. The draft resolution was put to the vote on 26 July 1973 and received thirteen affirmative votes, but was vetoed by the US Government. China abstained.

The US veto which defeated the draft resolution was criticized by President Sadat of Egypt as indicative of partisanship on the part of the US Government. World opinion, including that of sectors of the public in America, was also critical of the US Government's attitude and of its endorsement of Israel's intransigent and unreasonable position. The *New York Times* pointed out that the US and Israel could not afford to ignore the widespread unease over Israeli policies that was reflected in the thirteen-to-nil vote for the resolution. It was evident, observed the paper, that

an overwhelming majority of nations — not just the Arabs — believe that Israel's 'creation of facts' in the occupied lands and demands for substantial border changes are also incompatible with resolution 242 and represent a serious obstacle to peace.

All the diplomatic efforts that Egypt exerted to secure Israel's withdrawal from the occupied territories thus failed. Similarly, President Sadat's threats of resuming hostilities were not taken seriously. Even the talk about a possible oil embargo by the Arab oil-producing countries against states that supported Israel were discounted as groundless by Zionist propaganda and by so-called 'experts' on the Middle East. In such circumstances, Egypt and Syria had no alternative but to wage war on Israel to recover their territories.

THE WAR AND ITS INTERNATIONAL REPERCUSSIONS

On 6 October 1973, Egyptian forces suddenly crossed the Suez Canal to the east bank, washed away with water-cannons the sand walls erected by the Israelis along the waterway, captured and destroyed the fortifications of the Bar-Lev line, and occupied the east bank to a depth of several miles. At the same time Syrian forces smashed their way into Syrian territory occupied by Israel in 1967. Jordan did not open hostilities. The Israeli air force, which Israel had repeatedly boasted would devastate Egypt in case of an attack on Israel, was itself devastated by Egyptian ground-to-air missiles. Israel suffered the same humiliating experience on the Syrian front. The fourth Arab-Israeli War, called by Israel the War of Yom Kippur, and by the Arabs the War of Ramadan, had started.

Israel's substantial losses of aircraft and armour in the first few days of the war were a matter of great concern both to the Israelis and to the US government. The latter, under the influence of the powerful Israeli lobby, undertook, on or about 10 October, a massive airlift to Israel and delivered by means of some 500 flights over 22,000 tons of tanks, guns, missiles and aircraft. Unlike the covert American participation in the War of 1967, this time the US military assistance was furnished quite overtly and was even formally announced by the State Department on 15 October.

The Arabs reacted to this American intervention by taking two measures affecting the production and supply of crude oil. The first measure was adopted on 17 October by the eleven members of the Organization of Arab Oil Producing Countries (OAPEC) and consisted of a cutback in oil production at the rate of five per cent every month until Israel should withdraw from the occupied Arab territories and the rights of the Palestinians should be restored. The cutback was aimed at countries the Arabs regarded as supporters of Israel. In fact, the cutback was implemented at the outset at the rate of ten per cent. Iraq, however, did not join in the cutback, preferring instead to nationalize US and Dutch oil interests. The second measure was taken on the following day and consisted of the imposition of a ban on oil exports by the Arab producing countries to the USA and the Netherlands because of their aid and support to Israel. (The embargo against the USA was lifted on 18 March 1974 and that against Holland was lifted on 10 July 1974.)

Having made up their losses with the American arms airlift, the Israelis mounted a counter-offensive against Egypt and Syria. They forced their way through Sinai between the Second and Third Egyptian Armies, and crossed to the west bank of the Suez Canal south of Ismailia. On the Syrian front, they recovered the terrain they had lost at the beginning of the war, and attempted to advance on Damascus.

Meanwhile the Security Council had been considering how it could bring the hostilities to an end. It finally adopted, on 22 October 1973, resolution 338, which ordered a cease-fire effective on that day, and called upon the parties to implement Security Council resolution 242 of 1967 and, under appropriate auspices, to start negotiations aimed at establishing a just and durable peace in the Middle East.

Although the cease-fire was accepted by all parties, it was not honoured by Israel, whose forces on the west bank of the Canal moved south towards Suez. As a result, a highly dangerous situation developed between 22 and 24 October, not only on the terrain but also between the USA and the Soviet Union. On 23 October, Egypt asked for a meeting of the Security Council to consider the non-implementation by Israel of the cease-fire. The Council met and adopted its resolution 339, which confirmed its decision of the day before calling for an immediate cessation of all military action, and urged the return of the two sides to the positions they had occupied on 22 October.

Instead of returning to the positions which they occupied on the preceding day, Israeli forces improved their position on the ground and moved further south. They cut the Cairo–Suez road, encircled the town of Suez, which they began to bombard, and also cut the vital supply line across the Canal to the Third Egyptian Army, which was thus isolated, if not trapped, in Sinai, without water and provisions. This behaviour was similar to Israel's action during its aggression of June 1967. At that time, four cease-fire orders were issued by the Security Council, but Israel ignored them, attacked Syria, and did not stop fighting until it had seized the Golan Heights and thus achieved its territorial objectives.

In this case, however, Israel's adventurous action almost led to a confrontation between the two superpowers. Following Israel's grave violation of the cease-fire, President Sadat requested Soviet and US military intervention to enforce the cease-fire, and to ensure a return to positions held at the time of the original truce deadline as it existed on 22 October. On the night of 24 October the Soviet Union urged the US government that they both send military forces to enforce the cease-fire, implying in its message that, in default, the Soviets might be obliged to act alone. Thereupon, fearing unilateral action by the Soviets, or maybe to discourage such a move, President Nixon called a military alert of US forces around the world.

The crisis was resolved by the Security Council's adoption on the following day, 25 October, of resolution 340, which demanded that an immediate and complete cease-fire be observed and that the parties return to the positions occupied by them at 1650 hours GMT on 22 October 1973. The resolution further decided that a UN

Emergency Force be immediately set up to supervise the cease-fire, such Emergency Force to be composed of personnel drawn from member states of the UN other than the permanent members of the Security Council.

Hostilities ended in October 1973 but the Arab oil boycott continued. Secretary of State Kissinger threatened retaliatory action if the Arab oil embargo continued. Saudi Arabia responded by declaring that if the US attempted to use military force it would blow up the oil fields. Although the oil embargo which caused a worldwide economic disruption was lifted, as we have noted, it led nonetheless to a continuous escalation of the price of crude.

Both sides have claimed to have won the war, but whatever the military evaluation of the conflict by strategic technicians might be, it is certain that the Arabs won an important psychological victory by destroying the myths of Israeli invincibility and of Arab military incompetence. They have also shown, contrary to the view of so-called 'experts' on the Middle East, that they can and would wield the oil weapon against those who endanger their vital interests by their support of Israel.

THE GENEVA PEACE CONFERENCE

Pursuant to Security Council resolution 338, which envisaged that peace talks be initiated under appropriate auspices, a Conference was convened by the Secretary-General of the UN at Geneva on 21 December 1973. The Conference was sponsored by the Soviet Union and the USA. The parties invited to attend, in addition to the sponsors, were: Egypt, Israel, Syria and Jordan. The Palestinians, who are at the root of the conflict, were ignored.

At the Conference, which lasted two days, the parties restated their well-known positions, both with respect to Israel's withdrawal and to the rights of the Palestinians. On the latter issue, while the Arab states maintained that Israel must respect the national rights of the Palestinians, Israel, in fact, denied that the Palestinians possessed any rights, and argued that the Palestinian Question merely involved a refugee problem which must be solved by the resettlement of the Palestinians outside Israel. The Soviet Union and the US both emphasized that a peace settlement should protect the 'legitimate rights' of the Palestinians, without defining what they meant by this expression.

After the exposition of the parties of their viewpoints, the

139

Conference adjourned and a military working group was formed to discuss the disengagement of military forces. On 18 January 1974 an agreement was reached between Egypt and Israel on the disengagement of their forces along the Suez Canal front, and on 31 May 1974 a similar agreement was reached between Syria and Israel on the disengagement of their forces on the Golan front. In both cases provision was made for the limitation of forces and arms on the lines of confrontation, and for the establishment of buffer zones between opposing forces, such zones to be manned by men of the UN Emergency Force (UNEF). These two agreements were signed at Geneva.

Apart from its formal opening, the Geneva Peace Conference made no progress towards its goal. It broke down over the issue of the representation of the Palestinians. Israel and the US took the position that the Palestinians could not be represented at the Conference by the PLO. Israel mentioned it would not in any event negotiate with the PLO but the US declared that the Palestinians must be involved in the peacemaking process on condition that they adhere to Security Council resolution 242. This meant that the Palestine Question would be treated not as one involving national rights, but as a question of refugees.

The Egyptian-Israeli Sinai Disengagement Agreement, 1975

The Agreements for disengagement of forces signed by Israel and Egypt on 18 January 1974 and with Syria on 31 May 1974 did not provide for withdrawal, but only for limitation of forces and the establishment of buffer zones between opposing forces, such zones to be manned by men of the UN Emergency Force (UNEF). Then following Secretary of State Kissinger's efforts as intermediary, Egypt and Israel initialled on 1 September and signed on 4 September 1975 an agreement providing for a limited Israeli withdrawal from Sinai. The Agreement further proclaimed the determination of the two parties to reach a final and just peace by means of negotiations within the framework of the Geneva Peace Conference in accordance with Security Council resolution 338.

US COMMITMENTS TO ISRAEL

The Sinai Disengagement Agreement of 1975 between Egypt and

Israel also contained secret provisions which have since been published and which concern:

(i) US commitments of economic and military aid to Israel;
(ii) a modest financial contribution to Egypt; and
(iii) an exchange of political assurances between the USA, Egypt and Israel.

These secret provisions are alarming for peace in the Middle East. The financial inducements offered by the US to 'persuade' Israel to sign the Disengagement Agreement are disturbing. More disturbing is the US commitment to supply Israel with aircraft, advanced weapons and missiles, including specifically Pershing missiles which can be fitted with nuclear warheads, enabling it to hit all the Arab countries including Saudi Arabia and Iraq. Still more disturbing are the political commitments because they have blocked the path to any settlement of the Question of Palestine and to the establishment of peace in the Middle East.

These commitments were set forth in Paragraphs 2 and 4 of a Memorandum of Agreement between the Governments of Israel and the US which states as follows:

2. The United States will continue to adhere to its present policy with respect to the Palestine Liberation Organization, whereby it will not recognize or negotiate with the Palestine Liberation Organization so long as the Palestine Liberation Organization does not recognize Israel's right to exist and does not accept Security Council resolutions 242 and 338. The United States Government will consult fully and seek to concert its position and strategy at the Geneva Peace Conference on this issue with the Government of Israel.

Similarly the United States will consult fully and seek to concert its position and strategy with Israel with regard to the participation of any other additional states. It is understood that the participation at a subsequent phase of the conference of any possible additional state, group or organization will require agreement of all the initial participants.

4. The United States will oppose and, if necessary, vote against any initiative in the Security Council to alter adversely the terms of reference of the Geneva Peace Conference or to change resolutions 242 and 338 in ways which are incompatible with their original purpose.

FORMAL END OF THE WAR OF 1973

The Sinai Disengagement Agreement of 1975 did not provide for complete Israeli withdrawal nor formally end the War of 1973. This was done in the case of Egypt in further negotiations that led to the Camp David Accords (1978) and the Egyptian-Israeli Peace Treaty (1979) which are the subject of the next chapter. As for Syria, the position is still governed by the Syrian-Israeli Disengagement Agreement signed on 31 May 1974.

142

22

The Camp David Accords (1978) and the Egyptian-Israeli Peace Treaty (1979)

The Camp David Accords and the Egyptian-Israeli Peace Treaty have achieved a peace of sorts between Egypt and Israel; their effect on the Palestine Question was negative, even prejudicial.

ANWAR SADAT'S PROPOSAL

The origin of the Egyptian-Israeli agreements can be traced to the unusual and controversial visit which Egyptian President Anwar Sadat made to Jerusalem on 19 November 1977. This visit by the head of state of the largest Arab country to Israel with which it had been at war for 30 years had the effect of a bombshell in the Middle East. The purpose of Anwar Sadat was to offer peace to Israel and in his address to the Israeli Knesset on 20 November he outlined the two basic points of his peace proposal:

(i) Total Israeli withdrawal from Arab lands occupied in 1967, such withdrawal, he said, being 'elementary, not negotiable and not subject to argument'.
(ii) Realization of the fundamental rights of the Palestinian people and of their right of self-determination, including the establishment of their own state.

ISRAEL'S REACTION

Sadat's proposal received a cool reception in Israel. The latter indicated a willingness to effect a partial withdrawal from Egyptian territory (Sinai) but would retain the settlements which it had established there since 1967. On the Palestine Question, Israel did not envisage any withdrawal from the West Bank and Gaza and suggested that the Palestinians in those territories be granted an obscure kind of 'autonomy' under Israeli rule. On 28 December 1977 Menachem Begin, the Israeli Prime Minister, submitted to the Knesset a plan for the West Bank and Gaza which he described in biblical language as Judea and Samaria. The plan envisaged autonomy for Arab residents without statehood. The Arab residents would elect an administrative council which would be charged with education, finance, commerce, agriculture, justice and control of a police force. A commission composed of representatives of Israel, Jordan and the administrative council would lay down rules for the return of Arab refugees in reasonable numbers, provided that its decisions were adopted unanimously. Security and maintenance of public order would remain in Israel's hands. The Israelis would have power to buy land and to settle in the occupied territories. As to the future, the plan stated that Israel maintained its right and its claims of sovereignty over Judea, Samaria and the Gaza Strip, but in view of the existence of other claims, it proposed that the question of sovereignty remain open.

DEADLOCK OF NEGOTIATIONS

In the negotiations that followed between Begin and Sadat, the latter showed infinitely more concern for the restitution of the Sinai than for the restitution of the West Bank and Gaza. A complete deadlock occurred between them regarding the question of Israeli withdrawal from Egyptian territory. Sadat declared: Egypt will insist on Israel's withdrawal from 'every inch of Sinai', on the dismantling of 'every Jewish settlement' established there and on the departure of 'every Israeli settler' from Egyptian territory. To which Begin retorted in Shylock fashion that Israel would not return 'one grain of sand' of Sinai without receiving value in return and would maintain its settlements and settlers.

President Carter's intervention

In the face of this impasse, US President Jimmy Carter offered his services as a mediator and invited the two men to come to Camp David to negotiate under his patronage. During two weeks of seclusion and intense negotiation, the three protagonists developed what they thought to be a suitable terrain for compromise: Palestinian rights and territory in consideration for withdrawal from Sinai.

Camp David formula

This formula inspired the Camp David Accords which were signed on 17 September 1978 and embodied a framework for peace in the West Bank and Gaza as well as provision for the Egyptian-Israeli Peace Treaty that followed and was signed on 26 March 1979.

In accordance with the Peace Treaty, Israel agreed to return the whole of Sinai to Egypt and to withdraw within three years behind the international boundary between Egypt and mandated Palestine. It also agreed to dismantle all 17 settlements it had established and to withdraw all its armed forces and 'civilians' from Sinai (Article I (2) of the Treaty). The price paid in return was Egypt's recognition of Israel, its abandonment of its original position on Palestinian rights (self-determination and a Palestinian state) and its acceptance of Begin's 'autonomy' plan for the West Bank and Gaza.

Amnon Kapeliouk, an Israeli writer and journalist, put it concisely when he said that 'the restitution of Sinai to Egypt serves as consideration (*monnaie d'échange*) for preserving what is essential: the West Bank and Gaza'.[1] Explaining Begin's plan Kapeliouk stated:

> To restore Sinai to Egypt in order to have a free hand in the West Bank and Gaza: such was the precise objective of the Israeli Prime Minister, Mr. Menachem Begin, when he signed the Camp David Accords. But in order that such an operation should become acceptable, it was necessary to create the impression that the Palestinian problem would also find its solution. Whence the plan for administrative autonomy which he proposed for the Arab territories occupied in 1967, not without declaring with insistence that a Palestinian state will never see the light of day in 'Judea and Samaria' [West Bank and Gaza].[2]

Let us now examine this autonomy more closely. The Camp David Accords provided that Egypt, Israel, Jordan and representatives of the Palestinian people should participate in negotiations on the resolution of the Palestinian problem in all its aspects. (It may be observed that neither Jordan, nor the Palestinians were consulted

145

concerning their willingness to participate in such negotiations. In fact, they condemned the Camp David Accords and never participated in such negotiations). The Accords stated that to achieve such an objective, namely to resolve the Palestine problem, negotiations relating to the West Bank and Gaza should proceed in three stages.

In a first stage transitional arrangements would be set up for a period not exceeding five years. Under these arrangements, the inhabitants would enjoy 'full autonomy' and elect a 'self-governing authority' (which was described as an administrative council). Upon such election, the Israeli military government and its civilian administration would be withdrawn but Israeli forces would be redeployed into specified security locations. In a second stage, Egypt, Israel and Jordan would agree on the modalities for establishing the self-governing authority and would define its powers and responsibilities. Finally, when the self-governing authority was established, the transitional period of five years would begin to run. As soon as possible, but not later than the third year after the beginning of the transitional period, negotiations would take place to determine the final status of the West Bank and Gaza and its relationship with its neighbours.

There followed provisions relating to the refugee problem. A special committee constituted of Egypt, Israel, Jordan and the self-governing authority would decide 'by agreement' on the modalities of admissions of persons displaced from the West Bank and Gaza in 1967. As for other refugees, Egypt and Israel would establish 'agreed procedures' for the resolution of their problem. The requirement that decisions on repatriation of the refugees should be subject to agreement meant that Israel reserved the right of veto over the matter.

It will have been noticed that the Camp David Accords substantially reproduced the main provisions of Begin's plan of 28 December 1977 for the West Bank and Gaza.

In a letter contemporaneous with the Egyptian-Israeli Peace Treaty Egypt and Israel agreed to negotiation at the earliest possible date for the establishment of the self-governing authority in the West Bank and Gaza in order to provide full autonomy to the inhabitants. These negotiations, in which the US government participated, commenced after ratification of the Peace Treaty and lasted three years.

From the outset Israel adamantly maintained that autonomy and the powers of the proposed self-governing authority should not go beyond the limited powers mentioned in the Begin plan of December

1977, i.e. regarding certain administrative or municipal matters, but excluding the exercise of national rights or legislative powers or any evolution into a sovereign state. Begin stated unambiguously that 'autonomy' does not mean sovereignty and that the 'full autonomy' offered to the Palestinians meant an autonomy for persons, not for territory. Israel, in his view, would retain sovereignty, including control over public land and water resources as well as the right of settling Jews in the area, and would never permit any 'foreign' sovereignty over Judea, Samaria and Gaza.

Collapse of autonomy negotiations

Both Egypt and the US did not subscribe to Israel's conception of autonomy for the Palestinians. Egypt maintained that autonomy should lead eventually to the establishment of a Palestinian state. Apart from the conflict on the meaning and scope of autonomy, there were other points of difference: Israel's demand to retain military control over the occupied territories, its insistence upon the creation of new settlements, its claim to control water resources and the status of the Old City of Jerusalem. The autonomy negotiations foundered over these differences and were suspended by Egypt as a result of Israel's invasion of Lebanon in 1982. In fact, they have died a natural death.

Israeli withdrawal from Sinai

Israel's withdrawal from Sinai in accordance with the Peace Treaty was completed on 25 April 1982. Israel took care before evacuation to bulldoze all Israeli settlements, including the town of Yamit, which it had established in Sinai.

The Peace Treaty had provided for the limitation of forces at the boundary between the two parties and for the permanent stationing of UN forces and observers as a security measure. The Security Council, because of the disagreement of most of its members with the provisions of the Peace Treaty, was unwilling to agree to the stationing of UN forces and observers as planned by the Treaty. As a result, the US government established in lieu thereof a multi-national force in which it largely participates.

Despite the collapse of the autonomy negotiations, the three protagonists of the Camp David Accords have continued to cling to

147

them: Israel clings to them because they pave the way for its usurpation of the whole of Palestine and the liquidation of the Palestine Question. The US government clings to them to satisfy Israel and the Jewish lobby. Egypt clings to what it describes as 'the Camp David peace process' because it does not wish to jeopardize the evacuation of Sinai, even though it does not subscribe to Israel's definition of autonomy and its denial of Palestinian national rights.

Condemnation of the Camp David Accords

The Camp David Accords and the Egyptian-Israeli Peace Treaty were denounced and condemned by the Palestinians and by all Arab States with the exception of Somalia, Sudan and Oman. They were also condemned by 95 states at the Conference of Non-Aligned Nations at Havana in September 1979 as being a sell-out by Egypt of Palestinian rights. All the Arab States — except Somalia, Sudan and Oman — severed diplomatic relations with Egypt and excluded it from the League of Arab States whose offices were moved from Cairo to Tunis. The Camp David Accords were also denounced and declared invalid in several resolutions of the General Assembly of the UN as being inconsistent with the inalienable rights of the Palestinian people.[3]

It is noteworthy that two of Sadat's Foreign Minsters resigned in protest against his dealings with Israel: Ismail Fahmy resigned in November 1977 in protest against Sadat's proposed visit to Israel and his successor, Muhammad Ibrahim Kamel resigned on the eve of the signing of the Camp David Accords of 17 September 1978. Both criticized Sadat for the conclusion of those agreements. Ismail Fahmy pointed out that Egypt's peace with Israel has encouraged the latter to undertake further aggressions against the Arabs. He said:

Israel's policies and practices after the peace agreement with Egypt lead one to believe that it perceives the Egyptian-Israeli peace as creating the proper circumstances for it to continue acquiring more land at the expense of the Arab side. It was after the peace that Israel annexed the Golan Heights and the Knesset voted to support Begin's statement that the Jewish settlements on the West Bank and Gaza would never be dismantled . . . All this happened after Sadat made peace with Israel.[4]

Israel's invasion of Lebanon in 1982 and its war against the PLO also took place after the Egyptian peace with Israel. Israeli General Shlomo Gazith, formerly chief of military intelligence, underscored the importance of Israel having a peace treaty with Egypt during the War of 1982, saying:

> Behind the victory of Lebanon, there is the peace treaty with Egypt. If we could not count on this treaty, the Israeli army would not have been able to send to the north such powerful troop concentrations as it did, nor exercise such menace on the Lebanese-Syrian front.[5]

The inappropriateness of the Camp David formula as a peace initiative for the solution of the Palestine Question will be discussed in Chapter 32.

NOTES

1. Translation from *Monde Diplomatique*, October 1978.
2. Translation from *Monde Diplomatique*, January 1979.
3. See Chapter 32.
4. Ismail Fahmy, *Negotiating for Peace in the Middle East* (Croom Helm, London, 1983), pp. 310–11.
5. *Yediot Aharonot*, 18 June 1982.

23

The War of 1982

Israel's War of 1982 was a flagrant and barbaric aggression against the PLO which Israel attempted to disguise under the spurious label of a 'Peace for Galilee' operation. In fact, the War of 1982 was the next stage of Israel's continuous war against Palestinian nationalism.[1]

PRETEXTS FOR THE WAR

The first pretext which Israel invoked for launching the war was that its invasion of Lebanon was for the purpose of establishing a *cordon sanitaire* extending 25 miles northwards from the Lebanese-Israeli border. From this area Palestinian 'terrorists' would be driven out in order to eliminate the danger of attacks across the border on Israeli settlements in Galilee.

Israel's allegation that its invasion of Lebanon aimed at stopping Palestinian guerrilla attacks on Israeli settlements in Galilee is utterly without foundation because there were then no guerrilla attacks to be stopped. All guerrilla attacks completely ceased after the cease-fire which was arranged by Ambassador Philip Habib, the US special envoy, between Israel and the PLO on 24 July 1981. The cease-fire put an end to the massive Israeli military operations against the Palestinians in Beirut and south Lebanon which had lasted two weeks in July 1981 and had caused the death of 500 and the wounding of 1,200 civilians as compared with 5 killed and 40 wounded in Israel. The PLO scrupulously respected the cease-fire despite a provocative Israeli bombing of Palestinian positions on 21 April 1982. The PLO did not respond to this provocation. Only after Israeli aircraft again bombed the Palestinians on 9 May 1982 causing

71 casualties did they retaliate by firing rockets into Galilee. This was the only action taken by the Palestinians subsequent to the cease-fire agreed in 1981 before Israel launched the War of June 1982. It follows, therefore, that Israel's allegation that by its War of June 1982 it aimed at stopping Palestinian guerrilla attacks was devoid of any truth whatsoever.

The pretext of security for Galilee was, therefore, a fake. At no time did Israel intend to establish, as it claimed, a *cordon sanitaire* 25 miles from the Lebanese border because the advance of its army which started on 6 June 1982 did not stop at this line but continued at full speed towards Beirut, bypassing Tyre and Sidon where it encountered fierce Palestinian resistance, and reaching the outskirts of Beirut three days later.

The second pretext which Israel invoked was that by waging the war it was acting in self-defence against attacks made on Jews in Europe. Israel referred to a number of incidents in which Jews had been attacked or killed in Europe and, without any proof, imputed them to the PLO. Even the attempted assassination of Israel's Ambassador in London on 3 June 1982 was attributed by Israel to the PLO when in fact, as officially established by the UK Government, it was committed by Palestinians opposed to the PLO (see Chapter 19). It is fitting to cite here John Reddaway's comment upon this flimsy argument:

> To try to make out that a number of isolated attacks on Jews, by unidentified assailants in Europe, presented such a danger to the state of Israel as to justify its invasion of a neighbouring state in the Middle East is making a mockery of the concept of self-defence.[2]

It is also relevant to refer in this context to the testimony of George W. Ball, former US Under-Secretary of State, given in July 1982 to the Senate Foreign Relations Committee:

> The invasion of Lebanon was not a defensive action; it was an attempt to crush the only legitimate and recognized Palestinian opposition so that Israel could proceed unchallenged to absorb the occupied areas.[3]

AIMS OF THE WAR

Israel's War of 1982 was not undertaken for security, nor in self-

151

defence, nor in retaliation: it was waged in execution of Israel's policy to destroy the PLO and to annihilate the Palestinian national movement. Michael Jansen pointed out that Israel's aggression in 1982 differed only in degree, not in kind, from earlier Israeli operations against the PLO.[4] In fact, the war was planned several months before it was launched. According to the *New York Times* of 26 February 1982 Moshe Arens, Israel's ambassador in Washington, predicted that Israel would have to take military action in southern Lebanon and that this would be a matter of time. On 14 August 1982 Ariel Sharon, Israel's Defence Minister and architect of the war, told the *Jerusalem Post* that he had been planning the operation in Lebanon since he took office in July 1981. General Rafael Eitan, the Israeli Chief of Staff, disclosed that 'the Israeli invasion of Lebanon had been planned to take place in July 1981 and had been postponed after the cease-fire arranged by Philip Habib, the US envoy'.[5] Jacobo Timerman, a Jewish writer, summarized the position by describing the War of 1982 as one whose preparation was known to everybody, whose necessity was never demonstrated and whose reasons were fabricated.[6] Again Ze'ev Schiff and Ehud Ya'ari, two leading Israeli journalists, have described Israel's war in Lebanon in the following critical terms:

Born of the ambition of one wilful, reckless man, Israel's 1982 invasion of Lebanon was anchored in delusion, propelled by deceit, and bound to end in calamity.[7]

In addition to the destruction of the PLO as a military and political force, and the crushing of Palestinian nationalism, Israel sought also to achieve the following objectives:

(1) To eliminate PLO influence in the West Bank and Gaza in the expectation that, being deprived of PLO support, the Palestinians in the occupied territories would drop their opposition to Israeli rule, submit to the Camp David formula of autonomy and facilitate Israel's annexation of the West Bank and Gaza.

(2) To expel the PLO, its armed forces and the Palestine refugees from Lebanon. This objective was shared by Israel's Phalangist allies.[8]

(3) To establish in Lebanon a friendly Lebanese Government with which Israel could conclude a peace treaty similar to that which was made with Egypt.

The invasion

The war began by massive aerial bombardments of Beirut and south Lebanon on 4 and 5 June 1982. These bombardments were followed by a land invasion on 6 June. On the same day the Security Council issued resolution 509 which demanded that Israel withdraw its military forces 'forthwith and unconditionally' to the internationally recognized boundaries of Lebanon. Israel stated it would not comply and the IDF (Israeli Defence Forces) continued to blast its way towards Beirut destroying towns, villages and Palestinian refugee camps. The invasion took the form of a four-pronged attack that aimed at Beirut, the Beirut–Damascus road and Syrian positions in the Bekaa valley and alongside Mount Hermon. It is estimated that Israel fielded a force of 120,000 men, 1,600 tanks, 1,600 armoured personnel carriers, 600 guns and 670 modern combat aircraft against the PLO fighters who were outnumbered in the ratio of 6 or 7 to 1 and who did not possess one single aircraft, no modern tanks and no heavy guns. Syrian forces numbered approximately 30,000.

DESTRUCTION OF REFUGEE CAMPS

On their way to Beirut, Israeli forces destroyed Palestinian refugee camps almost systematically. According to UNRWA's reports, the Ein Hilweh refugee camp, near Sidon, one of the largest refugee camps in the area, which housed 24,000 refugees was 'reduced to rubble'. Other refugee camps were partly destroyed. The intention to destroy Palestinian refugee camps is established by the fact that houses and shacks that survived the bombardment at Ein Hilweh and other camps were later bulldozed and razed to the ground after the invasion. Such systematic destruction of Palestinian refugee camps evidencing an intention to remove the refugees from Lebanon is confirmed by the issue of a directive by the Israeli Prime Minister to prevent the reconstruction of the ruined refugee camps in south Lebanon. The International Commission set up under the chairmanship of Seán MacBride in 1982 to inquire into violations of international law during Israel's invasion of Lebanon confirmed that the destruction of the refugee camps reveals that the main objective of the Israeli occupation policy 'was to push the Palestinian people out of the occupied zones and even out of Lebanon'.[9] Pierre Gemayel, the founder of the Phalangist party and Bashir Gemayel, its military leader, advocated the complete expulsion of all Palestinians from Lebanon, civilian and PLO alike.[10]

Vengeful bombing of Ein Hilweh camp

The savage destruction of Ein Hilweh refugee camp foreshadowed the terror bombing of Beirut. An Israeli war correspondent who witnessed the bombing of the camp wondered at the motivation for its ferocity. He said:

> For days a thick, black cloud of dust and smoke hung over Ein Hilweh as the artillery and planes pounded away . . . The air was suffused with a sickening stench of gunpowder, sewage and rotting corpses . . . The Israeli soldiers watching the devastation seem to become inured to the din and the smoke and the smell of death . . .
>
> Did they regard the pulverization of Ein Hilweh as just a grim necessity to be carried out as best they could? Or was this relentless battering a dose of retribution for all the acts of terrorism perpetrated against innocent Israelis? And was it perhaps fueled by an even deeper sense of vengeance for all the harm and hatred that the Jews had suffered at the hands of others over the centuries?[11]

IDF MARCHES ON BEIRUT

On 10 June Israeli troops, which had moved along the coast road and bypassed Tyre and Sidon, penetrated one of Beirut's suburbs and linked with their allies the Phalangists who controlled East Beirut. PLO forces were thus completely surrounded in West Beirut and then commenced their siege which was to last two and a half months.

IDF ENGAGES THE SYRIANS

In its other thrusts towards the Bekaa valley and the Beirut–Damascus highway the IDF encountered stiff opposition from Syrian forces which had been in Lebanon since 1976 to assist the Phalangists during the Lebanese civil war. The Syrians were not anxious to fight Israel but the war was thrust upon them. They lost a large number of planes in combat and had their missile batteries in the Bekaa valley destroyed.

Hostilities between Israel and the Syrians ended temporarily with a cease-fire which came into effect on 11 June. The cease-fire did not apply to the PLO. The cease-fire, however, prevented the IDF from gaining control over the Beirut–Damascus highway and the hills overlooking Beirut which were in Syrian hands. To overcome such a drawback, Israel's Defence Minister Ariel Sharon instructed his officers in the field to 'creep' hill by hill in order to seize the Syrian positions at Aley and Bhamdoun. This was called the 'creeping cease-fire'. However, the 'creeping cease-fire' did not creep fast enough to satisfy the Defence Minister and Israeli forces were ordered to disregard the cease-fire and to attack Aley and Bhamdoun and to secure the highway as far as those two towns. After this was done another and more lasting Israeli-Syrian cease-fire was concluded on 25 June.

Having thus ended its offensive against the Syrians, the IDF could now concentrate on the PLO which was completely surrounded in West Beirut.

Terror bombing of West Beirut

Israel's military leaders imagined that they would be able to reduce PLO forces and force them into surrender by massive terror bombing by land, sea and air. Accordingly, millions of bombs were poured on West Beirut between 10 June and 12 August 1982. It was estimated that on certain days 170,000 to 180,000 shells and bombs fell on West Beirut, including residential quarters. Professor Charlotte Teuber of the University of Vienna said that the TNT equivalent of explosives directed at West Beirut by Israeli forces in 1982 was equal to that used in the two nuclear attacks on Japan in 1945.

The bombardments were carried out with the latest deadly and destructive American weapons: cluster bombs, phosphorus bombs and suction bombs.[12] The bombing was indiscriminate: refugee camps, residential quarters, apartment buildings, schools, air raid shelters, hospitals and embassies were hit spreading death and destruction everywhere in the city.

To increase the terror, the bombing was accompanied by the dropping of leaflets warning the inhabitants to leave the city to save their lives. The International Commission stated that it considers that the Israeli plan was to terrorize the population, so as to make the situation for the PLO untenable by bringing to bear on it the wrath of the population for the horrors of the siege. But although 200,000 of the 500,000 living in West Beirut left, the terror bombing failed to break the spirit of those who remained or the PLO defenders.[13]

A 'tourist' attraction

What is incredible is that the Israeli authorities made of the terror bombing of Beirut, with its death scenes, raging fires and collapse of buildings, a tourist attraction. Two Israeli journalists reported that

> The Israelis took to busing delegations of honored guests from abroad to an observation point in East Beirut to watch as planes dropped their bombs from high altitudes and plumes of black smoke billowed up from the city — treating the war like a spectator sport.[14]

Blockade of West Beirut

Simultaneously with the terror bombing, the Israeli army imposed a blockade on the city: water, foodstuffs, electricity and petrol were cut off. Contrary to all civilized rules, even the entry of medicines, blood and medical equipment for hospitals, and, on certain occasions, of doctors, surgeons and nurses was not allowed into West Beirut. And this despite the protests of the International Committee of the Red Cross and UN resolutions. A complete famine was avoided by reason of the few convoys allowed to pass and because the PLO distributed free the foodstuffs, especially flour, taken from its stocks.[15] Like the bombardments, the blockade affected the civilian population above all. For this reason, it was contrary to the laws of war and to the Fourth Geneva Convention of 1949 which prohibits the starvation of civilians as a method of warfare.

The whole world which followed the horrors of the war in press reports, on radio and television was appalled by Israel's barbarity during its siege of Beirut. Dennis Walters, British MP, expressed the revulsion felt everywhere in a letter to *The Times* (7 August 1982) in which he said:

> For seven weeks now the Israeli Air Force, equipped with the full and latest might of American air power, has been pouring its high explosives and cluster bombs on military and civilian targets alike while the Israeli artillery and the Navy bombard the city from land and sea. Cruel psychological warfare, involving the cutting of water and electricity, shooting up food convoys and holding up medical supplies, have all been used.
>
> Elementary decency and humanity call for immediate action.

The Security Council demanded from Israel on 19 June (resolution 512), 4 July (resolution 513), 29 July (resolution 515) and again on 12 August (resolution 518) to lift the blockade on vital facilities, such as water, electricity, food and medical supplies for the civilian population. Israel, however, flouted those resolutions.

Negotiations for PLO withdrawal

Negotiations for the PLO's withdrawal from Beirut began at the outset of the Israeli invasion. They were initiated by US Ambassador Philip Habib who was sent by President Reagan to arrange for the withdrawal of the PLO from Beirut. Such withdrawal was a basic Israeli demand to which the US had agreed. The negotiations with the PLO were conducted by the Lebanese Government.

The terms which Israel sought to impose without a cease-fire and under the pressure of fierce bombardments were the laying down by the PLO of its arms and its unconditional surrender. Although the Palestinians were fighting one of the strongest armies in the Middle East, single-handed, without air power and without any assistance from the Arab States, they rejected Israel's terms. Yasser Arafat declared that the PLO would make of Beirut another Stalingrad. Yasser Arafat's declaration was no empty threat. Despite the huge disparity in numbers, weapons and armaments, the Palestinian soldiers displayed exceptional courage in standing up to the Israeli army. Two seasoned Israeli war correspondents who covered the war paid tribute to the Palestinian fighters in their book *Israel's Lebanon War* for their 'bravery' (p. 122), for fighting 'like tigers to the end' (p. 127), for 'their noble stand' which their victors would not deny (p. 129) and for their 'inordinate courage and determination' (p. 137). They further observed that 'the Israeli victors were astounded by the extraordinary valor of their adversaries' (p. 142). At Ein Hilweh, 'though estimates put the number of PLO fighters at 300 or less, they sometimes seemed to be doing the job of a division' (p. 150).[16]

However, because of huge civilian losses and large-scale destruction of Beirut, the Lebanese Government suggested that the PLO withdraw from the city. In the second week of July the PLO agreed with the Lebanese Government to pull out of Beirut subject to agreement on the conditions of withdrawal and subject also to guarantees for the safety of Palestinian civilians remaining in Lebanon. The conditions of withdrawal were the subject of prolonged negotiations between the American envoy Philip Habib, Lebanon, Syria, Israel and the PLO. On 29 July the League of Arab States endorsed the principle of the PLO withdrawal once the PLO was guaranteed safe passage out of Beirut and the security of Palestinians remaining in Lebanon was assured.

Israel attempts to storm Beirut

As the negotiations for the PLO withdrawal were about to produce agreement, they suffered a severe setback. Israel's military leaders favoured a military solution: the storming of West Beirut and the destruction of the PLO. The Israeli Cabinet discussed this option at several meetings and on 24 July the Cabinet was split over the question. The military, however, took matters into their own hands and intensified the bombing of Beirut by land, sea and air. The intensification of the bombing of Beirut led Saeb Salam, a former Lebanese Prime Minister in charge of negotiations with the PLO, to declare on 31 July that Israel did not want a PLO pull-out, but planned to destroy it as a military and political force.

The Israeli plan to storm Beirut was reportedly finalized on 30 July. On 1 August residential areas and refugee camps in West Beirut were subjected to fierce bombardment by land, sea and air. On 2 August the IDF concentrated tanks around West Beirut and an entire armoured brigade was stationed at the Museum crossing. Then on 3 August and the following day IDF armoured units attempted to force their way into West Beirut. The PLO put up a fierce resistance and inflicted heavy losses on the assailants. After losing a number of men and tanks, the IDF abandoned the attempt to storm West Beirut and resumed its fierce bombardments.

On 4 August the Security Council adopted resolution 517 in which it declared it was shocked and alarmed by the deplorable consequences of the Israeli invasion of Beirut on 3 August. It reconfirmed its previous resolutions, reiterated once again its demand for an immediate cease-fire and the withdrawal of Israeli forces from Lebanon. It also censured Israel for its failure to comply with its resolutions. The US abstained from voting on this resolution.

Israel paid no heed to the Security Council resolution and pursued its massive bombardments. It also renewed its attempts to storm West Beirut but without success. Fires raged throughout West Beirut. Casualties mounted. The stench of death was all over the city. Food, water, fuel and electricity remained cut off. Thousands fled from

West Beirut. However, 'only Lebanese, but no Palestinians were allowed to leave (Phalange say this was done at IDF orders)'.[17] The massive attacks and bombings continued daily and reached their climax on 12 August when IDF forces hit West Beirut with ferocious 11-hour bombing raids which were the heaviest of the war.

Collapse of negotiations

As a result of such massive and indiscriminate bombing, the negotiations for a PLO withdrawal collapsed. Shafik Wazzan, the Lebanese Prime Minister, told Philip Habib that talks could not continue under 'the blackmail and pressure' of the Israeli raids and Saeb Salam asked Philip Habib 'to go home'.

The collapse of the negotiations and the savage bombardment of West Beirut prompted President Reagan to telephone Menachem Begin on 12 August expressing his 'shock' and 'outrage' at the bombing of Beirut which he described as a 'holocaust'. President Reagan demanded a halt to the bombing and shelling of Beirut or else he would call back Philip Habib and cancel the American mediation. The disclosure that President Reagan had accused Israel of a 'holocaust' was made by Menachem Begin himself in a press conference during which he declared that he had been 'deeply hurt' by President Reagan in his telephone call of 12 August in which he had described the intense Israeli bombing of West Beirut by the words: 'This is holocaust' (*International Herald Tribune*, 30 August 1982).

President Reagan's telephone call to Begin was followed by a White House statement which said:

> The President expressed his outrage over this latest round of massive military actions and emphasized that Israel's actions halted Ambassador Habib's negotiations for the peaceful resolution of the Beirut crisis when they were at the point of success. The result has been more needless destruction and bloodshed.

On the same day the US at last joined the 14 other members of the Security Council in approving resolution 518 which 'demanded' strict observance of the Council's resolutions concerning the immediate cessation of all military activities in Lebanon, and particularly, in and around Beirut, the immediate lifting of the food blockade, and Israel's co-operation in the effective deployment of

UN observers (whom it had previously prevented from assuming their functions).

PLO WITHDRAWAL

As a result, a cease-fire came into force on 12 August which allowed the settlement of the final details of the plan for the departure of the PLO from Beirut. The agreed plan included a schedule of departure of the PLO to various Arab countries and envisaged the despatch to Beirut of a multinational force composed of French, Italian and US forces which would come to Lebanon upon the request of the Lebanese Government. The plan also provided for the assurances to be given by Israel and all armed elements for compliance with the cease-fire and the cessation of hostilities, the turning over of PLO heavy weaponry to the Lebanese army and recognition of the right of PLO personnel to carry with them their side arms and ammunition.

US guarantees for safety of Palestinians

An important provision of the evacuation agreement dealt under the title of 'Safeguards' with

    (i) an undertaking of all parties not to interfere with the safe departure of the PLO, and

    (ii) appropriate guarantees of the safety of non-combatants left behind in Beirut, including the families of those who had departed.

These 'guarantees of the safety' of Palestinian civilians were given by the Lebanese and US Governments. The US commitment was couched in the following terms:

> The United States will provide its guarantees on the basis of assurances received from the Government of Israel and from the leadership of certain Lebanese groups with which it has been in touch.

In addition to the US guarantees, Ambassador Philip Habib addressed a letter to the Lebanese Prime Minister in which he referred to the assurances that the Government of Israel would not interfere with the implementation of the plan for the departure of the PLO leadership, officers and combatants in a manner which would (a) assure the safety of such departing personnel; (b) assure the safety of other persons in the area. He further gave the following assurance:

I would like to assure you that the United States Government fully recognizes the importance of these assurances from the Government of Israel and that my Government will do its utmost to insure that these assurances are scrupulously observed.

On the basis of these assurances and after the arrival of the multinational force, the PLO withdrew its combatants from Beirut to various Arab countries between 21 August and 1 September.

EVENTS FOLLOWING THE PLO WITHDRAWAL

No later than nine days after the departure of the PLO, the multinational force hastened to withdraw. The withdrawal was carried out between 10 and 13 September and was opposed by Lebanon because, under the evacuation plan which had been agreed upon, the multinational force was expected to remain until 26 September.

On 14 September, the day following the departure of the multinational force, Bashir Gemayel, the Phalangist military leader and President-elect of Lebanon was killed in an explosion which blew up the Phalangist headquarters in Beirut. The authors of the deed were unknown. The death of Bashir Gemayel was felt as a great loss by Israel's leaders. This was because he was Israel's ally and had been elected as the future president of Lebanon with Israel's assistance in the expectation that he would, after assuming office, sign a peace treaty with Israel.

On the evening of the same day, Prime Minister Begin and Defence Minister Sharon took the decision for the immediate entry of the IDF into West Beirut. The decision to occupy West Beirut violated the undertaking given by Israel to observe the cease-fire and also breached the conditions of the agreement for the evacuation of the PLO. On 15 and 16 September the IDF occupied West Beirut. Both the Lebanese and US Governments objected to the Israeli action and called for an immediate Israeli pullback. Israel refused to withdraw because it still had some unfinished business to perform.

161

Then followed several dramatic events: the massacre between 16 to 18 September 1982 of about 3,000 unarmed Palestinian refugees at the Sabra and Chatila camps by Phalangist militiamen under Israeli supervision, an outrage which will be discussed in the following chapter; the return of the multinational force to Beirut (23 September) to protect the Palestinian refugees; the conclusion under American sponsorship of a Lebanese-Israeli troop withdrawal agreement which disguised a peace treaty (17 May 1983) and was one of the aims of the war; the outbreak of communal strife between Phalangists, Druze and Shiites; the involvement of the US in the internal political strife in Lebanon and its taking sides in the intercommunal conflict; the shelling by American warships of Druze positions in the Shouf mountains; the terrorist attacks on US and French army barracks in Beirut causing the death of 241 US marines and 58 French soldiers (23 October 1983); the withdrawal of the multinational force (February 1984); the revocation by Lebanon of the Lebanese-Israeli so-called troop withdrawal agreement (5 March 1984) and finally Israel's bloody conflict with the Shiites in south Lebanon which forced and hastened the Israeli withdrawal.

Eventually, Israel withdrew most of its armed forces from Lebanon on 6 June 1985, the third anniversary of its aggression, but retained what it described as a 'security zone' all along its northern borders which was twelve miles deep into Lebanon. It planned to police it with the help of its mercenary force, the army of south Lebanon under the command of General Lahoud.

RESULTS OF THE WAR OF 1982

In 1982, Israel failed in its new attempt to destroy the PLO and to liquidate the Palestine Question. On the contrary, the savage bombardment of Beirut, the systematic destruction of Palestinian refugee camps, the huge losses in civilian lives, tragically crowned by the Sabra and Chatila massacre, brought more vividly to the world's attention the tragedy of a people forcibly displaced from its homeland.

Although the PLO withdrew from Beirut and thus lost its territorial base in Lebanon, it retained its political structure and its international status. If by its war against the PLO in Lebanon, Israel did not succeed in destroying the Palestinian national movement, it did succeed in 'tarnishing its image in world public opinion'. In the words of two Israeli journalists: 'The war had not crowned their

162

country with a great political and military victory but had . . .
stained its honor indelibly.'[18]

ISRAEL'S VIOLATIONS OF THE UN CHARTER, INTERNATIONAL LAW AND THE GENEVA CONVENTION OF 1949

The war which Israel launched against the PLO in 1982 was a war
of aggression.

In the first place, the invasion of the territory of Lebanon, an
independent and sovereign state, was a blatant violation of the UN
Charter and international law. Regardless of whether the PLO had
its offices in Beirut or not, Israel possessed no right or justification
to invade the territory of Lebanon, to violate Lebanese sovereignty
and to bomb Beirut.

Moreover, the waging of war against the PLO was also a violation of the UN Charter and of international law. The PLO is the sole
and legitimate representative of the Palestinian people and is
recognized as such by the UN and by the majority of states. The
PLO is asserting the legitimate rights of the Palestinians in Palestine
and, in particular, their right to establish an Arab state in their own
homeland. They possess this right on the basis of their inherent
sovereignty and on the basis of General Assembly resolution 181 of
29 November 1947. Hence, Israel's war against the PLO, which
aimed at liquidating the Palestinian people's national representative
organization and at destroying Palestinian national rights was an
illegitimate and unjust war which violated the UN Charter, international law and UN resolutions.

Furthermore, in the conduct of the war, Israel committed
barbaric acts which shocked the world. A brief summary is given
below.

(i) Indiscriminate and massive shelling and bombing by air,
land and sea of civilians in refugee camps and in urban areas
causing the death or maiming of tens of thousands of
innocent persons. It has been estimated by UNICEF that the
percentage of civilian victims in the war in Lebanon was 97
per cent of the total casualties.

(ii) Use of weapons destined for massive and inhumane killing,
such as cluster, phosphorus and suction bombs, contrary to

163

the laws and customs of war and to the Hague Regulations of 1907.

(iii) Infliction of death and inhumane suffering on the civilians under siege in West Beirut by cutting off supplies of food, water, medicines and electricity.

(iv) Denial to captured Palestinian regular soldiers of prisoner of war status, their ill-treatment, and in some instances their torture, under the spurious allegation that their struggle for national rights made them common criminals and disqualified them from protection under international law or the Geneva Conventions of 1949.

(v) Unlawful detention of thousands of civilians, both Palestinian and Lebanese, in violation of the Fourth Geneva Convention of 1949 and the laws and customs of war. At one time, about 9,000 persons were unlawfully detained by Israel at Al Ansar camp in south Lebanon.

(vi) Systematic destruction of Palestinian refugee camps, even after fighting had ceased.

(vii) Plunder of the Palestinian cultural heritage, including the archives, manuscripts and other cultural material of the Palestine Research Centre in Beirut.

(viii) Complicity in the massacre of Palestinian refugees at the Sabra and Chatila camps which will be discussed in the following Chapter.

ROLE OF THE US GOVERNMENT IN THE WAR

Questions have been raised regarding the role played by the US government in the war in Lebanon. There exist some disturbing facts which are examined below.[19]

First, there is the question whether the war was launched by Israel with US encouragement, approval or acquiescence. Ariel Sharon, Israel's Defence Minister at the time and the architect of the war, visited Washington from 22 to 27 May 1982 and, according to a later statement, he disclosed to US Secretary of State Alexander Haig, the Israeli plan to invade Lebanon, to destroy the PLO, and to install a strong and friendly government in Beirut which would conclude a peace treaty with Israel. Sharon declared to the press that Haig approved the plan but the latter has denied that he gave his approval. Alexander Haig's denial has been questioned in several quarters. Two Israeli journalists in their book on the war in Lebanon have said that Sharon came out of his meeting with Haig with what he considered was a 'tacit agreement to a limited military operation'.[20] S.V. and W.T. Mallison are highly critical of Alexander Haig's role in the War of 1982 and charge him with making inaccurate statements concerning the war in his book *Caveat: Realism, Reagan and Foreign Policy*.[21] *Newsweek* magazine (20 February 1984) stated: 'Reagan administration officials denounced the invasion in public — but in private, many shared Sharon's goals. Insiders contend that Secretary of State Alexander Haig even gave Sharon a yellow light for the venture — a charge Haig has denied.' President Carter has confirmed that the US had advance knowledge of Israel's invasion plan and that 'General Haig gave the green light' (*Le Monde*, 7 October 1982). But whether or not Alexander Haig gave the green light it seems fairly clear that there was, at least, tacit approval by the American administration. This came out during the second televised Reagan–Mondale debate on foreign policy in the 1984 Presidential election campaign when President Reagan declared that 'Israel couldn't be blamed for chasing the terrorists all the way to Beirut'. Does not such a statement imply tacit acquiescence in the war?

A second disquieting fact is the US supply, and acquiescence in Israel's use, of aircraft and internationally forbidden weapons (phosphorus, fragmentation, cluster and suction bombs) during the siege of the PLO in Beirut. These weapons were given by the US to Israel for self-defence, not for aggression, devastation and mass slaughter of civilians. It would have been an easy matter for the US to put an end to the slaughter, if it wished, simply by halting military and financial aid to Israel on which it completely depended.

Criticism of the US government's failure to stop the slaughter with American weapons has come from many quarters. A Washington attorney, Franklin P. Lamb has pointed out that 'The White House, the State Department, the Pentagon and the CIA have all conceded that Israel flagrantly violated US arms laws during its invasion of Lebanon by its use of cluster bombs, not to mention other US arms. Yet, despite these findings, neither the President nor the Congress has acted to enforce the clear requirements of either the 1952 Mutual Defense Assistance Agreement or the 1976 Arms Export Control Act.'[22] Again former Under-Secretary of State George W. Ball said in his testimony to the Senate Foreign Relations Committee in July 1982:

Our most valuable asset is our standing as a nation and a people committed to justice and humanity, and we diminish ourselves when we allow our weapons (including cluster bombs) to be used in Israel's sanguinary adventure without even a whimper of protest. We are made to appear as an accessory to Israel's brutal invasion — or at least as a nation too weak and irresolute to restrain our client state whose military strength largely derives from our gift of deadly arms and whose economic life depends on the constant blood transfusion of our economic aid.[23]

Although certain American statesmen deplored the use by Israel of American weapons and equipment to spread death and destruction, yet some of the military establishment were impressed by Israel's performance. General David S. Jones, Chairman of the Joint Chiefs of Staff, told the National Press Club in June 1982 that the Israeli battlefield experience with US weapons shows that 'We don't have to be quite as pessimistic as we have been in the past about these systems.' Likewise, General Charles A. Gabriel, Air Force Chief of Staff, said in August of the same year that he found some reason for optimism from the performance of US equipment in the recent conflicts in Lebanon and the Falkland Islands.

Still another disturbing fact was the negative attitude of the US government at the UN with regard to the war. Although the US concurred with Security Council resolutions that called for Israel's withdrawal from Lebanon (resolution 509), for respect of the rights of civilians (resolution 512) and for lifting its blockade on vital facilities and supplies to the besieged civilian population (resolutions 513, 515 and 519), on several occasions it adopted a position that differed from the international community and deviated from the principles of the UN Charter:

— It vetoed on 9 June 1982 a Security Council resolution which condemned Israel and called for an immediate cease-fire.
— It vetoed on 26 June a Security Council resolution which called for an Israeli withdrawal. On the same day it voted against General Assembly resolution ES-7/5 which noted that the Security Council failed to take effective and practical measures to insure implementation of its resolutions and condemned Israel for its non-compliance. This resolution was adopted on 26 June 1982 by 127 votes to 2 against (Israel and the US) with no abstentions.
— It abstained on 4 August 1982 from Security Council resolution 517 which was adopted by all other members of the Council

and which censured Israel for its failure to comply with its previous resolutions.

— It vetoed on 6 August 1982 a Security Council resolution which condemned Israel and called for the imposition of an embargo on supplies of arms to it.

Finally, there is the question of US responsibility for its failure to honour its guarantees for the safety of the Palestinian civilians who remained after the PLO withdrawal from Beirut. Those guarantees were mentioned above and will be discussed in the next chapter in connection with the Sabra and Chatila massacre.

NOTES

1. On the War of 1982 see *Report of the International Commission, Israel in Lebanon* (Ithaca Press, London, 1983); Franklin P. Lamb (ed.), *Reason Not the Need* (Bertrand Russell Peace Foundation, Nottingham, 1984); 'The War in Lebanon', *Journal of Palestine Studies*, vols. 44/45 (1982); Ze'ev Schiff and Ehud Ya'ari, *Israel's Lebanon War* (Simon and Schuster, New York, 1984); George W. Ball, *Error and Betrayal in Lebanon* (Foundation for Middle East Peace, Washington, 1984); S.V. and W.T. Mallison, *Armed Conflict in Lebanon* (American Educational Trust, Washington, 1985).

2. John Reddaway, *Israel and Nuremberg, Are Israel's Leaders Guilty of War Crimes?* (EAFORD, London, 1983), p. 10.

3. *Middle East International*, 20 August 1982, p. 12.

4. Michael Jansen, *Why Israel Invaded Lebanon* (Zed Press, London, 1982).

5. *Financial Times*, 3 July 1982.

6. Jacobo Timerman, *The Longest War* (Alfred Knopf, New York, 1982).

7. Schiff and Ya'ari, *op. cit.*, p. 301.

8. The Phalangists are a group of Lebanese Christian Maronites.

9. *Report of the International Commission, op. cit.*, p. 138.

10. *Journal of Palestine Studies*, 44/45, p. 164, 1982.

11. Schiff and Ya'ari, *Israel's Lebanon War*, pp. 148–9.

12. For a description of these weapons and their devastating effects, see *Report of the International Commission*, pp. 152 *et seq.*, and pp. 230 *et seq.*; Franklin P. Lamb (ed.), *Reason Not the Need*, pp. 419–501, Kevin Danaher, 'Israel's Use of Cluster Bombs in Lebanon', *Journal of Palestine Studies*, vol. 44/45 (1982), pp. 48 *et seq.* One cluster bomb releases some 600 to 700 bomblets which can kill every human being in an area the size of a football field.

13. *Report of the International Commission*, p. 159.

14. Schiff and Ya'ari, *Israel's Lebanon War*, p. 218.

15. *Report of the International Commission*, pp. 154–9.

16. Schiff and Ya'ari, *Israel's Lebanon War*

17. *Journal of Palestine Studies*, vols. 44/45 (1982), p. 186.

18. Schiff and Ya'ari, *Israel's Lebanon War*, p. 280.

19. For a discussion of the US violations of international law in the case of the War of 1982, see S.V. and W.T. Mallison, *Armed Conflict in Lebanon*, pp. 92 *et seq.*

20. Schiff and Ya'ari, *Israel's Lebanon War*, p. 74.

21. S.V. and W.T. Mallison, *Armed Conflict in Lebanon*, p. 84.

22. Franklin P. Lamb (ed.), *Reason Not the Need*, p. 433.

23. *Middle East International*, 20 August 1982, p. 12.

24

The Massacre of Sabra and Chatila

MOTIVATIONS, PREPARATIONS AND EXECUTION

The Sabra and Chatila massacre is one of the most barbarous events in recent history. Thousands of unarmed and defenceless Palestinian refugees — old men, women and children — were butchered in an orgy of savage killing.[1] On 16 December 1982 the UN General Assembly condemned the massacre and declared it to be an act of genocide.

Background of the massacre

The Sabra and Chatila massacre was an outcome of the alliance between Israel and the Lebanese Phalangists. In its long-standing war against Palestinian nationalism and against the PLO, Israel found an ally in the Lebanese Phalangists. It exploited the resentment and hostility of a number of Christian Maronites in Lebanon, founders of the Phalangist Party, against the presence of a large number of Palestine refugees in their country. The arrival of the Palestine refugees in 1948, Moslem in their majority, disturbed in their view the communal balance that existed between Christians and Moslems in Lebanon. Despite the fact that Israel was itself responsible for the Palestinian exodus, the common feelings of hostility of Israel and the Phalangists to the Palestinians led to a secret alliance between them. In execution of this alliance Israel supplied the Phalangists with money, arms and equipment to fight the PLO which, following its conflict with Jordan in 1970, had been forced to move from Amman to Lebanon.

This is then how Israel came to play a role in the so-called 'civil war' in Lebanon which erupted on 13 April 1975 with the assassination by Phalangists of 27 Palestinian refugees travelling in a bus in Beirut. The incident opened a Pandora's box which for decades had concealed pent-up grievances and latent hostilities between different communities in Lebanon and degenerated into a 'civil war' between the Phalangists, on one side, and PLO forces and their Moslem allies, on the other side.

There exists no firm evidence concerning the date when Israel allied itself militarily with the Phalangists in their fight against the PLO in Lebanon. There is evidence, however, of a secret meeting in May 1976 between Israeli Prime Minister Rabin and Israeli Defence Minister Peres with Maronite personalities. In August 1977 Israeli Prime Minister Menachem Begin publicly disclosed Israel's military assistance to the Phalangists in their fight against the Palestinians in south Lebanon. Such assistance and co-operation continued after Israel's invasion of Lebanon in 1982.

History tends to repeat itself. Thirty centuries earlier, a similar alliance had been formed against the Philistines, ancestors of the Palestinians, between the Phoenicians and the Israelites:

> 'As the result of his military successes (King) David was now the neighbour of the Phoenician kingdom of Tyre, and these two semitic peoples had a common bond in their hatred of the Philistines.'[2]

Motivations

The massacre of Sabra and Chatila was not an act of revenge by the Phalangists against the Palestinian refugees for the assassination of their leader Bashir Gemayel. First, his assassins were not identified and there was no suggestion that the Palestinians were implicated in or had any connection with it; second, the massacre was planned some months in advance of Gemayel's assassination. The military correspondent of *Haaretz* reported for his paper on 28 September 1982 that

> this was not a spontaneous act of vengeance for the murder of Bashir Gemayel, but an operation planned in advance aimed at effecting a mass exodus by the Palestinians from Beirut and Lebanon . . . It appears that for some weeks the Phalange leaders had been known to talk about the need to take action to expel the Palestinians from all of Lebanon.[3]

In fact, there were two motivations for the massacre: one motivation on the part of the Phalangist militiamen, the other motivation on the part of Israel. The Phalangists were opposed to the presence of the Palestine refugees in Lebanon and the Phalangist political programme aimed at their elimination from the country. The Israeli Commission of Inquiry, established in September 1982 to inquire into the massacre, states in its report that during the meetings that the heads of the Mossad (Israeli secret service) held with Bashir Gemayel, he revealed his intention to eliminate the Palestinian problem in Lebanon when he came to power — even if that meant resorting to aberrant methods. There was a feeling among experienced Israeli intelligence officers that in the event that the Phalangists had an opportunity to massacre Palestinians, they would take advantage of it.[4] The Israeli Commission therefore rejected the plea that Israeli officials, including Prime Minister Begin, did not foresee the danger of massacre of the Palestinians.

On the other hand, there existed a motivation for the massacre on the part of Israel. Whereas resort to massacre of the Palestinians as a means of causing their exodus from Lebanon was simply a statement of intention on the part of the Phalangists before the Sabra and Chatila massacre occurred, in the case of certain Israeli leaders resort to massacre of the Palestinians was a policy which was successfully pursued from 1948. The International Commission of Inquiry which was established in 1982 as explained on p. 180, stated:

> The Commission can also not overlook the extent to which Israeli participation in prior massacres directed against Palestinian people creates a most disturbing pattern of a political struggle carried on by means of mass terror directed at the civilians, including women, children and the aged.[5]

Thus the Israeli journalist Ammon Kapeliouk wrote: 'A small massacre to frighten the Palestinians and lead them to escape from Lebanon; a new Deir Yassin, this time by Phalangists as surrogates.'[6]

Terror had led to the exodus of a large number of Palestinians in 1948. Therefore, the motivation for causing by similar means another exodus of Palestinians, this time from Lebanon, was a common objective of Israeli leaders and their Phalangist allies. Proof of their complicity, however, will be discussed when we come to consider Israeli responsibility for the massacre.

Israel moves into West Beirut

The hasty and premature departure of the multinational force from Beirut, which we noted in the preceding chapter, paved the way for Israel's occupation of West Beirut. With the departure of the PLO and West Beirut completely undefended, Israel had a golden opportunity to move into it without opposition. Bashir Gemayel's assassination on 14 September 1982 was a convenient pretext that Israel could invoke in order to seize the Palestinian stronghold which it had been unable to capture during the siege of Beirut.

The decision to move into West Beirut was taken by Prime Minister Begin and Defence Minister Sharon although it constituted a violation of the cease-fire and the agreement which governed the PLO evacuation. It was also a breach of Israel's word to President Reagan not to enter West Beirut after the PLO's departure. On the morning of 15 September the IDF moved into West Beirut and completely occupied it by the following day, notwithstanding the protests of the Lebanese and US Governments. The IDF, however, did not enter the Sabra and Chatila refugee camps, but encircled and sealed them off with troops and tanks.

As to the decision for the entry of the Lebanese militiamen into the Sabra and Chatila camps, it appears from the testimony of Rafael Eitan, Israel's Chief of Staff, before the Israeli Commission of Inquiry that it was taken by him and by Defence Minister Ariel Sharon on 14 September 1982. This was followed by meetings between these two military chiefs and Phalangist commanders to coordinate the operation of the militiamen's entry into the camps. The decision to allow the militiamen's entry into the camps was approved by the Israeli Cabinet on 16 September after it began to be put into execution.

The massacre

The discussions between Israeli military chiefs and their Lebanese allies regarding their entry into the camps having been completed, three units of 50 militiamen each stood ready in the afternoon of Thursday 16 September 1982 at the edge of the Sabra and Chatila camps awaiting orders from the Israeli military command. At 5.00 p.m. they were sent into the refugee camps in accordance with the agreed programme of action and they then commenced an orgy of killing which lasted until the morning of Saturday 18 September.

During 40 hours, aided at night by flares fired by the Israeli army, they savagely knifed, tortured and killed defenceless old men, women and children.

Reports of atrocities started coming in to the forward Israeli command post overlooking Chatila camp within less than two hours from the militiamen's entry into the camps. At 8.00 p.m. on Thursday 16 September, according to the Israeli Commission of Inquiry, the Intelligence Officer at the Israeli forward command post received a report about a radio message to the Phalangists' liaison officer from one of the Phalangists inside the camps that he was holding 45 people and asked what he should do with them. The reply was: 'Do the will of God'. At about the same time or earlier, at 7.00 p.m., Lieutenant Elul, who was then serving as Chief of the Bureau of the Divisional Commander and was on the roof of the command post, overheard another conversation that took place over the Phalangists' transmitter in which a Phalangist officer in the camps informed the Phalangist commander on the roof of the Israeli command post that there were 50 women and children and asked what he should do with them. The answer was: 'This is the last time you're going to ask me a question like that, you know exactly what to do.' Lieutenant Elul understood that this meant the murder of the women and children.[7]

An additional report on the actions of the militiamen in the camps came from the Phalangist liaison officer. The Israeli Commission of Inquiry states that when this liaison officer entered the dining room in the forward command post at 8.00 p.m. on that evening he told various people that about 300 persons had been killed by the Phalangists, among them also civilians. He stated this in the presence of many IDF officers, including Brigadier General Yaron who was the division commander.[8]

Later that evening, at 20.40 hours, an update briefing was held in the forward Israeli command post building with the participation of various IDF officers, headed by Brigadier General Yaron. The Division Intelligence Officer said, *inter alia*, according to the transcript of a tape recording:

> The Phalangists went in today . . . They are pondering what to do with the population they are finding inside. On the one hand, it seems, there are no terrorists there in the camp; Sabra camp is empty. On the other hand, they have amassed women, children and apparently also old people, with whom they don't know what to do . . . I heard (from Phalangists' liaison officer) . . . 'Do

what your heart tells you, because everything comes from God.'
At this point, the intelligence officer was interrupted by Brigadier
General Yaron.[9]

The Israeli Commission of Inquiry commented on this interruption of the briefing

. . . it appears from the transcript of the conversation that took
place then that Brigadier General Yaron wished to play down the
importance of the matter and to cut off the clarification of the
issue at that briefing.[10]

At 11.00 p.m. the Israeli commander in Beirut was informed by
radio contact with a militia officer in the camps that 'until now 300
civilians and terrorists have been killed'. This report was
immediately given to Chief of Staff Eitan and to more than 20 high-
ranking officers in Tel Aviv. However, despite such a report, no
action was taken by the Israeli command and the massacre
continued.

Reports of the massacre circulated during the night and the early
morning hours of Friday 17 September. At 8.00 a.m. Ze'ev Schiff,
military correspondent of *Haaretz*, received a report from the
General Staff in Tel Aviv that there was a slaughter going on in the
camps. At 11.00 a.m. Schiff went to Communication Minister
Zipori and conveyed to him the report. The latter relayed the report
to Foreign Minister Yitzhak Shamir and asked him 'to check the
matter'. It appears from Shamir's testimony, however, that although
he had heard about 'some rampage' by the Phalangists, 'he did not
remember' that Minister Zipori had spoken to him of a massacre or
slaughter. He, therefore, neither checked the matter nor made any
mention of it to anyone and he explained his inaction in his testimony
to the Commission 'that the matter did not bother him'.[11]

Don't interfere

The Israeli Commission of Inquiry further states:

On Friday, 17.9.82, already from the morning hours, a number
of IDF soldiers detected killing and violent actions against the
people from the refugee camps. We heard testimony from
Lieutenant Grabowski, a deputy commander of a tank company,

who was in charge of a few tanks which stood some 200 meters from the first buildings of the camps. In the early morning hours he saw Phalangist soldiers taking men, women and children out of the area of the camps and leading them to the area of the stadium. Between 8.00 and 9.00 a.m. he saw two Phalangist soldiers hitting two young men. The soldiers led the men back into the camp, after a short time he heard a few shots and saw the two Phalangist soldiers coming out. At a later hour he went up the embankment with the tank and then saw that Phalangist soldiers had killed a group of five women and children. Lieutenant Grabowsky wanted to report the event by communications set to his superiors, but the tank crew told him that they had already heard a communications report to the battalion commander that civilians were being killed, (and) the battalion commander had replied, 'We know, it's not to our liking, and don't interfere.'[12]

Thus the massacre was perpetrated under the eyes of Israeli soldiers and officers who reported the facts to their superiors, but nothing was done to stop it.[13] What adds to the tragedy is the fact that the massacre could have been stopped at an early stage. Two parachutists told reporters of the newspaper *Haaretz* on the day following the carnage:

The massacre could have been stopped from Thursday evening, if account were taken of what we told our officers.

Not only was nothing done to stop the massacre but, on the contrary, at 11.00 a.m. on Friday 17 September, the Phalangists asked for more ammunition as well as fresh militiamen to replace those who were tired.[14]

According to General Drori, Commander of the Israeli forces in Lebanon, Chief of Staff Eitan met the head of the Phalangist forces in East Beirut on Friday afternoon and congratulated 'the Phalangists on their smooth military operation inside the camps'.[15] At this meeting, the Phalangist leader asked for bulldozers. One or more were supplied. The bulldozers were used to dig mass graves into which were heaped the bodies of victims that filled the alleys. A number of houses were also bulldozed to cover up the bodies of victims. The Phalangist leader further asked Eitan 'for more time in order to clean them out' and Eitan reversed Drori's earlier order to the Phalangists to stop and allowed the Phalangists to remain in the camps until 5.00 a.m. on Saturday morning. Even then, the massacre did not stop.

Apparently, the massacre stopped only at about 10.00 a.m. on Saturday 18 September, just about the time at which Morris Draper, the US envoy to Lebanon, expressed his indignation to Defence Minister Sharon by addressing to him, through the Israeli Foreign Ministry, the following message:

> You must stop the massacres. They are obscene. I have an officer in the camps counting the bodies. You ought to be ashamed. The situation is rotten and terrible. They are killing children. You are in absolute control of the area, and therefore responsible for that area.[16]

Towards 11.00 a.m. on Saturday, horrified newspaper correspondents rushed to the camps and the news of the massacre was flashed around the world. They 'saw the corpses of a three-year-old boy shot in the back of the head, babies in diapers, old men, old women. They had escaped the bulldozers that the butchers thoughtfully brought with them to remove evidence of their "anti-terrorist" exertions' (*Washington Post*, 23 September 1982). Another description of the scene is given by Loren Jenkins of the *Washington Post* service:

> The scene at the Chatila camp when foreign observers entered Saturday morning was like a nightmare.
> Women wailed over the deaths of loved ones, bodies began to swell under the hot sun, and the streets were littered with thousands of spent cartridges . . .
> Houses had been dynamited and bulldozed into rubble, many with the inhabitants still inside. Groups of bodies lay before bullet-pocked walls where they appeared to have been executed. Others were strewn in alleys and streets, apparently shot as they tried to escape . . .
> Each little dirt alley through the deserted buildings, where Palestinians have lived since fleeing Palestine when Israel was created in 1948, told its own horror story . . .[17]

Thousands of photographs were taken depicting the utter savagery of the operation. Ralph Schoenman and Mya Shone, two American journalists who spent six weeks in Lebanon, gave evidence before the International Commission of Inquiry and the following is an extract from their testimony:

We entered Sabra-Chatila on the Saturday (18 September), the final day of the killing, shortly after 12 noon . . . When we entered we saw bodies everywhere . . . We photographed victims that had been mutilated with axes and knifes. Only a few of the people we photographed had been machine-gunned. Others had their heads smashed, their eyes removed, their throats cut, skin was stripped from their bodies, limbs were severed, some people were eviscerated.[18]

Under US pressure Israel withdrew its forces from Beirut on 26 September and three days later, at the Lebanese Government's request, the multinational force comprising US, French and Italian troops, returned to Beirut to provide security in the area. It should be noted that during their ten-day occupation of West Beirut, Israeli forces arrested several thousand Palestinians whom they detained at Al Ansar camp in south Lebanon or in Israeli prisons. They also found time to plunder Palestinian property as well as books, manuscripts and other cultural material from the Palestinian Research Centre in Beirut.

Number of victims

The precise number of victims of the massacre may never be exactly determined. The International Committee of the Red Cross counted 1,500 at the time but by 22 September this count had risen to 2,400. On the following day 350 bodies were uncovered so that the total then ascertained had reached 2,750.[19] Kapeliouk points out that to the number of bodies found after the massacre one should add three categories of victims: (1) those buried in mass graves whose number cannot be ascertained because the Lebanese authorities forbade their opening; (b) those that were buried under the ruins of houses and (c) those that were taken alive to an unknown destination but never returned. The bodies of some of them were found by the side of roads leading to the south. Kapeliouk asserts that the number of victims may be 3,000 to 3,500, one-quarter of whom were Lebanese while the remainder were Palestinians.[20]

ISRAEL ATTEMPTS TO CONCEAL ITS ROLE IN THE MASSACRE

When the news of the massacre spread worldwide and it became known that Israel had authorized the entry of the killers into the Sabra and Chatila camps, there was universal indignation and a demand for Begin's resignation. The Israeli authorities then sought to smother the scandal by a blatant distortion of the facts. Several communiqués were issued by the IDF and the Israeli Foreign Ministry which 'asserted explicitly or implied that the Phalangists' entry into the camps had been carried out without the knowledge of — or co-ordination with — the IDF'.[21] One of the communiqués even declared, according to *The Times* of 20 September 1982, that Phalangists 'broke into the camps' by a side entry point.

Official deceit by the Israeli Government

This official deceit received a stamp of approval from the Israeli Government. A communiqué issued by the Israeli Cabinet on 20 September indignantly declared that the charges made against Israel's forces were without foundation and that the government rejected them 'with the contempt that they deserve'. The communiqué further stated:

> In a place where there was no position of the Israeli army, a Lebanese unit entered a refugee centre where terrorists were hiding, in order to apprehend them. This unit caused many casualties to innocent civilians. We state this with deep grief and regret. The IDF, as soon as it learned of the tragic events in the Chatila camp, put an end to the slaughter of the innocent civilian population and forced the Lebanese unit to evacuate the camps. The civilian population itself gave clear expression to its gratitude for the act of salvation of the IDF.

The communiqué also alleged that the 'terrorists' (read Palestinians) had violated the evacuation agreement by leaving 2,000 'terrorists' behind. The communiqué further denounced as 'blood libel' the allegations made against the Israeli army. The Israeli Cabinet's communiqué was run as a full-page advertisement in the *Washington Post* and the *New York Times* and was published in other media. As is obvious from the account of the massacre given above, the Israeli

Cabinet's communiqué was nothing but a tissue of lies.

Its allegation that the massacre occurred 'in a place where the Israeli army had no position' is contradicted by the fact that the Israeli army was in occupation of all West Beirut, that it had encircled the camps with troops and tanks and had an observation post at 200 yards overlooking the scene of the massacre. Again the allegation that 'a Lebanese unit entered a refugee centre' without the knowledge of the Israelis does not square with the fact that the entry of the Lebanese units into the camps was arranged and co-ordinated between the Phalangists and the Israeli army at its highest levels, including the Defence Minister, Ariel Sharon, and the Chief of Staff, Rafael Eitan. To contend that the Lebanese unit entered 'a refugee centre where terrorists were hiding in order to apprehend them' is a lie because those fighters that Israel describes as 'terrorists' had been evacuated from Beirut under international supervision and there were no PLO armed men in the camps. This fact is confirmed by the Israeli Divisional Intelligence Officer on the first evening of the massacre who said, as we have noted above, that 'there are no terrorists in the camp'.[22] In fact, the allegation that there were terrorists in the camps was fabricated *ex post facto* to explain the authorization given by the Israelis to the Phalangists to enter the refugee camps.

Moreover, the Cabinet's communiqué is at variance with the reason given by Prime Minister Begin to Morris Draper on 15 September 1982 for the IDF's entry into Beirut. Begin greeted him with these words 'Mr. Ambassador, I have the honour to advise you that since 5.00 a.m. this morning our forces have advanced and taken positions inside the city. With the situation created by the assassination of Bashir Gemayel it was necessary to protect the camps' (*Maariv*, 26 September 1982). The sending of assassins into the camps can hardly be meant for their 'protection'.

Again, the allegation that 2,000 PLO men were left behind in the camps was rejected by Lebanese Prime Minister Shafik Wazzan who is quoted by the *Washington Post* of 18 September 1982 as saying that Sharon's allegation about PLO guerrillas remaining was 'a disingenuous excuse to justify the invasion which he had already planned'. Moreover, the allegation must also be rejected on the basis of simple logic. If there were any truth in the suggestion that 2,000 PLO fighters were left in the camps it is unbelievable and incongruous that Israel would send 150 Lebanese militiamen 'to mop them up', particularly after the PLO fighters had resisted successfully for over two months the onslaught and the might of the entire Israeli army.

Finally, to contend that as soon as it learned of the slaughter the IDF put an end to it is untrue since the atrocities were known to the IDF as soon as they began i.e. on the evening of Thursday 16 September and the killers were even given more time on Friday 17 September by the Chief of Staff to finish their dirty work. And on top of it all to seek also self-praise by stating that the civilian population expressed 'its gratitude for the act of salvation of the IDF' is another distortion and an insult to intelligence.

The Israeli Government's explanations convinced no one and it reluctantly accepted on 28 September 1982 under strong internal and external pressures to appoint a commission of inquiry 'into the events at the refugee camps' (see p. 186).

ISRAEL'S RESPONSIBILITY FOR THE MASSACRE

Israel's responsibility for the massacre was the subject of inquiry by two Commissions: the Israeli Commission mentioned above and an International Commission which was set up to inquire into reported violations of international law by Israel during its invasion of Lebanon.

International Commission of Inquiry

The International Commission of Inquiry was formed in July 1982 by a group of independent and qualified jurists and professors from the US, Canada, France, South Africa and Ireland under the chairmanship of Seán MacBride. The Commission toured the areas of fighting, examined witnesses in diverse countries in the Middle East and published its report in 1983. The Commission concluded that in its invasion of Lebanon the Government of Israel had committed acts of aggression contrary to international law, that the IDF made use of weapons or methods of warfare forbidden by the laws of war and that it violated international law in its conduct of hostilities and its actions as an occupying power. Specifically with regard to the issue of the Sabra and Chatila massacre, the Commission found the Israeli authorities or forces were involved, directly or indirectly, in the massacre and other killings that have been reported to have been carried out by Lebanese militiamen in the refugee camps of Sabra and Chatila in the Beirut area between 16 and 18 September. The Commission's report was published by the Ithaca Press in London under the title *Israel in Lebanon*.

Israel's responsibility for the massacre rests on two grounds: first, the breach of its obligations as an occupying power to assure the protection of civilians, and second, its complicity in the massacre.

Responsibility as occupier

Under accepted rules of international law and specifically under the Fourth Geneva Convention of 12 August 1949, to which Israel is a party, the residents of the Sabra and Chatila camps were 'protected persons' and Israel, as an occupying power, was under an obligation in accordance with Article 27 of the Convention to protect them against acts of violence. Article 73 of Protocol I expressly extends the status of protected persons to refugees and stateless persons. Hence, by allowing, or failing to stop the massacre it violated its duty as occupying power.

Responsibility as accomplice

Israel's responsibility as accomplice is established: by its instigation and masterminding of the massacre; by the execution of the massacre by its allies and mercenaries under its supervision; and by the aid and assistance it gave to the perpetrators during the massacre.

Instigation and masterminding of the massacre

The proof of the instigation and masterminding of the massacre is found in several facts: the statement of Prime Minister Begin to the Israeli Cabinet in June 1982 in which he explained his plan 'to get rid of the Palestinians' in Lebanon; the meetings between Israel's military leaders with Phalangist commanders during the two days which preceded the massacre and the minutes of the meeting of the Israeli Cabinet on Thursday 16 September 1982.

The Israeli plan 'to get rid' of the terrorists which in Israeli parlance means the Palestinians fighting for their homeland was disclosed by Prime Minister Begin to the Israeli Cabinet at the time of the link-up between Israeli and Phalangist forces around Beirut in mid-June 1982. He is reported to have told the Cabinet the following: 'The concrete proposal to the Phalange is that you can and must, in our opinion, capture the part of Beirut inhabited by the terrorists, and you must get rid of them . . .'[23]

181

The instigation of the massacre is further established by the meetings that took place between the Chief of Staff (Eitan) and the Minister of Defence (Sharon) with Phalangist commanders during the two days preceding the massacre in which the parties co-ordinated and planned the entry of the militiamen into the Sabra and Chatila camps. The co-ordination arrangements that were agreed between Israeli military chiefs and Phalangist commanders at their meetings on 15 and 16 September included the setting up of Israeli command posts overlooking the Sabra and Chatila camps and the stationing in the forward command posts of Phalangist liaison officers with radio communication with the militiamen entering the camps. Accounts of these meetings are given in the Report of the Israeli Commission of Inquiry. At the meeting on 15 September, the Defence Minister stated 'that he would send the Phalangists into the refugee camps'.

Moreover, in the evening on which the massacre started (16 September) the Israeli Cabinet convened at 19.30 hours and was informed of the Phalangists' entry into the camps. At this meeting the Israeli Chief of Staff outlined the programme of action which he had set for the Phalangists and made it clear that the Phalangists did not enter the refugee camps of their own volition, but were 'told' by him to do so. The minutes of the Cabinet of that meeting state:

> The Chief of Staff provided details about the IDF's operation in West Beirut and about his meetings with Phalangist personnel. He said, *inter alia*, that he had informed the Phalangist commanders that their men would have to take part in the operation and go in where they were told, that early that evening they would begin to fight and would enter the extremity of Sabra, that the IDF would ensure that they did not fail in their operation but IDF soldiers would not fight together with the Phalangists, rather the Phalangists would go in there 'with their own methods' (p. 16 of the minutes of the meetings, Exhibit 22). In his remarks the Chief of Staff explained that the camps were surrounded 'by us', that the Phalangists would begin to operate that night in the camps, that we could give them orders whereas it was impossible to give orders to the Lebanese Army . . .[24]

No one made any objection and the operation in the camps received the Cabinet's tacit approval.

Execution of the massacre by Israel's allies and mercenaries

The second ground for Israel's complicity is that the massacre was carried out by its allies and mercenaries. The Phalangists were openly Israel's allies even though they refrained from actively participating in the war, to Israel's disappointment.

The Phalangists, however, were not the only militia involved in the Sabra and Chatila massacre. Although the Israelis have attributed the massacre solely to the Phalangists, this was done to cover up the participation of their own mercenaries in the massacre. The Phalangists did not act alone: two other Israeli-controlled groups also took part in the operation. These were Major Saad Haddad's 'Army of Free Lebanon' and 'the Damour Brigade'. Major Haddad was a renegade Lebanese Army officer, who after Israel's invasion of south Lebanon in 1978 formed, in agreement with Israel, a combatant force of mercenaries called the Army of South Lebanon to fight the Palestinians and to protect Israel's northern borders. These mercenaries were trained, armed, equipped, fed and paid by Israel and were at all times under its control. As to the Damour Brigade, it was created by the Israelis after the beginning of the 1982 invasion and was entirely under their command. It was composed partly of habitual criminals and partly of villagers who had escaped from the village of Damour following its occupation and the killing of a number of its inhabitants by Palestinians in revenge for the bombardment and massacre of Palestinian refugees at Tal El Zaatar camp near Beirut in August 1976. According to testimony heard by the International Commission, it was the Damour Brigade which was in the forefront in the massacre of Sabra and Chatila.[25]

The Israeli Commission of Inquiry made no mention of the Damour Brigade or of its role in the massacre. Likewise, it denied any role of Major Haddad's militiamen in the massacre. The Israeli Commission accepted the Israeli Government's contention that the massacre was solely the work of the Phalangist militia. Unlike the International Commission which took the evidence of a number of witnesses to the massacre, including foreign doctors, medical personnel and journalists, the Israeli Commission confined the scope of its investigation mainly to testimony from Israeli military personnel, whereas a number of eyewitnesses testified before the International Commission that Haddad's militiamen participated in the massacre. Moreover, the report of the UN Secretary-General to the Security Council (S/15400) dated 18 September 1982 cites a message from the UN Observer Group which stated that 'according to information received from the Lebanese Army, the units seen in the Bir Hassan, Sabra and Airport areas were in fact Kataeb (Phalange) units mixed with Lebanese *de facto* forces from southern Lebanon'. Such forces from southern Lebanon were no other than Haddad's men. The participation of Haddad's men in the massacre is also confirmed by the International Commission,[26] Amnon Kapeliouk,[27] Franklin P. Lamb,[28] Robert Fisk[29] and by Nicholas Veliotes, US Assistant-Secretary of State for the Middle East who told a House subcommittee that militia forces of Major Saad Haddad had a role in the massacre.[30]

It is quite evident that participation in the massacre by Haddad's militia and the Damour Brigade as mercenaries or surrogates of Israel entails the latter's direct responsibility. Hence, it was more convenient for Israel and the Israeli Commission of Inquiry to throw all the blame for the massacre on the Phalangists alone.

Israeli control and supervision

Although the Phalangists and other militias were sent into the camps, they remained under the IDF's control and supervision throughout the massacre. This is confirmed by the orders that were issued by Defence Minister Sharon on 15 and 16 September. On 15 September at 9.00 a.m. Sharon arrived at the forward command post which overlooked the Chatila camp and he repeated his order to send them in 'under the IDF's supervision'.[31] Then on 16 September Sharon issued the following order: 'Only one element, and that is the IDF shall command the forces in the area. For the operation in the camps the Phalangists should be sent in.'[32]

Israeli control over the operation included visual and around-the-clock supervision. The IDF had an observation post at 200 yards from the Sabra camp and from the 7th floor of the building the Israelis had an unimpeded view over the inside of the camps. At night, they were able with infrared binoculars to see what was happening inside the camps. According to the Israeli Commission's report,

> Brigadier Yaron set up lookout posts on the roof of the forward command post and on a nearby roof even though he knew that it was impossible to see very much of what was going on in the camps from these lookouts. An order was also issued regarding an additional precautionary measure whose purpose was to ascertain the actions of the Phalangist forces during their operation in

the camps (this measure is cited in Section 5, Appendix B). It was also agreed that a Phalangist liaison officer with a communications set would be present at all times on the roof of the forward command post.[33]

In addition, Israeli forces were ordered to monitor from their observation posts the Phalange's communications network.

It is clear, therefore, that the massacre was carried out under Israeli control and visual supervision.

Aid and assistance to the killers

The third ground of Israel's complicity rests upon the aid and assistance it gave to the killers. In addition to the fact that the killers were all armed and equipped by Israel, they also received concrete assistance during the massacre in several ways: the camps were encircled and sealed off, as previously noted, by Israeli troops and tanks; maps and photographs of the two camps had been given to the militiamen;[34] flares were fired over the area of the camps to help the killers find their victims during the two nights that the massacre lasted; one or more bulldozers were supplied to them to dig up mass graves or to destroy houses over the heads of the victims; and on the second day of the massacre the militiamen were 'authorized' to bring in fresh troops, to restock their supplies of ammunition and to continue for another night. Another appalling form of assistance was the fact that the IDF turned back those refugees who attempted to escape from the horrors of the massacre. On 17 September some 400 refugees seeking to escape the massacre and carrying a white flag approached the Israeli soldiers at one of the camp's gates. According to *Time* magazine (4 October 1982): 'They were turned back to the camps at gunpoint.'

Testimony as to the IDF's complicity in the massacre was given in a radio report made on 20 September 1982 by Loren Jenkins, Beirut correspondent of the *Washington Post* on the American National Public Radio:

There is no doubt in my mind that Israel aided and abetted that whole operation! These troops were trained by them, they're equipped by them, these men passed through Israeli lines, they set up their command post just next to the Israeli command post. They came in and out of the camps. They were fed by the Israeli Army, given water between their shooting sprees and went back into the camp. The final proof to me was when I walked and found what was a mass grave in a part of the camp, that when you stand just on top of that, and you raise your head, and you look up at a seven storey building, about 300 yards away, which is the Israeli Army's main observation post . . . And as I stood there Saturday morning looking up, there were six Israelis looking straight down at me. They stood and watched through this whole horrible tragedy as people were brought here, shot, dumped in this grave and packed up![35]

Finally, the failure of the military and political authorities to stop the massacre in an area under their control after they received reports of the atrocities from their own soldiers and officers and their allowing the carnage to continue for two whole days and for two long nights, even silencing Israeli soldiers who made the reports and ordering them 'not to interfere'[36] confirm Israeli complicity beyond any doubt.

CRITICAL EXAMINATION OF THE REPORT OF THE ISRAELI COMMISSION OF INQUIRY

The Israeli Commission of Inquiry into the Sabra and Chatila massacre was established on 28 September 1982 by the Israeli Government and was composed of Yitzhak Kahan, President of the Supreme Court, Aharon Barak, a justice of the Supreme Court and Yona Efrat, a retired general. The Commission examined the responsibility of both Israel and individual political and military leaders in respect of the massacre.

Commission's findings regarding Israel's responsibility

The Commission cleared Israel of direct responsibility, both as occupier or as accomplice but held it was 'indirectly' responsible for the massacre.

Regarding Israel's responsibility as occupier, the Commission stated that the issue:

is not unequivocal, in view of the lack of clarity regarding the status of the state of Israel and its forces in Lebanese territory. If the territory of West Beirut may be viewed at the time of the

186

events as occupied territory — and we do not determine that such indeed is the case from a legal perspective — then it is the duty of the occupier, according to the rules of usual and customary international law, to do all it can to ensure the public's well-being and security.

The Commission's suggestion that Israel's status as occupier of Lebanese territory or of West Beirut 'is not unequivocal' has no justification whatsoever and amounts to equivocation on its part. Between 15 and 26 September 1982 Israel was in occupation of West Beirut and was undoubtedly and undeniably subject to the obligations of an occupier under international law and the Geneva Convention of 1949.

In several resolutions, the United Nations have considered Israel as a belligerent occupant of Lebanon and therefore bound by the international law of occupation. Even Israel's own High Court of Justice ruled on 13 July 1983 in a case concerning the status of detainees Israel holds in Lebanon that the Geneva Conventions applied and that Israel was an occupying power in Lebanon.

The Commission also cleared Israel of direct responsibility for the massacre on the ground that the evidence indicates that the massacre was perpetrated by the Phalangists. It rejected any suggestion that Major Haddad's militiamen (who were in Israel's pay and under its command) took part in the massacre. It has been seen in the preceding section that such findings are contradicted by the evidence.

The Commission tempered its conclusion that Israel is not directly liable by holding that it is indirectly responsible. The Commission stated:

If it indeed becomes clear that those who decided on the entry of the Phalangists into the camps should have foreseen . . . that there was danger of a massacre, and no steps were taken which might have prevented this danger . . . then those who made the decisions and those who implemented them are indirectly responsible for what ultimately occurred, even if they did not intend this to happen and merely disregarded the anticipated danger.

To sum up, we assert that . . . no direct responsibility devolves upon Israel or upon those who acted on its behalf. At the same time, it is clear . . . that the decision on the entry of the

Phalangists into the refugee camps was taken without consideration of the danger . . . that the Phalangists would commit
massacres and pogroms against the inhabitants of the camps . . .
Similarly, it is clear from the course of events that when the
reports began to arrive about the actions of the Phalangists in the
camps, no proper heed was taken of these reports . . . This both
reflects and exhausts Israel's indirect responsibility for what
occurred in the refugee camps.[37]

The Israeli Commission's arguments that Israel is not directly
responsible for the massacre do not stand on examination. The fact
that the Phalangists perpetrated the massacre does not exempt Israel
from direct responsibility. In law, direct responsibility for a crime
is not limited to the perpetrators, but extends to accomplices,
whether as accessories before the fact or as aiders and abettors.
Israel's direct responsibility is based upon its instigation of the
massacre, its execution by allies and mercenaries acting under its
control and supervision, and upon its aiding and abetting the
perpetrators. In arriving at its conclusion that Israel is not directly
responsible the Commission ignored patent facts, namely, that the
Phalangists were Israel's allies and in entering the camps they acted
under Israeli orders; that its mercenaries assisted in the massacre;
that the IDF was in command of the area at the time of the massacre
and had encircled and sealed off the camps; that the killers were sent
by Israel into the camps by Israel's highest officers and with Cabinet
approval and remained throughout the operation under the IDF's
supervision; that they were supplied with flares during two
successive nights to perform their macabre business and with
tractors to dig mass graves to hide the bodies of the victims; that
Israeli soldiers turned back refugees attempting to escape; and that
when atrocities were reported to the Israeli military command no
action was taken to stop them but those who reported them were
ordered 'not to interfere'. By ignoring such a mass of incriminating
evidence, the Israeli Commission acted improperly and
injudiciously.

All neutral observers who have considered the facts have come
to the conclusion that Israel is directly responsible. The International
Commission of Inquiry concluded that 'the Israeli authorities bear a
heavy legal responsibility, as the occupying power, for the
massacres at Sabra and Chatila. From the evidence disclosed, Israel
was involved in the planning and the preparation of the massacres
and played a facilitative role in the actual killings.'[38] Likewise,

Franklin P. Lamb criticized the Israeli Commission's finding that no direct responsibility devolves upon Israel and pointed out that 'This conclusion has no support in the evidentiary record which, on the contrary, strongly suggests that all the killer units inside the camps were under Israeli control and acting on Israel's behalf.'[39] Kapeliouk, a reputable Israeli journalist, declared that the conclusions of the Israeli Commission regarding responsibility for the massacre are in contradiction to the facts which it itself sets out and that there is a case of direct responsibility.[40] Israel bears clear responsibility for the massacre under international law without distinction between direct or indirect responsibility.

Responsibility of Israeli leaders

After discussing Israel's responsibility, the Israeli Commission considered the individual responsibility of the political and military leaders who were involved.

Starting with the Prime Minister, Menachem Begin, the Commission did not accept his claim 'that he was absolutely unaware of the danger of a massacre'. It considered such a claim to be inconsistent with the explanation he gave for his decision to have the IDF occupy West Beirut 'in order to protect the Moslems from the vengeance of the Phalangists'. The Commission stated that no report about the Phalangists' operations reached the Prime Minister, 'except perhaps about the Gaza Hospital', until he heard the BBC broadcast towards evening on Saturday 18 September. For two days after the Prime Minister heard about the Phalangists' entry, the Commission observed, he showed absolutely no interest in their action in the camps and it concluded: 'The Prime Minister's lack of involvement in the entire matter casts on him a certain degree of responsibility.'

It was unsatisfactory that the Commission should leave in doubt Begin's knowledge of the atrocities except those committed at the Gaza Hospital. Equally unsatisfactory was its failure to resolve the conflict of testimony relating to those issues. Chief of Staff Eitan had testified that Begin phoned him on Saturday morning and told him that the Americans had called him and complained that the Phalangists had entered Gaza Hospital and were killing patients, doctors and staff workers there. Begin stated in his testimony that he had had no conversation with Eitan on that morning; that there had been no American call to him regarding the Gaza Hospital; and therefore, the conversations regarding the Gaza Hospital about which the Chief of Staff testified had not taken place.

All that the Commission had to say on the conflict of testimony on this important issue was that 'it saw no need, for the purpose of determining the facts in this investigation, to decide between the two contradictory versions regarding the conversations about the Gaza Hospital'. It assumed, without any basis, that 'the contradictions were not deliberate, but stem from faulty memory'. The Commission's explanation is not acceptable because such a conflict of testimony between Begin and Eitan cannot be explained by a faulty memory: one of them was not telling the truth.

Likewise, the responsibility of others involved is played down. Thus Minister of Defence Ariel Sharon is simply found to have committed 'a blunder' in deciding to have the Phalangists enter the camps and in disregarding the danger of acts of vengeance by them against the refugees. Foreign Minister Yitzhak Shamir, 'erred in not taking any measures' after he was told by Minister Zipori about the atrocities in the camps. As to Chief of Staff Eitan, the Commission determined that his 'inaction' upon learning that the Phalangists had 'overdone it' and his order to provide the Phalangist forces with a tractor, 'constitute a breach of duty and dereliction of the duty incumbent upon the Chief of Staff'. The Director of Military Intelligence, Major General Yehoshua Saguy committed 'a breach of duty'. As to the head of the Mossad (Israel's secret service) 'his inaction should not be considered serious'. GOC Northern Command, Major General Amir Drori, and Division Commander, Brigadier Amos Yaron, were found guilty only of 'a breach of duty'.

It is evident that the Israeli Commission acted both as party and judge and wished to reduce the stain on Israel's image. In such an uncomfortable situation it put Israel's unquestionable liability at its lowest possible level: it minimized it from direct to indirect liability and it reduced the war crimes committed by Israel's political and military leaders to simple 'breaches of duty', 'blunders' or 'inactions'. In effect, the Commission's report is a cover-up of Israeli responsibility for the massacre.

The belittling by the Commission of Israel's responsibility is noted by Uri Avnery, an Israeli politician and writer, who said that its members 'acted as Israeli patriots, who refused to assign greater responsibility to the nation and its representatives than the minimum responsibility which they could not possibly have avoided . . .'[41]

The Commission's report is also vitiated by other flaws. Among the most important mention may be made of the following:

(i) The Commission injudiciously accredits the false and politically motivated charge — fabricated by Israel for propaganda purposes — that Palestinian freedom fighters are 'terrorists'. Such vilification was incompatible with a supposedly judicial investigation and it discredits the Commission's inquiry and its conclusions.

(ii) The Commission also injudiciously and improperly accredited the false claim made by Israel's Defence Minister (Sharon) and later adopted by the Cabinet in its lying communiqué that the PLO did not completely withdraw from Beirut but left behind '2,000 terrorists' with their arms. The utter falsity of this allegation was discussed above. By accepting it the Commission has not only acted injudiciously but has also disregarded evidence given before it by the Israeli intelligence officer who said that 'there are no terrorists in the camp'.

(iii) Apparently in its zeal to minimize Israel's responsibility the Commission exceeded the bounds of propriety by denying that it was possible to see from the top of the Israeli forward observation post what was happening in the camps. The Commission stated that from the roof of the Israeli forward command post it was possible to see generally the area of the two camps, but not what was happening in the alleys, not even with the aid of the 20 × 120 binoculars that were on the roof of the command post. This assertion is flatly contradicted by eyewitnesses and by those who, unlike the Commission, did go to the roof of the command post to check the visibility over the camps.

Jonathan Randal, of the *Washington Post*, wrote:

In its . . . obviously wrongheaded factual error, the Kahan Report insisted Israeli troops couldn't see into the camps' alleyways, even with giant telescopes on the command post roof. Journalists who climbed the seven-story building had no such difficulty with their own naked eyes.[42]

The *New York Times* (26 September 1982) reported that from the rooftop of the Israeli observation post one can look down into the Chatila camp and that 'it would not have been difficult to ascertain (what was happening in the camps) not only by sight but from the sounds of gunfire and the screams coming from the camps'.

The Israeli Commission itself asserted that Major General Drori 'followed the fighting as it was visible from the roof of the forward command post'.[43]

    (iv) The Commission reduced the number of the victims to the lowest level just as it reduced Israel's responsibility. The Commission stated: 'It would appear that the number of victims of the massacre was not as high as a thousand and certainly not thousands.' This is contradicted by the count of the total number of dead by the International Committee of the Red Cross which was 2,400 as of 22 September 1982. A further 350 bodies were uncovered on the following day.

    (v) The Israeli Commission was guilty of several misrepresentations. Thus the savage, large scale and indiscriminate terror bombing and shelling of West Beirut during two and a half months which caused tens of thousands of casualties and which President Reagan described as a 'holocaust' is referred to by the Commission as 'the occasional shelling' of some targets in Beirut.

    Again, the atrocities perpetrated during the massacre were at times referred to as being 'excesses' committed by the Phalangists. Is it reasonable for a judicial commission to describe the mass slaughter of men, women and children, rape and torture simply as 'excesses'?

    So also, in mentioning that Major General Drori was on the roof of the forward command post at 7.30 on 16 September, the Commission stated that 'he followed the fighting as it was visible . . . '. It is surely a serious misrepresentation to describe as 'fighting' what was undoubtedly a 'massacre' of unarmed and defenceless refugees that resulted in the slaughter of some 3,000 to 3,500 persons.

Those are the flaws and shortcomings of the Israeli inquiry. The value of the Israeli investigation is that it established and put on record certain important facts which otherwise might not have been brought to light, such as the meetings between Israeli military chiefs and Phalangist commanders to arrange and co-ordinate the militiamen's entry into the refugee camps, the report of atrocities by Israeli soldiers and officers whose conscience revolted over what they saw and the failure of the military and political establishment at the highest levels to move a finger to stop the two-day slaughter.

However, in its evaluation of the facts and the testimony given before it, the Israeli Commission was neither judicial nor judicious, but was politically oriented in an effort to minimize and dilute Israeli responsibility. This was hardly in keeping with the standing of a judicial tribunal.

Judging by appearances and taking into account the fact that an inquiry was held by Israel into the massacre, the US media hailed the report of the Israeli Commission as 'a tribute to the vitality of democracy in Israel and to the country's moral character'. The *Washington Post* described it 'as an impartial inquiry'. All this was certainly undeserved praise for what was, in fact, a whitewashing of Israel and its leaders of a most heinous crime.

Lebanese inquiry

Neither can praise be showered upon the Lebanese inquiry into the massacre. In fact, there was no real inquiry or investigation. In October 1982 the President of Lebanon, Amin Gemayel, appointed Assad Germanos, military prosecutor, to conduct an investigation into the Sabra and Chatila massacre. The investigator submitted his report in June 1983 to the Lebanese President but the report was not made public.

It seems, however, that the Lebanese inquiry exonerated the political leadership of the Phalangist party from responsibility for the massacre and imputed the blame to militiamen of Major Haddad. Moreover, the Lebanese authorities have ascribed overall responsibility to Israel which was in occupation of West Beirut and had control over the camps which it surrounded and sealed off before and at the time of the massacre. Like Israel's inquiry, the Lebanese investigation was also a whitewashing operation.

RESPONSIBILITY OF THE US GOVERNMENT

Finally, it is necessary to examine whether the US Government has incurred any responsibility in respect of the Sabra and Chatila massacre.

Israeli Commission's allegations of US responsibility

The Israeli Commission of Inquiry, as we have seen, found Israel was 'indirectly' responsible for the massacre. Presumably, to dilute Israel's responsibility, the Israeli Commission suggested that indirect responsibility may also fall upon other parties, namely, the Lebanese army and the Lebanese and US governments. The Commission stated:

> One might argue that such indirect responsibility falls, *inter alia*, on the Lebanese army, or on the Lebanese government . . . It should also be noted that in meetings with US representatives during the critical days Israel's spokesmen repeatedly requested that the US use its influence to get the Lebanese Army to fulfil the function of maintaining public peace and order in West Beirut, but it does not seem that these requests had any result. One might also make charges concerning the hasty withdrawal of the multinational force . . .[44]

The Israeli Commission's suggestion that the US government was at fault was answered by Franklin P. Lamb in these terms:

> The Commission implies (p. 56) that the United States may have liability for the massacre because it did not send the Lebanese army into the camps. This assertion has no juridical basis whatsoever, because it was not the US that was the occupying power, but Israel. Indeed, the evidence makes plain that Morris Draper, special American envoy to Lebanon, urged Israel not to invade West Beirut, and not to send the Phalangists into the camps . . . While the US has some degree of international legal responsibility based on its guarantees of the safety of the civilian population in the camps, its responsibility is not that which is suggested by the Kahan commission.[45]

The rejection of the Israeli Commission's suggestion that the US was at fault does not, however, dispose of the question of responsibility of the American government for the massacre. This responsibility rests on two specific grounds.

US guarantees of the safety of the Palestinians

The first ground of responsibility rests upon the US government's failure to honour the guarantees it gave for the safety of the Palestinians after the PLO departure from Beirut which we have noted in the previous chapter.[46] These guarantees were one of the basic conditions of the evacuation agreement. The fact that they were provided on the basis of assurances received by the US from Israel and Lebanese armed groups that they will comply with the cease-fire and with the cessation of hostilities does not in any way affect or impair their effectiveness. It is obvious that such guarantees acquire practical significance and require implementation only in the case of the breach of the assurances given by others. This is exactly what happened. Israel reneged on its word, invaded West Beirut and allowed or, even worse, as we have seen, it instigated the entry of Lebanese militiamen into the Sabra and Chatila camps. Moreover, the Israeli army remained in West Beirut from 15 September to 26 September and during this period it arrested several thousand Palestinian civilians whom it unlawfully moved out of Beirut and detained in Al Ansar camp in south Lebanon or in Israeli prisons.

In the light of these happenings, can one reasonably say that the US government honoured its guarantees of the safety of the Palestinians after the departure of the PLO? US diplomatic representatives had immediate knowledge of Israel's move to occupy West Beirut. They objected to it, but was that enough? Does a simple protest constitute a fulfilment of the guarantee?

Former Under-Secretary of State George W. Ball answered this question in these terms:

In America our nation's responsibility for the whole tragic incident has gone largely unnoticed, yet the facts are clear enough. We put our own good faith behind Israel's word of honor; otherwise the PLO would never have agreed to leave. The PLO leaders trusted America's promise that Palestinians left behind would be safeguarded. When America promised 'to do its utmost' to assure that Israel kept its commitments they took that commitment at face value. They would never have trusted an Israeli promise but they trusted us. We betrayed them.[47]

In addition to the US failure to prevent or to put an immediate halt to Israel's occupation of West Beirut, one must also consider whether the US could have prevented the massacre from reaching the magnitude it did unfortunately reach, or at least to cut it short after its outbreak. This raises the question as to the time when the US authorities received news of the massacre. The *Sunday Times* (30 January 1983) suggested that American intelligence officials heard that killings were taking place on the evening of Thursday 16 September 1982, that is, shortly after the entry of the militiamen into the camps. However, the US government states that it received news of the massacre only on Friday 17 September. A 'press guidance' paper issued by the State Department stated that on Friday 17 September 1982,

> we started to receive fragmentary information that something was amiss in the Chatila/Sabra refugee areas of Beirut. We did our best to find out what was happening. It was not until Saturday morning, 18 September, that an Embassy officer was able to enter the Chatila camp and observe directly the evidence of the massacre . . . In short, we had no advance warning.

However, despite the State Department's denial of definite knowledge of the massacre until Saturday 18 September, it seems clear that US representatives became aware of the massacre early enough on 17 September to be in a position to stop the slaughter if they wished and, in any event, to prevent its continuation for a second night. According to testimony given to the Israeli Commission of Inquiry, there was American pressure on Friday 17 September on the Phalangists 'to leave the camps'. The Israeli Commission states that 'at about 16.00 hours' on that day a meeting was held between the Israeli Chief of Staff Eitan and the Phalangists at which they were told to continue action, mopping up the empty camps south of Fakhani until tomorrow at 5.00 a.m. at which time they must stop their action due 'to American pressure'. The Commission continued: 'The Chief of Staff testified that the Phalangists had reported . . . that the Americans are pressuring them to leave . . .'[48] It goes then without saying that the US government was aware of the entry and doings of the militiamen in the Palestine refugee camps before 16.00 hours on 17 September since it had been pressuring them to leave.

In those circumstances was it not the duty of the US administration to take immediate and effective steps on 17 September to stop the massacre, not only with the Phalangists, but also with the occupying power, instead of allowing the killers to remain in the camps for another day and another night?

196

Writing in the *New Statesman* of 1 October 1982 Claudia Wright said that 'Reagan's officials had enough knowledge to intervene in the massacre — but chose not to . . . That they didn't try — out of negligence or out of conviction that the "purging operations" were acceptable — is now obvious.'

Use of American weapons

The second ground of American responsibility rests upon the supply of US weapons and their use by the killers in the Sabra and Chatila massacre. According to the *Philadelphia Inquirer* of 30 September 1982, Nicholas Veliotes, Assistant Secretary of State for the Middle East, told a House Foreign Affairs subcommittee that American weapons provided to Israel might have been transferred to the Christian militia forces in Lebanon that were involved in the Palestine refugee camp massacre, but that, if so, they had not been provided with American government approval. Rep. Paul Findley (R., Ill.) observed at the meeting of the subcommittee that in his judgement, the US, along with Israel, 'has a responsibility for the murders'. According to the *New York Times*, reporters who visited the two massacre sites found M-16 shell cases fired by the militiamen and boxes that had contained M-16 bullets. The M-16 is a US-made rifle.

American responsibility also rests upon more general grounds. In this context, it seems fitting to conclude this discussion with a quotation from an article by Joseph C. Harsch in the *Christian Science Monitor* of 21 September 1982. He wrote that as a US citizen he 'bristled' when he first read that PLO leader Yasser Arafat had held his country responsible for the massacre. But then he began to think about the chain of circumstances which has led to this horror and came to the conclusion

> . . . that this atrocity was made possible because American taxpayers have made Israel the dominant military power in the Middle East.
>
> Since the US is the supplier of the power it is responsible for the way in which that power is used. It has been used in a way which led President Reagan to say, 'All people of decency must share our outrage and revulsion over the murders, which included women and children.'

NOTES

1. On this massacre, see the *Report of the Israeli Commission of Inquiry* into the events at the refugee camps in Beirut, 1983, an official translation of which was published in the *Jerusalem Post*, 9 February 1983 and can also be found in *Journal of Palestine Studies*, vol. 47, 1983; Amnon Kapeliouk, *Sabra and Chatila, Enquête sur un Massacre* (Seuil, Paris, 1982); Franklin P. Lamb, *International Legal Responsibility for the Sabra-Shatila Massacre* (Tipe, Montreuil, France, 1983); *Israel in Lebanon, Report of the International Commission* (Ithaca Press, London, 1983); *Reason Not the Need*, edited by Franklin P. Lamb (Bertrand Russell Peace Foundation, 1984, Nottingham, UK); Ye'ev Schiff and Ehud Ya'ari, *Israel's Lebanon War* (Simon and Schuster, New York, 1984); *The Beirut Massacre* (Press profile, Claremont Research and Publications, New York, 1984); S.V. and W.T. Mallison, *Armed Conflict in Lebanon* (American Educational Trust, Washington, 1985).

2. Michel Join-Lambert, *Jerusalem* (Elek Books, Putnam, 1958), p. 36.

3. The Beirut Massacre (Claremont Research and Publications, New York, 1984), p. 32.

4. *Report of the Israeli Commission, Jerusalem Post*, p. 4.

5. *Report of the International Commission* (Ithaca Press, London, 1983), pp. 182–183.

6. *Monde Diplomatique*, p. 21, June 1983.

7. *Report of the Israeli Commission, Jerusalem Post*, p. 6.

8. *Report of the Israeli Commission, Jerusalem Post*, p. 6.

9. *Ibid.*, p. 6.

10. *Report of the Israeli Commission, Jerusalem Post*, p. 19.

11. *Report of the Israeli Commission, Jerusalem Post*, p. 8.

12. *Ibid.*, p. 8.

13. Kapeliouk, *Sabra and Chatila, Enquête sur un Massacre* (Seuil, Paris, 1982).

14. Franklin P. Lamb, *International Legal Responsibility for the Sabra-Shatila Massacre* (Tipe, Montreuil, France, 1983).

15. Kapeliouk, *Sabra and Chatila, Enquête sur un Massacre* (Seuil, Paris, 1982), p. 64.

16. This was the testimony of the Foreign Ministry official before the Israeli Commission of Inquiry (*International Herald Tribune*, 22 November 1982.

17. Extract from report by Loren Jenkins published in the *International Herald Tribune*, 20 September 1982.

18. *Report of the International Commission, op. cit.*, p. 276.

19. *Report of the International Commission, op. cit.*, p. 176.

20. Kapeliouk, *Sabra and Chatila, Enquête sur un Massacre* (Seuil, Paris, 1982), pp. 93–94.

21. *Report of the Israeli Commission, op. cit.*, p. 106.

22. *Report of the Israeli Commission, Jerusalem Post*, p. 6.

23. Schiff and Ya'ari, *Israel's Lebanon War* (Simon and Schuster, New York, 1984), p. 199.

24. *Report of the Israeli Commission, Jerusalem Post*, p. 7.

25. *Report of the International Commission, op. cit.*, pp. 118–19.

26. *Report of the International Commission, op. cit.*, pp. 171, 176, 177.

27. Kapeliouk, *Sabra and Chatila, Enquête sur un Massacre* (Seuil, Paris, 1982), pp. 44–46.

28. Franklin Lamb, *International Legal Responsibility for the Sabra-Shatila Massacre* (Tipe, Montreuil, France, 1983), p. 72.

29. Robert Fisk reported in *The Times* (London), 21 September 1982 that Israeli C-130 aircraft transported some of Haddad's forces to Beirut on the day of the massacre.

30. *Philadelphia Inquirer*, 30 September 1982.

31. Schiff and Ya'ari, *Israel's Lebanon War* (Simon and Schuster, New York, 1984), p. 254.

32. *Report of the Israeli Commission, Jerusalem Post*, p. 6.

33. *Report of the Israeli Commission, Jerusalem Post*, p. 6.

34. Schiff and Ya'ari, *Israel's Lebanon War* (Simon and Schuster, New York, 1984), p. 268.

35. Transcribed from 'All Things Considered' broadcast on National Public Radio, 20 September 1982, and cited by Linda A. Malone, 'The Kahan Report and the Sabra/Chatila Massacres in Lebanon', p. 44, thesis, University of Illinois, 1983.

36. Schiff and Ya'ari, *Israel's Lebanon War* (Simon and Schuster, New York, 1984), p. 267.

37. *Jerusalem Post*, p. 13.

38. *Report of the International Commission, op. cit.*, p. 190.

39. Franklin P. Lamb, *International Legal Responsibility for the Sabra-Shatila Massacre* (Tipe, Montreuil, France, 1983), p. 82.

40. Kapeliouk, 'Les Insuffisances de l'Enquête Israélienne sur les Massacres de Sabra et de Chatila', *Le Monde Diplomatique*, June 1983.

41. *Ha'alam Ha'zeh*, 16 February 1983, p. 186.

42. Cited by Franklin P. Lamb, *International Legal Responsibility for the Sabra-Shatila Massacre* (Tipe, Montreuil, France, 1983), p. 98.

43. *Jerusalem Post*, p. 6.

44. *Report of the Israeli Commission, Jerusalem Post*, 9 February 1983, p. 12.

45. Franklin P. Lamb, 'The Kahan Commission and International Law', *Middle East International*, no. 196, 18 March 1983.

46. The question of US responsibility under the guarantee given to the Palestinians is discussed by S.V. and W.T. Mallison, *Armed Conflict in Lebanon* (American Educational Trust, Washington, 1985), p. 82.

47. George W. Ball, *Error and Betrayal in Lebanon* (Foundation for Middle East Peace, Washington, D.C., 1984), p. 57.

48. *Report of the Israeli Commission, Jerusalem Post*, p. 9.

25

Colonization and Land Usurpation in the West Bank and Gaza

Israel's occupation of the West Bank and Gaza in 1967 was followed by a systematic colonization and usurpation of Arab land which have continued until the present day. Although Israel's Prime Minister Levi Eshkol proclaimed in June 1967 that Israel was waging a defensive war and entertained no territorial ambitions on the West Bank and Gaza, the deception was soon belied when Israel annexed the Old City of Jerusalem within three weeks of its capture and then proceeded to dispossess landowners, usurp their land and create Jewish settlements in the recently occupied territories.

NEW METHODS OF USURPATION OF ARAB LAND

The Palestinians did not oblige in 1967, as they had in 1948, by fleeing massively in the face of terror and hostilities. Only 410,000 were expelled or fled, the rest of the population remained. In consequence, the Israeli authorities could not lay their hands on Arab lands under the pretext that they had been abandoned or were absentee property, as they had done in 1948. The methods which they used for usurpation of the land of Arab residents, as explained in Chapter 13, such as requisition for military purposes, closing of areas, expropriation or appropriation of land registered in the name of the Jordanian government, were not suited or sufficient to permit the seizure of large areas. So other means had to be devised.

The first method that was adopted was 'land use planning and licensing'. Meron Benvenisti, an Israeli land expert, explained the use and effectiveness of this method:

Official land use planning and licensing procedures have been a major instrument in Israeli efforts to gain control over space in the territories . . . In 1977, the Likud planners sought to achieve firm Israeli control over the entire West Bank and severely to restrict Arab construction outside the nuclear towns and villages . . . Arab population and Arab land use are regarded as constraints. Arab areas are encircled in the first stage and are then penetrated and fragmented. The declared plan objective is *to disperse maximally large Jewish populations* in areas of high settlement priority . . . and to achieve the incorporation of the West Bank in the Israeli national system . . . The main principle of this scheme (new scheme of 1982 near Jerusalem) is simple: to check future expansion of Arab towns and villages.[1]

The second method was to issue a military order that would declare an area to be restricted or closed for military purposes. Restricted military areas covered 1.11 million dunums (a dunum equals 1,000 square metres) equivalent to one-fourth of the area of the West Bank. Benvenisti observed that 'large areas closed for military purposes or seized by the army have actually been given to settlements and other Jewish civilian uses'.[2]

Elon Moreh case

The third method of seizing Arab land was developed in 1980 in order to defeat the effect of the High Court decision in the *Elon Moreh* case.

Until 1979 the courts had shown no readiness to interfere with the illicit and highhanded acts of the authorities in seizing Arab property allegedly for military purposes (despite such lands being intended for the creation of settlements) because they considered the question of 'security' was within the exclusive province of the administration. Farmers whose lands were taken were helpless and could not seek the assistance of the courts. However, recourse to the spurious pretext of security was exposed by the Israeli High Court on 22 October 1979 in the case of Elon Moreh. In that case land near Nablus had been requisitioned by the military authorities 'for military needs' and given to Jewish settlers for the creation of a settlement. The owners complained to the High Court and requested the rescission of the requisition order. The authorities contended that they were entitled to take the land for building a settlement in reliance on Article 52 of the Hague Regulations of 1907 which reads: 'Requisition in kind and services shall not be demanded from local authorities or inhabitants except for the need of the army of occupation.' They further pointed out that 'requisition for military purposes' had been the method generally used until then to secure land for Israeli settlements.

The Israeli High Court of Justice rejected the Government's argument and held that in this case the land had been taken for 'political reasons', not for 'security needs'. The Court stated that Article 52 of the Hague Regulations

cannot include on any reasonable interpretation national security needs in the broad sense.

The Court ordered the rescission of the requisition because

The decision to establish a permanent settlement destined from the outset to remain in its place indefinitely . . . comes up against insurmountable legal obstacles, because no military government can create facts in its area for its military needs which are designated *ab initio* to persist even after the end of military rule in that area, when the fate of the area after the termination of military rule is still unknown.[3]

What greatly disturbed the Israeli authorities was the reasoning of the High Court which held the applicability to the case of the Hague Convention on the Laws and Customs of War on Land of 18 October 1907. In accordance with the Convention, no land or other property, whether private or public, can be permanently confiscated by the occupier, who can only requisition such land or property. The owners, even though dispossessed, retain ownership and are entitled to rent for use of their land.

Circumvention of the decision of the High Court

This High Court decision wrecked the Israeli plan to continue the construction of Jewish settlements on private or public lands. Israel was not interested in a temporary use or occupation of Arab land, but in its permanent and definitive appropriation. Accordingly, the authorities decided to abandon the method of requisition for security and put their 'legal' experts to work in order to circumvent the High

Court's decision and to devise a new procedure that would protect the operation of Arab land confiscation from court interference. Israel's 'legal' experts lost no time in devising a new formula based upon the proposition that all land under Israeli control constituted 'Israeli national patrimony', except that which the Arab villagers could prove to be theirs. The Zionist interpretation of the Bible, that God promised the land of Canaan (Palestine) to the Hebrews, and Menachem Begin's axiom, that Judea and Samaria, despite the passing of 25 centuries, belong to the Jews, coupled with the Ottoman feudal principle that the Sultan of Turkey 'theoretically' owned all land furnished a pseudo-religious and political pretext in support of such an extraordinary proposition. Accordingly, a procedure was devised that was extremely simple and expeditious: the administrator of government property can declare any area that he wishes to be state land. Such declaration is not required to be notified to the owners affected by it. They have 21 days from its date, even though they may know nothing about it, to make an opposition and to prove their title — not to any court — but to a committee of three members appointed by the regional military commander. The committee's decision is automatically referred to the civilian administrator of government property. If no opposition is made, or if the committee's decision, whether favourable or unfavourable to the opposer, is rejected by the administrator of government property, the declaration of state land becomes final and binding, with no right of recourse or redress whatsoever by the plundered owners. In May 1980 the Israeli Cabinet approved the new procedure which has since been in use for the usurpation of Arab land. Nothing more blatantly arbitrary and abusive can be imagined.

Benvenisti observes:

> The decision of the Israeli cabinet on state land should be regarded as a major step towards the annexation of the West Bank. Not only was 40 per cent of its total area thus taken from the Palestinians and put at the disposal of the Israelis for unlimited settlement, but the last pretense of maintaining the temporary nature of land seizure arrangements was dropped. The old devices of military acquisition and closure 'for the duration' were replaced by a new concept identifying government property in the West Bank and Gaza as Israeli national patrimony.[4]

No state succession

The procedure of land acquisition by means of an administrative declaration of state land is arbitrary, illegal and robbery disguised in pseudo-legal garb. But even apart from such consideration, Israel has not acquired title under the principle of state succession to state domain in the West Bank and Gaza. Israel is not the successor to the Arab State which the UN resolved in 1947 to establish in Palestine, nor a successor to the Kingdom of Jordan which was in control of the West Bank and Gaza before the 1967 aggression. Accordingly, Israel possesses no right or title to state domain in territories that lie outside the boundaries of the Jewish State as defined by the General Assembly of the UN in 1947.

Institutional robbery

The administrative or legislative methods used by Israel to appropriate Arab land and property, mentioned above, are illegal and null and void and have been described as 'institutional robbery'. To such illicit measures, one should add hundreds of cases of appropriation of land for Jewish settlements by means of the forgery of title-deeds and signatures of Arab owners in respect of which the police and the courts have refused to take action.[5] The total area of Arab land seized by Israel in the West Bank since 1967 was estimated by Benvenisti in 1984 at 40 per cent.[6] In 1985, the land area of the West Bank under Israeli control had increased to an estimated 52 per cent.[7]

UN INVESTIGATION

The usurpation of Arab land for the construction of settlements in the West Bank and Gaza was the subject of a UN inquiry in 1979. In its resolution 446 dated 22 March 1979 the Security Council established a Commission to examine the situation relating to settlements in the Arab territories, occupied since 1967, including Jerusalem. Israel refused to admit the Commission in the occupied territories to conduct its investigations, but after making its inquiries and hearing testimony, the Commission submitted on 12 July 1979 its report to the Security Council (S/13450).

The Commission found that since 1967 Israel had established 133 settlements: 13 in and around Jerusalem, 62 in the West Bank, 29 in the Golan Heights and 25 in the Gaza Strip and the Sinai. It also found that the land seized by the Israeli authorities covered 27 per cent of the West Bank. (This percentage has since increased as noted above). The following excerpts from the report are significant:

229. The Commission is of the view that a correlation exists between the establishment of Israeli settlements and the displacement of the Arab population. Thus it was reported that since 1967, when that policy started, the Arab population has been reduced by 32 per cent in Jerusalem and the West Bank . . .

230. The Commission is convinced that in the implementation of its policy of settlements, Israel has resorted to methods — often coercive and sometimes more subtle — which included the control of water resources, the seizure of private properties, the destructions of houses and the banishment of persons, and has shown disregard for basic human rights, including in particular the right of refugees to return to their homeland.

The Commission was again requested in 1979 and 1980 to examine the situation relating to settlements and to investigate the reported serious depletion of water resources. The Commission submitted two additional reports: S/13679 and S/14268, in which it stated, *inter alia*:

— that the Israeli Government was actively pursuing its wilful, systematic large-scale process of establishing settlements in the occupied territories;

— that the establishment of settlements had resulted in the displacement of the Arab population;

— that 33.3 per cent of the West Bank had been confiscated to date;

— that Israeli occupying authorities continued to deplete the natural resources, particularly water resources, for their advantage and to the detriment of the Palestinian people;

— that Israel employed water both as an economic and even political weapon to further its policy of settlements.

NUMBER OF SETTLEMENTS

Estimates of the number of settlements in the West Bank and Gaza range from 114 (Benvenisti) to 204 (UN). The same variation exists with respect to the number of settlers: 28,000 to 42,500. It should be noted that a large number of so-called settlers are suburban residents of Jerusalem and Tel Aviv in search of cheap housing in massive apartment buildings erected around those two cities.

Illegality of Israeli settlements

The creation of settlements by Israel in the occupied territories is illicit under international law. It violates the Hague Convention on the Laws and Customs of War on Land of 18 October 1907 and the Fourth Geneva Convention Relative to the Protection of Civilian Persons in Time of War of 12 August 1949. Both forbid a military occupier to appropriate, confiscate or expropriate private or public property in the occupied territory. It may be remarked that the creation of settlements involves two elements: the appropriation of land and the establishment of settlers on such land, both acts being specifically forbidden by Articles 147 and 49 of the Geneva Convention of 12 August 1949. Article 147 considers as 'grave violations' of the Convention 'the appropriation of property which is not justified by military necessity' and 'illegal transfers' of persons. Article 49 provides that the occupying power cannot 'transfer a part of its own civilian population to the occupied territory'.

Since 1967, the UN has deplored or condemned, in dozens of resolutions, the establishment by Israel of settlements in the occupied territories, including Jerusalem, and has declared that Israel's actions in this regard have no legal validity. The last resolution adopted by the General Assembly on 14 December 1984 (resolution 39/95) 'strongly deplored' the establishment of settlements in the occupied territories and 'strongly condemned the establishment of new settlements on private and public Arab lands, and transfer of an alien population thereto'.

Dismantling of settlements

Of particular importance is Security Council resolution 465 of 1 March 1980 which not only proclaimed the legal invalidity of Israeli settlements, but also called for their dismantlement. The resolution stated, *inter alia*, that the Security Council:

5. *Determines* that all measures taken by Israel to change the physical character, demographic composition, institutional structure, or status of the Palestinian and other Arab territories occupied since 1967, including Jerusalem, or any part thereof, have no legal validity and that Israel's policy and practices of settling parts of its population and new immigrants in those territories constitute a flagrant violation of the Fourth Geneva Convention Relative to the Protection of Civilian Persons in Time of War and also constitute a serious obstruction to achieving a comprehensive, just and lasting peace in the Middle East;

6. *Strongly deplores* the continuation and persistence of Israel in pursuing those policies and practices and calls upon the Government and people of Israel to rescind those measures, to dismantle the existing settlements and in particular to cease, on an urgent basis, the establishment, construction and planning of settlements in the Arab territories occupied since 1967, including Jerusalem;

7. *Calls upon* all states not to provide Israel with any assistance to be used specifically in connexion with settlements in the occupied territories.

Needless to say, Israel paid no heed to this and other resolutions.

NOTES

1. Meron Benvenisti, *The West Bank Data Project* (American Enterprise Institute, Washington, DC, 1984), pp. 27–8.
2. Meron Benvenisti, *The West Bank Data Project*, p. 23.
3. High Court of Justice, Case 390/1979, Jerusalem.
4. Meron Benvenisti, *The West Bank Data Project*, p. 32.
5. See *Newsweek*, 16 September 1985, p. 26.
6. Meron Benvenisti, *The West Bank Data Project*, p. 32.
7. *Middle East International*, 27 September 1985, p. 12.

26

Israel's Policies and Practices

Israel's wars, aggressions and terrorist raids, its usurpation of Palestine, the eviction of its inhabitants, their spoliation and the confiscation of their lands and homes, its war on Palestinian nationalism and its smear campaign against the PLO, its colonization of the West Bank and Gaza have been already considered in the preceding chapters. Hence, the discussion here will be limited to other Israeli policies and practices that were not discussed elsewhere in this book, the violations of human rights, racism and obliteration of the name, history and culture of Palestine.

VIOLATIONS OF HUMAN RIGHTS AND FUNDAMENTAL FREEDOMS OF THE PALESTINIANS

In the matter of violations of human rights and fundamental freedoms of the Palestinians, it seems necessary, for purposes of clarity, to distinguish between three classes of Palestinians:

(i) Those who were uprooted or expelled in 1948 and in 1967 and were denied repatriation to their homes, i.e. the Palestine refugees.

(ii) Those who remained since 1948 under Israeli occupation and became citizens of the State of Israel.

(iii) Those who came under Israeli occupation after Israel's seizure of the West Bank and Gaza in 1967.

The Palestine refugees

The Palestinians of the first category are refugees and exiles. As we

208

have noted in Chapter 10, they numbered over 2,500,000 of whom 2,145,794 only were registered as refugees with UNRWA in June 1986. The remainder are unregistered with UNRWA as explained in Chapter 10. These refugees are denied their human, legal and fundamental rights. They cannot, in particular, return to their homes or recover their other property; live, work and die in their ancestral homeland; exercise their civil and political rights. In short, they are deprived of their dignity and their rights as citizens and even as human beings.

Arab citizens of Israel

The second category of victims are those who remained in 1948 and became Israeli citizens. They number at present over 700,000 (Israel's statistics of September 1985) and represent 17 per cent of the population of Israel. On the surface, they appear to enjoy equal rights with Israeli citizens of the Jewish faith: they are entitled to vote and to elect representatives at the Knesset and are assured by Israel's 1948 proclamation of independence of 'complete equality of social and political rights for all citizens without distinction of creed, race or sex'. But, in actual fact, they are treated as second-class citizens and are subjected to discrimination. They are victims of various forms of oppression and repression: arrest, detention, expropriation of their properties, and, in a number of cases, destruction of their homes and villages. They do not enjoy freedom of political expression or activity. Arab workers are paid half the rate that Jews receive for the same job. A description of living conditions of Israeli Arabs is given by Sabri Jiryis, a Palestinian lawyer who lived in Israel until 1966, in *The Arabs in Israel*.[1]

In addition, Israeli Arabs are subject to special repressive laws that are not applied to Jews (e.g. the Emergency Defence Regulations; see pp. 212–13). Until 1966, the Palestinians who remained in Israel were subjected to a regime of military occupation. Although in that year military government was abolished, in their case, this made no change in the strict regime applied to them.

Inhabitants of the territories occupied in 1967

The third category of Palestinians is the inhabitants of the territories which Israel occupied in 1967. Their present number amounts to about 1,300,000. They are subject to oppression and repression. They are denied the protection of civilians in time of war for which provision is made in the Fourth Geneva Convention of 12 August 1949. As a result, Palestinians in the West Bank and Gaza enjoy no rights whatsoever.

A detailed and documented list of human rights violations in the occupied territories is given, *inter alia*, by Israel Shahak,[2] Felicia Langer,[3] and the *Report of the National Lawyers Guild*, 1977, Washington, D.C.[4] and in a number of General Assembly resolutions, the last of which is resolution 40/161 dated 16 December 1986.

UN investigations

Since 1968 the UN has focused attention on the violations of the human rights of Palestinians in the West Bank and Gaza and established on 19 December 1968 the Special Committee to Investigate Israeli Practices Affecting Human Rights of the Population in the Occupied Territories. Israel refused and still refuses to co-operate with the Special Committee or to allow it access to the occupied territories. Moreover, it has prevented witnesses in the occupied territories from appearing before it to testify. Despite such obstructive tactics, the Special Committee has conducted its investigations and submitted annual reports to the General Assembly.[5] On its part, the General Assembly has condemned Israel each year for diverse violations of the human rights of the population in the occupied territories.

Without attempting a complete enumeration, these violations of human rights include occupation; annexation; establishment of settlements and transfer of an alien population into the occupied territories and Jerusalem; deportation and expulsion of Palestinians (including the mayors of Jerusalem, Hebron, Halhul and Bireh) and denial of their right to return; confiscation of private and public property; exploitation of Arab labour which is paid lesser wages than Jews; prohibition under penalty of imprisonment for Arab workers who go over to work in Israel to spend the night there; interference with the educational system in Arab schools; demolition of Arab houses; collective punishment; mass arrests; administrative detention, ill-treatment and torture of persons under detention. Moreover, the Palestinians under occupation are deprived of freedom of expression, their newspapers and their books are censored, their political demonstrations brutally repressed, sometimes with bullets.

Economic strangulation

Israel Shahak gives examples of Israeli measures in the West Bank and Gaza which tend to bring about the economic strangulation of the Palestinians: land 'taken over', that is, stolen, is deemed to be 'redeemed' and is reserved for the sole use of the Jews; the authorities forbid the opening in the occupied territories of factories to manufacture products for sale in the territories themselves; exports by Israel to the occupied territories are allowed, but exports from the occupied territories to Israel are forbidden or restricted; worse still, exports of oranges from the Gaza Strip to the West Bank are forbidden, their export being permitted only to other countries while Israel can freely export to the West Bank.[6] A particularly objectionable form of oppression of Arab cultivators is the prohibition of the planting of trees or of the growing of vegetables, even of a tomato, 'without a written permit of the military authorities' (see *Haaretz*, 27 September 1985).

All those measures and violations of human rights or even simple liberties are prompted by one political objective: the psychological oppression and the economic strangulation of the Palestinians so as to force their emigration. Such overall purpose is recognized by the Commission appointed by the Security Council on 22 March 1979 to investigate the question of settlements in the occupied territories which stated in paragraph 231 of its report S/13458:

> 231. For the Arab inhabitants still living in those territories, particularly in Jerusalem and the West Bank, they are subjected to continuous pressure to emigrate in order to make room for new settlers who, by contrast, are encouraged to come to the area . . .

In addition to economic strangulation of the occupied territories, Israel exploits their markets and taxes their inhabitants. Meron Benvenisti states that according to his calculations, the occupation is not a bad deal for Israel which has levied one billion dollars in taxes over the past 19 years from the West Bank and Gaza (*Newsweek*, 12 May 1986), p. 60.

RACISM

Israel: a racist state

In accordance with the UN partition plan of 1947 the proposed

Jewish state would have had a starting majority of Palestine Arabs in the proportion of 509,780 Moslems and Christians to 499,020 Jews.[7] In the Zionist concept, it would be a contradiction to describe as Jewish a state in which the Jews would be a minority. The well-known Jewish orientalist Maxime Rodinson has observed that the Jewish character of the state is 'the prime aim and postulate of Zionist ideology'.[8] This explains why the founders of the State of Israel resorted in 1948 to the brutal and barbarous method of uprooting and expelling the majority of the Palestinian population, refusing their repatriation and opening the gates to a massive Jewish immigration. The Israelis thereby transformed the demography of Palestine, the Jews having now become the majority of the population.

The racist policy of the State of Israel prompted the UN General Assembly to adopt a resolution on 10 November 1975 which equated Zionism with racism and racial discrimination. This moral condemnation of Israel caused an uproar in Zionist circles, arousing even the wrath of the US whose Secretary of State (Henry Kissinger) threatened retaliation in the form of economic sanctions against those that voted in favour of the resolution.

The charge of racism which was levelled at Israel does not rest on mere opinion or appreciation, but is grounded on undeniable facts. Palestinians were evicted and expelled from their homeland to make room for Jewish immigrants; they were denied repatriation to their homes, villages and cities which were given to the new settlers; Jewish immigrants were granted automatic citizenship on arrival under the Law of Return while Palestinians who were born in Palestine and had remained in territory held by Israel were required to prove their citizenship and to be naturalized; Arab land was massively confiscated to be given to the new settlers; no Palestinian Arab, though he may be an Israeli citizen, may purchase, occupy or lease 'redeemed' land from any Jew or from the Israeli authorities; Palestinian Arabs are treated as second-class Israeli citizens. One can also explain by racism and discrimination the fact that; although the Israeli Arabs represent 17 per cent of the population of Israel, only 16 Arabs out of 1,839 senior officials are listed in the Israeli government yearbook.

Application of special repressive laws to Arabs but not to Jews

An undeniable example of racism and discrimination is found in the application of special laws to repress the Palestinians regardless of whether they are Israeli citizens or inhabitants of the territories occupied in 1967. These laws are contained in the Emergency Defence Regulations which were enacted by the British Government in Palestine in 1936 to repress the Palestinian rebellion and were preserved by Israel (see Chapter 19) for use against the Arabs. These regulations were supplemented by the Israeli Defence Laws of 1945. Under such legislation, the authorities can arrest, detain without trial for successive and unlimited periods of six months each, banish, destroy property, impose curfews, try suspects by military courts with no possibility of redress or recourse to any civil court. In contrast, a Jew is never detained without trial, whether under the Emergency Defence Regulations or otherwise. Moreover, if charged with an offence, a Palestinian Arab is tried by a military court under the Emergency Defence Regulations, whereas a Jew, if charged with a similar offence, is tried by a civil court.

Although the Emergency Defence Regulations do not specifically state that they apply to Palestinians only, such has, in fact, been the case. Israel Shahak, a courageous defender of human rights and Chairman of the Israeli Human and Civil Rights League stated in a commentary dated 18 November 1983:

> The numerous 'experts' who assert (especially in the USA) that Israel is a democracy, with 'the rule of law' even for its citizens, are not only lying, but are racists as well. *Israeli democracy is strictly for Jews only.* All non-Jewish citizens of Israel live under the Defence Regulations 1945 Code, which was truly described when it was applied by the British to the Jews, as 'worse than the Nazi laws'. From 1951, those truly Nazilike laws are applied *only to* the Palestinian citizens of Israel.

Racism in Israeli education

The educational system in Israeli schools, in particular, in the religious schools, is permeated with racism. According to *Yediot Aharonot* of 20 March 1985 an opinion poll conducted among thousands of students in the secondary schools revealed that 50 per cent are for denial of the rights of the Arabs in Israel including the right to vote. *The Economist* of 20 July 1985 reports that 'opinion polls have consistently chalked up a majority, especially among young Israelis, in favour either of expelling West Bank Arabs altogether (15% according to a survey last year in *Al Hamishmar*) or of allowing them to live there but with no civil or electoral rights (43.5% according to the same poll).

The racist anti-Arab attitude displayed by Israel's youth should

213

not come as a surprise because racism is *taught* to the young in government religious schools. Just to take one example: a new three-volume series called *On the Good Land*, written for elementary government religious schools by the Department of the Israeli Ministry of Education states, *inter alia*:

> Jew and Arab sitting under one tree as a symbol of peace between them is a utopia of Zionism's creation. The Arabs have no roots in the Land of Israel. They did not plant any trees here, and therefore they will not 'eat the fruit of those trees'. If they are sitting under trees, these trees do not belong to them. The connection of Arabs to the land is a material one, while the relation of the Jew to the land is historical and religious.

The distortion of the Arab image is current in Israeli children's books. An analysis of such distortion has been made of 520 books.[9] Among them, one writer described the Arab as 'vicious as a Chinese snake, daring as an Indian tiger, treacherous as a Syrian fox . . . a criminal even in his mother's womb'. The extent to which Israeli youths are imbued with racism and even with hatred of the Palestinian Arabs is explained by an Israeli educator, Shlomo Ariel, who writes:

> As part of my job, I organize some seminars about current issues for youngsters about to be conscripted into the Israeli army. I met ten such groups of 50 boys each who can be described as a representative, random sample of Israeli-Jewish population . . . I chose as one of my topics the attitude towards the Arabs of Israel. Almost all . . . said they identified with Finkelstein's racist attitude towards the Arabs. [Finkelstein had conducted a campaign to expel the Arabs from Upper Nazareth — Ed.] When I argued that the Arabs in question were citizens accorded equal rights by our laws, the typical response was that they should be deprived of Israeli citizenship . . . There were several boys who argued that the Arabs of Israel should be physically eliminated, including the old, women and children. When I drew comparisons with Sabra and Shatila and with the Nazi extermination campaign, they voiced their approval . . . Some did say that there was no need for physical extermination. It was enough to expel the Arabs across the border. Many argued for South African style *apartheid* . . . In any one group there were never more than two or three boys with humanitarian and anti-racist opinions . . .[10]

Racism in Israel is epitomized by the draft laws which Rabbi Meir Kahane, a member of the Knesset, has presented to the Israeli legislative body for adoption. Their provisions are summarized by *Haaretz* of 27 March 1985 and include, *inter alia*, the following:

> A citizen can only be who belongs to the Jewish people . . . a non-Jew who wants to live in Israel must observe the seven commandments of the Jewish religious law . . . a foreign resident must accept the burden of taxes and slavery . . . if he does not accept slavery, he shall be deported . . . a foreigner shall not reside in the area of Jerusalem . . . shall not vote to the Knesset.

Another of Kahane's draft laws prescribes the establishment of separate beaches for Jews and non-Jews, prohibits mixed marriages as well as relations out of wedlock between Jews and non-Jews. Such laws are not dissimilar to Nazi legislation against the Jews and South African apartheid regulations against blacks.

Racism and the Knesset

The spread of racism in Israel is exemplified by the politico-racist-religious campaign launched by Rabbi Meir Kahane against the Palestinians calling for their expulsion from Israel and the introduction of apartheid-style regulations against the Arabs. Some Israelis, however, deplore racism. Thus certain political parties have been led to initiate at the Knesset a law against racism. This law, however, met with stiff opposition from the religious parties because the Old Testament itself embodies what can be considered racist teaching and discrimination against non-Jews. Thus, for example, Deuteronomy (7:3), says:

> Neither shalt thou make marriages with them; thy daughter thou shalt not give unto his son, nor his daughter shalt thou take unto thy son.

Again, it is stated in the Book of Exodus,

> (23:27) I will send my fear before thee, and will destroy all the people to whom thou shalt come, and I will make all thine enemies turn their backs unto thee.
> (23:28) And I will send hornets before thee, which shall drive out the Hivite, the Canaanite, and the Hittite, from before thee.
> (23:29) I will not drive them out from before thee in one year; lest the land become desolate, and the beast of the field multiply against thee.

215

(23:30) By little and little I will drive them out from before thee, until thou be increased, and inherit the land.

(23:31) And I will set thy bounds from the Red Sea even unto the sea of the Philistines, and from the desert unto the river: for I will deliver the inhabitants of the land into your hand; and thou shalt drive them out before thee.

Accordingly, the anti-racism law was so diluted in the Knesset by pressure from the religious factions that although it was eventually adopted on 5 August 1986 and did provide for punishment of a person for urging discrimination on the basis of race, colour or ethnic background, yet it did not cover religious racism or discrimination and further stipulated that calls to safeguard the Jewish character of Israel cannot be viewed as racist. The religious parties warned that it might otherwise become an offence to quote publicly biblical passages referring to the Jews as 'God's chosen people'. Given that the Bible ordains racism and discrimination, Rabbi Meir Kahane, whose activities the new law was originally aimed at stopping, voted for the measure, raising both hands.

OBLITERATION OF THE NAME, HISTORY AND CULTURE OF PALESTINE

The obliteration of everything relating to Palestine is also a manifestation of Israel's racism. Its actions since its emergence have sought and succeeded in the judaization of dominion, demography and land ownership in the territories under its occupation. They also sought to suppress the name, history and culture of Palestine. The object has been to obliterate the centuries-old Arab and Christian character of the country, in particular, the Arab character of Jerusalem, and to exhume the Jewish kingdom which disappeared more than 25 centuries ago in the dust of history. Israel considers it necessary for the success of its process of judaization to draw a veil over the history of Palestine. This fact is noted by Father Joseph L. Ryan who observes: 'As a result of Zionist presentations, the impression is at times given — and taken — that history of any consequence stopped in Palestine in the year 70 AD and only began again with the Zionist movement under Herzl.'[11] On the other hand, a Jewish source confirms this politically inspired suppression of Palestinian history. Jane M. Friedman wrote in the *International Herald Tribune* (May 1979):

Ever since the establishment of the Jewish state in 1948, the diaspora — 2,000 years of Jewish existence in exile, beginning with the Roman destruction of the second temple in AD 70 — has been regarded by Israel as history they would prefer to forget.

For many Israelis, their history began with the Bible, ran to the Bar Kochba revolt against the Romans in AD 132 and then jumped to the Holocaust and the Jewish state in 1948. And this view has been encouraged by the government.

As part of the process of obliterating Palestinian history and culture, the history of Palestine is not taught in Israeli schools. Israel Shahak, Professor at the Hebrew University of Jerusalem and Chairman of the Israeli Human and Civil Rights League states (translation): 'In schools, no mention is made of the history of Palestine during the two thousand years of the diaspora, neither in books, nor in lectures.'[12] Not only is the history of Palestine not taught in Jewish schools, it is almost not allowed to be taught in Arab schools within Israel. A Palestinian education officer who taught in Israel writes:

In short, Israeli education and cultural policies for Arabs aimed at nothing less than the de-Palestinization and de-nationalization of those Arabs under its control since 1948 . . . Education of Arabs in Israel has been perceived and used as an instrument of ideology through which the Zionist entity can, so it had hoped, achieve the goal of annihilation of Palestinian cultural and national identity . . . The modern history of Palestine is distorted and reduced to the 'history of the lands of fathers', of the desert which was transformed into paradise by Zionist settlers and 'newcomers'.[13]

The teaching of the virtues of Zionism to Arab boys in the syllabus imposed by the Israeli authorities in Arab schools is carried out unabashedly. Adel Mana'a, an Israeli Arab who lectures in Islamic history at the Hebrew University at Jerusalem, states: 'It was my fate to grow up in our village in Galilee, and to be taught in its school to love Zionism, which was said to have "redeemed our empty country".'[14] Sabri Jiryis points out that in Arab secondary schools in Israel in the whole of the four years of secondary education only 32 hours are devoted to Arab history and, in contrast, 384 hours are devoted to Jewish history.[15]

After the 1967 occupation, Israel sought 'to impose its syllabus

217

on the inhabitants of East Jerusalem'.[16] However, in consequence of strong opposition against this initiative, Israel was compelled to allow the Jordanian syllabus to be taught in the schools 'but only if expurgated of all reference to Palestine or its people'.[17] No Palestinian history is taught in those schools because, according to a teacher, it is too 'risky'.

The continual closure of the four Palestinian universities in the West Bank for long periods of time is part of the Israeli plan to disrupt and obliterate Palestinian culture. Likewise, the prohibition imposed by the Israeli authorities on the importation or publication of a large number of books is inspired by the same motive.

Israel's policy of annihilating Palestinian history, culture and identity has aimed also at the elimination of the name of Palestine. In fact, Palestine is referred to as 'Israel', or 'the land of Israel'. The territories of Palestine occupied in 1967 — which were regrettably called 'the West Bank of the Jordan', or 'the West Bank' by the Jordanian authorities after 1948, thus unwittingly contributing to the suppression of the name of Palestine — are now referred to by the Israeli authorities by the biblical names of Judea and Samaria or as the 'administered territories'. Accordingly, the term 'Palestine' or 'Palestinian' is taboo in Israel. The Palestinians are officially referred to as 'the Arabs of the land of Israel' and, if they have any connection with the PLO they are described — in furtherance of Israel's smear campaign against Palestinian nationalism — as 'terrorists'. The *New York Times* of 30 March 1982 mentioned deletions and changes made by the Israeli censor on newspaper articles relating to Palestine or the PLO:

In one story, the description of the PLO as a 'national liberation movement' was stricken. In a report on a call by an Israeli committee for 'the death penalty against Palestinian commandos', the censor changed 'commandos' to 'terrorists'. In an article about 'Palestinian graduates inside Palestine', the censor changed 'Palestine' to 'Israel' and the phrase 'outside Palestine' to 'abroad'.

Israel's antagonism to anything Palestinian has even become paranoiac. A Palestinian press agency which was established in 1977 in Jerusalem under the name 'Palestine Press Service' was refused registration as a press agency on account of its name. On appeal to the court against such refusal, the court upheld the administration's refusal to register the agency on the ground that the use of the word

218

Palestine in its name 'was offensive to the sentiment of the Israeli public'.

Moreover, to eliminate the physical reminders of the Arab presence in Palestine for centuries prior to the emergence of Israel, in 1948 the new state destroyed and ploughed the site of 385 villages as mentioned in Chapter 10. This massive destruction also served to prevent the return of the refugees and enabled the confiscation of their lands for Jewish resettlement. The names of Arab villages that were destroyed are listed by Israel Shahak[18] who observed that Israel maintains a complete silence over the villages that were destroyed so as to give credence to the myth taught in Israeli schools and repeated to visitors that Palestine was 'a desert country' before Israel was established. As no trace was left of those villages, even their cemeteries were destroyed, visitors may well accept the idea that Palestine was a desert country. They may even accept the slogan of 'a land without people for a people without land' which was coined by the Zionists to gain support for the establishment of a Jewish state in Palestine.

This deceitful slogan about Palestine was re-invoked by two Israeli Prime Ministers who denied the existence of the Palestinians. Levi Eshkol, in answer to the question put to him by a journalist: 'If the Jews are entitled to a homeland, aren't the Palestinians similarly entitled to their own country?' replied

What are Palestinians? When I came here there were 250,000 non-Jews — mainly Arabs and Bedouins. Palestine was a desert — more than underdeveloped. Nothing. It was only after we made the desert bloom and populated it that they became interested in taking it from us.[19]

Levi Eshkol's statement is simply a tissue of untruths. When he emigrated to Palestine, its population was almost three times the figure he mentions. His description of its inhabitants as being 'mainly Arabs and Bedouins' is deliberately pejorative and is calculated to convey the false impression that the Palestinians were a nomad population; in fact, the Palestinians, unlike the wandering Jew, have lived in Palestine since the dawn of history. His suggestion that the country was desert and was developed by the Jews is a plain distortion of the truth.

Likewise, Mrs Golda Meir, another Israeli Prime Minister, followed the same line and denied the existence of the Palestinians. She said:

219

There was no such thing as Palestinians . . . It was not as though there was a Palestinian people in Palestine considering itself as a Palestinian people and we came and threw them out and took their country away from them. They did not exist.[20]

The obliteration of the history of Palestine is now attempted by deformation of historical facts. Zionist apologists have reached a new stage in deceit by suggesting that not only the Palestinians did not exist in Palestine, but that Palestine was essentially 'uninhabited' by Arabs before the Zionist movement began towards the end of the nineteenth century, and that the Arabs came in large numbers after that, from nearby countries, drawn by the economic benefits of Jewish settlements. This extraordinary statement serves as the theme of a book *From Time Immemorial* by Joan Peters, published by Harper and Row in 1984. A number of critics, including Jews, have severely criticized this worthless book, one of them describing it as 'the most spectacular fraud ever published in the English language on the Arab-Israeli conflict' (*Middle East International*, p. 16, 21 December 1984). Anthony Lewis observes that a 1893–4 census by the Ottoman Empire showed 'a total of 9,817 Jews in all of Palestine and 371,969 Moslems'. In other terms, the Jews represented no more than 3 per cent of the population of Palestine. The untruths published in the book in question are not surprising because political Zionism has thrived on the distortion of history.

PRACTICE OF DECEIT

The practice of deceit is deeply ingrained in Zionist political ideology and in Israeli policy. Israel's recourse to deceit is systematic, and, without being exhaustive, a few choice examples will be mentioned here:

— That Russian, Polish and other converts to Judaism who emigrated to Palestine during the mandate are descendants of the biblical Israelites and hence possess a claim over Palestine.[21]
— That the displacement of one million Palestinians in 1948 was not the result of Jewish terror and expulsion, but took place at the request of the Arab States.[22]
— That Israel's annexation of Modern Jerusalem in 1948 and of the Old City in 1967 did not involve annexation.[23]
— That the Jews living in Arab countries had fled to Israel after

its creation to escape Arab persecution when, in fact, they were 'persuaded' to emigrate to Israel and, when persuasion failed, Zionist agents blew up synagogues as in Iraq in order to spread terror among them and force them to emigrate to Israel.[24]
— That the cause of the War of 1967 was an Egyptian air attack on Israel.[25]
— That Palestinians demanding self-determination and independence in their own country are 'terrorists'.
— That Israel had no connection with the Sabra and Chatila massacre and that such an allegation against it was 'a blood libel'.[26]

The latest act of deceit was practised by Israel spying on its American ally and benefactor, as we shall see in the next chapter, in discussing the Pollard affair.

Security of Israel

There exists one act of Israeli deceit which has developed into a course of conduct. This is the argument repeatedly invoked to justify Israel's wrongs, namely, the security of Israel.

Thus, in 1948 Israel invoked the pretext of security to expand the territory that was designated for the Jewish state by the UN. In 1956, it invoked the pretext of security to seize the Gaza Strip and the Sinai Peninsula. Under the pretext of security, in 1967 it seized the West Bank and Gaza which it is in the process of colonizing. Again under the pretext of 'security for Galilee', in 1982 it launched the war in Lebanon with the aim of destroying the PLO and Palestinian opposition to its occupation of the West Bank and Gaza. And, upon its withdrawal from Lebanon three years later, it retained a strip of Lebanese territory which it claimed it needed as a 'security zone'. This prompted Michael Bar-Zohar, an opposition member of the Knesset, to ironize on Israel's pretext of security in these terms: 'We've seen that scenario before. First we'll claim the area as vital for our security. The historic and religious claims will follow — and we'll never leave.'[27]

The argument of Israel's security has been exploited not only for territorial expansion, but also for other purposes. In fact, this argument is put to multiple use. It was invoked to deny to the Palestine refugees the right to return to their homes. It was invoked to misappropriate Arab land until the Israeli High Court, as we have seen in the preceding chapter, exposed such spurious pretext and held that the land in the case before it was not taken for 'security' but for 'political purposes'. The argument of preserving its security has been and is still being used by Israel to secure from the US Goverment huge quantities of arms to enable it to undertake all kinds of military adventures in the Middle East.

The argument of security is invoked by Israel also for another purpose, namely, to justify its repression in the occupied territories. This is noted by Michael Adams who wrote after a recent visit to the West Bank:

> No word in the Israeli vocabulary has a greater resonance than 'security'. In the name of 'security' every aspect of life in the occupied territories is rigidly controlled by Israeli soldiers masquerading as a 'civilian administration'. It is for the sake of 'security' that refugee camps are blockaded and subjected to long curfews; that any political activity on the part of the Palestinian population is banned; that the Palestinian press is rigidly censored; that student life in Palestinian universities is subjected to the minutest control; that schoolboys of twelve and fourteen are imprisoned for throwing stones at the soldiers of the occupation army; 'security' becomes the justification even for the fact that a Palestinian painter may be sent to jail if he uses the wrong colours in his composition.[28]

The argument of Israeli security has been stressed so much that, through incessant repetition, it has been accepted and, more importantly, it has come to be considered by Western statesmen and political commentators as the premiss for a solution of the Middle East conflict. In discussing the Reagan Peace Plan in Chapter 32 we shall see how solicitous President Reagan is about Israel's 'security concerns'. To quote a more recent example: 'The subjective national concern for security must be accepted as an objective factor in any Middle East peace plan', writes Joseph Weiler.[29] Israeli security now overshadows everything else. It is not on the basis of justice or international law, nor of UN resolutions, nor of the principles of the Charter that a solution for the Palestine Question is being sought but on the basis of Israel's security. This implies, of course, that security becomes the means for rewarding aggression and for justifying Israel's retention even of the territories which it seized in excess of the limits of the Jewish State as defined by the UN.

NOTES

1. Sabri Jiryis, *The Arabs in Israel* (Institute of Palestine Studies, Beirut, 1968).

2. Israel Shahak, *Le Racisme de l'Etat d'Israël* (Guy Authier, Paris, 1975).

3. Felicia Langer, *With My Own Eyes* (Ithaca Press, London, 1975).

4. The Report was published under the title: *Treatment of Palestinians in Israeli-Occupied West Bank and Gaza.*

5. The Commission's report for 1984 is contained in UN Doc. A/39/591.

6. Israel Shahak, *Zu Haderech,* 13 November 1985.

7. UN Doc. A/AC/14/32, p. 291.

8. Maxime Rodinson, *Israel and the Arabs* (Penguin Books, London, 1968), p. 228.

9. See Adir Cohen, *Ugly Face in the Mirror, The Reflection of the Jewish-Arab Conflict in Hebrew Children's Literature* (Rishafim Publishers, Haifa).

10. *Haaretz,* 1 December 1983, cited at p. 15 in the North American NGO Symposium on the Question of Palestine, held at the UN, 25–27 June 1984.

11. Cited in O. Kelly Ingram (ed.), *Jerusalem* (Triangle Friends of the Middle East, Durham NC, 1978), p. 26.

12. Israel Shahak, *Le Racisme de l'Etat d'Israël* (Guy Authier, Paris, 1975), p. 236.

13. Sami Khalil Mar'i, *Education, Culture and Identity Among Palestinians in Israel* (EAFORD, London, 1984), pp. 6–9.

14. *Middle East International,* 13 July 1984, p. 17.

15. Sabri Jiryis, *The Arabs in Israel,* p. 154.

16. *Middle East International,* 1 June 1984, p. 13.

17. *Ibid.,* p. 14.

18. Israel Shahak, *Le Racisme de l'Etat d'Israël,* p. 156.

19. *Newsweek,* 17 February, 1969.

20. *Sunday Times,* 15 June 1969.

21. Henry Cattan, *Palestine and International Law,* 2nd edn. (Longman, London, 1976), p. 49.

22. *Ibid.,* p. 138.

23. *Ibid.,* pp. 181 and 253.

24. 'One prime example is the burning of the synagogues in Iraq sixteen years ago, not by anti-Jewish enemies but admittedly by Zionist emissaries who actually succeeded in uprooting a Jewish commuity that had endured literally for thousands of years'. (Extract from monograph of American *Naturei Karta,* October 1978, New York. *Naturei Karta* is a Jewish Orthodox anti-Zionist group).

25. Henry Cattan, *Palestine and International Law,* p. 168.

26. See Chapter 24.

27. *Newsweek,* 27 February 1984, p. 16.

28. *Journal of Palestine Studies,* vol. 56 (Summer, 1985), pp. 62–3.

29. Joseph Weiler, *Israel and the Creation of a Palestinian State* (Croom Helm, London, 1985), p. 20.

27

US Patronage of Israel

EVOLUTION OF US POLICY IN REGARD TO PALESTINE

Politically, the US began to take an interest in Palestine and other Arab territories at the end of the First World War. In his speech to the American Congress on 8 January 1918 President Wilson proclaimed the principles which should be applied to the peoples and territories detached from Turkey in the war, namely, the rejection of any territorial acquisition by conquest and the recognition of the right of self-determination of peoples. These two principles were incorporated in 1919 in Article 22 of the Covenant of the League of Nations and served as the basis for the institution of mandates (Chapter 4). Thus, the US brought into existence in the sphere of international relations two fundamental and ethical principles: the inadmissibility of the acquisition of territory by conquest and the right of self-determination of peoples.

The application of these principles to Palestine was, however, thwarted, as we have seen, by the incorporation of the Balfour Declaration into the Palestine mandate without the consent of the Palestinians, by the imposition of a massive Jewish immigration into Palestine during the period of the mandate and eventually by the UN vote for the partition of Palestine. The role played by President Harry Truman in improperly influencing the UN vote for partition and creation of the state of Israel was discussed in Chapter 6.

Despite President Truman's devotion to the Zionist cause, yet at the time of the Lausanne Conference which sought in 1949 under the aegis of the UN to settle the Palestine Question he attempted to correct some of Israel's excesses. He addressed a note to Israel on 29 May 1949, through US Ambassador James G. McDonald, which was critical of its attitude at the Conference. The note:

expressed disappointment at the failure of Eytan (Israel's representative) at Lausanne to make any of the desired concessions on refugees and boundaries; interpreted Israel's attitude as dangerous to peace and as indicating disregard of the UN General Assembly resolutions of 29 November 1947 (partition and frontiers) and 11 December 1948 (refugees and internationalization of Jerusalem); reaffirmed insistence that territorial compensation should be made for territory taken in excess of the 29 November resolution and that tangible refugee concessions should be made now as an essential preliminary to any prospect for general settlement.[1]

However, despite his 'disappointment' over Israel's actions, President Truman failed to take any concrete steps or exercise any pressure to secure Israel's observance of UN resolutions concerning territory, the Palestine refugees and Jerusalem. In effect, the US government acquiesced in the grave wrongs done to the Palestinian people.

President Eisenhower acted differently in regard to Israel's Suez aggression of 1956. He upheld UN resolutions and the principles of the UN Charter and insisted upon, and effectively secured, Israel's withdrawal from the Sinai Peninsula and the Gaza Strip, despite the electoral pressures which Israel and the Jewish lobby brought to bear upon him (Chapter 16). Although President Eisenhower was then primarily concerned with putting an end to the Suez aggression, he did in his famous televised address on 20 February 1957 look beyond the Suez crisis and he emphasized

that upon the suppression of the present act of aggression and breach of the peace there should be greater effort by the United Nations and its members to secure justice and conformity with international law. Peace and justice are two sides of the same coin.

Perhaps the world community has been at fault in not having paid enough attention to this basic truth. The United States, for its part, will vigorously seek solutions of the problems of the area in accordance with justice and international law.[2]

US policy since the mid-1960s

Unfortunately, however, US policy regarding the problems of the

225

area — the most important of which is undoubtedly the Palestine Question — did not seek their solution in accordance with justice and international law. On the contrary, it radically changed course by supporting the Israeli aggressor militarily, economically and politically, and acquiescing in the wrongs done in Palestine.

The turning point in US policy with regard to the Arab-Israeli conflict occurred in the mid-1960s under the administration of President Lyndon Johnson. Kennett Love states:

> Johnson had been firmly in Israel's camp since his days in Congress and had opposed Eisenhower during the 1956 Suez War. In 1967 he directed US policy to be unabashedly pro-Israel. The difference in policy reflected the difference in the political philosophies of the two presidents. Eisenhower, who was fundamentally a nonpolitician, preferred the upholding of principle to the exercise of power. Johnson, like Kennedy before him, brought to the White House a professional's delight in the exercise of power, sometimes at the expense of such cardinal principles as truth, justice and peace. The urban Jewish vote meant power in America and Israel's fighting forces meant power in the Middle East.[3]

MILITARY AND ECONOMIC ASSISTANCE TO ISRAEL

Until the mid-1960s, American economic assistance to Israel was minimal and military aid was virtually non-existent. In 1950 the US even refused Israel's request for arms. The situation, however, soon changed under the Johnson Administration. From $40 million in US assistance in fiscal year 1964 under the Kennedy Administration, both US military and economic aid shot upward. George W. Ball, former Under-Secretary of State, remarks that

> in the fiscal year 1966 alone, we provided more military assistance to Israel than we had cumulatively provided during all the years since its establishment as a nation . . . President Johnson, responding to domestic pressures and the urging of political friends, transformed the fundamental American-Israeli politico-military relationship. For the first time, America became Israel's military arms supplier, economic benefactor and political supporter, as a torrent of US money and military material began flowing to Israel.[4]

226

Since then American military and economic aid have increased massively and reached astronomical levels under Presidents Nixon, Carter and Reagan. And to win the support of the Jewish electorate, each President has boasted of his role in increasing aid to Israel. On 4 September 1980 President Jimmy Carter told a Jewish convention 'I am proud since I have been President, we have provided half the aid Israel has received in the 32 years since its independence.'

The escalation and size of aid to Israel are shown in the following table:

Table 27.1: American aid to Israel (US $m)

Date	Military	Economic	Total
1948–61	0.9	593.6	594.5
1962–73	3,911.6	713.7	4,625.3
1974–78	4,000.0	2,679.9	6,679.9
1979–84	11,500.0	4,931.1	16,431.1
Total	19,412.5	8,918.3	28,330.8

Source: George W. Ball, *Error and Betrayal in Lebanon* (Foundation for Middle East Peace, Washington, DC, 1984), p. 96.

Commenting on the above figures, George W. Ball observed that, as the table shows, US military aid to Israel for the 13 years from 1948 to 1961 amounted to less than one million dollars and economic aid amounted to barely half a million dollars; then, in the twenty-two years from 1962 through 1984, military aid rose to a total of over $18 billion while economic aid reached almost $9 billion.[5] Referring to a proposal presently made to put Israeli aid to $5 billion yearly, George W. Ball remarks:

Such a level of aid is approaching the ridiculous . . . it means that American taxes are being used to provide Israel with an annual sum roughly equal to $1,500 for every Israeli man, woman and child; or $7,500 for each Israeli family of five.[6]

STRATEGIC CO-OPERATION

Strategic co-operation is another form of military assistance. Strategic co-operation has existed between the US and Israel since the mid-1960s and was concretized by massive deliveries of American military equipment, by the testing of new American weapons in Israel's armed conflicts with the Arabs, in particular, during the War of 1973 and the invasion of Lebanon in 1982, and by covert military assistance extended by Israel at the request of the US to American client states in Africa, Asia and Latin America.

However, the role played by Israel has not been confined to the execution of covert operations requested by its American ally. Early in 1985 Israel itself instigated the shipment of American arms to Iran with the approval of the White House in violation of US law and without the knowledge of the American Congress. The operations were further aggravated by the diversion of millions of dollars of the profits of the deals to US-backed contras (rebels) in Nicaragua. The uncovering of the story of such arms shipments by a Beirut newspaper in the fall of 1986 caused a political uproar in the US and came to be considered as a most scandalous episode in the life of the American administration. Both the Senate and the House of Representatives appointed commissions of enquiry into the scandal. The enquiries began in January 1987 and it appeared from a preliminary report of the Senate Select Committee on Intelligence and from classified documents released by the White House on 9 January 1987 that Israel instigated the arms deals between the US and Iran *purportedly* 'to bring about a more moderate government in Iran' and 'to achieve the release of American (hostages) held in Beirut'. But Israel's real motivation for its instigation of the US supply of arms to Iran was primarily to prolong the seven-year-old war between Iran and Iraq and to weaken both of them as its regional foes in a mutually destructive conflict. This is confirmed by the Tower Commission's report on 26 February 1987 (appointed by President Reagan) which stated that 'it was in Israel's interest to prolong the war between two of its adversaries'. The report says that Israel pressed the programme for the sale of arms to Iran by the Reagan administration in pursuit of its own interests, 'some in direct conflict with those of the United States. One of those interests was to distance the United States from the Arab world and ultimately to establish Israel as the only real strategic partner of the United States in the region.'

Fearful of the backlash which the scandal may have on American economic and military aid, Israel sought to disengage itself by disclaiming responsibility. An official statement issued by the Israeli government stated that in helping 'to convey weapons and spares from the United States to Iran, Israel acted in response to a request by the US government'. Moreover, Shimon Peres, the Israeli

Foreign Minister, declared in the Knesset: 'This is not an Israeli operation. This is a matter for the United States, not for Israel. Our purpose was to help a friendly country save lives. Israel was asked to help and it did.' The Israeli Government is now at pains to stifle the disclosure of its connection with the scandal.

Israel's strategic co-operation with the US goes beyond extending covert assistance in American military adventures. Not content with repeated US assurances about its security, Israel

> wanted an arrangement that would visibly symbolize America's commitment to it, assure that supplies would be available for sustained conflict without the need for another airlift, and, by the stationing of forces, guarantee America's immediate involvement in case of another Arab assault.[7]

In contrast, the US administration is not worried by the eventuality of an Arab assault upon Israel, which in any case is not likely, and, in any event, could easily be handled by Israel. The US is concerned with what President Reagan described as 'the increased Soviet involvement in the Middle East'. Oblivious of the fact that Soviet involvement in the Middle East is spawned by Israeli aggressions, the Reagan administration considers Israel to be, since the fall of the Shah of Iran in 1979, 'the only remaining strategic asset in the region' on which it can rely to restrict Soviet options.[8]

Such converging motivations, although not identical, had led to the conclusion on 30 November 1981 of the Strategic Co-operation Agreement between the US and Israel. This Agreement did not achieve all of Israel's aims, but some of them. The main terms of the Agreement, in so far as they were made public, provided for:

   (i) The establishment of a US-Israeli military committee for permanent consultation.
  (ii) The holding of joint naval and aerial manoeuvres.
 (iii) The prepositioning of military supplies in Israel for use by the US Rapid Deployment Force.
 (iv) The use of Israeli ports by the US Navy.
  (v) An increase in US military grants to Israel and negotiations for a free trade agreement.
 (vi) The resumption of shipments of US-made cluster bombs — which had been liberally used by Israel in South Lebanon in 1978 (and 1982) in violation of the conditions of their delivery to Israel.

Although the Agreement was suspended by President Reagan after Israel's annexation of the Golan in December 1981 and Prime Minister Begin retaliated by denouncing it, the US administration revived it on 28 November 1983.

The Arab states were angered by the conclusion of the Strategic Co-operation Agreement and considered it an alignment by the US on the side of Israel against them. It is doubtful, however, that the Strategic Co-operation Agreement makes of Israel a strategic asset for the US instead of a strategic liability by its alienation of the Arab world.

Furthermore, the UN General Assembly, confirming previous resolutions, declared on 16 December 1985 in its resolution 40/168 that it:

> 10. *Considers* that the agreements on strategic co-operation between the United States of America and Israel, signed on 30 November 1981, and the continued supply of modern arms and *matériel* to Israel, augmented by substantial economic aid, including the recently concluded Agreement on the establishment of a Free Trade Area between the two Governments, have encouraged Israel to pursue its aggressive and expansionist policies and practices in the Palestinian and other territories occupied since 1967, including Jerusalem, and have had adverse effects for the establishment of a comprehensive, just and lasting peace in the Middle East and would threaten the security of the region.

POLITICAL SUPPORT

Since the mid-1960s US policy became increasingly supportive of Israeli actions, even of those that are of an illicit character. US political support of Israel is of different kinds and takes various forms which are discussed below.

Acquiescence in Israeli aggressions

In 1967 the US administration failed to follow President Eisenhower's attitude at the time of Suez of condemning Israel's aggression and insisting upon its immediate and unconditional withdrawal from the West Bank and Gaza (see Chapter 17). This new attitude represented the turning point of the US government's policy with regard to the Arab-Israeli conflict. Pursuant to its new policy, in July 1967 the US government opposed and defeated a General Assembly resolution that condemned Israel's aggression and called for its withdrawal. The US position was that Israel could remain in occupation of the territories it had seized until a comprehensive settlement was reached. No such settlement has been reached in respect of the West Bank and Gaza so that Israel is still today in occupation of those territories and is, moreover, feverishly creating in them settlements with a view to their annexation.

The new American attitude of extending support to Israel was again followed during the War of 1973 in which Egypt and Syria sought to recover their own territories which Israel had seized in 1967. The US then actively intervened in the war by organizing a massive airlift during which it delivered to Israel great quantities of war material which changed the course of the war and left Israel in occupation of Egyptian and Syrian territories. Several years later, Israel withdrew from the Egyptian territory of Sinai under the Egyptian-Israeli Peace Treaty of 1979 but it still remains in occupation of the Syrian Golan which, moreover, it annexed in 1981.

American acquiescence in Israel's aggressions was also evident in 1982 in the case of its invasion of Lebanon and its war against the PLO. As noted in Chapter 23, this last aggression received the tacit assent of the US administration and was conducted with American aircraft and weapons.

American acquiescence in Israeli aggressions was also expressed at the highest level following the raid which Israel carried out on 1 October 1985 on the PLO's headquarters at Tunis. This raid was an act of war and aimed at assassinating Yasser Arafat, chairman of the PLO. However, it failed in its basic objective, but it destroyed Arafat's living quarters and PLO offices and killed over 70 persons. President Reagan then decribed the Israeli raid as 'a legitimate response' and 'an act of self-defence'. The whole world, including the Security Council, condemned this 'act of armed aggression' — except the US government which abstained from the Security Council's resolution.

Endorsement of Israel's opposition to the PLO, to Palestinian nationalism and to a Palestinian state

The US administration has fully espoused Israel's opposition to the

PLO, to Palestinian nationalism and to the creation of a Palestinian state. As previously noted in Chapter 21, it gave Israel a commitment not to recognize or to negotiate with the PLO which is the generally recognized representative of the Palestinian people. This commitment has been criticized by neutral observers. After his resignation as US Ambassador to the UN, Andrew Young said that US policy of not meeting with the PLO was 'ridiculous' and was not in the US interest. Nahum Goldmann, former president of the World Jewish Congress observed that it was 'foolish' for Israel and the US to refuse to negotiate with the PLO. Moreover, the US administration also endorsed Israel's opposition to the establishment of a Palestinian state, whether in the territory earmarked for such a state by the UN in 1947 or in the West Bank and Gaza.

US opposition to the establishment of a Palestinian state has been unequivocally formulated by American Presidents Jimmy Carter and Ronald Reagan. It is all the more surprising because in 1947 the US itself was responsible and the prime mover for the adoption of the UN vote for the creation of Arab and Jewish states in Palestine.

Although early in his term of office President Carter spoke on 17 March 1977 of 'the right of the Palestinians to have a homeland, to be compensated for losses they have suffered' and of Israel's 'withdrawal from territories occupied in the 1967 war', he abandoned this policy under Israeli and Zionist pressures and proclaimed his opposition to a Palestinian state. President Carter explained in an interview published by the *New York Times* (11 August 1979) US opposition to a Palestinian state in these terms:

> I am against any creation of a separate Palestinian state. I don't think it would be good for the Palestinians. I don't think it would be good for Israel. I don't think it would be good for the Arab neighbours of such a state.

It may be doubtful whether President Carter is a good judge of what is good for Israel, but he is surely not a good judge of what is good for the Palestinians and the Arab states. In any event, it is probably the first time that one hears the proposition that it is good for a people to be deprived of their human, legitimate and national rights to establish their own state.

It is pertinent to observe that the opposition of Presidents Carter and Reagan to the establishment of a Palestinian state does not stem from the same reason: in one case, the reason is religious while in the other, it is political. Speaking during a tour of the Middle East on 10 March 1983 at Tel Aviv University, President Carter, who is a Baptist, said: 'God has ordained the existence of the State of Israel as a permanent homeland for the Jews. This is my deep religious belief.'[9] He added, however, that 'the Palestinians had the right to have a voice in the shaping of their own destiny and the resolution of the Palestine issue in all its aspects. I am convinced that permanent peace without justice for all is not possible.'

As to President Reagan, although he has spoken of providing the Palestinians with 'something in the nature of a homeland' — whatever such vague formulation may mean — he also opposes in his peace plan a Palestinian state (see Chapter 32), his opposition being grounded in strategic considerations. As noted above, President Reagan considered Israel 'a strategic asset' and 'a barrier to Soviet expansionism' in the Middle East. 'It is foolhardy', he wrote, 'to risk weakening Israel, our most critical remaining ally, either through building the basis for a radical Palestinian state on her borders or through providing her with insufficient military assistance.'[10]

Voting with Israel at the UN General Assembly

US support for Israel has become almost a rule at the UN. In principle, any UN resolution which is opposed by Israel is automatically opposed by the US. Many General Assembly resolutions are adopted each year over the negative votes of Israel and the US. Thus the US government voted with Israel against resolutions of the General Assembly which, *inter alia*:

— recognised the rights of the people of Palestine to self-determination and sovereignty and their right to return to their homes;
— reaffirmed the inalienable rights of the people of Palestine;
— established a Special Committee to investigate Israel's violations of human rights in the occupied territories;
— declared that all measures taken by Israel to settle the occupied territories, including Jerusalem, are null and void;
— called upon Israel to rescind forthwith all measures violating the human rights of the population in the occupied territories;
— expressed grave concern at the violation in the occupied territories of the Geneva Convention of 1949 relating to the Protection of Civilian Persons in Time of War.

233

Moreover, in dozens of instances the US has been *alone* in voting with Israel against resolutions of the General Assembly adopted by the whole international community on the Palestine Question, thereby isolating itself politically from the whole world for the sake of Israel.

US vetoes in Security Council of resolutions that are critical of Israel or are not to its liking

A negative vote by the US does not prevent the adoption of a General Assembly resolution. The case, however, is different in the Security Council where a negative vote by a permanent member like the US defeats a decision or resolution and prevents its adoption.

For a long time the US government did not exercise the right of vetoing Security Council resolutions which condemned Israel's actions. In fact, it joined other members of the Security Council between 1948 and 1972 in condemning over forty Israeli attacks against the Arab States, Palestinian villages and refugee camps.[11] In addition, it concurred between 1968 and 1980 in nine Security Council resolutions which censured or condemned Israel for its actions in Jerusalem and the occupied territories.[12]

A change in US policy in this regard occurred in the early 1970s. On 10 September 1972 the US vetoed, as we have seen, a Security Council resolution that condemned massive Israeli reprisal raids after 'Munich' on Palestinian villages and refugee camps which killed hundreds of men, women and children (Chapter 19). This veto has since been followed by many others which defeated at the Security Council every resolution that is critical of Israel or is not to its liking. The vetoes exercised by the US in favour of Israel can be grouped into three categories:

(i) *Vetoes that defeated Security Council resolutions which provided for the establishment of a Palestinian state or the recognition of Palestinian national rights*

Thus the US vetoed on:

— 26 July 1973 a resolution which stressed respect for the rights and legitimate aspirations of the Palestinians.
— 26 January 1976 a resolution which recognized the right of the Palestinians to establish an independent state in Palestine.
— 29 June 1976 a resolution which affirmed the inalienable right

of the Palestinian people to self-determination, and their rights to return, to national independence and to sovereignty.

— 30 April 1980 a resolution which affirmed the right of the Palestinians to establish an independent state.

(ii) *Vetoes that defeated Security Council resolutions which condemned or censured Israel's illicit actions*

The US vetoed on:

— 10 September 1972 a resolution that condemned Israel's murderous raids on Palestinian refugee camps (as mentioned above).

— 8 December 1975 a resolution that condemned the bombings of Palestinian refugee camps.

— 25 March 1976 a resolution that censured Israel's actions in Jerusalem and the occupied territories.

— 2 April 1982 a resolution that condemned Israel's dismissal of two mayors in the West Bank.

— 9 June 1982 a resolution which condemned Israel for its aggression in Lebanon and called for an immediate cease-fire.

— 2 August 1982 a resolution that condemned attacks on civilians in Lebanon.

— 6 September 1984 and 12 March 1985 resolutions that condemned illicit measures taken by Israel against civilians in south Lebanon.

— 13 September 1985 a resolution that deplored the repressive measures taken by Israel against civilians in the West Bank and Gaza and called upon it to stop curfews, administrative detentions and deportations.

— 17 January 1986 a resolution which renewed the demand for withdrawal of Israeli troops from Lebanon and deplored Israeli acts of violence in south Lebanon.

— 30 January 1986 a resolution which strongly deplored provocative acts at the Mosque of Al-Aqsa.

— 6 February 1986 a Security Council resolution which strongly condemned Israel for an act of 'air piracy' in intercepting and forcing to land in Israel a Libyan civilian plane under the spurious pretext that it carried Palestinian 'terrorists'. In fact, the plane was carrying a Syrian political delegation from Tripoli to Damascus.

(iii) *Vetoes that defeated Security Council resolutions which imposed sanctions on Israel for illicit actions*

The US vetoed on

— 20 January 1982 a resolution that called for sanctions destined to reverse Israel's annexation of the Golan.

— 26 June 1982 a resolution calling for sanctions to ensure Israel's withdrawal from Lebanon.

— 6 August 1982 a resolution that called for an embargo on supplies of arms to Israel following its invasion of Lebanon.

The US vetoes at the Security Council have done much mischief in the Middle East. In the words of Rabbi Elmer Berger, they have given to Israel a 'blank check' to commit its aggressions — with American weapons. They have closed the door to the attainment by the Palestinians of their legitimate national rights by pacific means. They have encouraged Israel to continue its occupation of Palestinian and Arab territories thus foreclosing the restoration of justice and peace in the Middle East.

It is fitting to quote here the criticism made by the *New York Times* of the US veto on 26 July 1973 of a Security Council resolution because it referred, *inter alia*, to 'the rights and legitimate aspirations of the Palestinians':

It is also puzzling that the United States chose to echo Israel's objections to a passage in the resolution referring to the 'rights and legitimate aspirations of the Palestinians'. So long as this country — and Israel — refuse to recognize that the Palestinian people, central parties to this dispute since the original United Nations partition plan, also have rights and legitimate aspirations that must be taken into account, it is difficult to see how United States diplomacy can contribute to a lasting settlement.[13]

US abstentions at the Security Council

Another form of political support which the US extends to Israel at the Security Council that falls short of a veto is its 'abstention' from joining other member states in the condemnation of Israel. Unlike a veto, an abstention does not affect the adoption of the resolution but implies approval of the action condemned. A notable US abstention at the Security Council occurred on 1 September 1969 when, in connection with the arson committed at the Mosque of Al-Aqsa the Council condemned Israel's failure to comply with its resolutions. Again on 20 August 1980 the US abstained from Security Council resolution 478 which censured the enactment by Israel of a law proclaiming Jerusalem its eternal capital. Likewise, on 4 October 1985, the US abstained from a resolution adopted by all other members of the Security Council which condemned Israel's raid of 1 October 1985 on PLO headquarters at Tunis. So again, the US abstained on 23 September 1986 from a unanimous Security Council resolution calling for an end in southern Lebanon to any military presence which is not accepted by the Lebanese authorities. Israel, which occupies a so-called security zone in south Lebanon and maintains therein a mercenary army, rejected the resolution. So also on 8 December 1986 the Security Council deplored the shooting by the Israeli army of 'defenceless Palestinian students' (four of whom had been killed) during demonstrations against the closure of universities by the occupying authorities and urged Israel to abide by the 1949 Geneva Convention for the protection of civilians in time of war. All the members of the Security Council joined in the condemnation except the US which abstained. It is remarkable that Israel's Foreign Minister, Shimon Peres, *'deplored'* that the US failed to veto the resolution.

Exclusion of Israel from UN

The political support which the US extends to Israel includes its protection from exclusion under Article 6 of the UN Charter or from the rejection of the credentials of its representative for its violations of the Charter and UN resolutions. The rejection of credentials, as in the case of South Africa for reasons of apartheid, deprives such members of their seats at the General Assembly. In 1975, a movement developed among third world nations to seek the expulsion of Israel from the UN General Assembly or the rejection of the credentials of its representative on account of its continued occupation of Arab territories and its flouting of UN resolutions. This move was thwarted by the US which threatened to walk out of the UN if Israel were expelled or the credentials of its representative were not accepted.

The US has made the same threats in the case of Israel's exclusion from UN agencies. Following Israel's destruction of the nuclear reactor in Iraq in June 1981 for which it was condemned by the

Security Council on 19 June 1981, the International Atomic Energy Agency voted in 1982 to reject Israel's credentials and, as a gesture of disapproval, the US walked out of the Agency and suspended its payments to it. In September 1985, the US threatened to quit the International Atomic Energy Commission if a motion calling for sanctions against Israel were adopted. The US made similar threats in respect of the possible exclusion of Israel from the International Labour Organization and the International Telecommunications Union.

In further application of its unstinted political support of Israel, the US displays irritation over any discussion at international conferences of the Palestine Question or of the creation of a Palestinian state or the condemnation of Zionism.

ISRAEL'S INFLUENCE ON US POLICY AND ITS CONSEQUENCES

Israel's influence on US policy with respect to the Middle East and, in particular, the Palestine Question, is a recognized fact.[14] Lieutenant-General Burns, former Chief of Staff of the UN Truce Supervision Organization, wrote:

> The United States Jewish community, through its economic power especially as related to many media of mass information, under the leadership of the well-organized Zionist pressure groups, exerts an influence on US policy which goes far beyond what might be calculated from a counting of the so-called 'Jewish vote' . . . Thus the Jews of the United States determine the degree of political as well as financial support that Israel receives from the USA.[15]

Such influence is perceptible, particularly at the time of presidential elections when candidates vie with each other in making political promises to Israel on the Palestine Question, on Jerusalem, on Israeli 'security' in order to show who of them is Israel's greatest friend. Most members of Congress also court the Jewish vote and give Israel generous assurances regarding its security and their support. One example deserves mention. The American Israel Public Affairs Committee which acts as Israel's lobby published in 1974 in the press a letter signed by no less than 71 Senators and addressed to President Ford which urged 'support of Israel and rejection of the PLO'. Columnist William F. Buckley Jr, ironically commented on such letter in these terms:

> Two years ago I proposed that the US incorporate Israel as the 51st state of the union — which once and for all would have ended the problem of Israeli insecurity. The proposal, for some reason, was not seriously debated. The only argument I heard against it is that it would not be acceptable to the Israelis on the ground that they would then be represented by only two senators instead of 100. But surely they could be asked to make this sacrifice?[16]

In other terms, instead of Israel being a 'strategic asset', as President Reagan would like his countrymen to believe, Israel constitutes an 'electoral asset' for American politicians.

This, in short, has been US policy since the mid-1960s with regard to the Question of Palestine. Gone are the beautiful ideals of President Wilson about the self-determination of peoples and the inadmissibility of conquest by war. Gone is the urging of President Eisenhower to resolve the problems of the Middle East in conformity with justice and international law. Gone is President Jimmy Carter's insistence in 1977 on the need for the respect of ethical standards in US foreign policy. Moreover, if as President Reagan claims, Israel must be strengthened as a strategic asset against the Soviet Union and the creation of a Palestinian state should for that same reason be opposed, then it is obvious that the Palestinians and their national and human rights are sacrificed contrary to all moral and legal considerations. In the case of Palestine, therefore, the ethical and democratic principles which have characterized American policy in the past have been cast away as something that is worn out.

The US has replaced those principles by acquiescence in the wrongs committed by Israel since 1948 against the Palestinians although the latter never caused harm or showed hostility to the US or to American interests. On the contrary, the Palestinians were from the outset well disposed towards America to the extent that when consulted in 1919 by the King–Crane Commission sent by President Wilson to the Near East to investigate the wishes of the peoples detached from Turkey regarding the choice of a mandatory, the Palestinians, among others, indicated to the Commission that 'America was the first choice'. The Commission stated that 'they declared their choice was due to knowledge of America's record: the unselfish aims with which she had come into the war . . .'[17] Accordingly, it recommended that the USA be asked to undertake the mandate for Syria, including Palestine. Zionist intrigues, however, thwarted implementation of this recommendation and the Supreme Council of the Principal and Allied Powers decided in 1920 to entrust the Palestine mandate to Great Britain.

The generous patronage extended by the US government to Israel and the 'special relationship' that exists between them did not deter Israel from conducting espionage and other unlawful operations against its ally. In 1986, a member of an Israeli spy network, Jonathan Jay Pollard, a former US Navy counter-intelligence analyst, was charged with spying and pleaded guilty to participating in espionage operations directed by Israeli officials. It was reported that he gave to Israel more than 1,000 secret US documents, including aerial photographs, which helped it to bomb the head-quarters of the PLO in Tunis in 1985 causing the death of 70 persons. And to contradict Israel's allegation that it was not aware of his spying activities he informed the court before sentence that he was congratulated by 'the highest levels of the Israeli government' for the secret documents he turned over on 'their outer ring of enemies, namely Libya, Algeria, Iraq and Pakistan'. He was sentenced on 4 March 1987 to life imprisonment. The case was described as one of the most serious breaches of security in American history and caused friction between the US and Israel. But Israel sought to bury the affair. The Israeli Prime Minister shrugged it off as a 'rogue operation' unknown to the Israeli authorities. Then adding insult to injury, the Israeli government promoted the two Israeli officials who had supervised Pollard's spying activities. The Israeli actions offended American public opinion and, in particular, Jewish Americans because Pollard was himself a Jew. Columnist William Safire wrote in the *New York Times* (12 March 1987): 'Most of us were offended as Americans at seeing our foreign aid dollars used to buy US secrets . . . The Israelis invite . . . a slash in foreign economic aid . . . (which) is likely to be proposed.'

Moreover, Israel came under investigation for illegally attempt-ing to acquire US machinery to manufacture cluster bombs after their shipment to Israel was halted by the US administration follow-ing their use during Israel's invasion of Lebanon in 1982 in violation of the terms under which the US made them available to Israel. The US authorities also discovered in 1985 a plot for smuggling to Israel high-speed electronic switches, known as krytons, that act as triggers for nuclear weapons. The Justice Department's probes into Israeli activities of spying and smuggling have brought it into conflict with the State Department which is subject to the influence of the Israeli lobby and desires to show leniency towards Israel's violations of US law. Moreover, those probes caused great displeasure in Israel because they represented a distressing change of attitude on the part of its 'ally'. As noted by *Newsweek* (21 July 1986):

> Over the years, the Israelis have used daring — and sometimes unscrupulous — means to obtain whatever they thought they needed to ensure their own survival. In the late 1940s and 50s, they smuggled quantities of surplus World War II equipment under the noses of US authorities. Later they allegedly did the same with US nuclear materials. Sometimes they were caught in the act, but usually the administration quietly looked the other way.

These Israeli activities do not seem to have shaken the 'special relationship' that existed between the US and Israel before the Pollard and Iranian arms scandals. In its annual report on US-Israeli relations submitted to its members on 6 April 1986, the American Israel Public Affairs Committee, which acts as Israel's lobby, stated:

> We are in a midst of a revolution that is raising US-Israel relations to new heights . . . Gone are the days when some US officials considered Israel a liability and a hindrance to America's relationship with the Arab world . . . Gone, too, is the dark period during 1982 and 1983, when Israel's invasion of Lebanon strained the longstanding special relationship that goes back to Israel's founding in 1948.

Apart from not serving the cause of peace and justice, it is doubtful that present American policy serves American interests in the Middle East. *The Economist* (25 July 1981) wrote:

> Mr Menachem Begin, Israel's Prime Minister, is using American money and America's arms to do things that are contrary to America's interests. There is no reason why this should be tolerated by President Reagan. Those Americans who have slipped into the habit of defending Israel-right-or-wrong are performing a disservice to their own country and not, in the slightly longer run, helping Israel either.

241

Ironically, American policy in regard to the Palestine Question and its support of Israel are not serving even the beneficiary of such policy. Nahum Goldmann, former President of the World Zionist Organization, wrote:

> I have maintained for years that America, by its reluctance to influence Israel and through having given in to too many Israeli demands — for instance, with regard to the Jarring mission, the Rogers Plan, etc. — not only failed to help Israel but harmed it in the long run.[18]

The conclusion is clear: the misguided US patronage of Israel has caused great harm not only to the Palestinians, but also to America itself, to Israel and to the cause of peace.

NOTES

1. James G. McDonald, *My Mission to Israel* (Simon and Schuster, New York, 1951), pp. 181–2.

2. Address of President Eisenhower on the situation in the Middle East, 20 February 1957, 36 Dept. State Bulletin, 387–91 (11 March 1957) and *The Arab-Israeli Conflict* (Princeton University Press, New Jersey, 1974), vol. III, pp. 64–8.

3. Kennett Love, *Suez* (McGraw-Hill, New York, 1969), p. 685.

4. George W. Ball, *Error and Betrayal in Lebanon* (Foundation for Middle East Peace, Washington, DC, 1984), pp. 93–4.

5. *Ibid.*, p. 95.

6. *Ibid.*, p. 118.

7. *Ibid.*, p. 81.

8. Ronald Reagan, *International Herald Tribune*, 17 August 1979.

9. President Carter's admission that his religious biblical belief has influenced his policy is a reminder of the influence exercised by American evangelists on US policy in favour of Israel. On the role played by American evangelists in this regard, see Ruth W. Moly, *The Evangelical Dimension* (National Council on US-Arab Relations, Washington, DC), Occasional Paper Series: Number 3; and Grace Halsell, *Prophecy and Politics*, Lawrence Hill, Westport, Conn., 1986.

10. *International Herald Tribune*, 17 August 1979.

11. See Henry Cattan, *Palestine and International Law*, 2nd edn (Longman, London, 1976), pp. 156–8.

12. See Henry Cattan, *Jerusalem* (Croom Helm, London, 1981), pp. 124–5.

13. See *International Herald Tribune*, 30 July 1973.

14. On the question of Zionist influence on US policy with regard to Israel, see R.P. Stevens, *American Zionism and US Foreign Policy*

1942–1947 (Pageant, New York, 1962); Harry N. Howard, 'The United States and Israel: Conflicts of Interest and Policy', *Issues* (Summer 1964), pp. 14 *et seq*; Paul Findley, *They Dare to Speak Out: The Struggle Against the Zionist Lobby in the USA* (Lawrence Hill, Westport, Conn., 1985).

15. E.L.M. Burns, *Between Israeli and Arab* (Harrap, London, 1962), p. 288.

16. *International Herald Tribune*, 29 September 1977.

17. *The Arab-Israeli Conflict*, ed. John Norton Moore, *op. cit,* vol. III, 1974, p. 60.

18. Nahum Goldmann, 'Zionist Ideology and the Reality of Israel', *Foreign Affairs* (Fall 1978), p. 81.

Part III

The Problem of Jerusalem

28

Jerusalem Before the Emergence of Israel

THE FOUNDING OF JERUSALEM

Jerusalem is one of the oldest cities in the world. According to Josephus who wrote in the first century of our era, it was founded by the Canaanites. Josephus wrote:

> But he who first built it [Jerusalem] was a potent man among the Canaanites, and is in our tongue called Melchisedek, *The Righteous King*, for such he really was; on which account he was (there) the first priest of God, and first built a temple (there), and called the city Jerusalem, which was formerly called Salem.[1]

As Melchisedek was a contemporary of Abraham (Genesis 14:18), this would date the founding of Jerusalem in the eighteenth century BC. Hence, the city was in existence several centuries before the arrival of the Israelites in the land of Canaan. In fact, the *Jewish Encyclopedia* mentions that in Hebrew annals 'Jerusalem is expressly called a "foreign city" not belonging to the Israelites (Judges 19:12), and the Jebusites are said to have lived there for very many years together with the Benjamites.'[2]

Jerusalem was inhabited by the Jebusites, a Canaanite subgroup. It was one of the oldest and most illustrious royal cities in the land of Canaan and for some 800 years it remained a Canaanite city. Around 1000 BC it was captured by David. It should be noted, however, that when David captured the city, he did not displace its original inhabitants allowing them to remain in their city, but not in the fortress.[3] The continued existence of the Canaanites in Jerusalem, which became the capital of the new Jewish kingdom that was established by David, is confirmed by the Bible which refers to the people whom Israel was not able to destroy and upon whom David's son, Solomon, levied a tribute of bondservice (1 Kings 9:20–1).

It is necessary to stress the fact that Jerusalem was founded by the Canaanites and inhabited by them for several centuries, long before its capture by David, because some present-day Israeli politicians falsely claim that it was founded by the Jews. Thus at the time of the capture of the Old City of Jerusalem in June 1967, Ygal Allon, then Israel's Deputy Prime Minister, was reported by the press to have said: 'The world must reconcile itself to the fact that the city has at last returned to the nation that founded it and turned it into a Holy City' when, in fact, Jerusalem existed as a Canaanite sacred city for several hundred years before the Israelites set foot in Palestine.

JERUSALEM, AN ARAB CITY FOR 18 CENTURIES

The history of Jerusalem is linked with the history of Palestine which was briefly reviewed in Chapter 1. A chronology of the city is given in Appendix VII. As we have seen, many nations ruled Jerusalem but its demography did not always follow its political rule. The Assyrians, the Egyptians, the Babylonians, the Persians, the Romans, the Greeks, the Moslem Arabs, the Crusaders, the Turks and the British ruled Jerusalem, at one time or another, but none of those peoples implanted themselves in the city or became part of its traditional population. Only three peoples have through the ages constituted the population of Jerusalem. These are the Canaanites, the Jews and the Palestinian Arabs.

Contrary to a common error, as explained in Chapter 1, the Canaanites and the Jews cohabited peacefully together until the massacre and deportation of the Jews by the Romans, first in AD 70 and finally in AD 132–135.

The Palestinian Arabs, descendants of the Canaanites and the Philistines (Chapter 1), remained and constituted the main element of the population of Jerusalem from the second until the twentieth centuries. They survived all subsequent conquests, massacres and vicissitudes. More than once, they changed their religion, adopting the religion of the conquerors. Pagans originally, they were converted to Christianity and many, though not all, accepted Islam after the Moslem Arab conquest of Jerusalem in the seventh century. Until the nineteenth century, the Palestinian Arabs were practically the only inhabitants of Jerusalem. For eighteen centuries, Jerusalem was essentially and fundamentally an Arab city. As previously mentioned in Chapter 1, neither the Moslem conquest of Palestine in the seventh century, nor the Turkish conquest in the sixteenth century, involved any demographic change or colonization by the conquerors. The latter were in small numbers and were interested solely in establishing their dominion over the conquered population.

As for the Jews, they completely disappeared from Jerusalem after their deportation by the Romans. Following their first revolt, in AD 66–70, Titus destroyed Jerusalem and the Temple. After its destruction in AD 70, Jerusalem 'never again revived as a Jewish city'.[4] After their second revolt, in AD 132–135, the Jews were either killed or sold into slavery and dispersed to the far corners of the Roman Empire. When Jerusalem was rebuilt after AD 135 by the Roman Emperor Hadrian, it was given the name of Aelia Capitolina and a decree was issued which prohibited under penalty of death the presence of Jews in the city. The prohibition of the presence of Jews in Jerusalem was continued for several centuries until it was lifted by the Arabs after the Moslem Arab conquest. As from Hadrian's time until the reign of Constantine in the fourth century, the population of Jerusalem consisted only of Christians and pagans, the latter worshipping Roman deities and idols. As from the reign of Constantine who made Christianity the religion of his empire, no pagans were left in Jerusalem which became a wholly Christian city.

It may be observed that despite the abrogation by the Arabs of Hadrian's prohibition of the presence of Jews in Jerusalem, very few Jews lived in the city. M. Franco, who made a special study of the position of the Jews in the Ottoman Empire, mentions that the famous Spanish traveller Benjamin of Tudela found two hundred Jews in Jerusalem in the year AD 1173. M. Franco observes that, apparently, the Jews who lived at the time that Benjamin of Tudela visited the city were expelled, for in AD 1180 another traveller, Petahia of Ratisbon, found in Jerusalem one co-religionist only. In AD 1267, a Spanish rabbi, Moïse Ben Nahman, found two Jewish families in Jerusalem.[5]

During the following centuries there was a trickle of Jews into Palestine. In consequence of their persecution in Western Europe and their expulsion from Spain (1492) and Portugal (1496), some of them sought refuge in Palestine and in other Mediterranean countries. As a result, a small number of Jews came to live in Jerusalem. According to Rappoport, there were 70 Jewish families in Jerusalem in 1488, 200 families in 1495 and 1,500 families in 1521.[6]

Again after the Russian pogroms of 1881–82, a number of Jews emigrated to Palestine and settled in Tiberias, Safad and Jerusalem. At the end of the First World War, in 1917, the Jewish population of Jerusalem numbered 30,000. The Arab character of Jerusalem was not affected by the small number of Jews who had emigrated to Palestine during Turkish times, in particular, in the nineteenth century. In fact, many of them were Arabized in language and lived on good terms with the Palestinian Arabs, Moslem and Christian.

However, the Arab character of Jerusalem began to change during the British mandate (1922–48) when a massive Jewish immigration into Palestine was permitted by the British government in implementation of the Balfour Declaration and against the will of the original inhabitants. As a result, the Jewish population of Jerusalem tripled, rising from 30,000 in 1917 to 99,690 in 1946 as compared with 105,540 Moslems and Christians.[7] In consequence, Jerusalem became at the termination of the British mandate a city with a mixed population which comprised an almost equal number of Arabs and Jews. This situation, however, was to change radically after the emergence of Israel in 1948 and its resort to a racist demographic policy as we shall see in the following chapter.

NOTES

1. Josephus Flavius, *The Great Roman-Jewish War AD 66–70* (Gloucester, Mass., 1970), p. 250.

2. *The Jewish Encyclopedia*, vol. VII, p. 120.

3. Henrich Graetz, *History of the Jews* (Elek Books, London, 1958), vol. I, p. 55.

4. Albert Hyamson, *Palestine Old and New*, p. 83.

5. M. Franco, *Histoire des Israélites de l'Empire Ottoman* (Durlacher, Paris, 1897), pp. 4, 5.

6. A.S. Rappoport, *Histoire de la Palestine* (Payot, Paris, 1932), p. 210.

7. Official Records of the 2nd session of the General Assembly, Ad Hoc Committee on the Palestine Question, p. 304.

29

Israel's Illicit Actions in Jerusalem since 1948

After its emergence in 1948 Israel reversed 1800 years of history, usurped Jerusalem and transformed it from an Arab into a Jewish city, in violation of international law, UN resolutions and the rights of its original inhabitants. Israeli aggressions against Islamic and Christian Holy Places and their implications for world peace will be discussed in the following chapter.

USURPATION OF JERUSALEM

Israel has unlawfully usurped Jerusalem. Regardless of whether Jerusalem is considered to be the capital of Palestine and hence falls under Palestinian sovereignty, or whether Jerusalem is considered to be a territory which, under General Assembly resolution 181 of 29 November 1947, is subject to an international régime to be administered by the UN, in either case the Jewish state possessed no right to seize, occupy and annex the city. The usurpation of Jerusalem was carried out in two stages.

In a first stage, in 1948, Israel seized and annexed Modern Jerusalem or the New City and its western environs. Modern Jerusalem is partly Jewish and partly Arab. In 1948 the majority of the Palestine Arab population of Jerusalem — Christian and Moslem — lived in 15 residential quarters in Modern Jerusalem and owned most of its lands and buildings. Arab residential quarters in Modern Jerusalem were completely undefended and 13 of them were then occupied by Israeli forces with almost no opposition. Hence, it is an error to imagine that in 1948 the Jews seized the Jewish section of Jerusalem while the Arabs seized its Arab part.

After the Jews overran the Arab quarters of Modern Jerusalem they attacked the Old City and attempted to take it by storm. Between 14 and 18 May 1948 the Palestinians defended the Old City and repelled Jewish attacks thanks to their courage and the massive walls built around it in the sixteenth century by Suleiman the Magnificent, the Sultan of Turkey. On 19 May Jordan's regular army, called the Arab Legion, came to their assistance and occupied the Old City.

The Old City remained in the hands of Jordan until 1967. In the first two days of the war which Israel launched on 5 June of that year against Jordan, Egypt and Syria, it captured the Old City and annexed it three weeks later as explained in Chapter 17. Then on 30 July 1980, in defiance of world opinion, Israel enacted a law which proclaimed Jerusalem its 'eternal capital'. On 20 August 1980 the Security Council censured in the strongest terms Israel's action by 14 votes to 0 (with the US abstaining), declared the Israeli law invalid and called upon those states that had established diplomatic missions in Jerusalem to withdraw them from the city.

EVICTION OF THE PALESTINIAN INHABITANTS

Israel's objective in 1948 was not simply to seize Jerusalem, but to seize it without its Arab inhabitants. To achieve this objective Jewish terrorist organizations perpetrated several outrageous deeds against the Arab inhabitants. The most notorious of those deeds (described in Chapter 7) was the massacre on 9 April 1948 of Deir Yassin, a peaceful and undefended Arab village which lies one and a half miles to the west of Jerusalem where 300 men, women and children, defenceless and unarmed, were savagely slaughtered. The purpose of the massacre was to spread terror among the Palestinians and to force them to flee. And to make sure that the massacre had its intended effect, the few survivors, including some women, were paraded by Irgun forces as war trophies in three trucks in the streets of Jerusalem. Terrorized by the Deir Yassin massacre, the Arab inhabitants of Modern Jerusalem estimated in 1945 to number 24,000 Christians and 21,000 Moslems (UN Document A/1286) fled or were killed when Jewish forces attacked Jerusalem in May 1948. As a result, Jewish forces occupied Modern Jerusalem empty of its inhabitants.

Likewise, upon its seizure of the Old City in 1967 Israel repeated its attempt to force the Arab inhabitants by threats and intimidation to evacuate the city. Immediately after their occupation of the Old

City Israeli troops ordered the inhabitants on loudspeakers to leave and seek refuge in Jordan 'while the road was still open'. The number of Palestinians who were displaced in 1967 from their homes in Jerusalem has not been determined with precision. Estimates of the number vary from 7,000 according to the International Red Cross to 30,000 according to other sources.

It was noted in Chapter 17 that, as a result of international pressure, Israel made a token gesture for the repatriation of refugees of the 1967 War. In this token gesture, Israel repatriated 14,000 but at the same time it expelled 17,000. What is noteworthy is that Israel deliberately excluded from its token repatriation those refugees whose homes were in Jerusalem. This significant fact was brought to light by John H. Davis, Commissioner-General of UNRWA (UN Relief and Works Agency for Palestine Refugees) who reported: 'Among those permitted to return, it appears that there were very few former inhabitants of the Old City of Jerusalem' (UN Document A/6713, p. 4). The reason for this veto on the return of the inhabitants of Jerusalem is obvious: the return of the original inhabitants does not fit into the Israeli scheme of judaization of the city.

PLUNDER OF ARAB REFUGEE PROPERTY

The Arab refugees from Jerusalem, like other Palestinian refugees, were despoiled in 1948 of all their property, movable or immovable. It was a massive plunder. All Arab homes and their contents, lands, businesses in Modern Jerusalem were confiscated under the Absentee Property legislation of 1948 and 1950 as explained in Chapter 12. The magnitude of this plunder can be appreciated when it is realized that the Palestinians owned 40 per cent of Modern Jerusalem as compared with 26.12 per cent owned by the Jews. The rest belonged to Christian religious communities, the government, municipality, roads and railways.[1] In other words, some 10,000 Palestinian homes were plundered and confiscated by Israel in Modern Jerusalem in 1948.

JUDAIZATION OF THE POPULATION

During many centuries, as we have seen in the preceding chapter, the population of Jerusalem was almost exclusively Arab. The opening of the gates of Palestine to Jewish immigration during the British mandate substantially increased the number of the Jewish inhabitants in Jerusalem and changed the traditional Arab character of the city.

After the emergence of the state of Israel, the change of demography of Jerusalem was carried out in a more radical manner. In addition to the eviction of the Palestinians and to barring their repatriation, Israel enacted in 1950 the *Law of Return* which granted to every Jew in the world potential citizenship, the right of residence and automatic acquisition of nationality on arrival in Israel. As a result of those measures about 94,000 Jewish immigrants were settled in Modern Jerusalem after 1948, and over 60,000 were settled in the Old City and its environs after 1967. Hence, the Jewish population of Jerusalem has risen from 99,690 in 1946 to 330,000 in 1987, compared with 100,000 Palestinian Arabs presently residing in the city.

The figure of 100,000 Palestinian Arabs includes 10,000 Christian Arabs. Such a small figure of the number of Christians is striking since it means that the number of Christian Arabs in Jerusalem — who form the earliest and oldest Christian community in the world — which stood in 1948 at 25 per cent of the total population of Jerusalem has now dropped to 2.5 per cent of such total. Hence, one of the results of the judaization of the population of Jerusalem has been the de-Christianization of the city.

There exists another striking aspect of the racist policy pursued by Israel in Jerusalem. Not only does Israel bar the return of the Palestinians to their own homes in Jerusalem while it welcomes with open arms any foreign Jew to come and settle in the city, it denies to the Arabs generally, whether Palestinian or not, the right to come and reside in Jerusalem. This prohibition applies even in the case of a Palestinian resident in Jerusalem who marries a non-resident Arab. Such a resident cannot bring his or her spouse to come and reside with him or her in Jerusalem and he or she must in such event emigrate out of Jerusalem to live with his or her spouse.

COLONIZATION OF THE CITY AND ITS ENVIRONS

Immediately following the occupation in 1948 of Modern Jerusalem and the western part of the *corpus separatum* of the city of Jerusalem, as delimited by the UN, Israel undertook a massive colonization of those areas without the least regard to the rights of their Arab owners or to the international régime prescribed by the UN for the city of Jerusalem. All Arab homes and lands in Modern Jerusalem were, as we have seen, confiscated. Outside Modern Jerusalem, Arab villages were destroyed and their lands confiscated for building settlements. The Knesset (Israel's legislative chamber) itself was erected on confiscated Arab land.

Again in 1967, after the capture of the Old City, Israel undertook a massive colonization in and around Jerusalem. Land was expropriated and the owners refused the derisory compensation offered to them. In the case of Christian religious institutions which own considerable urban areas in Jerusalem, the Israeli authorities were able through pressures or greed of the institutions to acquire from them a number of important lands and buildings, such as the Russian compound (*Al Mascobia*) which includes several important buildings in the centre of Jerusalem (the law courts, the government hospital, the prison and police headquarters), Schneller's orphanage, Fast Hotel and the lands of the Orthodox Convent of the Cross.

On 22 March 1978 the Security Council appointed a Commission to examine the situation relating to settlements in the territories occupied since 1967, including Jerusalem (Chapter 25). In its report dated 12 July 1979 (S/13450) the Commission stated that 13 settlements were established in and around Jerusalem and that in the Old City 320 housing units were established for Jews, 160 Arab houses were destroyed, 600 houses expropriated and 6,500 Arab residents evicted. It is estimated as a result of expropriations, confiscations and expulsions of Palestinians in the Old City the old Jewish quarter has grown to four times its size.

The settlements and fortress-like apartment buildings reserved for habitation by Jews which have been built since 1948 and now encircle Jerusalem have disfigured the Holy City. Condemning such disfigurement the former Archbishop of Canterbury, the Right Reverend Michael Ramsey said:

It is distressing indeed that the building programme of the present authorities is disfiguring the city and its surroundings in ways which wound the feelings of those who care for its historic beauty and suggest an insensitive attempt to proclaim as an Israeli city one which can never be other than the city of three great religions and their peoples.[2]

DEMOLITIONS AND EXCAVATIONS

During the first week of their occupation of the Old City, the Israelis razed to the ground the historic Mughrabi quarter which dated back to AD 1320, destroying, in the words of journalist David Hirst, 'seven hundred years of Muslim history' in order to make a parking lot in front of the Wailing Wall. Similarly, a large area of the historic cemetery of Mamillah which contained the tombs of many famous or pious Moslems was bulldozed and converted into a car park. Ambassador Thalmann, representative of the UN Secretary-General, mentions that the dynamiting and bulldozing of 135 houses in the Mughrabi quarter involved the expulsion of 650 poor and pious Moslems from their homes.[3] There was also a number of other demolitions of Arab-owned buildings in and around the Old City.[4]

In addition to demolitions, in an attempt to search for ancient Jewish vestiges, the Israeli authorities undertook extensive excavations in the vicinity of and underneath the *Haram Al-Sharif*.[5] As these acts endangered Moslem Holy Places, vigorous protests were made by the Moslems. In several resolutions, the General Assembly and the Security Council censured Israel for its archaeological excavations and appealed to it — without avail — to preserve the historical and religious heritage in the city. Similarly, the UN Educational, Scientific and Cultural Organization (UNESCO) showed great concern over Israel's actions in Jerusalem. Since 1968 UNESCO has repeatedly called on Israel to desist from its excavations in Jerusalem and from the alteration of its features or its cultural and historical character, but again without avail. Since 1974 UNESCO has repeatedly condemned Israel's persistence in altering the historical features of Jerusalem.

The damage done to the historical and religious heritage in Jerusalem by Israel's destructions and excavations in the Old City was described by Mr René Maheu, former Director-General of UNESCO, in these terms:

> Between the summer of 1967 and the summer of 1969 the western side of the sacred enclosure (*Haram Al-Sharif*) called the Wailing Wall, was cleared over a distance of 140 metres, and a vast esplanade was opened in front of the Wall by destroying a medieval quarter which formed part of the traditional urban structure of the Old City. Besides, this quarter contained some buildings of architectural value or of undoubted cultural character . . .

The works undertaken on this site of the Old City have robbed it of its picturesqueness and have given it the appearance of a gaping wound in the flesh of the City . . . Again in order to clear the sacred enclosure, tunnels were dug in 1970–1971 over a distance of 215 metres. But certain movements of the earth above these tunnels were observed which are likely to put in danger the buildings in the quarter overhead . . . Beyond these particular aspects, the greater danger which threatens Jerusalem in its entirety is an erratic urbanization of a modern style like that which has disfigured so many ancient cities in various countries . . . The alterations that have occurred since 1967 in the sites and the appearance of the City are very grave. If such evolution were to be pursued, the personality of Jerusalem, its unique charm, the extraordinary physical radiance of its spirituality, would be doomed within a short time.[6]

Israeli excavations under and in the vicinity of the *Haram Al-Sharif* area have continued until today (UNESCO Doc. 23/C15 of 9 August 1985). In its resolution 11.3 adopted at its General Conference at Sofia (8 October–9 November 1985) UNESCO deplored that the works carried out in the Old City by Israel have put in peril important historical monuments. The present length of the tunnel (in 1985) has reached 305 metres.

NULLITY AND UN CONDEMNATIONS OF ISRAEL'S ILLICIT ACTIONS IN JERUSALEM

Israel's actions in Jerusalem are null and void, both under international law and UN resolutions. It is obvious that in accordance with international law, Israel is a military occupier of Jerusalem, whether of Modern Jerusalem or its Old City. In accordance with the universally recognized principle of the inadmissibility of acquisition of territory by war Israel has not acquired, nor could it acquire, sovereignty over Jerusalem. Its usurpation of Jerusalem, regardless of its duration, gives it no title nor any right to continue in occupation of the city. Likewise, Israel's actions in Jerusalem are null and void under UN resolutions.

In this regard, a difference may be observed between UN resolutions adopted with regard to Jerusalem before and after 1967. The former dealt with the *corpus separatum* of Jerusalem as defined by the General Assembly in 1947 while the latter dealt with the Old City

257

and adjoining territory seized in 1967. The most relevant resolution adopted before 1967 was General Assembly resolution 181 of 29 November 1947 which recognized an international régime for the City of Jerusalem. This resolution was reaffirmed by resolutions 194 of 11 December 1948 and 303 of 9 December 1949. It is significant that such reaffirmation was made *after* the occupation of Modern Jerusalem by Israel and of the Old City by Jordan and despite their rejection of the international régime for the City of Jerusalem. Only *de facto* recognition of such occupation was granted to the occupying powers by third states. The reason for not according *de jure* recognition was based upon the recognition of the international status for the *corpus separatum* of Jerusalem by a UN resolution which is still valid and operative. One consequence of such non-recognition was the refusal of most states to establish their diplomatic missions in Jerusalem.

Since 1967 UN resolutions have dealt specifically with the Old City. The UN has:

(1) affirmed 'the legal status' of Jerusalem;
(2) condemned or censured Israel's actions in Jerusalem and proclaimed the nullity of all legislative and administrative measures taken to change the status and historic character of the city, including expropriations of land and properties and transfer of populations;
(3) called upon Israel:
    (a) to withdraw from the territories occupied in 1967 which include the Old City of Jerusalem;
    (b) to rescind all measures taken to change the legal status, geography and demographic composition of Jerusalem;
    (c) to permit the return of the Palestine refugees displaced in 1967;
    (d) to dismantle and cease the establishment of settlements in the occupied territories, including Jerusalem.[7]

No distinction in nullity of Israeli actions in Old City and in Modern Jerusalem

Although UN resolutions have emphasized since 1967 the illegality and nullity of Israeli actions in the Old City of Jerusalem, this does not mean that similar Israeli acts in Modern Jerusalem are any less tainted with illegality and nullity. Whether it be the usurpation of

Modern Jerusalem, or the expulsion of its inhabitants, or the confiscation of Arab property, or the transfer of Jews to the city, all those acts are illegal and null and void both under international law and UN resolutions.

NOTES

1. Sami Hadawi, *Palestine, Loss of a Heritage* (Naylor, San Antonio, Texas, 1963), p. 141.

2. *Diocesan Newsletter*, January 1971.

3. UN Doc. 6793, p. 21.

4. See the various complaints made by Jordan to the Security Council, and in particular, UN Docs. S/9001, S/9197, S/9284 and S/10882.

5. Rouhi Al-Khatib, *The Judaization of Jerusalem* (Research Centre, Beirut, 1972), pp. 19–20. See also Jordan's complaints to the UN concerning excavations in UN Docs. S/10169, S/10882 and S/11246.

6. Translation from *Le Monde*, 21 November 1974.

7. For the text of the principal UN resolutions on Jerusalem, see Henry Cattan, *Jerusalem* (Croom Helm, London, 1981), pp. 160–220.

30

Perils to Jerusalem and its Holy Places

RELIGIOUS SIGNIFICANCE OF JERUSALEM

Jerusalem is unique among all the cities of the world because of its association with three great religions. It is the spiritual and religious heritage to one half of humanity and is holy to one thousand million Christians, to eight hundred million Moslems and to fourteen million Jews.

Jerusalem is the birthplace of Christianity. All the Holy Places, sacred shrines and sanctuaries connected with the birth, life and death of Christ are found in Jerusalem and in nearby Bethlehem: the Holy Sepulchre, the Via Dolorosa, the Church of the Nativity, the Cenacle, the Garden of Gethsemane, the Mount of Olives and 38 churches.

Jerusalem is also holy for Islam:

> All Islamic traditions and sacred writings point to the unmistakable fact that Jerusalem is holy for all Moslems, second only in holiness to Mecca and Medina. It is the *qibla* (direction of prayer) and the third of the sacred cities.[1]

The name of Jerusalem in Arabic is *Al Qods*, which means 'The Holy'. On the site of the *Haram Al-Sharif* (sacred enclosure) in the Old City of Jerusalem stand two famous Islamic sanctuaries: the Mosque of the Dome of the Rock (commonly but erroneously called the Mosque of Omar) and the Mosque of Al-Aqsa. The first was built in the seventh century and is associated by Islamic tradition with the intended sacrifice of Isaac by Abraham. The second, meaning 'the farthest', was built in the eighth century on the place from which, in accordance with Islamic tradition, the Prophet ascended to Heaven during his Night Journey. It is mentioned in the *Qur'an* (surah xvii:1) as 'the farthest Mosque'.

To Judaism, Jerusalem has been a holy city since the building of the Temple of Solomon. This temple, completed in 962 BC, was destroyed by the Babylonians in 587 BC. A second temple of a humble character was built around 515 BC after the return of the Jews from captivity but was again destroyed by the Macedonians in 170 BC. It was reconstructed in Herod's time only to be destroyed for a third time by the Romans following the Jewish insurrection in AD 70. Today the most important Jewish sanctuary in Jerusalem is the Wailing Wall which the Jews consider to be a remnant of the western wall of Herod's temple.

The significance of Jerusalem, however, does not lie merely in the Holy Places and sanctuaries of the three monotheistic religions as all three have a vital interest in preserving the living presence of the adherents to their faith in the Holy City.

Jerusalem has been the scene of many dramatic events and the cause of many wars during the 38 centuries of its known existence. It has suffered more than 20 sieges, changed hands more than 25 times, was destroyed 17 times, and its inhabitants were massacred on several occasions. The last act in the drama of Jerusalem occurred in our lifetime: it was seized and annexed by the State of Israel which, as we have seen, has displaced most of its original Arab inhabitants. Israel's usurpation of Jerusalem has created an explosive conflict of world importance which has engaged the attention of the UN for more than three decades and was the subject of scores of decisions and resolutions of the international organization which have remained without implementation.

DESIGNS ON ISLAMIC AND CHRISTIAN HOLY PLACES

Intoxicated by their capture of the Old City in 1967, some prominent officers of the government of Israel caused world concern by asserting claims against Islamic Holy Places in Jerusalem and Hebron. Ambassador E. Thalmann of Switzerland, charged by the Secretary-General of the UN with a fact-finding mission on the situation in Jerusalem, reported: 'Statements by Israel official representatives and Jewish personalities concerning Jewish claims and plans in the Temple area had an alarming effect.'[2] The Israeli Minister for Religious Affairs was reported to have declared at a press conference at Jerusalem on 12 August 1967 that the authorities considered

261

the site of the Mosque of the Dome of the Rock as their property 'by past acquisition or by conquest'[3] and that there was question of rebuilding the Temple of Solomon in the area of the *Haram Al-Sharif*. He was also reported to have said:

> As to the Holy Ibrahimi Mosque, the Cave is a Jewish shrine which we have bought, in the same way that we bought the Holy Rock in the days of David and the Jebusites and our rights in the Cave and the Rock are rights of conquest and acquisition.[4]

The matter did not rest at ominous threats but soon evolved into provocative acts. Ambassador Thalmann reported:

> Most of the Arabs interviewed by the Personal Representative stated that the Moslem population was shocked by Israeli acts which violated the sanctity of the Moslem shrines. It was regarded as a particular provocation that the Chief Rabbi of the Israeli Army, with others of his faith, conducted prayers in the area of the *Haram Al-Sharif*.[5]

AGGRESSIONS AGAINST ISLAMIC AND CHRISTIAN HOLY PLACES

An outrage which shocked world opinion and was strongly condemned by the Security Council was the arson committed on 21 August 1969 at the Mosque of Al-Aqsa. The culprit told the authorities that his purpose was to burn the mosque so that the Temple of Solomon could be built on its site. Extensive damage was caused to the roof of the mosque and a historic twelfth century carved wooden pulpit was gutted by the fire. The culprit, an Australian, was deported on the plea that he was mentally deranged.

Christian Holy Places also were not spared and there were desecrations of shrines and cemeteries on Mount Zion. More recently Christian clergymen were harassed and church property in Jerusalem was vandalised in a series of attacks on Baptists, Roman Catholics and Orthodox.[6] 'It is a Jewish obligation to destroy graven images. The Christians have no place in Jerusalem, which is the Jewish capital', declared one of those detained for vandalism at Christian sites.[7]

Aggressions against Islamic and Christian Holy Places have increased in the last few years. Among the most serious mention may be made of the arrest of two Israeli soldiers in possession of explosives in 1980 in the Old City who were charged by the authorities with the intention of blowing up churches and mosques in Jerusalem; the shooting by an Israeli soldier in April 1982 of worshippers at the Mosque of the Dome of the Rock and the planting of explosives in various churches, convents and mosques during 1983. The most odious outrage, and the most dangerous in its sequels had it succeeded, was the attempt made during the night of 26/27 January 1984 to blow up the Mosques of the Dome of the Rock and of Al-Aqsa. The attempt was foiled by the Moslem guards of the mosques. A quantity of arms and explosives stolen from the army were found on the site.

In May 1984 27 Jewish terrorists who belonged to the Gush Emunim, an extremist settler group, were arrested and indicted with several crimes, including the plot to blow up the two mosques. The police investigation yielded the information that the terrorists had also planned to bomb the mosques from a helicopter but abandoned the idea for fear that they might damage the Wailing Wall. The crimes for which the accused were charged included the attempt in 1980 to assassinate three Palestinian West Bank mayors, two of whom were maimed; the murder in 1983 of three Arab students in Hebron University; the planting of bombs in 1984 at the mosque in Hebron; and conspiracy to blow up the two mosques in January 1984 in Jerusalem. Two of the accused pleaded guilty to conspiracy to blow up the two mosques and were sentenced to five and ten years. On 22 July 1985 the District Court of Jerusalem convicted three Jewish settlers and sentenced them to life imprisonment for murdering Arabs and sentenced eleven others to terms of imprisonment that varied from three to seven years. The accused were confident that they would be set free, if not by a court decision, then by a pardon. 'We were acting in the interests of the state' they frequently repeated during their trial. And their principal defence argument was that Shin Bet (the Israeli secret service) knew and approved of their attitudes.[8] During their detention before the trial, the accused enjoyed preferential treatment as well as moral encouragement and financial backing from a section of the population. Several highly placed politicians assured the convicted prisoners of an early reprieve. In fact, at the time of writing, most of them have been reprieved and released.

Israeli designs on the *Haram Al-Sharif* area did not cease with the condemnation of the assailants in the 1984 outrage. During a visit to the Al-Aqsa Mosque in January 1986 by a number of Knesset members, one of them pulled out a prayer book and began reciting Jewish prayers in violation of the ban by the Israeli authorities on Jewish worship at Temple Mount. Some young men planted an Israeli flag on the esplanade while others attempted to force their way into the underground chambers under the mosque. A scuffle broke out which involved several hundred Moslems and 600 Israeli policemen as a result of which 12 Arabs were injured and 19 arrested. The Arab and Islamic states complained to the Security Council against this new outrage to Islamic Holy Places.

Although the aggressions committed against Holy Places are the work of terrorists, yet the Israeli government has some share in responsibility for their acts. The claims made by Israeli official representatives on the Temple area in 1967; the proclamation made by the Knesset in 1980 that Jerusalem is the eternal capital of Israel; the constant biblical claims made by Israeli ministers to Judea and Samaria; the inaction, if not the deliberate laxity, of Israeli security forces in bringing to justice those responsible for the aggressions and the sympathy that the perpetrators enjoy in certain government quarters are no doubt contributory causes.

The danger to Holy Places, in particular, the Islamic mosques in the area of the *Haram Al-Sharif* should be taken seriously. The aggressions made against them are not the work of extremists or mentally deranged individuals as sometimes alleged by the Israeli government. Journalist David K. Shipler writes:

> Officially, Israel recognizes Moslem control over the Temple Mount and its mosques. But in the last few years, the yearning to remove the mosques and build a Jewish temple there has begun to spread from a few religious fanatics into more established rightist political groups (*International Herald Tribune,* 11 July 1984).

The aggressions against Holy Places bring back to memory the fears that were voiced by the King–Crane Commission which prophetically warned of the danger to Christian and Moslem Holy Places were they to fall into Jewish hands. The King–Crane Commission was appointed in 1919 by the Supreme Council of the Allied Powers at the Paris Peace Conference at the insistence of President Wilson to elucidate the state of opinion in Palestine and Syria regarding the mode of settlement of their future following their detachment from Turkey. With respect to the Holy Places in Palestine the Commission said:

There is a further consideration that cannot be justly ignored, if the world is to look forward to Palestine becoming a definitely Jewish state, however gradually that may take place. That consideration grows out of the fact that Palestine is 'the Holy Land' for Jews, Christians and Moslems alike. Millions of Christians and Moslems all over the world are quite as much concerned as the Jews with conditions in Palestine, especially with those conditions which touch upon religious feeling and rights. The relations in these matters in Palestine are most delicate and difficult. With the best possible intentions, it may be doubted whether the Jews could possibly seem to either Christians or Moslems proper guardians of the holy places, or custodians of the Holy Land as a whole. The reason is this: the places which are most sacred to Christians — those having to do with Jesus — and which are also sacred to Moslems, are not only not sacred to Jews, but abhorrent to them. It is simply impossible, under those circumstances, for Moslems and Christians to feel satisfied to have these places in Jewish hands, or under the custody of Jews . . . It must be believed that the precise meaning, in this respect, of the complete Jewish occupation of Palestine has not been fully sensed by those who urge the extreme Zionist program. For it would intensify, with a certainty like fate, the anti-Jewish feeling both in Palestine and in all other portions of the world which look to Palestine as 'the Holy Land'.[9]

The fears expressed by the King–Crane Commission about the dangers involved in the Jewish domination of Palestine and its Holy Places, and confirmed by Israeli actions in Jerusalem, constitute a writing on the wall.

EQUALITY OR PRIORITY OF RELIGIONS?

Israel has exploited the existence in biblical times of Solomon's Temple at Jerusalem for political purposes and for usurpation of the Holy City. It now seeks, after its occupation of Jerusalem, to establish pre-eminence for Judaism over the other two religions in Jerusalem. Abba Eban, at one time Israel's Foreign Minister, and presently Chief of the Knesset's Foreign Relations Committee, writes:

It is true that many outside Israel and the Jewish people have an interest in Jerusalem. But it is an offence against scholarship and historical truth to speak of 'equality' between the Jewish connection and anything else. Israel should not claim exclusiveness of concern but it has an immaculate claim of priority. Jerusalem is a theme of reverence in Christianity and Islam as a reflection and consequence of its Jewish sanctity.[10]

Despite his boast of 'scholarship and historical truth', Abba Eban's attempt to belittle and play down the religious significance of Jerusalem to Christians and Moslems for the purpose of justifying Israel's usurpation of the Holy City is hollow and misconceived. This is all the more so because — unlike the Christians who have almost all their Holy Places relating to the life and crucifixion of Christ in Jerusalem and unlike the Moslems who have two of their most sacred historic mosques in that city — the Jews do not actually own or possess any Holy Places in Jerusalem. This was expressly stated by Chaim Weizmann, the author of the Balfour Declaration and the first President of Israel. In his autobiography he wondered at the reason for opposition to Zionism by the Vatican and also why the issue of the Holy Places should arouse so much interest. To soothe fears, he wrote:

There were no Holy Places in Palestine to which the Jews laid actual physical claims — except perhaps, Rachel's tomb,[11] which was at no time a matter of controversy. The Wailing Wall we did not own, and never had owned since the destruction of the Temple.[12]

Following the bloody riots in 1929 over an incident at the Wailing Wall, an international commission was appointed in 1931 by the British Mandatory, with the approval of the League of Nations, to inquire into the rights over the Wailing Wall. The commission found that 'the ownership of the Wall accrues to the Moslems . . . and that the pavement in front of the Wall, where the Jews perform their devotions, is also Moslem property'.[13]

The problem of Jerusalem and its Holy Places transcends the Middle East in its importance and dimensions. The issues which it involves are emotional and explosive and could well lead to a conflict of unpredictable consequences. Already twice in history these issues have given rise to bloody wars: the Crusades (for the control of the Holy Sepulchre and Jerusalem) which lasted for several generations and the Crimean War (over the disappearance of the silver star at the Church of the Nativity at Bethlehem). Since 1969, after the arson committed at the Mosque of Al-Aqsa, there have been rumblings of a *jihad* (sacred war) in world Islamic conferences over Israel's occupation and actions in Jerusalem.

Israel's usurpation and its continued occupation of the Holy City constitute a danger to Islamic and Christian Holy Places. They put in peril the religious heritage of Christianity and Islam, and create a great risk to world peace. The future of Jerusalem will be discussed in Chapter 34.

NOTES

1. H.S. Karmi, *Islamic Quarterly Magazine*, vol. 14 (1970), p. 69.
2. UN Doc. A/6793, p. 21.
3. The term 'past acquisition' refers to the Jewish tradition that David purchased the land on which Solomon's Temple was built from a Jebusite.
4. UN Doc. A/6793, p. 53. The Ibrahimi Mosque is located in Hebron and contains the cave of Machpela in which are buried Abraham, Sarah and Jacob. The Rock refers to the Rock over which the Mosque of the Dome of the Rock is built.
5. UN Doc. A/6793, p. 21.
6. *International Herald Tribune,* 29 January 1980.
7. *The Times*, 2 February 1980.
8. *Middle East International*, 21 December 1984, p. 14.
9. J.C. Hurewitz, *Diplomacy in the Near and Middle East*, (Van Nostrand, Princeton, 1956), vol. II, p. 70.
10. *Daily Telegraph,* 8 September 1980.
11. Rachel's tomb is located outside Jerusalem on the road to Bethlehem.
12. Chaim Weizmann, *Autobiography* (Hamish Hamilton, London, 1949), p. 355.
13. Muhammad H. El-Farra, 'The UN and the Palestine Question', *The Arab-Israeli Conflict* (ed.) John Norton Moore (Princeton University, New Jersey, 1974), vol. III, p. 515.

Part IV

The Road to Peace

31

The Dimensions of the Palestine Question

EVOLUTION OF THE PALESTINE QUESTION

In examining the developments that have taken place in the Palestine Question, we have seen that its evolution has been from bad to worse, namely, from the Balfour Declaration which envisaged a national home for the Jews in Palestine, to the UN partition of Palestine into Arab and Jewish states, to the creation of a Jewish state which, after its emergence, displaced most of the Arab population and expanded by aggression to an area which exceeded its territory as defined by the UN partition plan, and finally to the seizure of the whole of Palestine. Such evolution signifies that political Zionism which was forcibly implanted in Palestine, constitutes a malignant growth in the body politic of the Middle East.

THREE MAIN ISSUES

In essence, the Palestine Question involves three main issues: territorial, human and religious.

The territorial issue

The territorial issue has two aspects: the theft of the territory of Palestine, on the one hand, and the theft of its cities, towns, villages, lands and properties, on the other. Israel's seizure and annexation in 1948 of most of the territory of Palestine, and its occupation of the remainder in 1967, are nothing but a theft of the country which has belonged for many centuries to the Palestinians. It was frankly recognized as such by David Ben Gurion, the founder and first Prime Minister of the state of Israel. Nahum Goldmann, President of the World Zionist Organization, reported a conversation which he had with Ben Gurion in 1956 in which they discussed the prospects of peace with the Arabs. Nahum Goldmann said:

> We had a forthright discussion on the Arab problem. 'I don't understand your optimism', Ben Gurion declared. 'Why should the Arabs make peace? If I was an Arab leader I would never make terms with Israel. That is natural: we have taken their country. Sure, God promised it to us, but what does that matter to them? Our God is not theirs. We come from Israel, it's true, but two thousand years ago, and what is that to them? There has been antisemitism, the Nazis, Hitler, Auschwitz, but was that their fault? They only see one thing: we have come here and stolen their country. Why should they accept that?'[1]

The second aspect of the theft of Palestine consists of the seizure, confiscation, expropriation, whether as absentee property or under a variety of other unlawful pretexts, of the cities, towns, villages and lands of the Palestinian people. This aspect was already described in Chapter 12 in the case of the 1948 plunder of Arab property and in Chapter 25 in the case of the 1967 land seizures. The theft embraces urban built-up property and lands, public or private.

The size of urban built-up property which was taken from the Palestinians comprises several cities, towns and villages, including Modern Jerusalem (largely Arab-owned), Jaffa, Lydda, Ramleh (wholly Arab-owned), Haifa (partly Arab-owned), Nazareth and Acre (wholly Arab-owned). The massive land robbery committed in Palestine can be judged from a comparison between land owned by the Jews at the end of the British mandate with land possessed by them today. This is given by an Israeli land expert, Meron Benvenisti:

> We should bear in mind that 37 years ago, in 1947, the Jews possessed less than 10 per cent of the total land of Mandatory Palestine. In 1983, they possessed 85 per cent of the area, and the Palestinians (including Israeli Arabs) controlled less than 15 per cent.[2]

Since the process of Arab dispossession is still continuing, the percentage of land in Jewish possession is certainly more than 85 per cent today.

Benvenisti's estimate of Jewish-owned land calls for some comments. First, Jewish-owned land in 1947 amounted not to some 10 per cent, but exactly, in accordance with the Palestine Government Statistics, to 1,491,699 *dunoms* (a dunom is equal to 1,000 square metres) or 5.67 per cent of the land area of Palestine as explained in Chapter 6. Second, at the date of the Balfour Declaration the Jews owned some 2 per cent, or, in other words, one-fiftieth of the land area of Palestine.

The massive theft of the lands of Palestine by Israel prompted Israel Carlbach, chief editor of *Ma'ariv*, the most widely read daily in Israel, to publish on 25 December 1953 a satire on Israel's methods of dispossessing the Palestinian Arabs of their lands. His satire takes the form of the following dialogue with his daughter:

This land was Arab land in the old days which you can't remember. The fields and villages were theirs. But you don't see many of these now — there are only flourishing Jewish colonies where they used to be . . . because a great miracle happened to us. One day those Arabs fled from us and we took their land and farmed it. And the old owners went to other countries and settled there.

But here and there you do sometimes see some Arab villages. These are the villages of the few who remained among us . . . they have become citizens of our state . . .

'Where are the fields?' you will ask.

There are none, my dear.

'What happened to the fields?'

We simply took them.

'But how? How can one take land belonging to someone else, someone living among us and cultivating that land and living off it?'

There is nothing difficult about that. All you need is force. Once you have the power, you can, for example, say: 'These fields are a closed area,' and stop anyone from getting to them without a permit. And you only give out permits to your friends, to people living in the *kibbutzim* nearby, whose eyes have feasted on that

273

land. It is really very simple.

'But is there no law? Are there no courts in Israel?'

Of course there are. But they only held up matters very briefly. The Arabs did go to our courts and asked for their land back from those who stole it. And the judges decided that yes, the Arabs are the legal owners of the fields they have tilled for generations, and even the police saw no reason why they should not sow the land and harvest it . . .

'Well then, if that is the decision of the judges . . . we are a law-abiding nation.'

No, my dear, it is not quite like that. If the law decides against the thief, and the thief is very powerful, then he makes another law supporting his view.

'How?'

All those who took part in the robbery gather in the Knesset. And who hasn't? The land was taken . . . by the departments of government, by Mapai and Mapam and the religious parties — all of them. They say: 'We are used to this land and we don't want the courts to disturb us and stop us farming it. Come, let us make a law that will make it impossible for anyone to take this land from us.'[3]

The human issue

The second issue concerns the tragedy that has befallen the five million Palestinian Arabs, one-half of whom live as refugees and exiles from their country and are denied the right to return to their homes and to their lands while the other half live under Israeli domination, oppression and repression, whether as citizens of Israel or as residents of the West Bank and Gaza. This was the result of the Zionist plan to establish in the twentieth century a Jewish state in a country inhabited since time immemorial by the Palestinians. Maxime Rodinson, a leading Jewish orientalist, comments on the Zionist plan to create a Jewish state as follows:

But this Jewish state had to be located somewhere. As a result of circumstances, of the ideological weight of the past, of the ignorance of many, and of the imperial interests with which the movement was to link itself in order to become effective, the land chosen was Arab Palestine . . . Logically, there were only two ways of transforming a land inhabited by Arabs into a Jewish territory: the subjection or expulsion of the indigenous inhabitants.[4]

Israel had recourse to both methods: it expelled the majority of the Palestinians and subjugated those who remained.

The Palestine refugee problem is unique in modern annals. There exist many refugee problems in the world today, some possessing even greater dimensions, but none of its tragic features, namely, the uprooting and spoliation of a people settled on its land for centuries, not for its domination or exploitation as in the case of past colonialist ventures, but for its expulsion and the usurpation of its homeland. Sir John Glubb, the former British Commander-in-Chief of Jordan's Arab Legion, emphasized the unique character of the Palestine refugee problem in these terms:

> It is quite essential vividly to grasp the unique conditions of the struggle in Palestine. We have witnessed many wars in this century, in which one country seeks to impose its power on others. But in no war, I think, for many centuries past, has the objective been to remove a nation from its country and to introduce another and evidently different race to occupy its lands, houses and cities and live there. This peculiarity lends to the Palestine struggle a desperate quality which bears no resemblance to any other war in modern history.[5]

The religious issue

The religious issue concerns Jerusalem and its Holy Places. As already pointed out, the significance of Jerusalem transcends Palestine and is of grave concern to one-half of humanity. Israel's occupation of Jerusalem has no legal or moral basis and contravenes international law and UN resolutions, in particular, General Assembly resolution 181 of 29 November 1947. Moreover, such occupation seriously endangers Islamic and Christian Holy Places. It is inadmissible that 3 million Israeli Jews who represent a fraction of 1 per cent of those to whom Jerusalem is sacred should usurp the Holy City and endanger its Holy Places. Israeli control over Jerusalem is all the more unacceptable and irrational when it is

275

realized that, as we have seen in the preceding chapter, the Jews do not own or possess any Holy Places in the Holy City.

TWO NEW FACTORS

The three issues set forth above represent, in essence, the original dimensions of the Palestine Question. Since the mid-1960s, however, the Palestine Question has been dangerously aggravated by two new factors. First, its exploitation in American domestic politics, including the highest holders of office, who vie with each other in order to gain the favours of the Jewish Zionist lobby and of Israel. Second, the special relationship which was forged between Israel and the US government which, as explained in Chapter 27, prevents any equitable redress of the wrongs done to the Palestinians.

Here then is a general bird's-eye view of the Palestine Question which constitutes one of the scandals of the twentieth century. A proper understanding of the real issues that it involves provides a gauge for weighing the value, if any, of the so-called peace initiatives which have been, and are still being, suggested for its resolution. It is essential to keep sight of the basic issues involved because each new wrong blurs and overshadows the previous one. Thus the massive Palestine refugee problem of 1948 came to dominate the picture to the extent that the world lost sight of the basic Palestine Question. Over the years the Security Council, as we have seen, came to consider the Palestine Question as involving simply a refugee problem. Likewise, after the 1967 aggression and Israel's seizure of the remaining territory of Palestine, the perspective of the Palestine Question, as viewed by many politicians, changed. Just as after 1948 the Palestine Question came to be considered as involving merely a refugee problem, so after 1967 the Palestine Question came to be considered and is still considered today as involving simply Israel's occupation of the West Bank and the Gaza Strip. The basic Palestine injustice is thus overshadowed and remains unresolved.

NOTES

1. Nahum Goldmann, *The Jewish Paradox* (Weidenfeld and Nicolson, London, 1978), p. 99.
2. Meron Benvenisti, *West Bank Data Project: A Survey of Israeli*

Policies (American Enterprise Institute, Washington, DC, 1984), p. 19.

3. Cited in *Journal of Palestine Studies*, vol. 54, pp. 23–4, 1985.

4. *Journal of Palestine Studies*, vol. 51 (Spring 1984), p. 19.

5. Sir John Glubb, *The Middle East Crisis* (Hodder and Stoughton, London, 1967), p. 41.

32

Abortive Initiatives for a Solution

Two kinds of initiatives have been taken since 1948 to liquidate or to resolve the Palestine Question: military and political.

Of the five wars that were fought between the Arabs and Israel, three of them, namely those of 1948, 1967 and 1982, sought, though without success, to liquidate the Palestine Question. The two other wars had no such objective: the War of 1956 had an expansionist Israeli objective while in the War of 1973 Egypt and Syria sought only to recover their territories which Israel had seized in 1967.

The various political initiatives that were taken in regard to the Palestine Question are set forth below.

1. MEDIATION AND CONCILIATION

We have seen in Chapter 14 that the UN attempted mediation and conciliation for the settlement of the Palestine Question but without success. Count Folke Bernadotte, the UN Mediator on Palestine, put it on record in his Report to the General Assembly dated 16 September 1948 that 'neither agreement nor a basis of agreement had been found between the parties'. He stated that 'vital decisions will have to be taken by the General Assembly if a peaceful settlement is to be reached'.[1] Likewise, the Conciliation Commission for Palestine consistently failed in its mediation and abandoned any attempt to achieve a settlement of the conflict.

The futility of mediation and conciliation as a means to settle the Palestine Question is obvious. Israel's avowed and determined policy to retain the whole of Palestine regardless of the boundaries of the UN partition resolution, its seizure of the territory earmarked for the Arab State, its opposition to the establishment of such a state, its rejection of the repatriation of the Palestine refugees and its determination to keep Jerusalem as its 'eternal capital' completely rule out any role for mediation and conciliation in order to settle the conflict.

2. THE PALESTINIAN PEACE PLAN

The original Palestinian Peace Plan

The Palestinian plan for the settlement of the Palestine Question was originally formulated at the UN in 1947 and adopted in the Palestine National Charter of 1964. The plan rests upon the premise of the establishment of a unitary and democratic state in the whole of Palestine with equal rights for all citizens, without distinction of race, creed or religion. Only Jews of Palestinian origin were considered by the Palestine National Charter to be Palestinian citizens. Since then, however, such limitation was abandoned. In his speech to the UN General Assembly on 13 November 1974 Yasser Arafat, Chairman of the PLO, declared that 'when we speak of our common hopes for the Palestine of tomorrow we include in our perspective all Jews now living in Palestine who choose to live with us there in peace and without discrimination'.

Evolution of the Palestinian position

However, a more decisive evolution occurred in the Palestinian national programme with the PLO's acceptance of a solution on the basis of UN resolutions. Such acceptance was made in a declaration of the PLO to the UN on 19 April 1981. The General Assembly took note of this declaration in its resolution 37/86D of 10 December 1982 which stated that the General Assembly:

1. Takes note of the declaration of the Palestine Liberation Organization of 19 April 1981 to pursue its role in the solution of the Question of Palestine on the basis of the attainment in Palestine of the inalienable rights of the Palestinian people in accordance with the relevant resolutions of the United Nations.

A similar acceptance of UN resolutions was also made by Yasser Arafat, Chairman of the PLO in 1982. On 25 July 1982 during the siege of Beirut, a visiting US congressional delegation obtained from him a written declaration which stated: 'Chairman Arafat accepts all UN resolutions relevant to the Palestine Question.' The document was countersigned by US Representative, Paul N. McCloskey, Jr.

This overture was rejected by Israel and by the US. Larry M. Speakes, then White House spokesman, said:

> The United States will not recognize or negotiate with the PLO until the PLO accepts United Nations Security Council resolutions 242 and 338 and Israel's right to exist. We have indicated this must be done in a clear and unequivocal way. The statement by Arafat does not meet these conditions.

The White House statement means not only Palestinian recognition of Israel, but also of its territorial conquests in excess of the UN partition resolution. Such a negative American reaction prompted *The Times* of London to observe that the US response 'suggests that the United States is not interested in obtaining the PLO's participation in a peaceful settlement of the conflict'.[2]

The US rejection of the PLO's overture was in execution of the secret commitment which Secretary of State Henry Kissinger gave to Israel, in connection with the Sinai Disengagement Agreement of September 1975, that the US will not recognize or negotiate with the PLO until the latter recognizes Security Council resolutions 242 and 338 and Israel's right to exist.[3] The reasons which explain why Security Council resolutions 242 and 338 are unacceptable to the Palestinians are discussed in the following section.

While the evolution of the Palestinian position in regard to the settlement of the Palestine Question has moved toward acceptance of UN resolutions, Israel, which was itself a creation of those resolutions, has, with US backing, moved away from them to the point of their rejection.

3. SECURITY COUNCIL RESOLUTION 242

Resolution 242 was adopted by the Security Council on 22 November 1967 for a 'just and lasting peace in the Middle East'. Resolution 338 was adopted in the wake of the War of 1973 and called for the implementation of resolution 242 and for negotiations between the parties aimed at establishing a just and durable peace in the Middle East. In pursuance of resolution 338 the Geneva Peace Conference on the Middle East was convened in December 1973 but, apart from the conclusion of agreements for the disengagement of the military forces of Israel, Egypt and Syria, it led to no other result (Chapter 21).

The basic provisions of resolution 242 were set out in Chapter 18. Hence, the discussion here will be limited to examining whether it provides a suitable and acceptable peace plan for the settlement of the Palestine Question.

Inadequacy as a peace plan

Viewed as a measure designed to restore the territorial situation to what it was before Israel's aggression of 5 June 1967, and to the extent that it emphasized the principle of the 'inadmissibility of the acquisition of territory by war' and required withdrawal of Israeli armed forces from territories occupied in that conflict, resolution 242 can be considered to be a positive step. But if, as it expressly states, it purports to bring about a 'just and lasting peace in the Middle East', it obviously misses the mark widely and should be rejected as totally inadequate for that purpose.

Resolution 242 has entirely bypassed and ignored the basic Palestine injustice which is the core of the Arab-Israeli conflict. It treated the Palestine Question as being a simple 'refugee problem', a view held by many statesmen in the 1960s. Henry Kissinger, former US Secretary of State, said in this regard:

> We had assumed that the Palestinians could be dealt with in a settlement purely as a refugee problem. Instead, they had become a quasi-independent force with a veto over policy in Jordan, and perhaps even in Lebanon . . .[4] The *fedayeen* were as yet unrecognized as a political entity — treated as refugees internationally . . .[5]

The Security Council's misjudgement — intentional or unintentional — of the nature of the conflict ignored crucial issues such as the restoration of the national and legitimate rights of the Palestinians and the restitution of their homeland and their homes.

Incompatibility with international law and UN resolutions

In fact, by resolution 242 the Security Council sought to dispose of the Palestine Question in a manner incompatible with international law and UN resolutions. In essence, it provided that Israel should withdraw from the territories it seized in June 1967 and that the Arab states should recognize Israel's sovereignty and territorial integrity. This meant recognition of Israel's sovereignty over the territory of Palestine which it had occupied in 1948 and 1949 in excess of the area of the Jewish State as defined by the UN in 1947. Thus, the conflict was presented as if it concerned Israel and the Arab States solely and exclusively and as if the Palestinians who are the victims of such conflict did not exist — except as refugees — and did not possess any political and national rights.

Moreover, by limiting the Israeli withdrawal to territories seized in 1967, resolution 242 implied that all other territories occupied by Israel, including most of the territory of the Arab State described in the partition resolution of 1947, would be considered as Israeli territory. In other words, the recognition of Israel's sovereignty and territorial integrity required by resolution 242 would mean the abrogation of the partition resolution of 1947 and the recognition of Israel's sovereignty over most of the territory of the Arab State. Such recognition implies the condoning of Israel's conquest and usurpation in 1948 and 1949 of Palestinian territories earmarked for the Palestinian Arab State, a reward for its aggression. Resolution 242 is self-contradictory as one does not see how the Security Council can reconcile its giving effect to the principle of 'the inadmissibility of the acquisition of territory by war' and requiring withdrawal therefrom in the case of territories seized in 1967, but not in regard to territories seized in 1948 and 1949 outside the boundaries of the Jewish State. This principle was equally in force in 1948 as in 1967 and it is obvious that Israel did not and could not gain any title over territory it seized beyond the boundaries of the intended Jewish State. Hence, the Security Council did not thereby conform to international law, to the principles of the UN Charter or to General Assembly resolution 181 of 29 November 1947.

To this should be added the fact that Israel did not then, and does not now, possess recognized boundaries. The Armistice Agreements of 1949 laid down armistice lines, not final political boundaries, and expressly reserved the rights, claims and positions of the parties in an ultimate peaceful settlement. By confining the Israeli withdrawal to the armistice lines that existed prior to the aggression of June

1967, the Security Council was, therefore, treating such armistice lines as definitive political boundaries contrary to the intention of the parties in the Armistice Agreements and to the accepted meaning of armistice lines in international law. Quincy Wright pointed out this anomaly:

> The resolution of November 22nd 1967 is advantageous to Israel in requiring withdrawal only from territory occupied in 1967. The territory occupied by Israel under the 1949 Armistice beyond the UN partition line of 1947 might have been added . . .[6]

Moreover, to the extent that by its silence over withdrawal from territories destined by General Assembly resolution 181 of 1947 for the establishment of a Palestinian Arab State the Security Council purports to ratify their usurpation by Israel, its action is null and void and is not conducive to peace. The Security Council cannot override or abrogate a resolution of the General Assembly. The Security Council is a body which was entrusted with certain powers delegated to it by Article 24 of the Charter of the UN. In discharging these duties the Security Council 'acts on behalf of the Members of the UN' (Paragraph 1 of Article 24) and, moreover, is required 'to act in accordance with the Purposes and Principles of the UN' (Paragraph 2 of Article 24). In accordance with general principles of law, a mandatory to whom authority is delegated cannot exceed the powers granted to him by the principal. In other terms, the Security Council possessed no authority to abrogate, alter or modify General Assembly resolution 181 which called for the creation of an Arab State and demarcated its territory. It follows that if resolution 242 were to be construed as having the effect of reducing the territory of the Palestinian Arab State from that defined in General Assembly resolution 181 to the West Bank and the Gaza Strip, then it is *ultra vires* and null and void.

Resolution 242 sought the liquidation of the Palestine Question

One might wonder how the Security Council came to adopt resolution 242 which, by implication, purported to ratify Israel's conquests of Palestinian territories in excess of the partition resolution. The explanation is found in the fact that resolution 242 was concocted by the US and Israel as a formula designed to liquidate the Palestine Question and to legitimate Israel's illicit territorial expansion beyond its frontiers under the partition resolution. In fact, the principles embodied in resolution 242 were set forth by the US at the fifth emergency special session of the General Assembly which was convened on 17 June 1967 to consider the situation. At this session the US opposed the adoption of a resolution submitted by the Soviet Union calling upon Israel to withdraw its forces from all territories which it had occupied and submitted instead a resolution which aimed at achieving peace through 'negotiated arrangements on the basis of the recognition of Israel's boundaries,' and 'the mutual recognition of the political independence and territorial integrity of all countries in the area'. This language was eventually incorporated into resolution 242. It may be observed that such language represented the Israeli position at that time.

Israel's equivocation

Israel's equivocation about resolution 242 is remarkable. Originally, it used its influence with the US government to secure its adoption because it was obviously for its benefit: the Palestine Question would be practically disposed of by becoming simply a refugee problem, the territorial issue would be reduced to the West Bank and Gaza Strip, that is to say, to 20 per cent of the area of Palestine, and finally Israel would be accepted by the Arab world and its sovereignty affirmed over 80 per cent of Palestine. However, when the question of the implementation of the resolution arose, Israel formally informed Ambassador Jarring on 26 January 1971 that it refused to withdraw 'to the pre-5 June 1967 lines' (Chapter 18). According to Israel's interpretation, the provision in resolution 242 for Israel's withdrawal from territories occupied in the recent conflict does not mean what it says and does not require withdrawal from all occupied territories. But despite its rejection of the implementation of the resolution, it secured a secret commitment from the US, as we have seen in Chapter 21, in 1975 to veto at the Security Council any change in the terms of resolution 242.

Franco-Egyptian proposed amendment thwarted

The US commitment to Israel to veto any change in resolution 242 thwarted the attempt made at the UN in 1982 to amend it in a manner that would make it acceptable to the Palestinians. On 28 July 1982

Egypt and France submitted to the Security Council a draft resolution (S/15317) which, while reaffirming the right of all states in the region to existence and security in accordance with resolution 242, also reaffirmed 'the legitimate national rights of the Palestinian people, including the right to self-determination with all its implications . . .'. This draft resolution was not put to a vote because the US intimated it would veto it despite the fact, now generally recognized, that resolution 242 is deficient in failing to recognize the national rights of the Palestinians.

Harm done to the cause of peace

Thus, instead of leading to a solution, Security Council resolution 242, coupled to the US commitment to Israel to veto any initiative in the Security Council to amend it, blocks the way to a settlement of the Palestine Question and to peace in the Middle East. In fact, the adoption of resolution 242 did not serve the cause of peace but has done much harm by giving the impression, and to some an argument, that it furnishes a solution to the Arab-Israeli conflict, including the Palestine Question, thereby preventing a serious and rational approach to the problem. As we shall observe in examining the so-called peace initiatives taken since 1967, the US government and Israel still cling to resolution 242 and assert that it represents the only solution of the Arab-Israeli conflict.

4. US-SOVIET STATEMENT OF 1977

Apart from its opening session in December 1973 the Geneva Peace Conference on the Middle East which was established pursuant to Security Council resolution 338 after the War of 1973 was still bogged down in 1977 without any progress having been made. President Carter, who after assuming office had come out with a declaration in favour of a 'homeland' for the Palestinians, decided to reactivate the Geneva Peace Conference. To that end, he initiated negotiations between the US and the Soviet Union in their capacity as co-chairmen to the conference. These negotiations resulted in the issuing on 1 October 1977 of a joint US-Soviet statement which contained guidelines for the work of the Conference.

The statement referred to the necessity of achieving a just and lasting settlement of the Arab-Israeli conflict as soon as possible, such settlement to be comprehensive and to incorporate all parties and all questions. In its operative provision, the statement declared:

> The United States and the Soviet Union believe that, within the framework of a comprehensive settlement of the Middle East problem, all specific questions of the settlement should be resolved, including such key issues as withdrawal of Israeli armed forces from territories occupied in the 1967 conflict; the resolution of the Palestine Question including ensuring the legitimate rights of the Palestinian people; termination of the state of war and establishment of normal peaceful relations on the basis of mutual recognition of the principles of sovereignty, territorial integrity and political independence.

The statement referred to the need for the participation of representatives of all the parties involved, including representatives of the Palestinian people. This disposed of a point which had become an issue that had blocked the resumption of the conference, namely, Israel's opposition to the participation of Palestinian representatives chosen by the people of Palestine.

In addition, the statement spoke of the possibility of the establishment of demilitarized zones, the stationing of UN troops and observers and international guarantees of borders. It further affirmed the intention of the two superpowers to facilitate the resumption of the work of the conference not later than December 1977.

The US-Soviet statement's recognition of the need to resolve the Palestine Question in addition to Israel's withdrawal

The US-Soviet statement was of paramount importance in several respects. For the first time, there was agreement between the two superpowers on the need for the resolution, not only of the question of Israel's withdrawal from the territories seized in 1967, that is the West Bank and Gaza, but also of 'the Palestine Question, including ensuring the legitimate rights of the Palestinian people'. This represented a new and rational development as compared with Security Council resolution 242. It is noteworthy that the statement did not mention or make any reference to Security Council resolution 242. In this regard, the US-Soviet statement of 1977 stands in contrast to current initiatives to settle the Arab-Israeli conflict, including the Palestine Question, simply on the basis of an Israeli withdrawal from the territories occupied in 1967.

It is also significant that for the first time the US subscribed to the need of ensuring the 'legitimate rights of the Palestinian people' instead of their 'interests' as was the case in its past declarations.

Israel's veto

Hopes of achieving a settlement, however, were dashed and the initiative was nipped in the bud by Israel's veto. Israel was particularly angered by the fact that the US should concede the need to resolve 'the Palestine Question' and to ensure 'the legitimate rights' of the Palestinian people, considering that these questions had been, in its opinion, done away with and buried. On being apprised of the contents of the US-Soviet joint statement by the American ambassador, Israel's Prime Minister Menachem Begin had to be hospitalized. Furthermore, Israel criticized the US government for ignoring its commitment of September 1975 not to allow any alteration of the terms of reference of the Geneva Conference or of resolution 242 which formed the basic guideline of the Conference (Chapter 21).

As a result of Israel's fierce opposition and the bombardment of President Carter with 8,000 telephone calls, telegrams and written protests, the US President caved in and abandoned pursuit of the US-Soviet joint initiative. He told a group of Jewish congressmen that he 'would rather commit political suicide than harm Israel'.[7] Then in a 'working paper' concerning the Geneva Peace Conference (published by *Le Monde* of 15 October 1977), Israel and the US declared that 'the agreed basis for negotiation at the Geneva Peace Conference on the Middle East is formed by resolutions 242 and 338 of the Security Council' which, it will be recalled, limited the Palestine Question to a refugee problem. In fact, the 'working paper' spoke of discussing 'the problem of the Arab refugees and the Jewish refugees' and 'the problem of the West Bank and Gaza'. Thus the Palestine Question had evaporated. In effect, this working paper nullified the joint US-Soviet statement and sought to bury the Palestine Question.

The Geneva Peace Conference was eventually torpedoed by Egyptian President Sadat's direct peace overtures to Israel during his visit to Jerusalem in November 1979. The Conference never resumed and the peace formula envisaged by the US-Soviet statement never had a chance of being discussed or implemented. Once again, the road to peace was blocked by Israel and, under its influence, by the US government.

5. CAMP DAVID ACCORDS OR PAX HEBRAICA

The provisions of the Camp David Accords were considered in Chapter 22. Only the question as to whether the formula by which they proposed to achieve peace in the West Bank and Gaza is at all suitable will be discussed here. Their provisions concerning peace between Egypt and Israel were discussed earlier.

The Camp David Accords were presented widely and loudly by their three authors — Anwar Sadat, Menachem Begin and Jimmy Carter — as a panacea for the ills of the Middle East and as the solution of the Arab-Israeli conflict. In their view, the Accords constituted a great diplomatic achievement which will go down as a landmark in history. The real facts, however, are otherwise, for the Camp David Accords did not constitute a contribution to peace, but a sham by which Israel sought to liquidate the Palestine Question and to legitimize its territorial conquests.

Liquidation of Palestine Question

It should first be observed that although the Accords spoke of a framework for peace in the West Bank and Gaza, their purpose was to liquidate the Palestine Question in its entirety. This is clear from their provision for the holding of negotiations 'on the resolution of the Palestine problem in all its aspects'. The limitation of the Palestine problem in the Accords to the West Bank and Gaza is in line with the Israeli position that after Israel's occupation and annexation of the territory of Palestine, except the West Bank and Gaza, the Palestine Question was, or should be, in its opinion, limited geographically and politically to those two areas. As to the territories which Israel seized in 1948 and 1949 in excess of the boundaries of the Jewish State as defined by the UN in 1947, they should not be the subject of any discussion.

Let us now examine the Camp David peace formula in the light of the principles of the Charter, international law and UN resolutions.

Incompetence of authors of Camp David Accords

The first question which one must ask is: what competence or capacity did the three authors of the Camp David Accords possess to decide the Palestine Question or even the future of the West Bank and Gaza?

Israel is the military occupier of the West Bank and Gaza. The status of a military occupier is well defined under international law: an occupier does not acquire sovereignty and can only act as an administrator; he cannot colonize the occupied territory, nor establish settlements, nor implant immigrants, nor expropriate or confiscate property. These are well-settled principles of international law and the Fourth Geneva Convention of 12 August 1949. In a number of resolutions, the UN condemned Israel for its violations of international law and the Geneva Convention of 1949 in respect of such prohibited acts. There exists no rule of international law which confers on a military occupier any power to decide the political and constitutional future of the inhabitants or the status of the occupied territory. By assuming in the Camp David Accords a right to decide these matters and to sit as arbiter over the destinies of the Palestinian people, Israel was usurping a power in violation of the law of nations.

Similarly, Egyptian President Anwar Sadat possessed no right or power to decide the future of the Palestinians or to barter away their national rights and territory. He was not their guardian, nor did he hold a mandate to represent them.

As to President Carter, one fails to see on what basis he purported to negotiate with Begin and Sadat the future of the Palestinians and of Palestinian territory. It is obvious that President Carter had as much a right to decide the future of the Palestinians and Palestinian territory as the Palestinians have a right to decide the future of US citizens or of US territory.

The conclusion is obvious that the three parties who concocted the Camp David Accords concerning the West Bank and Gaza were neither qualified nor competent to do so. Consequently the Camp David Accords are completely null and void in so far as they relate to the West Bank and Gaza or to the Palestinians.

Camp David Accords violate rights of Palestinians

The Camp David Accords must also be rejected because they violate

289

the fundamental and inalienable rights of the people of Palestine. The Palestinians are the masters of their own destiny and no state, much less an aggressor, possesses the power to decide their future or to prevent them from the exercise of their sovereignty.

Many people were misled by the Camp David Accords which they hailed as a contribution to peace. This is because they were framed so as to deceive and to give an illusion about their recognition of Palestinian rights. Thus the Accords speak of 'full autonomy' to the inhabitants, 'a self-governing authority', recognition of 'the legitimate rights of the Palestinian people' and 'carrying out the provisions and principles of resolutions 242 and 338' while in the same breath they deny all such things. The 'full autonomy' is hollow and, as we have noted in Chapter 22, completely nonexistent; the 'self-governing authority' is not self-governing at all since its competence is to be restricted to municipal matters; the 'legitimate rights of the Palestinian people' are not recognized but denied and the provisions in Security Council resolutions 242 and 338 for an Israeli withdrawal are not carried out but, on the contrary, are discarded since, instead of withdrawing from the West Bank and Gaza in accordance with those resolutions, Israel would maintain its military forces and even assert a claim of sovereignty over them, in violation of these resolutions.

As to the granting of a so-called 'autonomy' to the Palestinian inhabitants of the West Bank and Gaza, such generosity on the part of the Jews who came to Palestine as immigrants is both farcical and insulting. Farcical, because such grant purports to be made to the original inhabitants who shared with the Turks sovereignty over Palestine before its detachment from the Ottoman Empire and who enjoyed full political rights and elected their representatives to the Turkish Chamber of Deputies. Insulting, because the Palestinians are not a people who are emerging from a barbaric status to be accorded autonomy.

The insignificant 'rights' which are recognized by the Camp David Accords in favour of the Palestinians were ridiculed by Fayez Sayegh, then a member of the Kuwait delegation at the UN, in these terms:

A fraction of the Palestinian people (under one-third of the whole) is promised a fraction of its rights (not including the national right to self-determination and statehood) in a fraction of its homeland (less than one-fifth of the area of the whole); and this promise is to be fulfilled several years from now, through a step-by-step process in which Israel is able at every point to exercise a decisive veto-power over any agreement. Beyond that, the vast majority of Palestinians is condemned to permanent loss of its Palestinian national identity, to permanent exile and statelessness, to permanent separation from one another and from Palestine — to a life without national hope or meaning![8]

Camp David Accords violate UN resolutions

Moreover, the Camp David Accords are in flat contradiction to UN resolutions, in particular, resolution 181 of 1947 which called for the establishment of a Palestinian State, resolution 194 of 1948 which called for the repatriation of the refugees, and numerous other resolutions which affirmed the national and inalienable rights of the Palestinians.

Condemnation by General Assembly

The General Assembly of the UN proclaimed the invalidity of the Camp David Accords. In its resolution 33/28 of 7 December 1978 the General Assembly declared in Paragraph 4 that

> The validity of agreements purporting to solve the problem of Palestine requires that they lie within the framework of the United Nations and its Charter and its resolutions on the basis of the full attainment and exercise of the inalienable rights of the Palestinian people, including the right of return and the right to national independence and sovereignty in Palestine and with the participation of the Palestine Liberation Organization.

This was followed by resolution 34/65 of 29 November 1979 in which the General Assembly declared in Paragraph 4 that

> The Camp David Accords and other agreements have no validity in so far as they purport to determine the future of the Palestinian people and of Palestinian territories occupied by Israel since 1967.

Resolution 34/65 was reaffirmed by the General Assembly on 16 December 1981 in its resolution 36/120F which rejected any accords that ignore, infringe, violate or deny the inalienable rights of the Palestinian people, including the rights of return, self-determination, national independence and sovereignty in Palestine.

Camp David Accords were a sham

The Camp David Accords were completely misjudged in the West. Two of their protagonists, Begin and Sadat, were even awarded the Nobel Peace Prize for their great political achievement. However, the great political achievement which the Camp David Accords purported to represent was nothing but a sham which concealed a sordid deal between Anwar Sadat and Israel for the return of Egyptian territory at the expense of the people of Palestine. In reality, the Accords sought to achieve three objectives: the first was to return Sinai to Egypt in consideration for Egypt's acceptance of the autonomy plan for the Palestinians; second, to conclude peace with Egypt and hence to neutralize it and put it out of the military equation in the Middle East conflict and in this Israel has succeeded; third, to usurp the remainder of Palestine and to dominate the Palestinians in perpetuity in the West Bank and Gaza under the spurious pretence of according them autonomy and in this Israel has failed. In short, the Camp David Accords were nothing but an attempt to liquidate the Palestine Question and to impose a *Pax Hebraica* under the pretence of an illusory autonomy for the Palestinians.

6. THE EUROPEAN INITIATIVE

What has been described as 'the European initiative' was the outcome of the Arab-Israeli War of 1973. The oil embargo which the Arab oil producing states imposed against the US and the Netherlands during the war because of their support of Israel and the cut in crude oil production had threatened to cause the collapse of the world's economy and industry. This highly dangerous development awakened the European powers to the imperative need of eliminating the root cause of the Middle East conflict. Since then the Council of Europe has issued several declarations which have upheld the legitimate rights of the Palestinian people. In a declaration issued on 29 June 1977 the Council of Europe took the position that to the principles outlined in Security Council resolutions 242 and 338 there should be added the due recognition of the legitimate rights of the Palestinian people which should find their expression in an effective national identity and in a homeland. This was intended to remedy the deficiency in Security Council resolution 242.

In the spring of 1980 the Council of Europe decided to take more specific action on behalf of the Palestinian people, particularly since the futility of the Camp David formula for peace in the West Bank and Gaza had become apparent. In May 1980, François Poncet, the French Foreign Minister said in Washington that he expected that the European allies would take a Middle East initiative to meet Palestinian aspirations because of the deadlock in the Israeli-Egyptian negotiations on autonomy under the Camp David Accords. It was understood that such an initiative would lead to the amendment of Security Council resolution 242 so as to provide for the recognition of Palestinian national rights. Such a move would formalize the failure of the so-called Camp David 'peace process' which was moribund anyway. The proposed European initiative, however, aroused the wrath of President Carter who believed that the Camp David formula would go down in history as his great political achievement. Accordingly, on 1 June 1980 he expressed in a televised address his concern about the intention of the European powers to take a new Middle East initiative and warned them that the US would veto any attempt to introduce a resolution on Palestinian self-determination in the Security Council. He said:

We will not permit in the UN any action that would destroy the sanctity [*sic*] of and the present form of Security Council resolution 242. We have a veto power that we can exercise, if necessary, to prevent this Camp David process from being destroyed or subverted, and I would not hesitate to use it, if necessary.

The Venice declaration

President Carter's threat to veto any European initiative to amend Security Council resolution 242 blocked any action to this end at the UN. Such a threat, however, did not prevent the European powers from adopting a declaration at Venice on 13 June 1980 which stressed the deficiency of Security Council resolution 242. The Venice declaration stated that on the basis of resolution 242 and of the position adopted by the European Economic Community (EEC) on several occasions, two principles are universally admitted: the right to existence and security of all states in the region, including Israel, on the one hand, and justice for all peoples which implies recognition of the legitimate rights of the Palestinian people, on the other hand. Contradicting resolution 242, the Venice declaration stated that the Palestinian problem is not simply a refugee problem and that the Palestinian people should be able to exercise fully their right of self-determination. The declaration also called for the PLO to be associated with the peace settlement and for Israel to withdraw from the territories which it occupied in 1967. The declaration further considered that Israeli settlements and colonization in the West Bank and Gaza constitute a grave obstacle to peace and are illegal under international law. In an announcement made on 23 February 1987 by which the European Community gave its support for an international conference to resolve the Arab-Israeli conflict (see Section 12 hereinafter), it also declared that the Venice declaration remained the basis for a Middle East peace.

Although no concrete steps were taken to give effect to the Venice declaration, it possessed the merit of having emphasized the inadequacy of Security Council resolution 242, the right of the Palestinians to self-determination and the need to associate the PLO as the representative of the Palestinian people to any peace negotiations.

7. A JEWISH PEACE INITIATIVE: RECIPROCAL RECOGNITION

Declaration by Jewish leaders

Shocked by Israel's invasion of Lebanon in the summer of 1982 for the avowed purpose of destroying the PLO, three leading Jewish personalities, Pierre Mendès France, a former French Prime Minister, Nahum Goldmann, former President of the World Jewish Congress and of the World Zionist Organization, and Philip Klutznick, former US Secretary of Commerce, launched a peace initiative of their own. They issued a declaration in *Le Monde* on 3 July 1982 in which they called for an end to the war and for reciprocal recognition between Israel and the Palestinian people. The declaration stated the following (translation):

Peace is not made between friends, but between enemies who

have fought and suffered. Our sense of Jewish history and the moral imperatives of this moment require us to insist that the time is urgent for mutual recognition between Israel and the Palestinian people. A stop must be put to the sterile debate whereby the Arab world challenges the existence of Israel and Jews challenge the political legitimacy of the Palestinian fight for independence.

The real question is not whether the Palestinians possess the right to independence, but how to implement it while at the same time guaranteeing Israel's security as well as the stability of the region.

Concepts such as 'autonomy' do not suffice, because they have been utilized more to elude rather than to clarify. What is imperative now is to find a political accord between Israeli and Palestinian nationalism.

The war in Lebanon should cease. Israel should lift the siege of Beirut to facilitate negotiations with the PLO that would lead to a settlement. Reciprocal recognition should be sought without respite. Negotiations should be initiated in order to achieve the coexistence between the Israeli and Palestinian peoples on the basis of self-determination.

Although the authors of the declaration were in error about the alleged need of Israel for 'security', it was refreshing to have from them a stinging condemnation of the concept of 'autonomy' which, they declared, has been utilized 'to elude'. Furthermore, the declaration was certainly a great improvement on the requirement demanded by the US of a unilateral and unqualified recognition by the PLO of Israel's right to exist as a condition precedent to any peace negotiation. Finally, the declaration was remarkable for the fact that it was the first time that a group of distinguished Jewish statesmen formally recognized 'the right of the Palestinians to independence'. Yasser Arafat, Chairman of the PLO, considered the declaration 'a positive initiative toward a just and durable peace in the Middle East' (*Le Monde*, 4–5 July 1982).

Rejection by Israel

Despite the favourable response on the part of the PLO, nothing came out of this initiative by reason of Israel's rejection of its terms and its determination to continue the war and to annihilate the PLO.

295

The siege of Beirut was not lifted and the war continued with increasing ferocity. Menachem Begin told a delegation of US congressmen that 'in no circumstances would he accept any dialogue with the PLO, even if Yasser Arafat were to recognize Israel's right to exist and to accept Security Council resolutions 242 and 338' (*Le Monde*, 29 July 1982). Amnon Kapeliouk, an Israeli journalist, added that Yitzhak Shamir held the same view and quoted his statement: 'All we want from the PLO is that it disappears from the face of the earth.' Kapeliouk comments thereon: 'The reason for this attitude is simple: the Israeli Government does not want to negotiate because it refuses to contemplate the idea of returning territory occupied since 1967.'[9] Much less, it goes without saying, would Israel entertain the idea of returning other territories which it seized in excess of the UN boundaries of the Jewish state.

Evaluation of reciprocal recognition

It is pertinent to observe that a reciprocal recognition between Israel and the PLO does not carry the same significance for each party or imply equality in equities. Recognition of Israel by the PLO would or could imply acceptance of the usurpation of Palestine and could impair the legal and political position of the Palestinians whereas recognition of the PLO by Israel entails no prejudice to the latter.

8. REAGAN PEACE PLAN, 1982

Its basic points

President Ronald Reagan launched his peace plan for the Palestine Question on 1 September 1982 following Israel's war against the PLO in Lebanon. He declared that Israel's military successes alone could not bring a just and lasting peace and said: 'The question now is how to reconcile Israel's legitimate security concerns with the legitimate rights of the Palestinians.' The answer, he added, could only come through negotiations 'on the basis of the Camp David Agreement'.

Regarding Israel's 'security', he stated that Palestinian political aspirations are inextricably bound to recognition of Israel's right to a secure future, that America's commitment to the security of Israel was ironclad and that the US would oppose any proposal that threatened it. He emphasized a principle, which supposedly was 'enshrined' [*sic*] in Security Council resolution 242 and was incorporated in the Camp David Accords, that the conflict should be resolved upon the basis of 'an exchange of territory for peace'.

President Reagan's insistence on Arab recognition of Israel's right to a secure future was coupled with a strong plea for Arab recognition of the legitimacy of Israel. He declared:

> The State of Israel is an accomplished fact, it deserves unchallenged legitimacy within the community of nations. But Israel's legitimacy has thus far been recognized by too few countries, and has been denied by every Arab state except Egypt. Israel exists, it has a right to exist in peace behind secure and defensible borders and it has a right to demand of its neighbours that they recognize those facts.

As to Palestinian rights, President Reagan said that the Palestinians felt strongly that their cause was more than a question of refugees to which he agreed, adding: 'The Camp David Agreement recognized that fact when it spoke of the legitimate rights of the Palestinian people and their just requirements.' It should be observed that when President Reagan spoke of 'the Palestinian people' he meant the Palestinian inhabitants of the West Bank and Gaza, not the far greater number of Palestinians who are refugees and are deprived of all rights. In one respect only, the Reagan plan departs from the Camp David formula: instead of autonomy, it proposes self-government — though not self-determination — for the inhabitants of the West Bank and Gaza in association with Jordan.

The specific proposals made in the Reagan Peace Plan may be summarized as follows:

(1) Full autonomy for the Palestinians in the West Bank and Gaza during a transitional period of five years which would begin to run after election of a self-governing authority.

(2) A freeze on Israeli settlements during the transitional period, because further settlement activity is in no way necessary for the security of Israel and only diminishes the confidence of the Arabs that a final outcome can be freely and fairly negotiated.

(3) The US will not support the establishment of an independent Palestinian State in the West Bank and Gaza, nor their annexation or permanent control over them by Israel.

297

(4) The final status of the West Bank and Gaza must be decided through negotiations, but it is the firm view of the US that self-government by the Palestinians of the West Bank and Gaza in association with Jordan offers the best chance for a durable, just and lasting peace.

(5) In return for peace, Israel would withdraw from the West Bank and Gaza, except from such part as would be required to assure its security. The plan specifies that the extent to which Israel should be asked to give up territory will be heavily affected by the extent of true peace and normalization and the security arrangements offered in return.

(6) Jerusalem must remain undivided, but its final status should be decided through negotiations.

Those are the main principles of the Reagan Peace Plan. The plan was disclosed in a secret memorandum delivered a few days in advance of its publication to Israel and to certain Arab states. The memorandum dealt with two points which were not mentioned in the published plan. These concerned the PLO and Israeli settlements. On the first point, the memorandum declared that the US would not alter its refusal to deal with the PLO until it recognized Israel's right to exist and Security Council resolutions 242 and 338. Regarding the question of settlements, the memorandum indicated US opposition to their dismantlement during the transitional five-year period.

Reactions to the plan

The reactions to the Reagan plan were varied.

The Israeli government rejected it flatly and unequivocally and, to give more weight to its rejection, it announced its intention to establish new settlements in the occupied territories. The attitude taken by the Israeli government was not shared by the Israeli Labour opposition which considered that the plan offered a suitable basis for negotiation with Jordan. In fact, the Reagan plan corresponded in many respects to Labour's political programme which it had advocated for some time past and had come to be described as the 'Jordanian option'. According to the Israeli Labour plan, Israel, while maintaining its opposition to the establishment of a Palestinian state and insisting upon the preservation of Jewish settlements, would accept handing over to Jordan under a peace treaty the West Bank, excluding the Old City of Jerusalem, subject to the amputation from the West Bank of such territory as Israel would consider necessary for its security.

As to the Palestinians, they saw two positive aspects in the Reagan plan, namely, its rejection of Israel's claim of sovereignty or control over the West Bank and Gaza and the call for a freeze on settlements, but they did not accept its other provisions. In one of the resolutions adopted at Algiers in February 1983, the Palestine National Council declared that the Reagan plan failed to conform to international legality and did not provide for the attainment by the Palestinians of their inalienable rights of return and self-determination. Hence, the Council did not consider that it constituted a valid basis for a just and durable settlement of the Palestine problem and of the Arab-Israeli conflict.

Evaluation of the Reagan Peace Plan

The Reagan plan rests upon an erroneous perspective of the Palestine Question and of its dimensions. The plan is restricted to the West Bank and Gaza and ignores the other basic issues involved in the Palestine Question. It is in no way concerned with the territory of Palestine which was earmarked by the UN for the Palestinian Arab State, nor with the two and a half million Palestinians who were evicted from their homeland. It takes no account of the scores of UN resolutions which since 1948 have called for the repatriation of the Palestinians, for the respect of their inalienable rights and for the restitution of their homes. By ignoring the basic issues involved in the Palestine Question, the plan wrongly assumes that no Palestinian problem existed prior to 5 June 1967 and that consequently the only two issues to be resolved are the questions of the future of the West Bank and Gaza and Israel's alleged 'security needs'. This erroneous approach to the Palestine Question implies that the grave wrongs and injustices inflicted on the Palestinians prior to 1967, comprising the eviction and dispersal of one-half of the people of Palestine, the subjection of the other half and the usurpation of 80 per cent of their homeland, would remain without redress.

The Reagan Peace Plan invokes a principle allegedly 'enshrined' in Security Council resolution 242 of 'an exchange of territory for peace.' The statement that this principle is 'enshrined' in resolution 242 is unwarranted because the resolution lays down just the opposite, namely, the inadmissibility of the acquisition of territory by war. Furthermore, the alleged principle of the exchange of territory for peace when such territory was seized in an aggression is inadmissible because territory should be restored to its lawful owner unconditionally and without any reward to the aggressor.

Moreover, except for the rejection of the Israeli claim to annex the West Bank and Gaza, not one of the proposals made in the plan can be supported on moral, political or legal grounds. Thus, the Reagan plan's opposition to the establishment of an independent Palestinian State is irrational. Why of all peoples the Palestinians alone should be deprived of their natural, democratic and universally recognized right to establish their own state in their own homeland is not explained. US opposition to the enjoyment by the Palestinians of their independence and sovereignty is all the more surprising coming from a country which has always upheld respect for justice and democracy and was even the party primarily responsible for the UN vote on the partition of Palestine and the creation of Arab and Jewish States. The only explanation that one can give for such an attitude is a desire to conform to Israeli wishes regarding the Palestine Question.

Turning to the question of Israel's security, the Reagan plan abounds with safeguards in this regard: the need to reconcile Palestinian rights with Israeli security concerns; the necessity for recognition of Israel's right to a secure future; America's ironclad commitment to Israeli security; the principle of exchange of territory for peace subject to offering Israel in return satisfactory security arrangements. Thus, the security of Israel is treated as the primordial and paramount consideration. In this respect, one may ask two questions.

First, which Israel whose security requires to be assured? Is it the State of Israel with its boundaries as defined by the UN in 1947? Or is it the State of Israel expanded by seizure of most of the territory of the Arab State as defined by the UN?

Second, who is in need of having its security assured? Is it Israel or its neighbours? Who was the aggressor in the wars of 1948, 1956, 1967 and 1982? Is there any doubt that Israel's concern for its security is anything but a concern to keep the territorial gains it achieved in excess of the boundaries of the Jewish State as defined by the UN? Can there be any doubt that those in need of security from Israeli aggression are the Palestinians and the Arab States?

As to the plea made in the Reagan plan for recognition of Israel's legitimacy, such an appeal is misconceived. Arab recognition of Israel's legitimacy without redress of the Palestine injustice would be tantamount to condoning the wrongs done to the Palestinians and to acceptance of their eviction and the usurpation of their homeland. The illegitimacy of Israel does not stem from its 1967 aggression. Israel's illegitimacy is organic and stems from the succession of wrongs and violations of international law, Palestinian rights and UN resolutions.[10]

The weapon of non-recognition of states is not new or limited to the Arab-Israeli conflict. It has been resorted to in numerous instances and by many states, including the US. Oppenheim, one of the leading authorities in international law, gives the following justification for its use:

> . . . non-recognition is admittedly an imperfect weapon of enforcement. However, in the absence of regularly functioning international machinery for enforcing the law, it must be regarded as a supplementary weapon of considerable legal and moral potency. It prevents any law-creating effect of prescription. It constitutes a standing challenge to the legality of the situation which results from an unlawful act . . .[11]

It has been claimed that President Reagan has shown independence of judgement in proposing a plan which does not entirely conform to Israeli policy. This is quite true in so far as he rejects Israel's claim to annex the West Bank and Gaza and calls for a freeze on Israeli settlements. In all other respects, however, the Reagan plan faithfully conforms to the basic tenets of Israeli policy: opposition to the creation of a Palestinian state; no repatriation of the refugees; refusal to deal with the PLO; limitation of the Palestine Question to the West Bank and Gaza; autonomy for the Palestinians in association with Jordan and amputation of the West Bank for Israel's alleged security in line with the political programme of the Israeli Labour party.

It is clear then that the Reagan plan does not offer an appropriate solution of the Palestine Question. In accordance with its own terms, it is founded on the Camp David formula and on Security Council resolution 242. It, therefore, combines the flaws of both and is not conducive to the establishment of a just and durable peace.

9. THE FEZ PEACE PLAN, 1982

The Fez Peace Plan was originally proposed by Prince Fahd, then Crown Prince of Saudi Arabia, on 7 August 1981.

Although the proposed plan represented an improvement over Security Council resolution 242, it fell far short of Palestinian rights and expectations. Submitted to a summit of Arab states held at Fez (Morocco) on 25 November 1981, it failed to secure unanimous approval. Following further negotiations among the Arab states, including the PLO, the plan was substantially redrafted and was submitted again to a summit of Arab states which approved it at Fez on 9 September 1982. The redrafted Fez plan now comprises the following points:

1. Israeli evacuation of all Arab territories seized in 1967, including the Arab city of Jerusalem.
2. Dismantling of all settlements established by Israel in the Arab occupied territories since 1967.
3. Guarantee of worship for all religions in the Holy Places.
4. Reaffirmation of the right of the Palestinian people to self-determination and to the exercise of its national imprescriptible and inalienable rights under the leadership of the Palestine Liberation Organization, its sole and legitimate representative, and compensation to all those who do not wish to return to their homeland.
5. Placing the West Bank and the Gaza Strip under UN trusteeship for a transitional period of a few months.
6. Establishment of an independent Palestinian State with Jerusalem as its capital.
7. The Security Council guarantees peace among all states in the region, including the independent Palestinian State.
8. The Security Council guarantees respect of these principles.

The principal distinction between the original Saudi Peace Plan which was rejected in 1981 and the revised plan finally adopted in 1982 lies in the difference in their conceptual approach to the settlement of the Palestine Question. This is clear from the preamble to the plan as finally approved which stated, *inter alia*, that the summit of Arab states had taken into account 'the plan of President Habib Bourguiba (the Tunisian President) which considers international legality as the basis of a solution to the Palestine Question'. President Bourguiba considered that 'international legality' called for the implementation of the partition resolution of 1947 and the creation of Arab and Jewish States with the boundaries set forth in that resolution.

The Fez Peace Plan was flatly rejected by Israel, both in its original and in its final form. Israel reiterated its opposition to the establishment of a Palestinian state and to withdrawal from territories occupied in 1967. The US withheld its blessing of the Fez plan. The European powers approved certain, though not all, points of the plan. In its policy statement issued at Algiers on 22 February 1983 the Palestine National Council considered the plan as 'the minimum level for a political initiative by the Arab states'.

The Fez plan lay dormant after its adoption. Then suddenly, out of the blue, King Hassan II of Morocco, acting on his own initiative and without concerting his move with the other Arab states and the PLO, invited Shimon Peres, Israel's Prime Minister, to meet him at his summer residence in Morocco (Ifrane) in July 1986 to discuss a solution based on the Fez plan. Following meetings lasting two days the two men disagreed fundamentally following the rejection by Shimon Peres of the two principal demands made by the King, namely, negotiations with the PLO and evacuation of Arab territories seized in 1967.

Shimon Peres offered to negotiate with 'authentic' Palestinians as if those who support the PLO and who constitute the great majority were fake Palestinians. Irked by the Israeli attitude, King Hassan II broke off the talks. This did not prevent most of the Arab world from condemning the Moroccan-Israeli meeting. Syria severed diplomatic relations with Morocco and the Moroccan embassy in Beirut was ransacked and burnt. Despite the encounter ending in a fiasco, Shimon Peres expressed his 'satisfaction' that a meeting between him and an Arab king had taken place at all.

10. THE JORDANIAN OPTION

The 'Jordanian option' is based upon the concept of settling the Palestine Question in association with Jordan. Originally, the idea was suggested by Count Folke Bernadotte, the UN Mediator on Palestine. He mentioned in his report to the General Assembly of 16 September 1948 (A/648) the possibility of merging with Transjordan, in full consultation with the Arab inhabitants of Palestine, the territory of Palestine which was earmarked for the Arab State in accordance with the UN partition resolution. Israel's seizure and annexation of most of the area of Palestine in 1948 and 1949, including most of the territory earmarked for the Arab State, prevented the pursuit of Count Bernadotte's suggestion.

The idea of the merger of Jordanian and Palestinian territories

303

was carried out by King Abdullah in 1950 when he arranged a parliamentary vote for the unification of Transjordan and Palestine (as noted in Chapter 13).

Israel's Jordanian option

The question arose again in 1967 after Israel had occupied the West Bank and Gaza. The idea of settling the problem in association with Jordan was revived, this time by Israel, in order to resolve the issue, not with regard to the territory of Palestine that was reserved for the Arab State under the partition resolution as had been suggested by Count Bernadotte, but with regard only to the West Bank and Gaza. As we have seen in discussing the Reagan Peace Plan, such a plan was substantially based upon the political programme of the Israeli Labour party.

One should not be misled by Israel's willingness — at least the willingness of the Israeli Labour party — to make a territorial 'compromise' with Jordan concerning the West Bank. The motive is not generosity but is entirely selfish. If Israel were to absorb the territories occupied in 1967 and their Arab population of over 1,400,000, the number of Palestinians, added to Israel's present Arab citizens of 700,000, would comprise 40 per cent of Israel's total population. This would dilute the Jewishness of Israel and would be in contradiction with the Zionist concept of a purely Jewish state. Moreover, with the higher Arab birthrate, non-Jews could within the foreseeable future become the majority of the population. Hence, by effecting a so-called 'compromise' over the West Bank with Jordan under a peace treaty, Israel would achieve several objectives: it would 'get rid' of a large number of Palestinians, obtain Arab ratification of its conquests and liquidate the Palestine Question.

The above considerations, however, did not cause any concern to Menachem Begin who rejected the Jordanian option after becoming Prime Minister of Israel in 1977. His policy was not to return to the Arabs a single inch of the West Bank. The annexation of the West Bank and Gaza, which he described as the Judea and Samaria of biblical times, was his paramount objective which he sought to achieve by the multiplication of Jewish settlements. As to the problem posed by the number of Palestinians, it could be settled by expulsion, apartheid (which is already in application)[12] or by the grant of autonomy to the Palestinians in municipal affairs in accordance with the Camp David formula. This has been the policy of the Likud in contradiction to the Israeli Labour party.

Jordan's Jordanian option

A somewhat different Jordanian option was adopted as Jordan's policy by King Hussein after the capture of the West Bank and Gaza by Israel in 1967. In an attempt to counter Israeli efforts to annex the occupied territories by the creation of settlements, King Hussein proposed on 15 March 1972 the unification of the West Bank and the East Bank of the Jordan in a 'United Arab Kingdom'. The proposal was rejected by the PLO. Again on 22 June 1977, Jordan revived the proposal and suggested a federation between an autonomous West Bank State of Palestine and an East Bank State of Jordan. The proposal was again rejected by the PLO.

Then in 1982 when President Reagan offered his peace plan of Palestinian autonomy in association with Jordan, King Hussein seized the occasion to offer to the Palestinians a confederation between the West Bank and Jordan. This assumed the future establishment of a Palestinian State and was meant as a compromise between the Fez and Reagan Peace Plans. King Hussein's proposal was discussed by the Palestine National Council at Algiers in February 1983. The principle of a Palestinian-Jordanian confederation was approved, but only on condition that each of the members of the confederation was established as an independent state.

Jordan-PLO agreement of 11 February 1985

At the initiative of King Hussein of Jordan an agreement was reached on 11 February 1985 between the government of Jordan and the PLO on a joint initiative to promote a settlement of the Arab-Israeli conflict on the basis of UN resolutions and in the context of a confederation. The agreement provided for the implementation of the following principles: total withdrawal by Israel from the territories it occupied in 1967 in consideration of a comprehensive peace; right of the Palestinian people to self-determination, such right to be exercised within the context of the proposed confederated Arab states of Jordan and Palestine; solution of the Palestine refugee problem in accordance with UN resolutions; solution of the Question of Palestine in all its aspects. Negotiations for the implementation of the above principle would be conducted by a joint Jordanian-Palestinian delegation under the auspices of an international conference including the five permanent members of the Security Council.

The joint peace initiative encountered a number of difficulties. The US and Israel opposed the holding of negotiations with PLO representatives and the holding of negotiations in the context of an international conference. Regarding the composition of the Jordanian-Palestinian delegation, the US and Israel claimed the right to approve of the Palestinian members. Moreover, a difference also arose between Jordan and the PLO concerning the point whether Security Council resolution 242 would serve as the guideline for the negotiations. King Hussein showed readiness to accept resolution 242 while the PLO rejected it because it does not guarantee the national rights of the people of Palestine.

Eventually the plan for a Jordanian-PLO joint peace initiative collapsed in February 1986 over disagreement between King Hussein and the PLO regarding Security Council resolution 242.

11. RECOMMENDATIONS OF THE UN COMMITTEE ON THE EXERCISE OF THE INALIENABLE RIGHTS OF THE PALESTINIAN PEOPLE

The Committee on the Exercise of the Inalienable Rights of the Palestinian People was established by the General Assembly in its resolution 3376 of 10 November 1975. The Committee which is composed of a number of member states was entrusted with the task of recommending a programme designed to enable the Palestinian people to exercise their inalienable rights recognized in resolution 3236 of 22 November 1974, including self-determination, national independence and sovereignty, and return of refugees to their homes and property. The Committee submitted its recommendations to the General Assembly which approved them at its thirty-first session by its resolution 31/20 dated 24 November 1976. The Committee emphasized in its report the natural and inalienable right of the Palestinians to return to their homes and suggested its implementation in two phases. The first phase would involve the return of the Palestinians displaced in 1967 while the second phase would cover the return of those displaced between 1948 and 1967. Palestinians choosing not to return should be paid just and equitable compensation as provided in resolution 194 of 11 December 1948.

As to the implementation of the rights of the Palestinians to self-determination, national independence and sovereignty, the Committee considered that their exercise was dependent upon the return of the Palestinians to their homes and property and to Israel's evacuation of the territories occupied by force and in violation of the principles of the Charter and relevant UN resolutions. Its principal recommendations in this regard were:

(i) A time-table should be established by the Security Council for the withdrawal of Israeli forces from areas occupied in 1967 not later than 1 June 1977.

(ii) The evacuated territories, with all property and services intact, should be taken over by the UN which will subsequently hand them over to the PLO as the representative of the Palestinian people.

(iii) As soon as the Palestinian entity has been established in the evacuated territories, the UN, in co-operation with the states directly involved and the Palestinian entity, should, taking into account General Assembly resolution 3375 of 10 November 1975,[13] 'make further arrangements for the full implementation of the inalienable rights of the Palestinian people, the resolution of outstanding problems and the establishment of a just and lasting peace in the region, in accordance with all relevant UN resolutions'.

Although the Committee's report has been approved (except by Israel and the US) at every session of the General Assembly since 1976 and the Security Council was repeatedly urged to take urgent and positive action on its recommendations, none was taken. In fact, in June 1976, the US by its veto prevented the adoption of any decision by the Security Council on the Committee's report. Thus the implementation of the Committee's recommendations is blocked by US opposition at the Security Council.

12. INTERNATIONAL PEACE CONFERENCE ON THE MIDDLE EAST

Suggestions for the calling of an international conference for the settlement of the Palestine Question and the Arab-Israeli conflict were made on several occasions by the General Assembly of the UN, by the Soviet Union and also by the PLO and the Arab states.

A call for the convening of a UN sponsored peace conference was also formulated on 7 September 1983 by an international conference on the Question of Palestine held at Geneva under UN sponsorship.[14] It was proposed that such a conference be convened under the auspices of the UN on the basis of the principles of the Charter and relevant UN resolutions with the aim of achieving a comprehensive, just and lasting solution of the Arab-Israeli conflict, an essential element of which would be the establishment of an independent Palestinian state in Palestine.

On 13 December 1983 the General Assembly endorsed in its resolution 38/58C the call made at the Geneva Conference on 7 September 1983 for an international peace conference on the Middle East with the following guidelines:

    (i) The attainment by the Palestinian people of their legitimate inalienable rights, including the right of return, the right to self-determination and the right to establish their own independent state in Palestine;

    (ii) The right of the PLO, the representative of the Palestinian people, to participate therein;

    (iii) The need to put an end to Israel's occupation of Arab territories, in accordance with the principle of the inadmissibility of the acquisition of territory by force, and, consequently, the need to secure Israel's withdrawal from the territories occupied since 1967, including Jerusalem;

    (iv) The need to reject such Israeli policies and practices in the occupied territories, including Jerusalem, and any *de facto* situation created by Israel as are contrary to international law, particularly the establishment of settlements;

    (v) The need to reaffirm as null and void all legislative and administrative measures and actions taken by Israel which have altered the character and status of the Holy City of Jerusalem, and in particular, the so-called 'Basic Law' which declared Jerusalem the capital of Israel;

    (vi) The right of all states in the region to existence within secure and internationally recognized boundaries, with justice and security for all the people, the *sine qua non* of which is the recognition and attainment of the legitimate, inalienable rights of the Palestinian people as stated in subparagraph (i) above.

The General Assembly invited all parties to the Arab-Israeli conflict, including the PLO, as well as the USA and the Soviet Union and other concerned states, to participate in the conference on an equal footing and with equal rights and requested the Secretary-General, in consultation with the Security Council, to undertake measures to convene the conference. The resolution was adopted by 124 votes against the negative votes of Australia, Canada, Israel and the US. The Western countries abstained.

Pursuant to the General Assembly's directive, the Secretary-General of the UN contacted the members of the Security Council in order to convene the conference. The US opposed the convening of the conference, objected to PLO participation and stated its determination to confine peace talks to the sphere of the Camp David Accords. This was in conformity with Israel's attitude. The four other permanent members of the Security Council were evasive concerning their participation. Of the ten non-permanent members, only the Netherlands opposed the conference.

On 12 December 1985 the General Assembly by its resolution 40/96 reaffirmed again its endorsement of the call for convening the International Peace Conference on the Middle East in conformity with the provisions of General Assembly resolution 38/58C of 13 December 1983.

In February 1987 certain changes occurred in the international attitude concerning the holding of an international peace conference for the resolution of the Arab-Israeli conflict. On the one hand, a split occurred between the two main constituent elements of the Israeli government. Labour, represented by Shimon Peres, the Israeli Foreign Minister, supported the idea of an international conference as an umbrella for direct negotiations between Israel and the Arab countries, in particular, with King Hussein of Jordan. But the Likud, represented by the Israeli Prime Minister, Yitzhak Shamir, opposed such a conference. On the other hand, the US and the European powers modified their past attitudes regarding the international conference. The US abandoned its previous opposition and gave half-hearted support for the holding of an international conference, essentially, however, in order to promote Arab-Israeli negotiations. The twelve European powers abandoned their previous evasiveness and came out on 23 February 1987 with an announcement which backed the convening of an international peace conference under the auspices of the UN to resolve the Arab-Israeli conflict. The European Community's statement further said that the principles set forth in the Community's 1980 Venice declaration (Section 6 above) remained the basis for a Middle East peace and

309

that the international conference can provide the framework for 'negotiations between the parties directly concerned.'

It seems doubtful, in the author's judgement, that such a change of position on the part of the US and the European powers predicated as it is upon reaching a solution by means of negotiations between the parties would resolve the Arab-Israeli conflict. The failure of the Geneva Peace Conference of December 1973 (see Chapter 21) to achieve peace is sufficient proof in this regard. Reliance on 'negotiations' with Israel to secure its voluntary abandonment of Palestinian territories wrongly seized and annexed, or the repatriation of the Palestine refugees, or generally the implementation of UN resolutions is wishful thinking. This will appear clearly in the discussion of the next chapter on whether negotiations could lead to a settlement.

It also seems doubtful that the provision in the European Community's statement that the international conference be held under UN auspices is sufficient to give a proper and effective role to the UN in this matter. In the absence of a clear directive to the conference to seek a solution based on justice, international law and UN resolutions and also in the absence of a provision for the recourse to coercive measures, in case of need, to implement such a solution, the attainment of a fair and equitable settlement of the Arab-Israeli conflict, and in particular of the Palestine Question, will remain a distant mirage.

NOTES

1. UN Doc. A/648, 16 September 1948, p. 3.
2. Quoted in the *International Herald Tribune*, 28 July 1982.
3. See Chapter 21.
4. Henry Kissinger, *The White House Years* (Weidenfeld and Nicolson, London, 1979), p. 573.
5. *Ibid.*, p. 600. *Fedayeen* is the Arabic name of the Palestinian guerrillas and means fighters who are ready to sacrifice their lives.
6. Quincy Wright, 'The Middle East Crisis', *American Journal of International Law* (September 1970), p. 74.
7. *Newsweek*, 17 October 1977.
8. Fayez A. Sayegh, *Camp David and Palestine* (New York, 1978).
9. *International Herald Tribune*, 5 January 1984.
10. Regarding the illegitimacy of Israel, see Henry Cattan, *Palestine and International Law*, 2nd edn (Longman, London, 1976), pp. 91–104.
11. *Oppenheim's International Law*, 8th edn (Longman, London, 1955), vol. I, p. 145.

12. See Chapter 26 and also Orit Shohat in *Haaretz*, 27 September 1985 where he compares Israeli apartheid with South African apartheid.

13. Resolution 3375 requested the Security Council to adopt necessary resolutions and measures to enable the Palestinian people to exercise its inalienable national rights and called for the invitation of the PLO to participate in all conferences on the Middle East.

14. The Conference was convened in pursuance of General Assembly resolutions 36/120C of 10 December 1981, ES-7/7 of 19 August 1982 and 37/86C of 10 December 1982. For the text of the recommendations made by the Conference, see UN Doc. A/Conf. 114/4, 16 September 1983.

33

The Mechanics of Peace

As we have seen in the preceding chapter, all attempts to achieve a settlement of the Palestine Question and the resulting Arab-Israeli conflict have failed. How then is peace to be achieved?

Three means have been suggested to settle the Palestine Question: negotiation, Arab recognition of Israel and its right to exist, and UN intervention. We shall examine hereinafter their appropriateness or otherwise for this purpose.

NEGOTIATION

There exists a prevalent misconception that the Palestine Question can and should be resolved by negotiation between Arabs and Jews. Indeed, negotiation is a civilized way for the settlement of disputes between nations. It is incumbent, therefore, to examine whether negotiation is feasible and could lead to peace between the parties after several decades of bloody conflict.

Competence to negotiate

Before considering the practicability of negotiation as a means of settlement of the Palestine Question, it is necessary to discuss the preliminary question of competence. Who is qualified to negotiate on the Arab side: the Arab states or the PLO as representative of the Palestinian people?

The Arab states possess important ties with Palestine and with the Palestinian people: Palestine is an Arab country; the Palestinians are part of the Arab nation and possess common bonds of history, culture, language and, in their majority, religion with other Arabs; Islamic Holy Places, particularly in Jerusalem and Hebron, are of direct concern to Arab and Islamic peoples. These common bonds have caused the Arab states to express their solidarity with the people of Palestine and to take up the Palestine Question as their own.

Although they possess a vital interest in the Palestine Question, the Arab states do not possess sovereignty over Palestine which is vested in the Palestinian people, who alone are competent, through their representative the PLO, to decide their future and that of their country. As noted in Chapter 20 the principle that the PLO is the sole legitimate representative of the Palestinian people was confirmed in 1974 both by the General Assembly of the UN and by the Rabat Summit of Arab States. Hence, no Arab state is qualified to negotiate the future of Palestine or to alienate any part of its territory.

Yet, despite the fact that the Palestinians alone are competent to negotiate and to settle the Palestine Question, attempts have been made by two Arab heads of state — though without success — to negotiate with Israel over the heads of the Palestinians a settlement of the Palestine Question. On the first occasion, King Abdullah of Jordan sought to consider himself the sole representative of the Palestinians and even excluded spokesmen for the Palestine refugees from participating in the mediation talks which were initiated in 1949 by the Conciliation Commission for Palestine with the Arab states and Israel. Moreover, he conducted secret negotiations with Israel for settling the Palestine Question and concluding peace without the agreement, or even the knowledge, of the Palestinians. When this became known, he was assassinated at Jerusalem on 20 July 1951. On the second occasion, Egyptian President Anwar Sadat, in a deal with Israel for the restitution of Sinai, purported to liquidate the Palestine Question over the heads of the Palestinians by accepting in the Camp David Accords an Israeli proposal to grant the Palestinians a fictitious autonomy. Although he succeeded in recovering Sinai, he failed in his attempt to liquidate the Palestine Question (see Chapter 22). This was one of the reasons for his assassination at Cairo in October 1981.

Can negotiation resolve the Palestine Question?

Turning to the basic issue: is negotiation between Israel and the

313

Palestinians likely to resolve the Palestine Question? The answer lies in the existence of two insurmountable obstacles: first, the organic contradiction that exists between Zionist aims and the rights of the Palestinians, and second, the fact of the theft of Palestine by Israel.

First obstacle: contradiction between Zionist aims and the rights of the Palestinians

The organic contradiction that exists between the Zionist political programme and Palestinian rights is quite obvious. This programme which has been implemented by Israel since 1948 and has largely succeeded, entailed

    (i) the usurpation of the territory of Palestine 80 per cent of which has already been formally annexed with more to come;

   (ii) the eviction of the majority of its inhabitants; and

  (iii) the confiscation of most of their lands.

In such circumstances, negotiation does not seem to be a promising prospect. Is it likely or reasonable to expect that Israel would accept in any negotiation to undo any of its acts, or to abandon its territorial conquests, or to permit the return of the Palestinians to their homes which it has refused to do up to now or to disgorge spoliated Arab property? The futility of negotiating with Israel to settle the Palestine Question is perceived by Middle East observers. Harold H. Saunders, a former US Assistant Secretary for Near Eastern and South Asian affairs, has observed that 'an Israeli commitment to negotiate would automatically put Israel in a situation where the only reasonable outcome has to include some withdrawal from the West Bank and Gaza' . . . but 'the government's stated objective now is to keep all that territory.'[1] If Harold Saunders finds that 'some withdrawal from the West Bank and Gaza' does not appear possible by reason of Israel's stated objective to keep all that territory, how much more difficult, if not impossible, would it be to secure by negotiation Israel's withdrawal from the territory of the Arab State as defined by the UN which it has usurped? In such circumstances, what would the parties negotiate about?

Second obstacle: the theft of Palestine by Israel

The second obstacle to any successful negotiation was recognized by Israel's first Prime Minister, David Ben Gurion. The conversation between him and Nahum Goldmann, former President of the World

314

Zionist Organization was cited on this matter in Chapter 31. 'Why should the Arabs make peace? . . . They see only one thing: we have come here and stolen their country', said Ben Gurion.[2] Can one imagine that any negotiation between the victim and the thief would lead to redress, particularly since Israel has made it abundantly clear that it would not return one inch of the land of Palestine to its owners? Moreover, is there any chance of success in a negotiation in which the Israeli attitude invariably enjoys approbation from the US? And then, with Israel being armed to the teeth with the most modern and destructive weapons, is there the least chance for the force of arguments, however justified, to prevail over the force of arms?

Israel's policy rules out negotiation

Israel's policy since 1948 confirms that it rules out negotiation for settlement of the Palestine Question. Israeli policy has always been to attempt to settle the Palestine Question by force of arms. This policy was laid down by Israel's first Prime Minister, David Ben Gurion, who said: 'The Arabs are barbarians . . . the only thing they understand is force.'[3] This policy has been followed and applied by his successors in several wars and in hundreds of Israeli attacks and bombings of Palestinian villages and refugee camps. Levi Eshkol launched the War of 1967 and seized the West Bank and Gaza. Golda Meir denied the existence of the Palestinians.[4] Yitzhak Rabin, a former Israeli Prime Minister, declared in 1975: 'I don't see any room for negotiations with the Palestinians'[5] and in 1977 he stated: 'There can be no negotiations with the PLO. Dialogue with the PLO is only possible on the battlefield.'[6] Menachem Begin treated Palestinian nationalists as 'two-legged animals' and sought to settle the Palestine Question by the war which he and his Defence Minister Ariel Sharon launched in 1982 against the PLO in Lebanon. Then on 1 October 1985, Israel's bombers blew up the PLO's headquarters at Tunis in an air raid and buried the 'peace process' under its ruins.

Israel has always refused to negotiate with the PLO claiming that it did not represent the Palestinians and that it was a 'terrorist' organization. Both those arguments are falsehoods as we have noted in Chapter 19. Their purpose is simply to mask and obliterate Palestinian nationalism under a spurious charge of terrorism. Furthermore, Menachem Begin has repeatedly said that even though the PLO may recognize Israel, the latter would not negotiate with it.

Negotiations for a *Pax Hebraica*

The only readiness shown by Israel to negotiate is on the basis of the Camp David Accords, i.e. 'autonomy' for the West Bank and Gaza under Israeli subjection, this being the Likud's position, or on the basis of 'the Jordanian option', i.e. return of the West Bank to Jordan, minus Jerusalem and territory needed for security, this being the Israeli Labour party's position. In both cases, the negotiations would be conducted by Israel not with the PLO since there is no chance of their acceptance, but, as suggested by Shimon Peres, with Jordan and 'authentic' Palestinians. And in both cases such negotiations would lead to the imposition of a *Pax Hebraica* and the liquidation of the Palestine Question.

The futility of negotiations with Israel to settle the Palestine Question is thus evident.

ARAB RECOGNITION OF ISRAEL AND ITS RIGHT TO EXIST

The recognition of Israel, and of its legitimacy and its right to exist, by the Arab states and the PLO have been suggested in various so-called peace initiatives — the Jewish peace initiative and the Reagan Peace Plan — as being conditions or preconditions of peace. It is necessary, therefore, to clarify the position in this regard.

Significance of recognition under international law

The primary function of the recognition of a state, says J.L. Brierly, is to acknowledge as a fact the independence of the body claiming to be a state, and to declare the recognizing state's readiness to accept the usual courtesies of international intercourse.[7] Recognition is neither evidence of the legitimacy, nor a means of legitimation, of states. Moreover, recognition under international law is a discretionary act which can be neither exacted, nor imposed. A state can exist without recognition by other states.

The Soviet Union and China, for example, existed and continued to exist for a long time without recognition by many states. Even today West Germany and East Germany coexist without recognition of each other. Likewise, Israel exists as a matter of fact — it has a government, an army, a population and a territory which it controls — though such territory is largely usurped. Hence, its factual existence needs no recognition. As to its legitimacy, and its right to exist, Golda Meir, a former Israeli Prime Minister, declared that Israel is in no need of Arab recognition because 'this country exists as a result of a promise by God himself. It would be ridiculous to ask for recognition of its legitimacy.'[8]

But, notwithstanding the alleged divine promise and its feigned indifference to Arab recognition, Israel has at all times been anxious to secure recognition by the Arab states and by the Palestinians. However, neither the Arab states, nor the Palestinians are under any obligation to recognize Israel.

Recognition of Israel by the Arab states

Although the Arab states have refused to recognize Israel, the latter was able to extract an acknowledgement from Egypt of its 'territorial integrity' and from Lebanon of its 'sovereignty, political independence and territory integrity' in agreements which it 'negotiated' with those two countries under US patronage while their territories were under Israeli military occupation.

The Egyptian-Israeli Peace Treaty of 26 March 1979 which was concluded in pursuance of the Camp David Accords provided in Article II that 'each party will respect the territorial integrity of the other'. The same Article also provided that the permanent boundary between Egypt and Israel is the recognized international boundary between Egypt and the former mandated territory of Palestine, 'without prejudice to the issue of the status of the Gaza Strip'. There was no reservation with regard to the status of the West Bank and of territories, other than the Gaza Strip, which Israel had seized in excess of the boundaries of the Jewish state as defined in 1947 by the UN.

The Israeli-Lebanese troop withdrawal agreement of 17 May 1983, which was extracted during Israel's 1982 invasion of Lebanon, was taken as a pretext by Israel to impose a provision which corresponded to the language of Security Council resolution 242. This was despite the fact that the agreement purported to deal only with withdrawal and was not meant to constitute a peace treaty. Article I of the agreement stated:

1. The parties agree and undertake to respect the sovereignty, political independence and territorial integrity of each other.

317

The Israeli-Lebanese troop withdrawal agreement, however, was not ratified and was revoked by the Lebanese Government on 5 March 1984.

The question arises as to the significance of the recognition by Egypt of Israel's 'territorial integrity' in its peace treaty. Does it signify recognition of Israeli title or sovereignty over the territory which is under its occupation? In other terms, does Israel's territorial integrity encompass only the territory of the Jewish State as defined by the UN in 1947 or such territory enlarged by Israeli conquests and aggressions? The answer is found in two universally recognized principles of international law.

The first is that recognition of a state is neither attributive of legitimacy nor translative of sovereignty. Hence, Egyptian recognition of Israel's territorial integrity does not confer on Israel any right of sovereignty over territory under its occupation regardless of whether such territory is that defined by the UN for the Jewish state in the 1947 partition resolution or whether such territory was seized by Israel in excess of such resolution. The second is the inadmissibility of the acquisition of territory by war. In consequence, Egyptian recognition of Israel's territorial integrity does in no way cure the illegitimacy of Israel's occupation and annexation of territories which it seized in excess of the partition resolution.

Recognition of Israel by the Palestinians

Before the emergence of the Palestinian national movement in the 1960s as an organized political and military force, Israel was not much concerned with its recognition by the Palestinians. The situation changed when the PLO acquired an international status and the UN adopted several resolutions, commencing with General Assembly resolution 2535 of 10 December 1969, which affirmed 'the inalienable rights of the people of Palestine' as well as their rights of self-determination and sovereignty. The situation caused more concern to Israel as the UN recognized the PLO in General Assembly resolution 3210 of 14 October 1974 as the representative of the Palestinian people and invited it to participate in the deliberations of the General Assembly on the Question of Palestine. In such circumstances Israel did not consider it sufficient to seek recognition from the Arab states only, and it sought to secure from the Palestinians the recognition of its 'right to exist'. This is not a normal or usual mode of recognition and it has no precedent in diplomatic history. But the usurpation of the land of Palestine and the eviction of its inhabitants are neither normal nor usual and also have no precedent in modern history. So Israel found it essential to obtain confirmation from the displaced and evicted owners of its right to exist in their homeland.

Israel found the opportunity to gain US support for its plan to secure Palestinian recognition of its right to exist on the occasion of the conclusion of the second Egyptian-Israeli Sinai Disengagement Agreement of 1 September 1975. It was then able, as we have seen in Chapter 21, to obtain from the US, through the good offices of Henry Kissinger, US Secretary of State, a secret commitment (since published) annexed to the Sinai Disengagement Agreement which aimed at securing from the Palestinians the desired recognition of Israel's right to exist. Paragraph 2 of the commitment stated:

> The United States will not recognize or negotiate with the Palestine Liberation Organization so long as the Palestine Liberation Organization does not recognize Israel's right to exist and does not accept Security Council resolutions 242 and 338.

Let it be observed in passing that the insistence by the US and Israel on the PLO's recognition of Israel's right to exist stands in flat contradiction to their oft-repeated argument that the PLO does not represent the people of Palestine.

What then is the purpose of such abnormal and unusual recognition which is demanded from the PLO? Is it the recognition of Israel's legitimacy? Is it the recognition of its title to the territory of the Arab State which it seized in excess of the boundaries of the Jewish state as defined in 1947? Does it imply the abandonment by the Palestinians of their lands and homes and their legitimate rights in Palestine? The answer is that it is all this together. Palestinian recognition of Israel's right to exist signifies recognition of its title over their homeland. It is clear then that Arab recognition of Israel's right to exist in 80 per cent of the area of Palestine would not help resolve the Palestine Question but, on the contrary, would result in its liquidation.

It is interesting to observe that the US commitment to Israel to insist upon recognition of Israel's right to exist was shifted in Reagan's Peace Plan from the PLO to Israel's neighbours. The plan insists, as we have seen, upon recognition 'by Israel's neighbours' of Israel's 'unchallenged legitimacy' and its 'right to exist' and makes no mention of Israel's recognition by the PLO. Presumably,

319

the omission by President Reagan of any reference to Palestinian or PLO recognition of Israel's legitimacy or right to exist is explainable by the fact that he is opposed to any separate political existence for the Palestinians who, under his plan, would be absorbed in Jordan. Since under the Reagan plan the Palestinians would cease to exist as a nation or political entity, there is no need to ask for their recognition of Israel or of its right to exist.

Recognition of the right of the Palestinians to exist in their homeland

One final comment is necessary concerning the right to exist in Palestine. If any right to exist in Palestine needs recognition it is surely the right of the Palestinian people to live in their homeland. The right of the Palestinians to live in their own homeland has not been trumpeted throughout the world like Israel's alleged right to exist in *another people's country and in their homes*. Furthermore, the right of the Palestinians to exist and to establish their state in their own homeland is even vigorously denied by Israel and by the US. A more glaring and ludicrous inversion of the situation cannot be imagined.

UN INTERVENTION

After the preceding review of the unsuccessful efforts to settle the Palestine Question, it seems reasonable to assume that it cannot be resolved by mediation, conciliation, negotiation or by the mere adoption of UN resolutions without their implementation. Hence, the only means left, aside from war, is an effective UN intervention that would redress the gross injustices done to the people of Palestine. Such intervention would define and effectively implement a fair and just solution.

Responsibilities

It may be asked why the Palestine Question should require international intervention as distinct from other world problems? The answer lies not only in the fact that all UN resolutions on Palestine have been ignored or flouted, but also in the fact that the major powers and the UN itself have incurred clear and unquestionable responsibilities in regard to the Palestine situation.

The responsibility of Great Britain in issuing, and of other powers in endorsing, the Balfour Declaration which led to the introduction of demographic and political changes in Palestine during the British mandate against the will of its original inhabitants is evident. Moreover, Great Britain failed to implement the safeguards and reservations which it made in the Balfour Declaration for the protection of the rights of the Palestinians. Again, in accepting the mandate over Palestine, Great Britain assumed the specific obligations in Article 2 of 'safeguarding the civil and religious rights of all the inhabitants' and in Article 6 of 'ensuring that the rights and position of other sections of the population' — meaning the Palestinians — 'are not prejudiced'. Great Britain has neither safeguarded their rights, nor ensured that their position is not prejudiced. In fact, the Palestinians were deprived of all rights (self-government and self-determination) while the number of the Jews was increased by immigration from 8 per cent to 33 per cent of the total population. It follows that Great Britain's responsibility for the redress of the distressing injustice suffered by the Palestinians is unquestionable.

On the other hand, by recommending in 1947 an unjust partition of Palestine and allocating 57 per cent of its territory to the Jewish immigrants that came to Palestine under the Balfour Declaration and the British mandate the UN helped to put in motion political forces which it did not contain or control. By its action the UN provided the Jewish immigrants with a pseudo-juridical pretext to set up a state which expelled the majority of the Palestinians and, disregarding the boundaries set for it by the UN, expanded and usurped most of the territory of Palestine and now occupies and plans to annex the remainder. In consequence, the UN also bears responsibility for the situation that resulted and now exists in Palestine.

Finally, a special and heavy responsibility rests upon the US Government which used its enormous influence to secure the General Assembly's vote on partition and which has extended and still extends to the Jewish State extensive political, military and economic support despite the latter's violations of UN resolutions, its occupation of the whole of Palestine and the eviction of the majority of its inhabitants. On top of all this, the US Government has prevented and still prevents redress and the restoration of justice in Palestine.

UN commitments

In addition to the basic responsibility it incurred by voting the partition of Palestine, the UN is under an obligation to intervene by reason of the commitments it assumed in the partition resolution itself. In 1947, the General Assembly gave a clear and unequivocal guarantee to the Palestinians who were to live in the proposed Jewish State in respect of their human rights and fundamental freedoms. The same guarantee was given to the Jews in the Arab State. The resolution of the General Assembly of 29 November 1947 stated in Article I of Chapter 4 of the Declaration required from the Jewish and Arab states as follow:

> 1. The provisions of Chapters 1 and 2 of the Declaration shall be under the guarantee of the United Nations and no modification shall be made in them without the assent of the General Assembly of the United Nations. Any member of the United Nations shall have the right to bring to the attention of the General Assembly any infraction or danger of infraction of any of these stipulations, and the General Assembly may thereupon make such recommendations as it may deem proper in the circumstances.

Chapter 1 of the Declaration concerned Holy Places, religious buildings and sites, while Chapter 2 concerned religious and minority rights.

The effect of this provision of the resolution was to place the rights of the Arabs in the Jewish State (and of the Jews in the Arab State) — whether such rights are political or human or proprietary — under the guarantee of the UN. What has happened since then is a matter of common knowledge. The Palestinian Arabs, who for centuries had lived in territories now occupied by Israel, were expelled from their homes and dispossessed of their properties or, in the case of those who remained, are subjected to oppression and repression and are deprived of their human and fundamental rights. Jerusalem and its Holy Places were occupied and annexed. Apart from the voting of resolutions, what has the UN done to remedy the breach by Israel of its obligation to respect Jerusalem and its Holy Places as well as the rights of the original inhabitants of Palestine? What has the UN done to honour its guarantee? What is the value of the guarantee given to the Palestine Arabs by the UN if it is not implemented? The UN is, therefore, under a duty to take concrete and effective action in order to honour its guarantee of the Holy Places and of the rights of the people of Palestine.

Israel's undertakings

The UN is also justified, if not obligated, in intervening in order to enforce the undertakings given by Israel as a condition of its admission to UN membership. We have noted in Chapter 15 that Israel was admitted to membership in the UN only after it gave certain undertakings and assurances concerning its observance of General Assembly resolutions, and in particular, concerning the implementation of the resolutions of 29 November 1947 and 11 December 1948. These two resolutions embody, *inter alia*, Israel's obligations concerning boundaries, respect for the human rights and fundamental freedoms of the Palestine Arabs, the return of the refugees to their homes, and the status of Jerusalem. Israel, as we have seen, has violated each and every provision of the above resolutions.

Scope of UN intervention

UN intervention should aim at the redress of the wrongs done by Israel since 1948 and at the remedy of their underlying cause. It does not require much perspicacity to see that the underlying cause of the whole mess was the partition resolution of 1947. Accordingly, it is essential to reconsider and reappraise the partition resolution and to determine the measures which should be taken in order to achieve a just and equitable solution of the Palestine Question that would be based on justice, international law and UN resolutions. The requisites of a just and equitable solution will be discussed in the following chapter.

NOTES

1. *International Herald Tribune*, 5 March 1984.
2. Nahum Goldmann, *The Jewish Paradox* (Weidenfeld and Nicolson, London, 1978), p. 99.
3. Nahum Goldmann, *The Jewish Paradox*, p. 97.
4. *The Sunday Times*, 15 June 1969.
5. *Newsweek*, 15 December 1975.
6. *Le Monde*, 22 March 1977.
7. J.L. Brierly, *The Law of Nations*, 6th edn (Clarendon Press, London, 1963), p. 139.
8. *Le Monde*, 15 October 1971.

34

Requisites of a Just and Equitable Solution

A just and equitable solution of the Palestine Question calls for the taking of several measures that are outlined hereinafter.

1. PROCLAMATION OF THE STATE OF PALESTINE

The first step is the proclamation of the State of Palestine. Such proclamation can be made on the basis of Palestinian sovereignty and also, subject to reservations, on the basis of General Assembly resolution 181 of 29 November 1947. Such a first step can be taken by the Palestinians alone, without UN intervention.

The establishment of a Palestinian State does not require Israeli or American consent, nor does it need any authorization from the Security Council or the General Assembly. Unlike the Jewish State which came into existence from nothingness under the purported authority of a General Assembly resolution, a Palestinian State would not be, strictly speaking, a creation of a UN resolution but would come into existence in exercise of inherent Palestinian sovereignty and in continuation of the State of Palestine which came into existence upon the detachment of Palestine from Turkey.

Palestinian sovereignty

The right of the Palestinian people to establish their own state in Palestine is rooted in their inalienable and imprescriptible right of sovereignty which, as we have seen in Chapter 1, they shared with the Turks over the whole Ottoman Empire, but which vested in them exclusively over Palestine at the time of the detachment of Palestine from Turkey at the end of the First World War. Upon detachment from Turkey, Palestine became a separate political entity and an independent state in which was vested sovereignty over the territory of Palestine. The independence of its inhabitants was provisionally recognized by Article 22 of the Covenant of the League of Nations (Chapter 4). Under international law, independence and sovereignty are synonymous.

The grant by the League of Nations of a temporary mandate to Great Britain to administer Palestine — in order to lead it to independence — did not divest its people of their right of sovereignty, nor Palestine of its statehood and international identity. Conflicting views were expressed in the past as to who possessed sovereignty in the case of a mandated territory, such as Palestine. Today the accepted view is that sovereignty was vested in the inhabitants of the mandated territory, despite that temporarily, during the period of the mandate, they were deprived not of sovereignty, but of its *exercise*.[1] It follows that on the termination of the British mandate on 15 May 1948 the Mandatory's powers of administration over Palestine came to an end so that legally the right to 'exercise' sovereignty over the State of Palestine was vested in the original inhabitants of the country. It is noteworthy that in a communication to the US Government in 1948 the British Foreign Office expressed the view that 'with the end of the mandate sovereignty will probably lie in the people of Palestine but it will be latent'.[2] In exercise of their sovereignty, the people of Palestine became entitled to rule themselves and to determine their future in accordance with normal democratic principles and procedures.

However, the events which occurred at the termination of the mandate, namely, the precipitous withdrawal of the Mandatory leaving the country in a state of chaos and turmoil, the emergence of the State of Israel, the War of 1948, the occupation of 80 per cent of the territory of Palestine by Jewish forces, prevented the people of Palestine who then constituted the majority of the population from setting up any government or administration. Moreover, by terror and expulsion, the great majority of the Palestinians were forced out of their homeland.

Although the exercise of statehood and sovereignty by the people of Palestine over their country was impeded by the emergence of Israel and its annexation of most of its territory such statehood and sovereignty were not destroyed, but are at present in abeyance as was the case of Poland following its partition and annexation by Russia, Austria and Prussia between 1795 and 1919, Ethiopia after its annexation by Italy in 1936, and other states like Austria, Czechoslovakia and Albania whose territories were occupied and annexed during the Second World War. All of those states recovered their statehood and their full sovereignty, even after their extinction as political entities, which goes to show that sovereignty can survive and remain in latent form even though it is dissociated from occupation and control. The dissociation of occupation and control from sovereignty can be either forcible as in the cases aforementioned, or contractual as was envisaged by the Panama Canal Convention of 18 November 1903 which provided that 'the use, occupation and control' over the Panama Canal Zone were granted to the USA while titular sovereignty over the Zone was preserved in Panama.

Accordingly, Palestinian sovereignty was not extinguished by the emergence of the State of Israel and its usurpation of most of the territory of Palestine. Israel did not acquire sovereignty over the territory reserved by the 1947 partition resolution for the Jewish State because the UN possessed no sovereignty itself over Palestine and hence had no power to dispose of any part of its territory to the Jewish immigrants who came in during the mandate or to impair the sovereignty of the people of Palestine (Chapter 6). Likewise, Israel acquired no sovereignty over the territories of the Arab State as defined by the UN's partition resolution which it seized in excess of the boundaries of the Jewish State because such territories belonged to the people of Palestine and it is inadmissible under international law that territory could be acquired by war. Hence, the State of Palestine can be legitimately proclaimed on the basis of inherent Palestinian sovereignty.

Resolution 181 of 29 November 1947

The State of Palestine can equally be proclaimed, with reservations, on the basis of General Assembly resolution 181 of 29 November 1947. Resolution 181 was reaffirmed or recalled by General Assembly resolutions ES-7/2 of 29 July 1980, 35/169 of 15 December 1980, 36/120 of 10 December 1981 and 37/86 of 10 December 1982. It should further be observed that in addition to it having been reaffirmed by the General Assembly, resolution 181 was not amended or abrogated and remains valid, binding and operative.

Although General Assembly resolutions are usually considered to be recommendations that do not possess executory force, the position is different in the case of resolution 181 which was given executory force by the Security Council in 1948 when Arab opposition developed against its implementation. In its resolution 42 of 5 March 1948 the Security Council called for consultations among the permanent members with a view to implementation of the partition resolution. Furthermore, in its resolution 54 of 15 July 1948 the Security Council 'determined that the situation in Palestine constitutes a threat to the peace within the meaning of Article 39 of the Charter of the United Nations'. Such 'determination' enables the Security Council to take enforcement measures under Chapter VII of the Charter. It follows therefore, that resolution 181 became and remains binding and executory.

Moreover, a resolution of the UN does not lapse by reason of its breach. Hence, Israel's occupation of the territory reserved by resolution 181 for the Arab State cannot affect the validity, and binding force, of such a resolution on Israel.

Palestinian reservations

The reservations that should be made by the Palestinians in proclaiming the State of Palestine under resolution 181 of 1947 concern the incompetence of the General Assembly to partition Palestine, the illegality of the resolution of partition and its injustice. These grounds of invalidity of resolution 181 were discussed in Chapter 6.[3] The formulation of such reservations implies that the Palestinians do not abandon their right to claim the rest of Palestine by lawful means.

The question may be posed as to whether there exists contradiction between invoking the incompetence of the General Assembly and the illegality and injustice of partition, on the one hand, and relying on the partition resolution to proclaim the State of Palestine, on the other hand. The incompetence of the General Assembly to adopt resolution 181 should not prevent its being invoked for the proclamation of the State of Palestine nor preclude the implementation of its territorial provisions, since such proclamation and implementation would strip Israel of the illicit fruits of its aggressions and restore to the people of Palestine an important part of their national heritage. Moreover, such implementation should not be considered an unqualified acceptance of partition by the Palestinians, but rather as a recognition of their antecedent and imprescriptible right of sovereignty over every part of Palestine and an application of the principle that Israel cannot retain possession of, or acquire title to, any territory which it seized in excess of the area designated by the UN to the Jewish State. In consequence, the recovery by the Palestinians of the territory designated for the Arab State by the partition resolution would not be translative of rights in their favour, but would simply be declaratory of their existing and inherent right of sovereignty over such territory.

Opposition to the establishment of the State of Palestine is unfounded and irrelevant

Opposition to the establishment of the State of Palestine comes from two quarters: Israel and the US. Otherwise, it is universally recognized. It is ironical to observe that such opposition comes from the author and the prime beneficiary of the partition resolution.

Israeli opposition

Israel opposes the establishment of a Palestinian State for the simple reason that this would result in its disgorgement of the territory of the Arab State which it has annexed. There exists no valid basis for Israel's opposition, nor any reason for obtaining its consent to the establishment of a Palestinian State. The Jews possessed no territorial rights in Palestine antecedent to the date of resolution 181. Hence, it is preposterous for Israel to challenge the implementation of the very resolution which brought it into existence or to claim any rights in excess of such a resolution.

Israel is estopped from contesting the establishment of a Palestinian State

Moreover, Israel is bound by resolution 181 and is estopped from contesting its binding force or the establishment of a Palestinian State under its provisions. Such estoppel rests upon the following grounds:

(1) *Israel's admission of the binding character of resolution 181.*
When the security situation deteriorated in Palestine following the adoption of the partition resolution and, as a result, the US submitted to the UN a proposal for a trusteeship over Palestine,[4] Moshe Shertok, as representative of the Jewish Agency, opposed the proposal on the ground that the partition resolution was binding and could not be modified. He told the General Assembly of the UN on 27 April 1948:

With regard to the status of Assembly resolutions in international law, it was admitted that any which touched the national sovereignty of the Members of the United Nations were mere recommendations and not binding. However, the Palestine resolution was essentially different for it concerned the future of a territory subject to an international trust. Only the United Nations as a whole was competent to determine the future of the territory and its decision, therefore, had a binding force. It was questionable whether the earlier decision could legitimately be revoked since it conferred statehood upon Jews and Arabs and each group acquired rights which it could not be forced to renounce. To reimpose at this date some form of tutelage would be to legislate an established fact out of existence.[5]

(2) *The proclamation of the state of Israel was made on the basis of resolution 181.*

As we have noted in Chapter 8, when on 14 May 1948 the Jews proclaimed the State of Israel they based the proclamation on 'the natural and historic right of the Jewish people and the resolution of the General Assembly of the United Nations'. Moreover, the proclamation also stated that 'the State of Israel is prepared to cooperate with the agencies and representatives of the United Nations in implementing the resolution of the General Assembly of the 29th November 1947'. Then on the following day the Foreign Secretary of the Provisional Government of Israel cabled the UN Secretary-General to inform him of the proclamation of the State of Israel and of the new state's readiness to co-operate in the implementation of the resolution of 29 November 1947. It is evident that Israel cannot claim the territory envisaged for the Jewish State under the partition resolution and deny the title of the Palestinians to the territory allotted to the Arab State under the same resolution.

(3) *Israel invoked resolution 181 as the only internationally valid adjudication of the question of the future government of Palestine.*

When Count Bernadotte, the UN Mediator on Palestine, submitted his suggestions to the parties for a solution of the Palestine conflict, the Provisional Government of Israel rejected them on 6 July 1948 on the ground that they 'appear to ignore the resolution of the General Assembly of 29th November 1947, which remains the only internationally valid adjudication on the question of the future government of Palestine'.[6]

(4) *Israel cannot both invoke and violate the partition resolution.*

Israel has both invoked the partition resolution to justify its occupation of the territory envisaged for the Jewish State, and has violated the same resolution by its seizure of territories earmarked for the Arab State.[7] In 1948 Count Bernadotte made it plain to Israel that it was not entitled to consider provisions of the partition resolution which were in its favour as effective and to treat certain others of its provisions which were not in its favour as ineffective. In his reply dated 6 July 1948 to the Israeli government's letter of the preceding day, wherein it objected to the Mediator's suggestions for a peaceful settlement of the Palestine Question on the ground of their 'deviations from the General Assembly resolution of 29 November 1947',[8] Count Bernadotte stated as follows:

> 2. . . . You have not taken advantage of my invitation to offer counter-suggestions, unless I am to understand that your reference in paragraphs 1 and 2 of your letter to the resolution of the General Assembly of 29 November 1947 implies that you will be unwilling to consider any suggestions which do not correspond to the provisions of that resolution.
> 6. As regards paragraph 4 of your letter, I note that your Government no longer considers itself bound by the provisions for Economic Union set forth in the 29 November resolution for the reason that the Arab State envisaged by that resolution has not been established. In paragraphs 1 and 2, however, the same resolution is taken as your basic position. Whatever may be the precise legal significance and status of the 29 November resolution, it would seem quite clear to me that the situation is not of such a nature as to entitle either party to act on the assumption that such parts of the resolution as may be favourable to it may be regarded as effective, while those parts which may, by reasons of changes in circumstances, be regarded as unfavourable are to be considered as ineffective.[9]

Israel may not have it both ways. It is elementary that Israel cannot claim title to the territory envisaged for the Jewish State under the General Assembly resolution and deny the title of the Palestinians to the territories envisaged for the Arab State under the same resolution. Such an attitude is tantamount to a denial by Israel of its birth certificate.

(5) *Formal Israeli commitments on its admission to UN membership for observance of resolution 181 and other resolutions.*

Furthermore, in 1949, at the time of its application for UN membership, Israel gave to the General Assembly a formal commitment concerning its observance of General Assembly resolutions, and in particular, resolutions 181 of 29 November 1947 and 194 of 11 December 1948 and it was admitted to UN membership on that basis (see Chapter 15).

On all the above grounds, Israel cannot question the applicability and binding force on it of the partition resolution and the creation of an Arab State under that resolution.

American opposition

American opposition to a Palestinian state is simply a consequence of Israel's attitude. Having itself engineered the partition of Palestine into Arab and Jewish states, the US cannot rationally turn around and oppose the creation of the Arab state.

Zionist propaganda about Palestinians not being in need of a state

Zionist Jews argue that the Palestinians do not need a state because they already have one in Jordan. They claim that since the British mandate included Jordan together with a vast expanse of the Arabian desert, the Jews should not be 'begrudged' possession of Palestine which represents 'a small portion of the mandated area and a smaller part of the Arab world'. This argument is utterly fallacious: Jordan is *not* Palestine and is *not* the homeland of the Palestinians. For several centuries Transjordan, as it was then called, was a distinct and separate entity from Palestine and formed part of the *vilayet* (province) of Syria. The fact that for political reasons the British government obtained the inclusion of Jordan with an expanse of desert under its mandate over Palestine does not mean that the Jews acquired any right over that country or over such desert.

Provisions of the proclamation of the State of Palestine

The proclamation of the State of Palestine would be made by the Palestinian National Council and would specify its boundaries, subject to the reservations made above, as being those described in resolution 181. The proclamation would further recognize the PLO as the Provisional Government of the State of Palestine and would make provision for the election of a Constituent Assembly and the framing of a constitution as soon as the repatriation of the Palestine refugees has been effected. Such a constitution should guarantee to all persons equal and non-discriminatory rights in civil, political, economic and religious matters and the enjoyment of human rights and fundamental freedoms, including freedom of religion, language, speech, publication, education, assembly and association.

2. REAPPRAISAL OF THE PALESTINE QUESTION, INCLUDING GENERAL ASSEMBLY RESOLUTION 181 OF 1947, ON THE BASIS OF JUSTICE AND INTERNATIONAL LAW

The second step for a solution requires a reappraisal of the Palestine Question by the UN General Assembly, including the partition resolution of 29 November 1947, on the basis of justice and international law. The situation which has prevailed since 1948 in Palestine is unnatural, illegal and intolerable. Too many wrongs have been accumulated and none redressed.

In Chapter 32 we have examined the various so-called peace initiatives undertaken and found that they all failed. Hence, it is indispensable that the General Assembly, where there is no veto that could stifle any discussion or bar any resolution, reappraises the situation with a view to the attainment of a just and equitable solution.

Options in reappraisal

A reappraisal of the Palestine Question could involve consideration of four options:

(i) To leave the Palestine Question unresolved. This approach might well suit Israel, but the pursuit of such an option would almost certainly lead to perpetual war between the Arabs and Israel and result one day in a cataclysm in the Middle East of unforeseeable consequences. Moreover, leaving the situation without redress would mean that the powers responsible for it and the UN have defaulted on their obligations to the Palestinian people.

(ii) To return to the borders that existed prior to 5 June 1967. This option constitutes the basis of the peace efforts that were pursued by the US, Jordan and Egypt until their collapse in February 1986. The question is: would Israel's return to the borders that existed prior to 5 June 1967 resolve the Palestine Question? The answer is obviously in the negative because the evacuation of the territories seized in 1967 would simply restore the situation of conflict that existed before that date. Moreover, the restoration of the West Bank and Gaza Strip would resolve merely a fraction of the problem.

(iii) To implement the partition resolution of 1947. The partition resolution of 1947 was rejected by both Arabs and Jews, by the Arabs in words, by the Jews in deeds. As we have seen, the Jews seized in 1948 not only the area of the Jewish State, but also most of the area earmarked by the UN for the Arab State. Although the implementation of the partition resolution would have the merit of reducing the size of Israel to that envisaged by the UN in 1947, yet it would leave unredressed the illegalities, the wrongs and the injustices inherent in the partition resolution.

(iv) To seek a solution based on justice and international law. Rationally, the only viable and equitable option would be a solution based on justice and international law for the simple reason that the Palestine Question has arisen, was aggravated and has worsened because of gross violations of justice and international law. Moreover, a solution based on justice and international law is the only one that in the long term would survive the vicissitudes of time.

Justice

The Charter of the UN has laid emphasis upon the principles of justice and international law. Its preamble proclaims the determination of the UN 'to establish conditions under which justice and respect for the obligations arising from treaties and other sources of international law can be maintained'. This is followed by Article 1, which prescribes that the purposes of the UN are, *inter alia*, to bring about by peaceful means, and 'in conformity with the principles of justice and international law', adjustment or settlement of international disputes or situations which might lead to a breach of the peace. It is significant that the Charter mentioned the principles of justice before international law as if it intended to give the principles of justice precedence over international law. The concept of justice is not an empty one, and should not be confused with international law. 'If we may judge by the wording of Article 1, paragraph 1 of the Charter, the "principles of justice" are something distinct from "international law".'[10] Kelsen, an authority on the UN Charter, also points out that: 'If justice is identical with international law, one of the two terms is superfluous.'[11] All were agreed during the debates that preceded the adoption of the Charter at San Francisco in 1945 that 'the concept of justice is a norm of fundamental importance'.[12] At the first meeting of Commission I (UNICIO Doc.1006, I/6) its President declared during the discussion of the Preamble and Article I of the Charter: 'We feel the need to emphasize that our first object was to be strong to maintain peace, to maintain peace by our common effort and at all costs, at all costs with one exception — not at the cost of justice.'[13]

The concept of justice is universal, and, unlike international law, is much less subject to divergence of opinion or interpretation. The concept of justice introduces into the international sphere a gauge of moral and ethical values which are not conspicuous in the field of international law in its strict sense. It follows that respect for, and observance of, the principles of justice constitute an essential condition of any solution of the Palestine Question. Moreover, in so far as the principle of justice was incorporated into Article 1 of the UN Charter as a criterion for the settlement of international disputes and situations, it has as a result become part and parcel of international law.

The principle of justice has not been respected in the Palestine Question which does not involve one wrong or one injustice, but an accumulation of a number of grave injustices, unparalleled in modern history. Its solution, therefore, must seek the redress of these injustices to the extent that is humanly possible.

International law

A reappraisal of the Palestine Question also necessitates consideration of the violations of international law that were committed since 1917: the violation of Palestinian sovereignty, the Balfour Declaration, the mandate, the partition of Palestine, the emergence of Israel, and the subsequent chain of wrongs.

Specifically, the appraisal would attempt to answer the following questions:

(1) Was the British government competent to issue the Balfour Declaration? Did the Balfour Declaration possess any legal validity or confer any political or territorial rights on the Jews over Palestine?

(2) In so far as the British mandate over Palestine included as one of its objectives the implementation of the Balfour Declaration and thus deviated from the basic purpose of Article 22 of the Covenant of the League of Nations, could it be considered to have been formulated in conformity with international law and the Covenant itself? Was not the British mandate, as finally drafted, incompatible with the rights and sovereignty of the people of Palestine and hence null and void?

(3) Was not the introduction by the British government as the Mandatory power of a mass of Jewish immigrants into Palestine against the wishes of the majority of the original population an illicit act and a breach of its obligation to safeguard the rights and position of the original population?

(4) Did the General Assembly of the UN possess any competence to recommend the partition of Palestine? Was not the partition resolution vitiated by the General Assembly's rejection of several requests by the Arab states to refer the question of its competence and other material legal points for an advisory opinion from the International Court of Justice? Was not the partition resolution invalidated by the exercise of undue influence by the US and its president Harry Truman to secure its adoption? Are not its provisions involving amputation of the territory of Palestine for the creation of a Jewish State an infringement of Palestinian sovereignty and of the Palestinian right of self-determination? Was the partition resolution compatible with Article 22 of the Covenant of the League of Nations, the Charter of the UN and international law? Was not the partition resolution inequitable, even iniquitous, as explained in Chapter 6?

(5) Did not the state of Israel violate international law, the UN Charter and UN resolutions by i) seizing the territory of the Arab State as defined by the partition resolution and 80 per cent of the area of Palestine? ii) evicting the majority of the Palestinians and refusing their repatriation? iii) plundering and confiscating Palestinian homes, lands and properties? iv) launching the War of 1967 and occupying the West Bank and Gaza, violating the human rights of their inhabitants and

establishing Jewish settlements with a view to the annexation of such territories? v) seizing and annexing Modern Jerusalem and the Old City? vi) conducting hundreds of raids and bombardments on Palestinian villages and refugee camps? vii) launching the War of 1982 in order to destroy the Palestine Liberation Organization and the Palestinian national movement?

(6) Finally, the reappraisal would consider whether the rights of the Palestinian people — national, political, civil, human and proprietary — are impaired by the *faits accomplis* carried out by Israel since 1948 in breach of international law or UN resolutions?

International Commission of Jurists

Since the Palestine Question involves important principles of law and also because it resulted from, and was aggravated by, political influences, it is incumbent that the General Assembly be assisted in its reappraisal by a neutral and independent body of international jurists. Accordingly, the General Assembly of the UN should refer the Palestine Question, including General Assembly resolution 181 of 29 November 1947, to an International Commission of Jurists for reappraisal and reconsideration.

In addition, the International Commission of Jurists would be charged:

(a) with an inquiry into the violations of justice and international law which have been committed in regard to the rights of the Palestinian people as set forth above and

(b) with making recommendations for their redress.

The Commission would lay down the procedure to be followed in its inquiry, would hear the parties and would submit its findings and recommendations to the General Assembly within a time to be fixed by the decision of the Assembly.

It is essential that the International Commission of Jurists be composed of a small number (say five to seven) of neutral jurists and that they should not belong to countries that voted in 1947 in favour of partition. The same concern about the neutrality of the Commission also requires that its members should be appointed by the General Assembly of the UN, not by any other organ of the organization.

3. REDRESS OF WRONGS

The third step for a just solution is the redress of the wrongs and the reversal of illicit *faits accomplis* created by Israel since 1948. Any solution that would attempt to build on, or to preserve these wrongs would be doomed to failure. Hence, a proper and equitable solution would necessitate the taking by the UN of several measures of redress tantamount to an operation of political surgery to excise the wrongs committed in Palestine. It would not be the first time that this has been done for history abounds with examples of the suppression of wrongs committed by colonialism. Let it be said here for the peace of mind of those who are concerned above all else about Israel's existence, regardless of the quality of its acts, that the purpose of such measures would not be the elimination or annihilation of the Jews in Palestine, but the redress of wrongs done and the creation of a new order which would be consonant with right and justice.

The measures of redress which are required to be taken would be the following:

(a) Implementation of General Assembly resolutions.

(b) Implementation of the conclusions reached by the General Assembly and the International Commission of Jurists upon reappraisal of the Palestine Question, including the partition resolution of 1947, as set forth above.

Implementation of General Assembly resolutions

General Assembly resolutions adopted since 29 November 1947 concerning the delimitation of the boundaries of the Jewish State, or the repatriation of the Palestinians, or the restitution of their homes and lands, or the City of Jerusalem were not implemented by reason of Israeli opposition. Hence, these resolutions should be implemented under UN supervision. Accordingly, it is suggested that the General Assembly would see fit to recommend and implement the following measures of redress.

(1) Establishment of a Provisional International Authority

Such authority would be established by the General Assembly and would be charged with the implementation of the measures of redress decided by the Assembly.

(2) Israeli evacuation of occupied territories

In execution of the principle of inadmissibility of the acquisition of territory by war, Israel is obligated to evacuate all territories it occupied or annexed outside the boundaries of the Jewish State, as defined by the partition resolution of 1947, including the city of Jerusalem, as defined by such resolution. The evacuation should include civilians who settled in such territories.

Israel's annexation of the territory of the Arab State has no validity

Israel's status in all the territories which it seized in excess of the area of the Jewish State as defined by resolution 181 and subsequently annexed is that of a belligerent occupant and it is a settled principle of the law of nations that a belligerent occupant cannot annex occupied territory nor acquire sovereignty by the fact of his occupation. In accordance with the Hague Regulations of 1907 and the Fourth Geneva Convention of 1949 the occupant is regarded only as an 'administrator' of the occupied territory. Likewise, the UN has emphasized by several resolutions the principle of the inadmissibility of the acquisition of territory by war.

Furthermore, lapse of time does not legitimize Israel's annexation of the territories which it seized in excess of the partition resolution. In contrast to private law, no prescription is envisaged by international law to regularize irregular situations. Oppenheim observes that since the existence of the science of the law of nations, there has always been opposition to prescription as a mode of acquiring territory. It is only when there is a complete absence of protests and claims and a general conviction that the present condition of things is in conformity with international order that prescription can be accepted. The fact that five Arab-Israeli wars have so far been fought, that more than two and a half million Palestinians are barred from returning to their homes and that an equal number are living under a repressive rule, show that Israel's occupation is not accepted by the Palestinians and is not in conformity with international order.

(3) Taking over of evacuated territories by the Provisional International Authority

Evacuated territories should be taken over by the Provisional International Authority which would in turn hand over the territory of the Arab State to the Provisional Government of the State of Palestine and the Golan to the Syrian government. The Provisional International Authority should temporarily retain possession of, and control over, the city of Jerusalem.

(4) Repatriation of the Palestine refugees

Such repatriation is required by UN resolutions adopted annually since 1948 and should be carried out under the supervision of the Provisional International Authority.

The repatriation of the Palestine refugees to their homes is not only an obligation required by UN resolutions, international law and the Universal Declaration of Human Rights (1948) which provided in Article 13 that 'everyone has the right to return to his country', it is no less an imperative political necessity for the maintenance of peace. The presence of the Palestine refugees in neighbouring countries has been resented and opposed and has led to violence and bloodshed, even on some occasions to their massacre. This was the case in Jordan in 1970/1 and in Lebanon since 1975.

At the time of writing, another page of the refugee tragedy is being written in 'the camps war' which broke out in Lebanon between the Palestinians and the Lebanese Shiite militias in 1986. The cause of 'the camps war' was the antagonism felt by the Shiites against the presence of the Palestine refugees in Lebanon. In October 1986 the Shiite militias besieged and blockaded the Palestinian refugee camps near Beirut, Sidon and Tyre, cut off water and electricity and prevented food and medical supplies from being brought into the camps. As the inmates faced death by starvation, their only recourse was to eat dogs, cats and rats. And when none of such delicacies to people dying of starvation were left, they petitioned their religious leaders in February 1987 for permission to eat the flesh of dead humans (see the *Sunday Times* of 15 February 1987). Several hundred of them died from starvation aside from bombardment. At the time of writing, this tragedy was still continuing.

Although some blame may be ascribed to certain elements in the host countries for the aggravation of the plight of the Palestine refugees, the real responsibility for their tragedy lies with Israel which expelled them from their country, confiscated their homes and lands and denied their repatriation. The Palestinians do not wish to live in any country other than their own ancestral homeland.

(5) Restitution of public and private lands, including homes and other property of Palestinian Arabs, whether refugees or residents, in whatever way they were taken and without regard to who is at present their owner or possessor

Israel is obligated under international law to restore private Arab and public property that it appropriated.

Regarding restitution of property taken by a military occupant — which is the status of Israel in all territories it seized outside the borders of the Jewish State as defined in 1947 — Oppenheim states with respect to private property

> Immovable enemy property may under no circumstances be appropriated by an invading belligerent. Should he confiscate and sell private land or buildings, the buyer would acquire no right whatever to the property.[14]

Regarding public property, Oppenheim states:

> Appropriation of public immovables is not lawful so long as the territory on which they are found has not become state property of the occupant through annexation. During mere military occupation of enemy territory, a belligerent may not sell, or otherwise alienate, public enemy land or buildings, but may only appropriate their produce. Article 55 of the Hague Regulations expressly enacts that a belligerent occupying enemy territory shall only be regarded as administrator and usufructuary of the public buildings, real property, forests and agricultural works belonging to the hostile state and situated in the occupied territory.[15]

In the case of Arab property located in the area of the Jewish State, its restitution is also required on an additional ground, namely that it was unlawfully taken from its owners in violation of the express provision of the 1947 partition resolution and hence such taking is null and void. The partition resolution (Part 1, Chapter 2, paragraph 8) stated:

> 8. No expropriation of land owned by an Arab in the Jewish state (by a Jew in the Arab state) shall be allowed except for public purposes. In all cases of expropriation full compensation as fixed by the Supreme Court shall be paid previous to dispossession.

Needless to say, property of Palestinian residents in Israel, like Arab refugee property taken by Israel under the Absentee Property Regulations of 1948 and other confiscatory legislation, was not expropriated 'for public purposes' but for political purposes so as to change its tenure into Jewish ownership. Moreover, no compensation for its taking was fixed by the Supreme Court or paid to its owners, in breach of the partition resolution.

(6) Indemnification for loss, damage, property use and income

Israel is obligated to indemnify the Palestine refugees for loss, damage, use and income of their property, movable or immovable, which it seized, confiscated, used, sold or otherwise alienated.

In its resolution 194 of 11 December 1948 the General Assembly stated that 'compensation should be paid for the property of those (refugees) choosing not to return and for loss or damage to property which, under principles of international law or in equity, should be made good by the Governments or authorities responsible'.

At the time that this resolution was adopted, the tragedy of the Palestine refugees was just beginning to unfold. In September 1948 Count Bernadotte, the Palestine Mediator, reported to the General Assembly:

> There have been numerous reports from reliable sources of large-scale looting, pillaging and plundering, and of instances of destruction of villages without apparent military necessity. The liability of the Provisional Government of Israel to restore private property to its Arab owners and to indemnify those owners for property wantonly destroyed is clear, irrespective of any indemnities which the Provisional Government may claim from the Arab States.[16]

Since then the dimensions of the tragedy have assumed catastrophic proportions as previously explained. In view of the massive spoliation and destruction of Arab refugee property, it seems proper that the provisions relative to compensation contained in resolution 194 should be reviewed and revised. In particular, considering the length of time during which the spoliation of the Palestinians has lasted, it is only equitable that owners should be indemnified for the income or use of their homes and lands during the period of their dispossession. Since 1981 the General Assembly has declared in several resolutions that 'the Palestine Arab refugees are entitled to their property and to the income derived therefrom, in conformity with the principles of justice and equity'.[17] Moreover, the General Assembly requested the Secretary-General to take all appropriate steps, in consultation with the UN Conciliation Commission for Palestine, for the protection and administration of Arab property, assets and property rights in Israel, and to establish a fund for the receipt of income derived therefrom, on behalf of their rightful owners. Israel, however, has ignored all these resolutions.

Furthermore, it seems appropriate that the provision of indemnification of the refugees contained in resolution 194 should also be amended to provide for the establishment of an independent and neutral body for assessment and payment under UN supervision of the indemnities due to the victims.

(7) Rehabilitation of the Palestine refugees

It is evident that the repatriated refugees would need aid and assistance since they would have to start from scratch to rebuild their lives and their homes. The need for their rehabilitation on their repatriation was emphasized by Count Bernadotte in his report of 16 September 1948.

(8) Provisions regarding the city of Jerusalem

The evacuation by Israel of the city of Jerusalem under Section (2) above, whether of the Old City or of Modern Jerusalem, does not resolve the problem of the Holy City. There remain two questions: the rescission of Israel's illicit acts in Jerusalem and the future administration of the city.

Rescission of Israel's illicit acts in the city of Jerusalem as defined by the partition resolution. A large number of UN resolutions adopted by the General Assembly and the Security Council since 1967 have declared that all legislative and administrative measures and actions taken by Israel which tend to change the legal status of Jerusalem are null and void and must be rescinded. These include expropriations of land and properties, transfer of populations, changes of the physical and demographic composition and institutional structure of the Holy City.[18] These resolutions should receive an effective implementation.

The above resolutions referred to Israel's actions in Jerusalem since 1967. As pointed out in Chapter 29, there exists no reason why one part of Jerusalem should be treated differently from the other part. Accordingly, all illicit Israeli measures and actions in the whole city of Jerusalem as delimited by resolution 181 should be rescinded. In particular, such rescission shall include

    (i) the withdrawal of civilians and other settlers brought by Israel to the city of Jerusalem since 1948 for political purposes causing a substantial change in the character and the demographic structure of the Holy City;

   (ii) the repatriation of the Palestinians who were displaced from Jerusalem in 1948 and 1967;

  (iii) the restitution of Arab property, movable and immovable, to its owners;

  (iv) the annulment of all registrations or transactions carried out since 15 May 1948 with regard to immovable property;

   (v) the repeal of the changes in the municipal boundaries of Jerusalem made by the Israeli authorities since 1967;

  (vi) the abrogation of all legislative and administrative measures taken since 1948 by Israel which alter the status, demographic composition and historical character of Jerusalem.

Future administration of the city of Jerusalem. The question of the future administration of Jerusalem is sensitive and explosive. There exist several options for the future administration of Jerusalem:

    (i) Internationalization as provided in General Assembly resolution 181 of 1947. This option was rejected by Israel and by Jordan, although the other Arab states showed readiness in 1949 to accept it (Chapter 14). It is doubtful, however, whether such readiness exists today.

   (ii) Temporary UN trusteeship over Jerusalem.

  (iii) A tripartite communal administration which would be formed of an equal number of Christians, Moslems and Jews. The concept underlying the proposal of a tripartite communal administration is based on the consideration that Jerusalem is sacred to the three monotheistic religions. The principle of equal communal representation was adopted by the Trusteeship Council in Article 21 of the Statute envisaged by the 1947 partition resolution for the Legislative Council in the city of Jerusalem.[19]

Arabs and Jews, however, insist on considering Jerusalem as the capital of their state. Historically, Jerusalem has been for 18 centuries an Arab city and the capital of Palestine so that it would be normal that it should be the capital of the Arab State of Palestine. However, until the basic Question of Palestine is resolved by implementation of the various measures discussed in this chapter, including the findings and recommendations of the International Commission of Jurists, it would be judicious for the General Assembly to provide that the city of Jerusalem should be demilitarized and placed under a temporary UN trusteeship. UN trusteeship would be exercised by the Provisional International Authority mentioned in Section 1 above with the understanding that the municipal affairs of the city would be entrusted to Arab and Jewish municipalities. The mayor and councillors of each municipality would be appointed by the Provisional International Authority.

The Arab municipality would exercise municipal powers in the Old City and in the Arab quarters of Modern Jerusalem as they existed on 14 May 1948, namely, Katamon, Musrarah, Talbieh, Upper Bakaa, Lower Bakaa, the Greek and German Colonies, Sheikh Jarrah, Deir Abu Tor, Mamillah, Nebi Daoud and Sheikh Bader. The Israeli municipality would exercise municipal powers in the Jewish quarters of Modern Jerusalem as they existed on 14 May 1948. Any difference between the two municipalities would be settled by a decision of the International Provisional Authority.

(9) Security and military matters

One important problem which would arise upon the establishment of the State of Palestine would be the question of *its* security. Israel possesses one of the strongest and best equipped armies in the Middle East. The huge military imbalance between Israel and an unarmed Palestinian State would be a danger to peace and to the security of the Arab State of Palestine.

It is, therefore, necessary that the UN should deal with the question of security and make provision for the limitation of armaments of each of the two states. In particular, the UN would need to provide for the destruction of Israel's atomic arsenal, the demilitarization of its nuclear plant at Dimona and its subjection to the control of the International Atomic Energy Agency in accordance with UN resolutions as set forth in the next chapter.

(10) Admission of the State of Palestine to UN membership

As soon as the proclamation of the State of Palestine has been made and a Provisional Government has been established, an application for admission of the State of Palestine to membership in the UN would be made in accordance with Article 4 of the Charter of the UN.

Implementation of the conclusions reached by the General Assembly and the International Commission of Jurists upon reappraisal of the Palestine Question, including the partition resolution of 1947

Following the proclamation of the State of Palestine and the implementation of UN resolutions as mentioned above, the two States of Palestine and of Israel reduced geographically to the area of the Jewish State as envisaged by the UN in 1947 would coexist side by side without recognition between them. Such a situation is not without precedent for it is akin in many respects to the situation that exists today between East and West Germany. This situation would prevail until the conclusion of the reappraisal by the General Assembly and the International Commission of Jurists of the Palestine Question, including the partition resolution of 1947, as mentioned in the preceding section. The General Assembly shall then, after consideration of the report and recommendations of the International Commission of Jurists, adopt a resolution which would embody the appropriate measures of redress for a final settlement of the Palestine Question and shall implement its terms.

Ordinarily, implementation of UN resolutions may be entrusted to the Security Council. In the case of the Palestine Question, however, the eventuality of a US veto which would paralyse action by the Security Council cannot be discounted. Therefore, it is incumbent to examine the power of the General Assembly to implement its resolutions. This matter will be discussed in the next section.

4. OBSTACLES TO REDRESS

The steps suggested above would not lead to a solution of the Palestine Question unless they are effectively implemented. Implementation is the key to any settlement. The first step, namely, the proclamation of the State of Palestine offers no difficulty since it can and should be taken by the people of Palestine themselves. Likewise, the reference of the Palestine Question, including the partition resolution, to an International Commission of Jurists for reappraisal and reconsideration, can be carried out by a decision of

345

the General Assembly of the UN. However, the implementation of the UN measures of redress suggested in section 3, in particular, the evacuation by Israel of territories occupied in excess of the boundaries of the Jewish State, the repatriation of the Palestine refugees and restitution of property are certain to encounter Israeli (and presumably American) opposition to any alteration of the *faits accomplis*. Are such obstacles insurmountable?

Israeli opposition to redress

It is evident that, without international pressure and coercion, Israel will not comply with UN resolutions or abandon the fruits of its military conquests or undo any of its acts that have caused the Palestine tragedy. The rationale of coercion lies in the total impossibility of securing by persuasion, negotiation or UN resolutions the restoration of right and justice in Palestine. Armed to the teeth, crammed with weapons, and possessing a worldwide and most efficient network of propaganda, Israel plans to hold the territories it occupies and to maintain the situation it has created, by force of arms, regardless of the rights of the original inhabitants it has displaced, and regardless of world opinion or UN resolutions. Is it realistic to assume that after having established a most amazing record of defiance of UN resolutions, Israel will graciously bow down, recognize its past errors and rescind the measures it has taken, allow the Palestine refugees to return to their homes, withdraw the settlers it has brought to Palestine and annul the confiscations and expropriations of Arab property? It is completely utopian to imagine that any of these things could be achieved by negotiation between the parties or by fresh UN resolutions or by any means short of recourse by the UN to sanctions or the use of force. This is, therefore, the crux of the matter: without coercion, there can be no solution, no restoration of right and justice, no peace in Palestine and in the Middle East. But how is coercion on Israel to be exercised? The answer is that coercion can be exercised by the US or by the UN or both.

The US could, if it were willing, exercise considerable pressure on Israel, which is dependent on it for military, political and economic assistance. In fact, the only cases where Israel was forced to abandon unlawful activities were the result of US pressure: the suspension by the US government of Mutual Assistance funds to Israel in September 1953 succeeded in securing the stoppage of the drainage work undertaken by it in the Syrian-Israeli Demilitarized Zone in contempt of the UN; the strong condemnation by President Eisenhower of the Suez aggression in 1956 and his threat to suspend public assistance and to eliminate the tax credits allowed on private contributions to Israel were instrumental in securing its withdrawal from the territories it had then occupied; the threat made by the US government in March 1975, following Henry Kissinger's failure to secure a partial Israeli withdrawal from Sinai, that it would undertake a 'reappraisal' of its policy in the Middle East, coupled to the deferment of arms deliveries, quickly led to Israel's acceptance of a partial withdrawal from Sinai. During the siege of Beirut, a telephone call by President Reagan to Begin on 12 August 1982 in which he accused him of a 'holocaust' succeeded in stopping the bombing of Beirut and the slaughter of civilians with American weapons (Chapter 23).

In addition, the UN can exercise coercion on Israel. The UN Charter contains a wide range of measures of coercion which can be taken by the Security Council to enforce UN decisions. But apart from the UN intervention in Suez in 1956/7, no recourse to such measures has been made so far in the Palestine Question. The reason for this is that the US is now opposed to the use of coercion against Israel by recourse to sanctions, whether by itself or by the UN. It has on several occasions used its veto at the Security Council to prevent the imposition of sanctions upon Israel (see Chapter 27).

Competence of General Assembly to take coercive measures to overcome US veto

However, the US power of veto at the Security Council cannot nullify or thwart action by the General Assembly. Several of the measures suggested in this chapter can be taken by the General Assembly where they cannot be blocked by a veto, e.g., the reference of the Palestine Question to an International Commission of Jurists for reappraisal and reconsideration. Likewise, the General Assembly can establish a Provisional International Authority. It will be recalled that it was the General Assembly in 1947 which established the Special Committee to investigate the Question of Palestine and to make recommendations for the future government of the country (UNSCOP). So also the General Assembly set up in the 1947 partition resolution the Palestine Commission to take over the administration of the country from the British government pending the establishment of the Arab and Jewish States.

Moreover, the General Assembly is competent to act in the event of a veto of a resolution of the Security Council. This can be done by the General Assembly on the basis of its resolution 377 (V) of 3 November 1950 which was discussed in Chapter 16 and was invoked in the cases of the Korean War (1950), the Suez Crisis (1956) and the Congo (1960). Recourse to resolution 377 (V) of 3 November 1950 would be justified under the terms of Article 1 of the UN Charter which states that the purposes of the UN are 'to take effective collective measures' for the prevention and removal of threats to the peace, and for the suppression of acts of aggression. Such action would also be justified by the terms of Article 24 of the Charter which provide that members of the UN confer on the Security Council 'primary responsibility' for the maintenance of international peace and security and agree that in carrying out its duties under this responsibility the Security Council acts under an authority 'delegated' to it by the members of the UN; in accordance with general principles of law, in the event that the mandatory to whom authority is delegated is prevented from its exercise, the members of the UN, in their capacity as principals, are entitled 'to take collective measures'.

Although a US veto that opposes the adoption of coercive measures against Israel by the Security Council can be overcome by the General Assembly, yet it is an unsatisfactory situation that the US should stand in opposition to right and justice and to the implementation of UN resolutions that seek redress of the wrongs done in Palestine. It is desirable, both in the interests of the international community and of the US itself, that the latter should give its support to the UN of which it was one of the principal founders and desist from supporting the wrongs which were committed by Israel and from resisting the redress of such wrongs, a course of conduct which is incompatible with American traditions of justice, fairness and democracy.

Change of American policy on the Middle East

But how can such important change take place in the US where, as we have seen in Chapter 27, the administration's policy does not deviate from Israel's wishes, even at the expense of US interests? Conceivably, there exist two means to achieve a change of American policy in this respect.

The first consists in neutralizing the Israeli and Zionist lobby and in putting an end to its influence over US policy in the Middle East, in particular, with respect to the Palestine Question. This may appear to be an impossible task, but it can be done by the American people. Paul Findley, a former Republican congressman, recently published a book entitled *They Dare to Speak Out*,[20] in which he documents how the pro-Israel lobby helps to shape important aspects of US foreign policy, as well as how it influences congressional, senatorial and presidential elections. In a recent interview he said:

> The American people don't know what's going on [in the Middle East] . . . That region has the makings of another Vietnam, or even a much larger conflict involving even the superpowers. If we continue our present course, allowing a small state in the region to control public discourse in this country, in effect decide what U.S. policy will be, we're putting ourselves in the hands of foreigners who could easily lead us into a terrible war.
>
> How long can it go on? I don't think anyone can answer that. My hope is that my book will help break the ice. I hope it will be read by many people in this country, but I also hope it will encourage others to write books and speak out. I'm an optimist and I believe it's possible that the course of events can be changed, that the American people can be informed about what's going on. If they are informed, I have no doubt that there will be decisive political action in this country to bring about a change.[21]

The second means would be to alert American public opinion to the inequity in the US administration extending support to Israel in respect of its wrongs and aggressions, to the heavy cost to the American taxpayer of such support, to the dangers of such a policy and to the risks involved in the US isolating itself from the international community by its unjustifiable blocking of UN measures of redress in the Palestine Question. The process of alerting American public opinion is an extremely difficult one, but as Congressman Paul Findley pointed out, it is an American issue and, hence, it should not be left to be undertaken by Americans of Arab ancestry alone. Much less should it be left to the Palestinians whose means of influencing American public opinion are insignificant, if not non-existent.

The importance and effectiveness of alerting American public opinion emphasized by Seán MacBride, Nobel Peace laureate, in a colloquium held at New York on 31 October 1985 on democracy and disarmament. Referring to Americans he said:

> I have a tremendous admiration for the people of this great republic and believe that when an injustice is clearly exposed to them, they will react courageously in defence of peace and human liberty, as their founding fathers did in the past. It is essential therefore that every possible effort should be made to mobilise public opinion in the United States in favour of world disarmament and in favour of the application of the Rule of Law in international affairs. Adequately informed, the American people can by their determination persuade or compel their rulers to respect the rules of International Law . . .

Likewise, if the American people were adequately apprised of the dimensions and enormity of the Palestine injustice and of the US administration's responsibility in its regard, they would almost certainly bring sufficient pressure to bear on the US Government to assure its redress. The popular condemnation of the war in Vietnam, of Watergate and of the recent scandal of the arms deal with Iran in violation of the law are fitting examples.

Role of European powers

There is little doubt that, for the effective implementation of measures which aim at the redress of the wrongs done by Israel to the Palestinians, the key role must be played by the US. It is the superpower which has been giving its support to Israel and the interruption of its financial, military and economic aid would bring Israel to its senses, if not to its knees. However, the European powers must also play their part, because they have a share in responsibility for the creation of the Palestine situation. Unfortunately the interest shown in the 1970s by the European powers in supporting the Palestinian cause has waned since President Carter's threat to veto any European initiative that would seek recognition of Palestinian national rights at the Security Council (see Chapter 32). It is an error, however, to allow the Middle East to be polarized between the two superpowers and to allow their strategic (and in the case of the US also electoral) interests to dominate the situation to the detriment of the Palestinian people. The interests of the Europeans in the Middle East, and in particular, in Palestine, whether they be economic or cultural, have been very strong in the past. The implementation of UN measures of redress of the Palestine Question being, as we have seen, an international obligation, it is incumbent upon all powers who shared in the creation of the Palestine tragedy to share in its redress. The decision of the European Community on 23 February 1987 supporting the call for an international peace conference to resolve the Arab-Israeli conflict (noted in Chapter 32) indicated a revival of interest in finding a solution to the conflict.

NOTES

1. For a discussion of the sovereignty of the Palestinians, see Henry Cattan, *Palestine and International Law*, 2nd ed. (Longman, London, 1976), pp. 112–26.
2. *Foreign Relations of the United States* (Department of State, Washington, DC, 1948), vol. V, p. 898.
3. For a discussion of the invalidity of the partition resolution, see also Henry Cattan, 1 above, pp. 75–90.
4. See Chapter 7.
5. *Official Records of the 2nd Special Session of the General Assembly 1948*, vol. II, p. 108.
6. Diary of Folke Bernadotte, *To Jerusalem* (Hodder and Stoughton, London, 1951), p. 149.
7. See Ben Gurion, *Israël, Années de Lutte* (Flammarion, Paris, 1964), pp. 59 and 61.
8. UN Document A/648, p. 9.
9. Count Bernadotte's Progress Report to the General Assembly dated 16 September 1948 (UN Document A/648) contains extracts only from the said letter. However, the full text of Count Bernadotte's letter to the Provisional Government of Israel dated 6 July 1948, which contains the passage quoted above, is set out in his diary published under the title *To Jerusalem* (Hodder and Stoughton, London, 1951), pp. 153–8.
10. P.E. Corbett, *Law and Society in the Relations of States* (Harcourt, New York, 1951), p. 268.
11. Hans Kelsen, *The Law of the United Nations* (Praeger, New York, 1950), p. 18.
12. *Ibid.*, p. 17.
13. *Ibid.*, p. 2.
14. Oppenheim, *International Law*, 7th ed. (Longman, London, 1952), vol. 2, p. 403.
15. *Ibid.*, p. 397.
16. Report of Count Bernadotte, UN Mediator for Palestine, UN Doc. A/648, p. 14.
17. See Chapter 14 and General Assembly resolutions 36/146 C of 16 December 1981, 37/120 H of 16 December 1982, 38/83 H of 15 December

1983, 39/99 H of 14 December 1984 and 40/165 of 16 December 1985.

18. See Chapter 29.

19. The proposal of a tripartite communal administration is discussed in Henry Cattan, *Jerusalem* (Croom Helm, London, 1981).

20. Published by Lawrence Hill, Westport, Conn., 1985.

21. *Journal of Palestine Studies*, vol. 57 (Autumn 1985), p. 112.

35

The Future

What does the future hold in store for Palestine and the Middle East? In this connection, the future needs to be viewed in terms of decades rather than years. Much of the future can be foreseen in the light of past and present events. What lessons can be learnt from them?

THE CREATION OF ISRAEL WAS A HISTORICAL ANACHRONISM AS WELL AS AN INTERNATIONAL WRONG WHICH HAS CAUSED A DANGEROUS UPHEAVAL IN THE MIDDLE EAST

No vision of the future can ignore certain tragic facts: the grave error of the Balfour Declaration, the forcing of a massive Jewish immigration on Palestine against the will of its inhabitants, the illegality and injustice of the UN partition resolution, the illegitimate creation of Israel, its usurpation of Palestine and its uprooting of its inhabitants. Nahum Goldmann, late President of the World Jewish Congress and of the World Zionist Organization (and hence by definition not an anti-Semite) wrote:

> The Zionist demand for a Jewish state was in full contradiction with all principles of modern history and international law.[1]

Can there be any doubt that to establish a Jewish State in a country which was exclusively Arab for at least 1800 years, to drive out its inhabitants and to usurp their homeland constitutes anything but an international wrong and a great injustice which can only lead to conflict and catastrophe as has happened since 1948?

In addition to the havoc wreaked on Palestine and its inhabitants,

Israel also wreaked havoc on the Middle East generally. It was the cause of the five wars of 1948, 1956, 1967, 1973 and 1982 in the region. Each of Israel's neighbours has also suffered from its aggressions: Lebanon's territorial and political unity were shattered by Israeli intrigues, bombings of Palestine refugee camps and invasions; Jordan had to bear the burden of a million Palestinian refugees; a part of Syria's territory was occupied and annexed; as to Egypt, Sinai was occupied for a number of years and was evacuated only after Egypt agreed to a peace treaty which Israel imposed upon it during the military occupation of its territory.

Thus, to the Palestine Question, Israel has added two other major problems: the Arab-Israeli conflict with its neighbours and a still wider conflict with the Islamic world that resulted from its occupation and annexation of Jerusalem and its Holy Places.

All those developments weigh heavily on the future and portend more tragedy.

ISRAELI ILLUSIONS

Having seized the whole of Palestine in a way that exceeded the most optimistic expectations of Zionism and having succeeded in evicting the majority of its inhabitants, the Israelis are determined to retain it as their own perpetual possession at whatever cost and by whatever means. This is the policy of the two main political parties in Israel, both Labour and Likud, subject to a minor difference, namely that Labour would return a morsel of the West Bank to Jordan against a peace treaty. They both equally and firmly reject the repatriation of the Palestine refugees, the restitution of their homes, the establishment of the Arab State envisaged by the UN and the implementation of the UN resolutions generally.

Israel's attitude rests upon a number of illusions. It expects that the Palestine Question will evaporate with time, or that it can be treated as a simple refugee problem, or can be settled by a *Pax Hebraica*, such as Security Council resolution 242 or the Camp David formula for 'autonomy'. Israel believes it can, with Jewish and Zionist control over the media, continue to fashion and to warp public opinion in its favour as it has succeeded in doing until now. It is confident that with American support and a strong army and air force, equipped with the most advanced weapons, it can resist redress of the wrongs done in Palestine and maintain peace by force of arms and that by means of the Israeli lobby it can continue to exert its influence upon US policy in the Middle East.

Amnon Kapeliouk, an Israeli journalist, devoted a book to the discussion of Israeli illusions about the Arab-Israeli conflict. Among those illusions, he cites the following which have become maxims of Israeli policy: 'We shall maintain the status quo in the region as long as we desire'; 'The Arabs understand only the language of force'; 'War is not a game which is known to the Arabs'; 'The Arab world is divided and without military perspectives'; 'The Palestinians in the occupied territories will resign themselves to their fate'; 'Time is in our favour'; 'It does not much matter what the Gentiles say, what counts is what the Jews do.'[2] The pursuit of such illusions has prevented a serious approach to a settlement. Is it likely that Israel will abandon such illusions in the future?

PALESTINIAN ILLUSIONS

It is not only the Israelis who harbour illusions about the future; the Palestinians also have illusions. The Palestinians have relied and still rely on the UN to resolve the Palestine Question, on the Arab states, on world opinion and on the principles of justice and international law. Will they continue to harbour these illusions in the future?

It is noteworthy that the illusions of the parties are quite the antithesis of each other: the illusions of the Palestinians seek to obtain redress on the basis of the principles of right and justice while the illusions of the Israelis aim at maintaining their territorial gains and preventing redress through recourse to force and even to nuclear deterrence.

Nuclear menace

Israeli illusions are not just fanciful for Israel has built up, with American help and money, one of the most formidably equipped armies in the Middle East. In addition, not content with the possession of conventional and most sophisticated weapons, it has also manufactured atomic bombs. Although for a number of years Israel was suspected of manufacturing atomic bombs at Dimona in the Negeb Desert, its activities in this regard were concealed and protected by deceit and a strict censorship. On 5 and 12 October 1986, the *Sunday Times* revealed the secret operation and its magnitude. According to this newspaper's account, the underground plant was established in 1957 with the assistance of the French Atomic

355

Commission and Israel is in possession today of 100 to 200 nuclear weapons, ranking as the world's sixth nuclear power. Moreover, it is presently producing 40 kilogrammes of plutonium a year, enough to make 10 bombs annually. The Israeli technician who made these disclosures, Mordechai Vanunu, was kidnapped by the Israeli secret services and brought to Israel where he was put on trial.

Whether the disclosure of Israeli nuclear activities despite strict censorship was a deliberate leak on the part of Israel to inspire fear and terror among the Arabs cannot be guessed. Israel always maintained that it would not be the first state to introduce nuclear weapons in the Middle East. This is clear deception. The manufacturing of nuclear weapons is dangerous to Israel itself for it will incite other states in the region to do the same, thereby putting its own heavily concentrated population at great risk in case of armed conflict.

An unrestrained Israel in possession of a nuclear potential also constitutes a danger to world peace. Unlike those cases where the Arab-Israeli conflict almost caused a nuclear confrontation between the superpowers, as in 1956 and 1973, now Israel is capable of triggering an independent nuclear attack against its neighbours which may lead to the Third World War. Israel has steadfastly rejected any control by the IAEA (International Atomic Energy Agency) despite the Security Council's directive in its resolution 487 of 7 June 1981 condemning Israel for its raid on the Iraqi nuclear reactor at Baghdad. In that resolution the Security Council called upon Israel urgently to place its nuclear facilities under IAEA safeguards, but Israel has not complied. On 12 December 1985 the General Assembly similarly noted in its resolution 40/93 Israel's persistent refusal to commit itself not to manufacture or acquire nuclear weapons and to place its nuclear facilities under International Atomic energy safeguards. It pointed out the grave consequences that endanger international peace and security as a result of Israel's development and acquisition of nuclear weapons and Israel's collaboration with South Africa to develop nuclear weapons and their delivery systems. The General Assembly reiterated its condemnation of Israel's refusal to renounce possession of nuclear weapons, requested the Security Council to take effective measures to ensure Israel's compliance with its resolution 487 of 1981 and reaffirmed its condemnation of the continuing collaboration between Israel and South Africa regarding nuclear weapons. It may be observed that the only two states that voted against this General Assembly resolution were Israel and the US which means that the nuclear menace hangs ominously over the Middle East.

356

In addition to its massive and advanced weaponry and its nuclear capability, Israel pursues the policy of not allowing any Arab state to acquire arms that might threaten or compete with its military power. Thus it has often succeeded, through its influence in the US Congress, to block the sale of arms by the US to Arab countries. Moreover, it has succeeded, by means of the Camp David Accords as well as by American pressure and financial persuasion, in neutralizing Egypt, the strongest Arab power and in removing it from the Arab-Israeli equation. It is now looking for a pretext to knock out Syria from the Middle Eastern chessboard. As for Jordan, it is incessantly manoeuvring to tempt it out from the Arab-Israeli conflict by giving it a morsel of the West Bank. This state of things contains the roots of one or more future wars. Israeli military power coupled with American support portend more tragedy for the Middle East and are not conducive to a settlement of the Palestine Question.

Ironically, despite Israeli military power, one writer observes 'that the most dangerous spot in the world for a sizeable Jewish community is Israel'.[3]

ISRAEL'S DISINTEGRATION

Although Israel is at the peak of military power and despite the success of its expansionist Zionist programme one cannot help but observe signs of the disintegration of Israel's artificial structure.

Economically, Israel lives on American loans, grants and other financial help. It has the highest foreign debt per capita in the world and requires several billion dollars each year as assistance from the US Government. Without US economic assistance, Israel would collapse.

Politically, its artificial organic structure is cracking as a result of its latent internal struggle between secular and religious Jews and also in consequence of the emigration of its citizens in large numbers. Several hundred thousand Israelis (estimated to be in excess of half a million) have departed and still depart as visitors to the USA and remain there. General Matti Peled wrote in *Hadashot* (3 December 1985) about emigration from Israel:

Last year alone over 96,000 people left without returning. At the same time, only slightly over 17,000 people immigrated formally to this country . . . The government is feeling powerless in the

357

face of the scale of immigration and rightly so, for emigration figures show a lack of confidence in Israel's future.

Israel has resorted to desperate expedients to secure Jewish immigrants. We have seen how it used its agents to blow up synagogues in Iraq in the 1950s to frighten the ancient and prosperous Jewish community established there for centuries and induce it to move to Israel (Chapter 26). It then induced several hundred thousand Jews to emigrate from Egypt, Yemen, Syria, Morocco and Lebanon in which countries they had been living for centuries in security, ease and comfort. When the emigration of Jews from Arab countries came to an end, Israel concentrated on securing the emigration of Jews from the Soviet Union. This move yielded a few hundred thousand immigrants in the 1970s reaching a peak of 51,330 in 1979. Since then the emigration of Soviet Jews to Israel has declined sharply and was reduced to a trickle. Thereupon, Israel mounted a virulent campaign against the Soviet Union charging it with violation of human rights for not permitting a free and unimpeded emigration of its Jewish citizens to Israel. It should be noted, however, that Russian Jews willing or permitted to leave the Soviet Union prefer to go to America rather than to Israel. Yet despite such preference, the Zionists persist in organizing 'demonstrations to improve the situation of the Jews in the Soviet Union whereas the real aim is to find immigrants for the Zionist state'.[4] In this connection, it is fitting to observe that, in contrast to its campaign for the emigration of Russian Jews, Israel does not consider that its denial of the repatriation of the Palestinians to their *own* homes constitutes a more serious violation of their human rights that the alleged violation of the human rights of Soviet Jews to emigrate out of their own country.

It is relevant to observe that in view of the preference shown by Soviet Jews to go to the US rather than to Israel, the Israeli government urged the US to stop giving special refugee status to Jews emigrating from the Soviet Union so as to force them to proceed to Israel. But the Jewish organizations in the US objected and the American government turned down such a proposal.

In its quest for immigrants Israel turned to the 'importation' of Ethiopian Falashas. The American *Naturei Karta* (a Jewish orthodox group) stated recently:

In the 1920s and 1930s when Jewish Americans called for Jews to help the Falashas in Ethiopia, the Zionists emphasized that this was not of interest to them. Now that for the past few years they have run out of Russian Jewish emigrants, the colored Falashas were suddenly one of the main objectives of their support.[5]

In 1984 over 10,000 Falashas were transported to Israel by an airlift at considerable cost to the American taxpayer, but to their distress the Falashas — who consider themselves to be Jews of the earliest times — found on arrival that the Israeli Chief Rabbis insisted that they were not authentic Jews but should be 'converted' to Judaism.

ISRAEL REJECTS COEXISTENCE WITH THE PALESTINIANS

A peaceful future in Palestine by necessity requires coexistence between Arabs and Jews. The Zionist Jews, however, emigrated to Palestine, not to coexist with the original inhabitants, but in order to displace them. This is what they have done and are still bent on doing in the future. Israel's rejection of coexistence with the Palestinians applies both to the creation of a Palestinian state and to living with them as individuals.

Israel is not only hostile to the creation of a Palestinian State by its side in accordance with the UN partition resolution, but it has repeatedly declared that it will prevent its establishment by force of arms. In consequence, it is unwilling to evacuate the territory of the Arab State which it occupied in 1948 and in 1967. Moreover, Israel is unwilling to coexist with the Palestinians as individuals, whether in the territory of Palestine which it calls Israel or in the West Bank and Gaza. Official Israeli policy excludes and resists the repatriation of the Palestine refugees. As to the Palestinians who live under Israeli control they are subject to racist and apartheid practices as we have seen in Chapter 26. These practices, coupled with the anti-Arab education and even the hatred against the Palestinians which is disseminated in religious schools and in the army are incompatible with coexistence with the Palestinian Arabs.

The problem of coexistence is a grave one for the future. Regardless of what constitutional and structural changes would be effected in the State of Israel following the reappraisal of the Palestine Question and the partition resolution (Chapter 34), the fact remains that — excluding those Jews who are openly racists or are known to have been responsible for Arab massacres and who should be returned to their country of origin — Jews and Arabs will have to coexist together, whether in one state or in two states. The

359

Palestinians have shown generosity in accepting that the Jews who came as immigrants against their wishes during the British mandate would continue to live with them and enjoy equal rights (Chapter 19). On their part, the Israelis have not displayed an equal readiness to coexist with the Palestinians and to recognize their enjoyment of equal rights but, on the contrary, they have manifested, at least in certain quarters, a desire to expel the remaining Palestinians from their own country.

Expulsion is considered by some Israelis as the solution for the increase in the Arab population that would result from Israel's annexation of the West Bank and Gaza. This is the consequence of the organic contradiction between Zionism and Palestinian national rights.

IS THE SITUATION IRREVERSIBLE?

Influenced by the creation of Israeli settlements in the West Bank and Gaza, Meron Benvenisti, an Israeli land expert, suggests that the situation is irreversible and will inevitably evolve into annexation by Israel of the territories occupied in 1967. Meron Benvenisti further states that if these territories were annexed, the number of Arabs under Israeli rule in the occupied territories and in Israel would reach 38 per cent of the total population and hence 'a new equilibrium' is needed.[6] Benvenisti gives no indication as to what 'the new equilibrium' would involve. Is it the expulsion of the Palestinians? Some estimate that in the year 2000 the Palestinians would, by reason of their higher birthrate, become the majority of the population. As to Benvenisti's argument that the situation is irreversible, this was rejected by Uri Avnery, Israeli author and politician, in regard to the whole Palestine Question, and not simply in regard to the problem of settlements in the West Bank. Avnery referred to the disappearance from Palestine of the first two Jewish kingdoms as well as of the Crusaders' Latin Kingdom of Jerusalem which had lasted some 200 years and said: 'Nothing is irreversible, not even our national existence in this country.'[7]

A PEACEFUL FUTURE DEPENDS ON CHANGE OF ZIONIST IDEOLOGY

Jews and Arabs lived in peace for centuries and the Jews found in the Arab and Islamic world a place of refuge from persecution by

Christians in Europe. This historic harmony was destroyed in the twentieth century by the emergence of political Zionism, its territorial ambitions in Palestine and its creation of a militant State of Israel which has usurped an Arab country and uprooted its traditional population. If peace between Arabs and Jews in Palestine is to be restored, it is essential that certain facts and trends are reversed.

Peace in the future largely depends less upon military considerations than upon psychological factors which would require a basic and radical modification of Zionist ideology, the abandonment of the Zionist plan to possess Palestine to the exclusion of its original inhabitants and a willingness to coexist with them. True peace is not that which is imposed on the battlefield: true peace must exist in the minds and in the hearts. Are the Israelis prepared to give up Zionism and accept coexistence with the Palestinians?

NO FUTURE FOR THE ISRAELIS WITHOUT PEACE WITH THE ARABS

The Israelis cannot hope to usurp Palestine, to uproot and expel its inhabitants, to pillage their homes and to live thereafter in peace. This is perceived by leading Zionists. 'Israel has no long-term future without accord with the Arabs', said Nahum Goldmann, late President of the World Jewish Congress.[8] He also quoted Ben Gurion's statement to him in 1956 that 'in ten years, fifteen years, I believe there will still be a Jewish state, but (thereafter) the chance of there being a Jewish state would be fifty-fifty'.[9] Nahum Goldmann thought that

the Zionist idea is thoroughly irrational: for a people to return to its former lands after two thousand years' absence goes against all reason. If Zionism had been rational it would have had to find another, more or less empty, country, which is what the great English writer Israel Zangwill advocated.[10]

He continued

It is utterly simple-minded to believe that in the end the Arabs will forget our presence in Palestine . . . They have proved that they will prolong the war until they regain their lands. So this whole policy of the *fait accompli* represents an enormous waste

361

. . . There is no hope for a Jewish state which has to face another fifty years of struggle against Arab enemies. How many will there be, fifty years from now?[11]

A keen political observer, Lord Mayhew writing in *Middle East International* (17 May 1985) states:

If Israel continues in its present path, relying solely on military firepower and the Washington lobby, its survival as a sovereign Jewish state into the next century seems problematical.

IS PEACE BETWEEN THE PALESTINIANS AND ISRAEL CONCEIVABLE?

The argument is made that the French and German peoples fought three wars in the space of 70 years and yet they have now made peace and are good friends. Why cannot the Palestinians and the Israelis do the same? The answer is that there exists no possible similarity between the two cases. In the Franco-German conflict, each of the two peoples remained in its homeland at the end of each war, with the exception of Alsace-Lorraine which Germany seized in 1870. And the conflict was settled only after the return of Alsace-Lorraine to France. In the Palestinian-Israeli conflict an alien people came to Palestine from the four corners of the world under the protection of British bayonets, forced the Palestinians out of their homeland and took over their homes, their lands and their country. In such circumstances, is peace conceivable unless the Palestinians regain their homes, their lands and their country?

PEACE MUST REST ON JUSTICE

Peace between the Palestinians and the Israelis is conceivable only on one condition: it must rest on justice. Such a necessary and indispensable condition is absent from the so-called 'peace process' that has been pursued during the last few years by the US and Israel which, by the false illusions it creates, has done more harm than good by preventing the deployment of efforts for a just peace.

There exist small well-meaning groups of Israelis who advocate peace with the Palestinians on terms of Israel's evacuation of the West Bank and Gaza and the creation of a Palestinian State in the evacuated territory. They argue that 'half a loaf is better than nothing'. But is the giving back of one-fifth of the loaf to one-fifth of the Palestinians a just solution for the theft of Palestine?

Israel Shahak, Professor at the Hebrew University of Jerusalem, stated in one of his periodical publications that:

> there is a great dividing line between those who merely want peace, and those who are devoted to justice first. Those who put the emphasis on peace forget that peace which is not based on justice will not be easy to achieve, and even if achieved will not endure.

Other Jewish intellectuals have underscored the concept of justice as an indispensable condition for peace.

Judah L. Magnes, the late Rector of the Hebrew University in Jerusalem, said:

> But, as far as I am concerned, I am not ready to achieve justice to the Jew through injustice to the Arab . . . I would regard it as an injustice to the Arabs to put them under Jewish rule without their consent.[12]

Albert Einstein also declared:

> I should much rather see reasonable agreement with the Arabs on the basis of living together in peace than the creation of a Jewish state.[13]

The attempt to establish peace without justice is like building a house on foundations of sand: it will not endure.

REALPOLITIK v. JUSTICE

The peace plan suggested in Chapter 34, namely the reappraisal of the Palestine Question, the reconsideration of the partition resolution of 1947 and the implementation of relevant UN resolutions concerning certain basic rights of the Palestinians constitutes a political and peaceful solution based on right and justice. Some critics may consider that it deviates from *realpolitik* which, in their view, has replaced the principles of justice and international law contained in the UN Charter and, according to their argument, should be taken as the criterion for resolving the Arab-Israeli conflict. According to such critics, to expect that Israel, which possesses a most powerful army and enjoys the massive support of one of the superpowers, would accept a reversal of the existing situation on the basis of right and justice is unrealistic and utopian. The answer to such criticism is that the suggested plan offers a viable and logical solution and constitutes the only road to peace because maintenance of the present situation can only lead to catastrophe. Moreover, the suggested plan is less unrealistic and less utopian than the attempt to settle the problem by chimeric means, such as Security Council resolution 242 or the Camp David Accords.

FACING REALITIES AND WASTING A CHANCE OF SURVIVAL

The Israelis should face realities: they have wrongfully taken the country of another people, their homes and their lands; they have displaced them by force and terror; such a situation is unnatural and calls for redress. It cannot in the long term be maintained by force of arms because a wrong done to a people by force of arms can be undone also by force of arms.

Until the middle of this century Israel was a Zionist dream. Today it is a nightmare. Its leaders and most Israelis are intoxicated. They are intoxicated with their military victories, with their superiority in armaments, with the massive aid which they receive from one superpower, and above all with their seizure of Palestine and their resurrection of a Jewish state after 25 centuries.

Actually the Israelis do not realize that they live in a fool's paradise if they imagine that five million Palestinians will ever accept the usurpation of their homeland and the theft of all that they own, that over one hundred and fifty million Arabs will forget Palestine and the Palestinians, and that eight hundred million Moslems will abandon to Israel Jerusalem and their Holy Places.

The Israelis have today a choice between peace with justice or perpetual war. By opting for the latter, they may be wasting their chance of survival.

NOTES

1. Nahum Goldmann, 'The Psychology of Middle East Peace', *Foreign Affairs* (October 1975), p. 114.

2. Amnon Kapeliouk, *La Fin des Mythes* (Albin Michel, Paris, 1975), pp. 183–222.

3. Joseph Weiler, *Israel and the Creation of a Palestinian State* (Croom Helm, London, 1985), p. 40.

4. *Naturei Karta's* notice in the *New York Times*, 11 March 1971.

5. *New York Times*, 26 April 1985.

6. Meron Benvenisti, *West Bank Data* (American Enterprise Institute, Washington, 1984), p. 69.

7. Uri Avnery, *Ha'olam Hazeh*, 25 March 1983.

8. Nahum Goldmann, *The Jewish Paradox* (Weidenfeld and Nicolson, London, 1978), p. 98.

9. *Ibid.*, p. 99.

10. *Ibid.*, p. 115.

11. *Ibid.*, p. 202–3.

12. See N. Bentwich, *For Zion's Sake* (Jewish Publication Society of America, Philadelphia, 1965), p. 188.

13. Albert Einstein, *Out of My Later Years* (Philosophical Library, New York, 1950), p. 263.

Appendices

Appendix I

ARTICLE 22 OF THE COVENANT OF THE LEAGUE OF NATIONS, 28 JUNE 1919

Article 22. To those colonies and territories which as a consequence of the late war have ceased to be under the sovereignty of the States which formerly governed them and which are inhabited by peoples not yet able to stand by themselves under the strenuous conditions of the modern world, there should be applied the principle that the well-being and development of such peoples form a sacred trust of civilization and that securities for the performance of this trust should be embodied in this Covenant.

The best method of giving practical effect to this principle is that the tutelage of such peoples should be entrusted to advanced nations who by reason of their resources, their experience or their geographical position can best undertake this responsibility, and who are willing to accept it, and that this tutelage should be exercised by them as Mandatories on behalf of the League.

The character of the mandate must differ according to the stage of the development of the people, the geographical situation of the territory, its economic conditions and other similar circumstances.

Certain communities formerly belonging to the Turkish Empire have reached a stage of development where their existence as independent nations can be provisionally recognized subject to the rendering of administrative advice and assistance by a Mandatory until such time as they are able to stand alone. The wishes of these communities must be a principal consideration in the selection of the Mandatory.

Other peoples, especially those of Central Africa, are at such a stage that the Mandatory must be responsible for the administration of the territory under conditions which will guarantee freedom of conscience and religion, subject only to the maintenance of public order and morals, the prohibition of abuses such as the slave trade, the arms traffic and the liquor traffic, and the prevention of the establishment of fortifications or military and naval bases and of military training of the natives for other than police purposes and the defence of territory, and will also secure equal opportunities for the trade and commerce of other Members of the League.

There are territories, such as South-West Africa and certain of the South Pacific Islands, which, owing to the sparseness of their population, or their small size, or their remoteness from the centres of civilization, or their geographical contiguity to the territory of the Mandatory, and other circumstances, can be best administered under the laws of the Mandatory as integral portions of its territory, subject to the safeguards above mentioned in the interests of the indigenous population.

In every case of Mandate, the Mandatory shall render to the Council an annual report in reference to the territory committed to its charge.

The degree of authority, control or administration to be exercised by the Mandatory shall, if not previously agreed upon by the Members of the League, be explicitly defined in each case by the Council.

A permanent Commission shall be constituted to receive and examine the annual reports of the Mandatories and to advise the Council on all matters relating to the observance of the mandates.

Appendix II

RESOLUTION 181 (II) ADOPTED BY THE GENERAL ASSEMBLY ON 29 NOVEMBER 1947 CONCERNING THE FUTURE GOVERNMENT OF PALESTINE

A

The General Assembly

Having met in special session at the request of the mandatory Power to constitute and instruct a special committee to prepare for the consideration of the question of the future government of Palestine at the second regular session;

Having constituted a Special Committee and instructed it to investigate all questions and issues relevant to the problem of Palestine, and to prepare proposals for the solution of the problem, and

Having received and examined the report of the Special Committee (document A/364) including a number of unanimous recommendations and a plan of partition with economic union approved by the majority of the Special Committee,

Considers that the present situation in Palestine is one which is likely to impair the general welfare and friendly relations among nations;

Takes note of the declaration by the mandatory Power that it plans to complete its evacuation of Palestine by 1 August 1948;

Recommends to the United Kingdom, as the mandatory Power for Palestine, and to all other Members of the United Nations, the adoption and implementation, with regard to the future government of Palestine, of the Plan of Partition with Economic Union set out below;

Requests that

(*a*) The Security Council take the necessary measures as provided for in the plan for its implementation;

(*b*) The Security Council consider, if circumstances during the transitional period require such consideration, whether the situation in Palestine constitutes a threat to the peace. If it decides that such a threat exists, and in order to maintain international peace and security, the Security Council should supplement the authorization of the General Assembly by taking measures, under Articles 39 and

41 of the Charter, to empower the United Nations Commission, as provided in this resolution, to exercise in Palestine the functions which are assigned to it by this resolution;

(c) The Security Council determine as a threat to the peace, breach of the peace or act of aggression, in accordance with Article 39 of the Charter, any attempt to alter by force the settlement envisaged by the resolution;

(d) The Trusteeship Council be informed of the responsibilities envisaged for it in this plan:

Calls upon the inhabitants of Palestine to take such steps as may be necessary on their part to put this plan into effect;

Appeals to all Governments and all peoples to refrain from taking any action which might hamper or delay the carrying out of these recommendations, and

Authorizes the Secretary-General to reimburse travel and subsistence expenses of the members of the Commission referred to in Part I, Section B, paragraph 1 below, on such basis and in such form as he may determine most appropriate in the circumstances, and to provide the Commission with the necessary staff to assist in carrying out the functions assigned to the Commission by the General Assembly.

B[1]

The General Assembly

Authorizes the Secretary-General to draw from the Working Capital Fund a sum not to exceed $2,000,000 for the purposes set forth in the last paragraph of the resolution on the future government of Palestine.

Hundred and twenty-eighth plenary meeting, 29 November 1947.

At its hundred and twenty-eighth plenary meeting on 29 November 1947 the General Assembly, in accordance with the terms of the above resolution, elected the following members of the United Nations Commission on Palestine:

BOLIVIA, CZECHOSLOVAKIA, DENMARK, PANAMA and PHILIPPINES.

---

1. This resolution was adopted without reference to a Committee.

PLAN OF PARTITION WITH ECONOMIC UNION

PART I

Future constitution and government of Palestine

A. TERMINATION OF MANDATE, PARTITION AND INDEPENDENCE

1. The Mandate for Palestine shall terminate as soon as possible but in any case not later than 1 August 1948.
2. The armed forces of the mandatory Power shall be progressively withdrawn from Palestine, the withdrawal to be completed as soon as possible but in any case not later than 1 August 1948.

The mandatory Power shall advise the Commission, as far in advance as possible, of its intention to terminate the Mandate and to evacuate each area.

The mandatory Power shall use its best endeavours to ensure that an area situated in the territory of the Jewish State, including a seaport and hinterland adequate to provide facilities for a substantial immigration, shall be evacuated at the earliest possible date and in any event not later than 1 February 1948.

3. Independent Arab and Jewish States and the Special International Regime for the City of Jerusalem, set forth in part III of this plan, shall come into existence in Palestine two months after the evacuation of the armed forces of the mandatory Power has been completed but in any case not later than 1 October 1948. The boundaries of the Arab State, the Jewish State, and the City of Jerusalem shall be as described in parts II and III below.
4. The period between the adoption by the General Assembly of its recommendation on the question of Palestine and the establishment of the independence of the Arab and Jewish States shall be a transitional period.

B. STEPS PREPARATORY TO INDEPENDENCE

1. A Commission shall be set up consisting of one representative of each of five Member States. The Members represented on the Commission shall be elected by the General Assembly on as broad a basis, geographically and otherwise, as possible.
2. The administration of Palestine shall, as the mandatory Power

withdraws its armed forces, be progressively turned over to the Commission; which shall act in conformity with the recommendations of the General Assembly, under the guidance of the Security Council. The mandatory Power shall to the fullest possible extent co-ordinate its plans for withdrawal with the plans of the Commission to take over and administer areas which have been evacuated.

In the discharge of this administrative responsibility the Commission shall have authority to issue necessary regulations and take other measures as required.

The mandatory Power shall not take any action to prevent, obstruct or delay the implementation by the Commission of the measures recommended by the General Assembly.

3. On its arrival in Palestine the Commission shall proceed to carry out measures for the establishment of the frontiers of the Arab and Jewish States and the City of Jerusalem in accordance with the general lines of the recommendations of the General Assembly on the partition of Palestine. Nevertheless, the boundaries as described in part II of this plan are to be modified in such a way that village areas as a rule will not be divided by state boundaries unless pressing reasons make that necessary.

4. The Commission, after consultation with the democratic parties and other public organizations of the Arab and Jewish States, shall select and establish in each State as rapidly as possible a Provisional Council of Government. The activities of both the Arab and Jewish Provisional Councils of Government shall be carried out under the general direction of the Commission.

If by 1 April 1948 a Provisional Council of Government cannot be selected for either of the States, or, if selected, cannot carry out its functions, the Commission shall communicate that fact to the Security Council for such action with respect to that State as the Security Council may deem proper, and to the Secretary-General for communication to the Members of the United Nations.

5. Subject to the provisions of these recommendations, during the transitional period the Provisional Councils of Government, acting under the Commission, shall have full authority in the areas under their control, including authority over matters of immigration and land regulation.

6. The Provisional Council of Government of each State, acting under the Commission, shall progressively receive from the Commission full responsibility for the administration of that State in the period between the termination of the Mandate and the establishment of the State's independence.

7. The Commission shall instruct the Provisional Councils of Government of both the Arab and Jewish States, after their formation, to proceed to the establishment of administrative organs of government, central and local.

8. The Provisional Council of Government of each State shall, within the shortest time possible, recruit an armed militia from the residents of that State, sufficient in number to maintain internal order and to prevent frontier clashes.

This armed militia in each State shall, for operational purposes, be under the command of Jewish or Arab officers resident in that State, but general political and military control, including the choice of the militia's High Command, shall be exercised by the Commission.

9. The Provisional Council of Government of each State shall, not later than two months after the withdrawal of the armed forces of the mandatory Power, hold elections to the Constituent Assembly which shall be conducted on democratic lines.

The election regulations in each State shall be drawn up by the Provisional Council of Government and approved by the Commission. Qualified voters for each State for this election shall be persons over eighteen years of age who are: (a) Palestinian citizens residing in that State and (b) Arabs and Jews residing in the State, although not Palestinian citizens, who, before voting, have signed a notice of intention to become citizens of such State.

Arabs and Jews residing in the City of Jerusalem who have signed a notice of intention to become citizens, the Arabs of the Arab State and the Jews of the Jewish State, shall be entitled to vote in the Arab and Jewish States respectively.

Women may vote and be elected to the Constituent Assemblies.

During the transitional period no Jew shall be permitted to establish residence in the area of the proposed Arab State, and no Arab shall be permitted to establish residence in the area of the proposed Jewish State, except by special leave of the Commission.

10. The Constituent Assembly of each State shall draft a democratic constitution for its State and choose a provisional government to succeed the Provisional Council of Government appointed by the Commission. The constitutions of the States shall embody chapters 1 and 2 of the Declaration provided for in section C below and include *inter alia* provisions for:

(a) Establishing in each State a legislative body elected by universal suffrage and by secret ballot on the basis of proportional representation, and an executive body responsible to the legislature;

(*b*) Settling all international disputes in which the State may be involved by peaceful means in such a manner that international peace and security, and justice, are not endangered;

(*c*) Accepting the obligation of the State to refrain in its international relations from the threat or use of force against the territorial integrity or political independence of any State, or in any other manner inconsistent with the purposes of the United Nations;

(*d*) Guaranteeing to all persons equal and non-discriminatory rights in civil, political, economic and religious matters and the enjoyment of human rights and fundamental freedoms, including freedom of religion, language, speech and publication, education, assembly and association;

(*e*) Preserving freedom of transit and visit for all residents and citizens of the other State in Palestine and the City of Jerusalem, subject to considerations of national security, provided that each State shall control residence within its borders.

11. The Commission shall appoint a preparatory economic commission of three members to make whatever arrangements are possible for economic co-operation, with a view to establishing, as soon as practicable, the Economic Union and the Joint Economic Board, as provided in section D below.

12. During the period between the adoption of the recommendations on the question of Palestine by the General Assembly and the termination of the Mandate, the mandatory Power in Palestine shall maintain full responsibility for administration in areas from which it has not withdrawn its armed forces. The Commission shall assist the mandatory Power in the carrying out of these functions. Similarly the mandatory Power shall co-operate with the Commission in the execution of its functions.

13. With a view to ensuring that there shall be continuity in the functioning of administrative services and that, on the withdrawal of the armed forces of the mandatory Power, the whole administration shall be in the charge of the Provisional Councils and the Joint Economic Board, respectively, acting under the Commission, there shall be a progressive transfer, from the mandatory Power to the Commission, of responsibility for all the functions of government, including that of maintaining law and order in the areas from which the forces of the mandatory Power have been withdrawn.

14. The Commission shall be guided in its activities by the recommendations of the General Assembly and by such instructions as the Security Council may consider necessary to issue.

The measures taken by the Commission within the recommendations of the General Assembly, shall become immediately effective unless the Commission has previously received contrary instructions from the Security Council.

The Commission shall render periodic monthly reports, or more frequently if desirable, to the Security Council.

15. The Commission shall make its final report to the next regular session of the General Assembly and to the Security Council simultaneously.

C. DECLARATION

A declaration shall be made to the United Nations by the provisional government of each proposed State before independence. It shall contain *inter alia* the following clauses:

GENERAL PROVISION

The stipulations contained in the declaration are recognized as fundamental laws of the State and no law, regulation or official action shall conflict or interfere with these stipulations, nor shall any law, regulation or official action prevail over them.

CHAPTER 1

Holy Places, religious buildings and sites

1. Existing rights in respect of Holy Places and religious buildings or sites shall not be denied or impaired.

2. In so far as Holy Places are concerned, the liberty of access, visit and transit shall be guaranteed, in conformity with existing rights, to all residents and citizens of the other State and of the City of Jerusalem, as well as to aliens, without distinction as to nationality, subject to requirements of national security, public order and decorum.

Similarly, freedom of worship shall be guaranteed in conformity with existing rights, subject to the maintenance of public order and decorum.

3. Holy Places and religious buildings or sites shall be preserved. No act shall be permitted which may in any way impair their sacred character. If at any time it appears to the Government that any

particular Holy Place, religious building or site is in need of urgent repair, the Government may call upon the community or communities concerned to carry out such repair. The Government may carry it out itself at the expense of the community or communities concerned if no action is taken within a reasonable time.

4. No taxation shall be levied in respect of any Holy Place, religious building or site which was exempt from taxation on the date of the creation of the State.

No change in the incidence of such taxation shall be made which would either discriminate between the owners or occupiers of Holy Places, religious buildings or sites, or would place such owners or occupiers in a position less favourable in relation to the general incidence of taxation than existed at the time of the adoption of the Assembly's recommendations.

5. The Governor of the City of Jerusalem shall have the right to determine whether the provisions of the Constitution of the State in relation to Holy Places, religious buildings and sites within the borders of the State and the religious rights appertaining thereto, are being properly applied and respected, and to make decisions on the basis of existing rights in cases of disputes which may arise between the different religious communities or the rites of a religious community with respect to such places, buildings and sites. He shall receive full co-operation and such privileges and immunities as are necessary for the exercise of his functions in the State.

CHAPTER 2

Religious and minority rights

1. Freedom of conscience and the free exercise of all forms of worship, subject only to the maintenance of public order and morals, shall be ensured to all.

2. No discrimination of any kind shall be made between the inhabitants on the ground of race, religion, language or sex.

3. All persons within the jurisdiction of the State shall be entitled to equal protection of the laws.

4. The family law and personal status of the various minorities and their religious interests, including endowments, shall be respected.

5. Except as may be required for the maintenance of public order and good government, no measure shall be taken to obstruct or

interfere with the enterprise of religious or charitable bodies of all faiths or to discriminate against any representative or member of these bodies on the ground of his religion or nationality.

6. The State shall ensure adequate primary and secondary education for the Arab and Jewish minority, respectively, in its own language and its cultural traditions.

The right of each community to maintain its own schools for the education of its own members in its own language, while conforming to such educational requirements of a general nature as the State may impose, shall not be denied or impaired. Foreign educational establishments shall continue their activity on the basis of their existing rights.

7. No restriction shall be imposed on the free use by any citizen of the State of any language in private intercourse, in commerce, in religion, in the Press or in publications of any kind, or at public meetings.[2]

8. No expropriation of land owned by an Arab in the Jewish State (by a Jew in the Arab State)[3] shall be allowed except for public purposes. In all cases of expropriation full compensation as fixed by the Supreme Court shall be paid previous to dispossession.

CHAPTER 3

Citizenship, international conventions and financial obligations

1. *Citizenship.* Palestinian citizens residing in Palestine outside the City of Jerusalem, as well as Arabs and Jews who, not holding Palestinian citizenship, reside in Palestine outside the City of Jerusalem shall, upon the recognition of independence, become citizens of the State in which they are resident and enjoy full civil and political rights. Persons over the age of eighteen years may opt, within one year from the date of recognition of independence of the State in which they reside, for citizenship of the other State, providing that no Arab residing in the area of the proposed Arab State shall have the right to opt for citizenship in the proposed Jewish

---

2. The following stipulation shall be added to the declaration concerning the Jewish State: "In the Jewish State adequate facilities shall be given to Arabic-speaking citizens for the use of their language, either orally or in writing, in the legislature, before the Courts and in the administration."
3. In the declaration concerning the Arab State, the words "by an Arab in the Jewish State" should be replaced by the words "by a Jew in the Arab State".

State and no Jew residing in the proposed Jewish State shall have the right to opt for citizenship in the proposed Arab State. The exercise of this right of option will be taken to include the wives and children under eighteen years of age of persons so opting.

Arabs residing in the area of the proposed Jewish State and Jews residing in the area of the proposed Arab State who have signed a notice of intention to opt for citizenship of the other State shall be eligible to vote in the elections to the Constituent Assembly of that State, but not in the elections to the Constituent Assembly of the State in which they reside.

2. *International conventions.* (*a*) The State shall be bound by all the international agreements and conventions, both general and special, to which Palestine has become a party. Subject to any right of denunciation provided for therein, such agreements and conventions shall be respected by the State throughout the period for which they were concluded.

(*b*) Any dispute about the applicability and continued validity of international conventions or treaties signed or adhered to by the mandatory Power on behalf of Palestine shall be referred to the International Court of Justice in accordance with the provisions of the Statute of the Court.

3. *Financial obligations.* (*a*) The State shall respect and fulfil all financial obligations of whatever nature assumed on behalf of Palestine by the mandatory Power during the exercise of the Mandate and recognized by the State. This provision includes the right of public servants to pensions, compensation or gratuities.

(*b*) These obligations shall be fulfilled through participation in the Joint Economic Board in respect of those obligations applicable to Palestine as a whole, and individually in respect of those applicable to, and fairly apportionable between, the States.

(*c*) A Court of Claims, affiliated with the Joint Economic Board, and composed of one member appointed by the United Nations, one representative of the United Kingdom and one representative of the State concerned, should be established. Any dispute between the United Kingdom and the State respecting claims not recognized by the latter should be referred to that Court.

CHAPTER 4

Miscellaneous provisions

1. The provisions of chapters 1 and 2 of the declaration shall be under the guarantee of the United Nations, and no modifications shall be made in them without the assent of the General Assembly of the United Nations. Any Member of the United Nations shall have the right to bring to the attention of the General Assembly any infraction or danger of infraction of any of these stipulations, and the General Assembly may thereupon make such recommendations as it may deem proper in the circumstances.

2. Any dispute relating to the application or the interpretation of this declaration shall be referred, at the request of either party, to the International Court of Justice, unless the parties agree to another mode of settlement.

D. ECONOMIC UNION AND TRANSIT

1. The Provisional Council of Government of each State shall enter into an undertaking with respect to Economic Union and Transit. This undertaking shall be drafted by the Commission provided for in section B, paragraph 1, utilizing to the greatest possible extent the advice and co-operation of representative organizations and bodies from each of the proposed States. It shall contain provisions to establish the Economic Union of Palestine and provide for other matters of common interest. If by 1 April 1948 the Provisional Councils of Government have not entered into the undertaking, the undertaking shall be put into force by the Commission.

(Paragraphs 2 to 21 of the Economic Union are omitted.)

E. ASSETS

1. The movable assets of the Administration of Palestine shall be allocated to the Arab and Jewish States and the City of Jerusalem on an equitable basis. Allocations should be made by the United Nations Commission referred to in section B, paragraph 1, above. Immovable assets shall become the property of the government of the territory in which they are situated.

2. During the period between the appointment of the United Nations Commission and the termination of the Mandate, the mandatory Power shall, except in respect of ordinary operations,

consult with the Commission on any measure which it may contemplate involving the liquidation, disposal or encumbering of the assets of the Palestine Government, such as the accumulated treasury surplus, the proceeds of Government bond issues, State lands or any other asset.

F. ADMISSION TO MEMBERSHIP IN THE UNITED NATIONS

When the independence of either the Arab or the Jewish State as envisaged in this plan has become effective and the declaration and undertaking, as envisaged in this plan, have been signed by either of them, sympathetic consideration should be given to its application for admission to membership in the United Nations in accordance with Article 4 of the Charter of the United Nations.

PART II

Boundaries

[omitted]

PART III

City of Jerusalem

A. SPECIAL REGIME

The City of Jerusalem shall be established as a *corpus separatum* under a special international régime and shall be administered by the United Nations. The Trusteeship Council shall be designated to discharge the responsibilities of the Administering Authority on behalf of the United Nations.

B. BOUNDARIES OF THE CITY

The City of Jerusalem shall include the present municipality of Jerusalem plus the surrounding villages and towns, the most eastern of which shall be Abu Dis; the most southern, Bethlehem; the most western, Ein Karim (including also the built-up area of Motsa); and the most northern Shu'fat, as indicated on the attached sketch-map (annex B).

C. STATUTE OF THE CITY

The Trusteeship Council shall, within five months of the approval of the present plan, elaborate and approve a detailed Statute of the City which shall contain *inter alia* the substance of the following provisions:

1. *Government machinery; special objectives.* The Administering Authority in discharging its administrative obligations shall pursue the following special objectives:

(*a*) To protect and to preserve the unique spiritual and religious interests located in the city of the three great monotheistic faiths throughout the world, Christian, Jewish and Moslem; to this end to ensure that order and peace, and especially religious peace, reign in Jerusalem;

(*b*) To foster co-operation among all the inhabitants of the city in their own interests as well as in order to encourage and support the peaceful development of the mutual relations between the two Palestinian peoples throughout the Holy Land; to promote the security, well-being and any constructive measures of development of the residents, having regard to the special circumstances and customs of the various peoples and communities.

2. *Governor and administrative staff.* A Governor of the City of Jerusalem shall be appointed by the Trusteeship Council and shall be responsible to it. He shall be selected on the basis of special qualifications and without regard to nationality. He shall not, however, be a citizen of either State in Palestine.

The Governor shall represent the United Nations in the City and shall exercise on their behalf all powers of administration, including the conduct of external affairs. He shall be assisted by an administrative staff classed as international officers in the meaning of Article 100 of the Charter and chosen whenever practicable from the residents of the city and of the rest of Palestine on a non-discriminatory basis. A detailed plan for the organization of the administration of the city shall be submitted by the Governor to the Trusteeship Council and duly approved by it.

3. *Local autonomy.* (*a*) The existing local autonomous units in

the territory of the city (villages, townships and municipalities) shall enjoy wide powers of local government and administration.

(b) The Governor shall study and submit for the consideration and decision of the Trusteeship Council a plan for the establishment of special town units consisting, respectively, of the Jewish and Arab sections of new Jerusalem. The new town units shall continue to form part of the present municipality of Jerusalem.

4. *Security measures.* (a) The City of Jerusalem shall be demilitarized; its neutrality shall be declared and preserved, and no para-military formations, exercises or activities shall be permitted within its borders.

(b) Should the administration of the City of Jerusalem be seriously obstructed or prevented by the non-co-operation or interference of one or more sections of the population, the Governor shall have authority to take such measures as may be necessary to restore the effective functioning of the administration.

(c) To assist in the maintenance of internal law and order and especially for the protection of the Holy Places and religious buildings and sites in the city, the Governor shall organize a special police force of adequate strength, the members of which shall be recruited outside of Palestine. The Governor shall be empowered to direct such budgetary provision as may be necessary for the maintenance of this force.

5. *Legislative organization.* A Legislative Council, elected by adult residents of the city irrespective of nationality on the basis of universal and secret suffrage and proportional representation, shall have powers of legislation and taxation. No legislative measures shall, however, conflict or interfere with the provisions which will be set forth in the Statute of the City, nor shall any law, regulation, or offical action prevail over them. The Statute shall grant to the Governor a right of vetoing bills inconsistent with the provisions referred to in the preceding sentence. It shall also empower him to promulgate temporary ordinances in case the Council fails to adopt in time a bill deemed essential to the normal functioning of the administration.

6. *Administration of justice.* The Statute shall provide for the establishment of an independent judiciary system, including a court of appeal. All the inhabitants of the City shall be subject to it.

7. *Economic union and economic régime.* The City of Jerusalem shall be included in the Economic Union of Palestine and be bound by all stipulations of the undertaking and of any treaties issued therefrom, as well as by the decisions of the Joint Economic Board.

The headquarters of the Economic Board shall be established in the territory of the City.

The Statute shall provide for the regulation of economic matters not falling within the régime of the Economic Union, on the basis of equal treatment and non-discrimination for all Members of the United Nations and their nationals.

8. *Freedom of transit and visit; control of residents.* Subject to considerations of security, and of economic welfare as determined by the Governor under the directions of the Trusteeship Council, freedom of entry into, and residence within, the borders of the City shall be guaranteed for the residents or citizens of the Arab and Jewish States. Immigration into, and residence within, the borders of the City for nationals of other States shall be controlled by the Governor under the directions of the Trusteeship Council.

9. *Relations with the Arab and Jewish States.* Representatives of the Arab and Jewish States shall be accredited to the Governor of the City and charged with the protection of the interests of their States and nationals in connexion with the international administration of the City.

10. *Official languages.* Arabic and Hebrew shall be the official languages of the City. This will not preclude the adoption of one or more additional working languages, as may be required.

11. *Citizenship.* All the residents shall become *ipso facto* citizens of the City of Jerusalem unless they opt for citizenship of the State of which they have been citizens or, if Arabs or Jews, have filed notice of intention to become citizens of the Arab or Jewish State respectively, according to part I, section B, paragraph 9, of this plan.

The Trusteeship Council shall make arrangements for consular protection of the citizens of the City outside its territory.

12. *Freedoms of citizens.* (*a*) Subject only to the requirements of public order and morals, the inhabitants of the City shall be ensured the enjoyment of human rights and fundamental freedoms, including freedom of conscience, religion and worship, language, education, speech and Press, assembly and association, and petition.

(*b*) No discrimination of any kind shall be made between the inhabitants on the grounds of race, religion, language or sex.

(*c*) All persons within the City shall be entitled to equal protection of the laws.

(*d*) The family law and personal status of the various persons and communities and their religious interests, including endowments, shall be respected.

(*e*) Except as may be required for the maintenance of public order and good government, no measure shall be taken to obstruct or interfere with the enterprise of religious or charitable bodies of all faiths or to discriminate against any representative or member of these bodies on the ground of his religion or nationality.

(*f*) The City shall ensure adequate primary and secondary education for the Arab and Jewish communities respectively, in their own languages and in accordance with their cultural traditions.

The right of each community to maintain its own schools for the education of its own members in its own language, while conforming to such educational requirements of a general nature as the City may impose, shall not be denied or impaired. Foreign educational establishments shall continue their activity on the basis of their existing rights.

(*g*) No restriction shall be imposed on the free use by any inhabitant of the City of any language in private intercourse, in commerce, in religion, in the Press or in publications of any kind, or at public meetings.

13. *Holy Places*. (*a*) Existing rights in respect of Holy Places and religious buildings or sites shall not be denied or impaired.

(*b*) Free access to the Holy Places and religious buildings or sites and the free exercise of worship shall be secured in conformity with existing rights and subject to the requirements of public order and decorum.

(*c*) Holy Places and religious buildings or sites shall be preserved. No act shall be permitted which may in any way impair their sacred character. If at any time it appears to the Governor that any particular Holy Place, religious building or site is in need of urgent repair, the Governor may call upon the community or communities concerned to carry out such repair. The Governor may carry it out himself at the expense of the community or communities concerned if no action is taken within a reasonable time.

(*d*) No taxation shall be levied in respect of any Holy Place, religious building or site which was exempt from taxation on the date of the creation of the City. No change in the incidence of such taxation shall be made which would either discriminate between the owners or occupiers of Holy Places, religious buildings or sites, or would place such owners or occupiers in a position less favourable in relation to the general incidence of taxation than existed at the time of the adoption of the Assembly's recommendations.

14. *Special powers of the Governor in respect of the Holy Places, religious buildings and sites in the City and in any part of Palestine.* (*a*) The protection of the Holy Places, religious buildings and sites

located in the City of Jerusalem shall be a special concern of the Governor.

(*b*) With relation to such places, buildings and sites in Palestine outside the city, the Governor shall determine, on the ground of powers granted to him by the Constitutions of both States, whether the provisions of the Constitutions of the Arab and Jewish States in Palestine dealing therewith and the religious rights appertaining thereto are being properly applied and respected.

(*c*) The Governor shall also be empowered to make decisions on the basis of existing rights in cases of disputes which may arise between the different religious communities or the rites of a religious community in respect of the Holy Places, religious buildings and sites in any part of Palestine.

In this task he may be assisted by a consultative council of representatives of different denominations acting in an advisory capacity.

D. DURATION OF THE SPECIAL REGIME

The Statute elaborated by the Trusteeship Council on the aforementioned principles shall come into force not later than 1 October 1948. It shall remain in force in the first instance for a period of ten years, unless the Trusteeship Council finds it necessary to undertake a re-examination of these provisions at an earlier date. After the expiration of this period the whole scheme shall be subject to re-examination by the Trusteeship Council in the light of the experience acquired with its functioning. The residents of the City shall be then free to express by means of a referendum their wishes as to possible modifications of the régime of the City.

PART IV

Capitulations

States whose nationals have in the past enjoyed in Palestine the privileges and immunities of foreigners, including the benefits of consular jurisdiction and protection, as formerly enjoyed by capitulation or usage in the Ottoman Empire, are invited to renounce any right pertaining to them to the re-establishment of such privileges and immunities in the proposed Arab and Jewish States and the City of Jerusalem.

Appendix III

UN PARTITION PLAN – 1947
AND
UN ARMISTICE LINES – 1949

LEBANON

SYRIA
o Quneitra

Tyre

Nahariyya
'Akko
Haifa
Shef ar'am
Nazareth

GOLAN
o Zefat
Lake
Tiberias
Tiberias
o Nawa

Hadera
Netanya
Kefar Sava
Hod HaSharon o
Tel Aviv
Yafo
(Jaffa)
Rishon Le Zion
Rehovot
Latrun

Jenin
Tulkarm
Qalqilya
Nablus
Lod
Ramallah
Jericho
Jerusalem
Bethlehem

Jordan

Amman

MEDITERRANEAN
SEA

Gaza
GAZA
Khan Yunis
Rafah

Hebron

Beersheba

Dead
Sea

JORDAN

o El Arish

ISRAEL

SINAI

EGYPT

The designations employed and the presentation of material on this
map do not imply the expression of any opinion whatsoever on the
part of the Secretariat of the United Nations concerning the legal
status of any country, territory, city or area or of its authorities, or
concerning the delimitation of its frontiers or boundaries.

Elat
Gulf of
Aqaba

—··— Boundary of Former Palestine Mandate

PLAN OF PARTITION, 1947

Arab State
Jewish State
Jerusalem

— — Armistice Demarcation lines, 1949
(shown where at variance with Mandate boundary.)

0   10   20   30km
0   10   20   30mi

MAP NO. 3067 Rev. 2   UNITED NATIONS
SEPTEMBER 1985

Appendix IV

Land ownership of Arabs and Jews in 1948

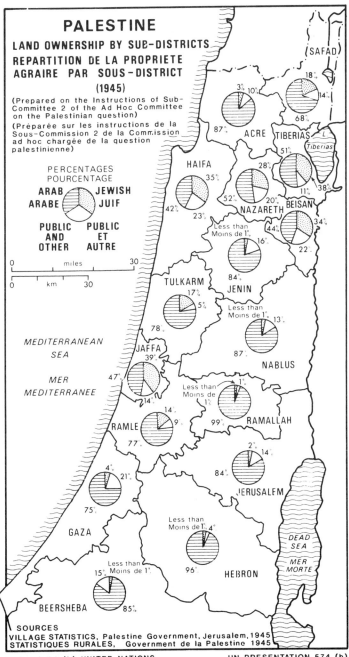

PALESTINE

LAND OWNERSHIP BY SUB-DISTRICTS

REPARTITION DE LA PROPRIETE AGRAIRE PAR SOUS-DISTRICT

(1945)

(Prepared on the Instructions of Sub-Committee 2 of the Ad Hoc Committee on the Palestinian question)

(Préparée sur les instructions de la Sous-Commission 2 de la Commission ad hoc chargée de la question palestinienne)

PERCENTAGES
POURCENTAGE

ARAB / JEWISH
ARABE / JUIF

PUBLIC / PUBLIC
AND / ET
OTHER / AUTRE

miles 0 — 30

km 0 — 30

MEDITERRANEAN SEA

MER MEDITERRANEE

SOURCES
VILLAGE STATISTICS, Palestine Government, Jerusalem, 1945
STATISTIQUES RURALES, Government de la Palestine 1945

MAP NO 94 (b) UNITED NATIONS   UN PRESENTATION 574 (b)
AUGUST 1950

Appendix V

Areas Seized by Israel in Excess of the Partition Plan

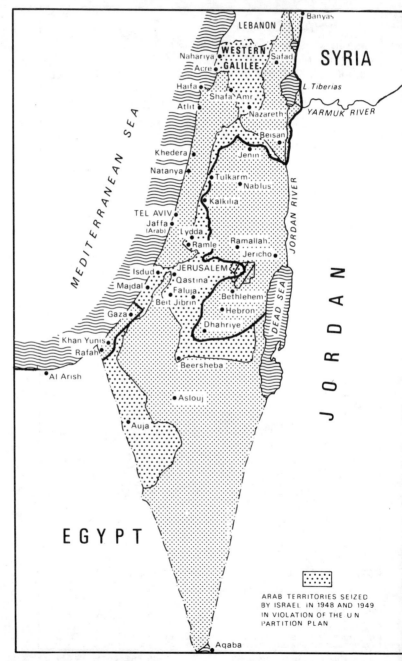

ARAB TERRITORIES SEIZED
BY ISRAEL IN 1948 AND 1949
IN VIOLATION OF THE U N
PARTITION PLAN

Appendix VI

Territories Occupied During Israeli Aggression of 1967

Appendix VII

Chronology of Jerusalem

Rulers		Years of occupation
Canaanites	From around 1800 BC or earlier until the capture of the city by David in about 1000 BC	800
Israelites (with intermittent occupations of the city by the Egyptians, the Philistines, the Syrians and the Assyrians)	From 1000 BC to capture of the city by the Babylonians in 587 BC (destruction of Jerusalem and the Kingdom of Judah)	413
Babylonians	From 587 to 538 BC	50
Persians	From capture of the city by Cyrus to Greek conquest: 538 to 332 BC	206
Greeks	Alexander's conquest of the city to its emancipation by the Maccabees: 332 to 141 BC	191
Jews	Maccabean rule: 141 to 63 BC	78
Pagan Romans	Roman conquest of the city to fall of paganism: 63 BC to AD 323	386
Christians	From Constantine to Persian conquest: 323 to 614	291
Persians	Persian rule: 614 to 628	14
Christians	Reconquest of the city by Byzantines: 628 to 638	10

Rulers		Years of occupation
Arabs	Conquest by the Moslem Arabs: 638 to 1072	434
Turks	Seizure of the city by the Turks: 1072 to 1092	20
Arabs	Reconquest of the city by the Arabs 1092 to 1099	7
Christians	Latin Kingdom of Jerusalem: 1099 to 1187	88
Arabs	Reconquest of the city by the Arabs: 1187 to 1229	42
Christians	City ceded by treaty for ten years to Frederick II: 1229 to 1239	10
Arabs	Revived Arab rule: 1239 to 1517	278
Turks	Occupation by the Ottoman Turks: 1517 to 1831	314
Arabs	Occupation of Jerusalem by Mohamed Ali and Egyptian rule from 1831 to 1841	10
Turks	Restoration of Turkish rule: 1841 to 1917	76
Christians	British occupation and mandate: 1917 to 1948	31
Israelis and Arabs	Modern Jerusalem occupied by Israel and Old City occupied by Jordan: 1948 to 1967	19
Israelis	Capture of Old City by Israel in 1967	

Index